1989

RADIO AND TV PROGRAMMING

GRID SERIES IN ADVERTISING AND JOURNALISM

Consulting Editors
ARNOLD M. BARBAN, University of Illinois
DONALD W. JUGENHEIMER, University of Kansas

Barban, Jurgenheimer, & Young, *Advertising Media Sourcebook and Workbook, Second Edition*
Burton, *Advertising Copywriting, Fifth Edition*
Burton & Ryan, *Advertising Fundamentals, Third Edition*
Burton & Sandhusen, *Cases in Advertising*
Fletcher & Bowers, *Fundamentals of Advertising Research*
Fletcher & Jugenheimer, *Problems and Practices in Advertising Research: Readings and Workbook*
Howard & Kievman, *Radio and TV Programming*
Jugenheimer & Turk, *Advertising Media*
Leckenby & Wedding, *Advertising Management: Criteria, Analysis and Decision Making*
Pickett, *Voices of the Past: Key Documents in the History of American Journalism*
Simon, *Public Relations: Concepts and Practices, Second Edition*
Simon, *Publicity and Public Relations Worktext, Fifth Edition*
Smeyak, *Broadcast News Writing, Second Edition*
Tan, *Mass Communication Theories and Research*
Zeigler & Howard, *Broadcast Advertising: A Comprehensive Working Textbook*
Zeigler & Johnson, *Creative Strategy and Tactics in Advertising*

OTHER BOOKS IN THE GRID SERIES IN ADVERTISING AND JOURNALISM

Francois, *Mass Media Law and Regulation, Third Edition*

RADIO AND TV PROGRAMMING

Herbert H. Howard
University of Tennessee
and
Michael S. Kievman
Cox Broadcasting Corporation

with the assistance of

Darrel Holt
University of Tennessee
Kent Sidel
New York Institute of Technology
Mark Banks
Marquette University

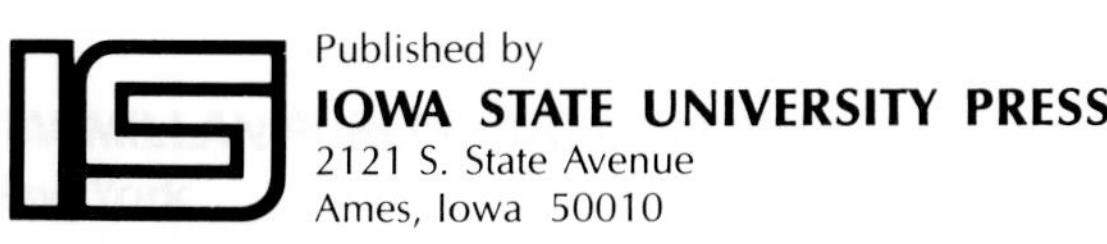

Published by
IOWA STATE UNIVERSITY PRESS
2121 S. State Avenue
Ames, Iowa 50010

ISBN 0-8138-0347-0

Macmillan Publishing Company
866 Third Avenue, New York, New York 10022
Collier Macmillan Canada, Inc.

Library of Congress Cataloging in Publication Data:

ISBN 0-02-357240-X

Printed in the United States of America

Printing 5 6 7 8 9 Year 6 7 8 9 0

Howard, Herbert H.
Radio and TV programming.

Includes index.
1. Radio programs—Planning. 2. Television programs—Planning. I. Kievman, Michael S. II. Title. III. Series.
PN1991.55.H68 384.54'0973 82-6079
AACR2

ISBN 0-02-357240-X

CONTENTS

PREFACE

For a majority of Americans, the time they spend with their radios and television sets surpasses any other single activity except working and sleeping. Even so, the tremendous number of programming choices available to each of us means that almost none of us can hear or view more than a few offerings. That fact poses a serious challenge to professional programming executives, whose success is measured largely by the size of the audiences they attract to their programs. Clearly, those who succeed most often are those who have the greatest knowledge and understanding of, as well as skill for the business/profession of competitive programming.

This book is intended as a textbook for those who want to increase their knowledge, understanding, and skill. Some readers will be university majors in telecommunications. Other users may well be junior staff members just at the start of their programming careers. To an extent, then, *Radio and Television Programming* is a how-to-do-it book to help enhance one's skills. Just as important, though, it probes into the when and why to help provide the perspectives and insights so necessary for fundamental knowledge and understanding. Thus, we have tried to provide an appropriate combination of both the practical and the cerebral, hoping the rest will be a sensitive and insightful examination of broadcast programming as practiced today.

Teachers of programming know that finding such a text is difficult, because so few exist. Having been a program manager and public affairs director before joining the academic ranks, I decided to undertake such a text. I then sought the assistance of one of the leading programming executives in the broadcasting industry. I am grateful that Michael S. Kievman, the Executive Vice President for Television at Cox Broadcasting Corporation, agreed to serve as my coauthor. His contemporary experience with a premier broadcast corporation assures readers that this textbook is sound in principle and as current as possible in such a dynamic, changing field.

In addition to Mike Kievman's broad experience and my own as both a professional broadcaster and educator, three other authors have contributed important chapters. Dr. Darrel W. Holt, professor and head of the Department of Broadcasting at The University of Tennessee, Knoxville, also has experienced program decision making first-hand as owner-manager of a North Dakota radio station. Two young broadcasting professors, Drs. M. Kent Sidel, New York Institute of Technology, and Mark Banks, Marquette University, have brought youthful insight to the book. Dr. Holt was responsible for the material on program criticism, while Dr. Sidel wrote on public broadcasting and Dr. Banks authored the chapter on broadcast programming in the future.

All of these efforts permit us to discuss in detail the organizational set-up of a broadcast program department, the responsibilities and duties of the program director, those of other key programming personnel, and the relationships between the program department and other units of radio and TV stations. Other practical subjects include designing competitive strategies and schedules for television stations, attractive formats for radio, and alternative programming approaches for public stations. However, because a successful programmer is more than a mere technician, this book provides a brief historical account of broadcast programming, as well as a look into its changing future. *Radio and Television Programming* also provides insight into such vital areas as audience behavior, audience measurement, broadcast regulation, and program criticism. We hope that you will find this book informative, even provocative, and especially, useful.

Finally, let me also acknowledge with gratitude the assistance of many individuals, broadcast stations, radio and TV networks, and other organizations whose contributions have helped make this book possible.

Special recognition is due to the following individuals who were generous with their assistance and advice during the preparation of this book: Hal Bouton, General Manager, KIXE-TV, Redding, California; Jay C. Bowles, General Executive, the Associated Press, New York; George E. DeVault, Jr., Vice President and General Manager, WKPT AM-FM-TV, Kingsport, Tennessee; Norris Dryer, Program Director, WUOT-FM, Knoxville, Tennessee; James H. Duncan, Jr., publisher of *American Radio;* Hop Edwards, Program Manager, WSJK-TV, Sneedville (Knoxville), Tennessee; Lawrence Frerk, Promotion Director, A.C. Nielsen Co., Northbrook, Illinois; Catharine Heinz, Broadcast Pioneers Library, Washington, D.C.; Jim Lewis, Director of Programming, KPTS-TV, Wichita, Kansas; Robert M. Ogles, Program Director, WHEL, Knoxville, Tennessee; W. Lawrence Patrick, Senior Vice President, National Association of Broadcasters, Washington, D.C.; John Reese, Program Manager, WATE-TV, Knoxville, Tennessee; James J. Ridings, Vice President, The Arbitron Co., New York; and John R. Wilson, Vice President for Information Services and Advertising, WTTW-TV, Chicago.

We are also grateful to the National Association of Broadcasters, as well as a large number of individual radio and television stations for photographs and other materials found throughout this volume. These stations include KDKA Radio, Pittsburgh; KEYA-FM, Belcourt, North Dakota; KING-TV, Seattle; KIXE-TV,. Redding, California; KPTS-TV, Wichita, Kansas; KRON-TV and KTVU-TV, San Francisco; KWGN-TV, Denver; WAGA-TV, Atlanta; WCCO Radio, Minneapolis; WGBH-FM, Boston; WGN

Radio, Chicago; WHIO AM-FM-TV, Dayton, Ohio; WINS, New York; WIOD/WAIA-FM, Miami; WKPT-TV, Kingsport, Tennessee; WMC-TV, Memphis; WSB AM-FM-TV, Atlanta; WSJK-TV, Sneedville (Knoxville), Tennessee; WSPA-TV, Spartanburg, South Carolina; and WUOT-FM, Knoxville, Tennessee.

Valuable assistance also was provided by the broadcast networks and other media-related organizations, including ABC Radio and ABC-TV; Ampex Corporation; The Arbitron Company; Broadcast Pioneers Library; CBS Radio and CBS-TV; Corporation for Public Broadcasting; Cox Broadcasting Corporation; Federal Communications Commission; Fulton High School, Knoxville, Tennessee; *The Knoxville Journal;* Market Evaluations, Inc; Metromedia, Inc.; Mutual Broadcasting System; The National Archives; National Association of Broadcasters; NAB Code Boards; NBC Radio and NBC-TV; National Black Network; National Public Radio; A.C. Nielsen Company; Public Broadcasting Service; Public Radio Cooperative; Radio Advertising Bureau; RKO General Corporation; Satellite Television Corporation, a Comsat Subsidiary; Scientific Atlanta, Inc.; Sheridan Broadcasting Network; Sony Corporation; TAT Communications Company; Television Bureau of Advertising; Television Digest, Inc.; Telemation Corporation; Viacom, Inc.; Warner-Amex Company; Westinghouse Broadcasting Company; WGN Continental Broadcasting Company; and *The Washington Post.*

Finally, we extend thanks to our wives, families, and colleagues for their patience and encouragement during the years we have devoted to the preparation of *Radio and Television Programming.*

1

AN INTRODUCTION TO BROADCAST PROGRAMMING

Radio broadcasting received a tremendous public welcome when the first regularly licensed stations began transmitting during the period from 1920 to 1922. Starting with KDKA, the Westinghouse station in Pittsburgh, the number of stations grew from three in 1920 to more than 500 at the end of 1922. Furthermore, the public was so captivated by the new medium that, by 1925, nearly one-fourth of all American families had bought receivers to tune in the wireless programs. Thirty years later, the scene was re-enacted with the beginning of television broadcasting.

Although the public no longer marvels at the technical miracles of radio and television, these two media have become immensely important instruments, depended upon by vast numbers of people for entertainment and information. Even in newly developing countries, broadcasting has become a vital tool for educating the populace and stimulating social and economic development.

The success of broadcasting as a communications instrument—regardless of the philosophical perspective or the criteria used for measuring success—depends squarely upon the creation and presentation of attractive programming. This fact is crystal clear. And, because audience-appealing programs are so vital in the broadcast undertaking, this book was developed as a text and guide for those who plan to serve the public and the broadcasting industry in program management. This first chapter focuses on the characteristics of radio and TV broadcasting in the United States, including an overview of programming practices and a comparison of the two electronic media.

PHILOSOPHIES AND SYSTEMS

Broadcast systems throughout the world differ in terms of station ownership, economic support, and programming philosophy. Since national governments determine the nature of the radio and TV systems within their boundaries, the characteristics of those systems always reflect the basic national economic and sociopolitical philosophies. It is no accident, therefore, that broadcasting in the United States is characterized by privately owned, advertising-supported networks and stations. Neither should it be surprising that broadcasting is a state-owned monopoly in the Soviet Union. Both approaches coincide with the basic philosophies of their home countries.

Three principal philosophical approaches determine the nature of broadcasting throughout the world, resulting in (1) authoritarian, (2) benevolent, and (3) competitive systems. The characteristics of these approaches are shown in Figure 1.1 and discussed next.

Figure 1.1 Broadcast Systems and Programming Goals

System	Usual Ownership	Usual Economic Support	Usual Program Goals	Prototype System
Authoritarian	State	Government	To implement governmental objectives	USSR
Benevolent	Public corporation	Tax on receivers; sometimes advertising and government subsidy	To uplift the public's taste and maintain an informed populace	BBC (UK)
Competitive	Private ownership	Advertising	To reach the maximum audience	USA

In an *authoritarian* society, the broadcasting system is a vehicle through which the government can communicate its policies and goals to the citizens and with which it can attempt to mold the culture. Because such governments strongly discourage dissent, their broadcast systems usually operate under very strict news controls. Entertainment programming is usually considered a waste of time, but cultural fare is emphasized because sports and the arts are also subsidized as vehicles to glorify the state. Other talk and informational programming tend to support state goals such as improving literacy, health conditions, and nutrition, as well as promoting national pride and unification.

Unlike the authoritarian plan, no attempt is made under the *benevolent* approach to control the news or other programming for thought control. Such systems, exemplified by the British Broadcasting Corporation (BBC), usually exist in democratic societies in which freedom of thought and expression are cherished rights. Extensive, but balanced, news programming is typical as part of the broadcasting system's effort to maintain a well-informed populace.

In entertainment programming, a typical benevolent system attempts to give the public a satisfying blend of "what it needs as well as what it wants." Thus, an attempt is made to lead public taste through exposure to quality, or "high brow," entertainment and culture, while also providing a modest amount of mass appeal fare. Increasingly, however, the BBC and other paternalistic radio and TV systems have responded to the wishes of the broad general public because of competition for audiences from rival systems.

In free enterprise societies in which private ownership of broadcast outlets is allowed, the government essentially serves as a licensing agent to place stations in the hands of qualified parties who pledge to serve the public's interest while attempting to earn a profit. In a *competitive* broadcasting environment, the government may establish basic public interest standards; but otherwise it exerts minimum, if any, control over specific program decisions. However, licenses, as we shall see in a later chapter, may be revoked when those entrusted with them abuse their trusteeships by malpractice or by ignoring the public interest.

Because profit making is enhanced among advertising-supported stations by reaching large audiences, networks and stations generally compete against each other with mass appeal entertainment and informational programming and/or with specialized fare. As a result, popular entertainment almost always overshadows cultural offerings. And news programming, which tends to be free from governmental control (though there are exceptions in some countries), is sometimes given an entertainment coating to attract a large audience.

In a free enterprise competitive system, the sponsors defray the cost of programs which inform, entertain, and provide service to the public. Despite the tendency toward popularizing the media, advertising serves to keep broadcasting relatively free from governmental control. In the final analysis, all programs broadcast by radio and television stations succeed or fail on the basis of public acceptance.

In reality, few "pure" systems of any of the three types exist among the leading nations of the world. Even authoritarian systems, such as the Soviet Union's, at times respond to public sentiment. And in both the United States and the United Kingdom, the traditional systems have been modified with the emergence of strong alternative media. In Canada and Japan as well, broadcasting also exhibits a dual nature, with influence from both government and private ownership. Thus, among many of the leading nations of the free world, "dualistic" is an appropriate adjective for describing broadcast systems.

THE BROADCAST MEDIA IN THE UNITED STATES

Broadcasting in the United States consists of two systems: (1) the commercial, advertising-supported stations and networks and (2) public broadcasting, supported by educational institutions, federal and state appropriations, grants from foundations and corporations, and funds from a variety of other sources. Commercial broadcasting was well entrenched long before public stations gained substantial funding with the passage of the Public Broadcasting Act of 1967. Although both systems have extensive coverage throughout the country, commercial broadcasting retains its dominance.

The nature of competitive broadcasting has produced a number of strategies designed to win listeners or viewers from the competition. These strategies will be explored in chapters 7 and 8. Although public broadcasting occasionally uses these same techniques, most noncommercial stations attract audiences through "alternative" programming.

RADIO AND TV STATIONS

Broadcast antennas dot the American landscape, sending entertainment, information, service programming, and advertising to vast audiences that include nearly every home in the United States. More than 10,000 broadcast stations, excluding translators and other low-power TV outlets, are licensed to communities of all sizes throughout the country. Approximately 9,000 stations (8,000 radio and 900 TV) operate as commercial outlets, and some 1,400 (1,100 radio and 300 TV) are licensed as noncommercial educational or public stations.

Radio and TV stations are each subdivided into two major categories based on technical considerations. Radio's two services, amplitude modulation (AM) and frequency modulation (FM) broadcasting, are divided further into classes of stations based on their geographical coverage. Television stations are licensed to either the very high frequency (VHF) or the ultrahigh frequency (UHF) band. These two services differ noticeably in effective coverage because of wave length characteristics in the two portions of the spectrum.

Radio stations exist in small towns (some even under 1,000 population), cities, and major metropolitan centers. On the other hand, because of economics, full-service TV stations are ordinarily located in metropolitan cities.

STATIONS AND REGULATION

Under the US system, a license to operate a radio or TV station is a public trust. The Federal Communications Commission (FCC), chartered under the Federal Communications Act of 1934, represents the public in awarding licenses to individuals, companies, corporations, and institutions which pledge to serve the interests and needs of their respective coverage areas. Although the Communications Act prohibits censorship of programs by the FCC, the courts have allowed the Commission to determine if a license should be renewed on the basis of how well the licensee has served the public during its trusteeship.

The rules and regulations governing broadcast stations have been relaxed greatly during the Carter and Reagan administrations. A more complete discussion of programming and regulation is given in chapter 3.

WHO OWNS THE BROADCAST STATIONS?

There are three principal forms of commercial station ownership in the United States. These are (1) network owned-and-operated (O & O) stations, (2) group-owned stations, and (3) independently owned stations. The networks and other group owners are limited to no more than seven stations in each broadcast service (AM, FM, and TV). In addition, common ownership of two stations of the same type (e.g., AM radio) which substantially overlap in geographical coverage is forbidden. And, under the rules adopted in 1975, the FCC forbids the formation of local crossmedia ownerships that consist of any combination of radio outlets, TV stations, and daily newspapers in the same market.[1] However, new AM-FM combinations still may be established at our date of publication.

Each major *network* company—ABC, CBS, and NBC—holds licenses for five important, major market TV stations and a number of radio outlets. These stations are among the most profitable and valuable properties in the broadcasting industry. The Mutual Broadcasting System, a radio network, owns a small number of radio stations. Other network organizations, including RKO General, the Spanish International Network (SIN), and the Christian Broadcasting Network (CBN), also own stations.

Whenever an organization owns two or more stations in different market areas, *group ownership* exists. This segment of broadcasting includes about 150 different TV ownerships and some 300 radio concerns. Although group owners usually strive for the maximum number of stations allowed (seven AM, seven FM, and seven TV), the average is about 3.5 per group.[2] Figure 1.2 lists the 25 largest TV groups, including network owned-and-operated stations, in order of weekly circulation as of January 1, 1982.

Group ownerships represent an important force in broadcasting, second only to the national networks. Such major groups as Storer, Metromedia, Group W (Westinghouse), Cox, and Multimedia regularly engage in program production and syndication and/or operate national news bureaus in addition to operating their stations.

Independently owned stations, which may be network-affiliated, involve station properties in only one broadcast market. This licensee pattern is most common among small market radio stations, but a few exceptions exist among larger markets. Some examples include WWL AM-FM-TV, New Orleans; WHAS AM-TV and WAMZ-FM, Louisville; KHQ AM-FM-TV, Spokane; and WSPA AM-FM-TV, Spartanburg, South Carolina.

A variety of types of organizations also hold licenses for public radio and TV stations. Major categories include (1) state network authorities; (2) state departments of education; (3) public and private colleges and universities; (4) local governments, including municipalities and boards of education; (5) nonprofit associations and corporations; and (6) public libraries.

Figure 1.2 25 Largest TV Station Groups (January 1, 1982)

Rank	Group	Net Weekly Circulation	Number of Stations
1	ABC O & O Stations	16,007,700	5
2	CBS O & O Stations	15,971,400	5
3	NBC O & O Stations	15,196,100	5
4	Metromedia	14,343,300	7
5	RKO General	10,025,200	4
6	Tribune Broadcasting	9,281,000	3
7	Westinghouse	9,116,500	6
8	Storer	7,318,700	7
9	Field Communications	6,944,100	5
10	Capital Cities	6.090,200	6
11	Gaylord	5,972,300	7
12	Taft	5,942,800	7
13	Cox	5,532,700	5
14	Scripps-Howard	4,283,200	6
15	Post-Newsweek	4,110,800	4
16	Golden West	4,068,400	3
17	Times-Mirror	3,954,000	7
18	Gannett	3,911,300	7
19	Corinthian	3,759,200	6
20	Hearst	3,675,800	4
21	Outlet	3,344,200	5
22	Chris-Craft	3,306,200	2
23	Meredith	3,010,300	6
24	Pulitzer	2,942,900	5
25	Evening News Association	2,836,900	5

Source: Arbitron data compiled from *Television Factbook, 50* (Washington: Television Digest, Inc., 1981).

TELEVISION BROADCASTING

Television stations in the United States utilize 82 different channels within the VHF and UHF bands. Varying amounts of power are allowed, depending upon channel number and band, to equalize coverage among competing maximum-service stations. In addition, in 1981, the FCC established a special class of low-power TV stations designed to serve small communities and urban enclaves.

Most TV stations tend to be *area stations,* reaching out some 65 to 80 miles. However, because of inherent technical limitations, UHF stations rarely attain coverage comparable to their VHF competitors. On the other hand, a few large market independent stations now serve national audiences through satellite distribution of their signals to widespread cable systems.

HOW ARE TV STATIONS CLASSIFIED?

Three principal methods are commonly used for classifying commercial television stations. These are (1) type of channel assignment, (2) size of market, and (3) network affiliation or independent status. Two other special categories are now included in the television industry. Stations which engage in subscription telecasting (STV) represent the fourth category, while the low-power TV service is a fifth category. Figures 1.3 and 1.4 show the studio/office facilities of two modern broadcast stations.

Figure 1.3 The ultramodern home of WSPA-TV, the CBS-TV affiliate for Greenville-Asheville-Spartanburg, the nation's 38th broadcast market (1982).

Photo courtesy of WSPA-TV, Spartan Radiocasting Co., Spartanburg, S.C.

Figure 1.4 The WGN-Continental Broadcast Center in Chicago houses both WGN-TV and clear-channel WGN Radio.

Photo courtesy of WGN Continental Broadcasting Co., Chicago.

Channel Assignment

Stations are frequently classified on the basis of their assignment to a VHF or a UHF channel. Wave lengths in the UHF band are much shorter than those in the VHF, which results in critical reception problems for many UHF stations. These problems become especially acute in hilly or mountainous regions.

Several attempts have been made by the FCC and Congress to reduce the disparity between UHF and VHF stations. Efforts have included (1) a requirement that all TV sets sold in interstate commerce have both UHF and VHF tuners; (2) a provision for UHF stations to transmit at power levels up to 5,000,000 watts; and (3) the designation of certain cities for all-UHF broadcasting. In addition, the FCC has authorized more than 50 UHF stations to provide over-the-air pay television programs. While all of these measures have helped, UHF stations continue to suffer a competitive disadvantage when competing against VHF outlets. Nevertheless, the number of UHF stations continues to grow as the public seeks greater diversity in its programming choices.

Market Rank

Another factor which affects TV programming is market rank. This item is very significant because the advertising potential for a television station correlates closely with the size of its market area. In turn, programming budgets, including prices expected for syndicated shows, also scale closely to market rank.

Some 240 TV markets in the United States are identified and ranked according to the number of TV households in each market. The markets themselves are delineated by the two principal audience research organizations on the basis of *predominance of viewing* within each county in the nation.

The Arbitron Company ranks US television markets by "Areas of Dominant Influence" (ADI), while the A.C. Nielsen Company similarly ranks "Designated Market Areas" (DMA). TV outlets in the top 50 markets are regarded as major market stations. Those located in markets 51 through 100 are considered secondary market stations, while those below the ADI/DMA rank of 100 are regarded as small market stations.

Network vs. Independent Status

Television stations are also classified as network affiliates or as independent outlets. Affiliation normally is desirable since it provides access to popular network programming and advertising revenue, while nonnetwork stations must defray the full costs of their programming. Affiliated TV stations usually obtain about 65 percent of their programming requirements from the network. Only in rare instances, however, does an independent station obtain network shows, usually when a particular program has been turned down by the primary affiliate in its market.

Independent television stations, which have far more programming flexibility than affiliates, usually rely upon feature movies, sports, and syndicated programs for their schedules. The syndicated programming often includes a hefty roster of network reruns. Independent stations also produce local live programs to varying degrees and in addition, some nonnetwork stations engage in cooperative ventures to increase the availability of program material. One such venture, "Operation Prime Time," produces occasional network-quality evening programs which are fed via satellite circuits to the subscribing stations. Another major program development for independent television was the launching of nightly national newscasts on an independent network basis. The "Independent Network News" is produced by WPIX-TV, New York, and relayed by communication satellite to more than 80 independent TV stations across the country.

Because of increased availablility of competitive programming, independent operation is far more viable now than during television's early decades.

Subscription Television

In 1968, after many years of deliberation, the FCC authorized over-the-air pay television. In subscription television (STV), a station encodes a scrambled signal from its transmitter, which then may be unscrambled by a decoding device attached to a customer's set. Stimulated by the cable television industry's successful pay TV efforts during the mid-1970s, a rush developed for STV franchises. The first such stations began operating in 1977. By January 1, 1982, subscribership to STV exceeded 1,500,000 households, with about 25 stations in service. It is likely that over-the-air pay television will be available in most top 50 markets by 1990.

Subscription television stations typically build their pay TV schedules around recent uncut and unedited movies, including PG and R titles, plus sports attractions and made-for-STV entertainment. Typical stations provide STV programming after 8:00 PM, when audience potential is greatest and when nonnetwork stations usually have difficulty competing against prime-time network fare. During their non-STV hours, usually most of the daytime, these stations compete as general or specialty independents. Formats such as all news, financial, religious, Spanish, and Black programming have been used.

The concepts for broadcast pay television programming are still emerging. New technology, including satellite distribution of material, already plays an important role in facilitating pay TV broadcasting. Although it is a recent adjunct to the broadcasting industry, pay television appears to have a bright future.

Low-Power Television

As the 1980s began, the FCC proposed to expand the number of television stations by permitting the operation of low-power outlets wherever they might fit without interfering with the reception of existing maximum power stations. This concept, however, was not entirely new. For many years, low-power *translator* stations have been used to bring TV signals to areas of poor reception. However, translators only repeat the programs of the originating station, whereas low-power stations may originate programs.

Typical low-power stations can effectively cover small communities or sectors of urban centers within a 5- to 10-mile radius. This limited coverage is suitable for localized service to small towns and to minority groups clustered in urban enclaves. Some low-power facilities are expected to rebroadcast pay TV and other nationally produced programs from distant sources to their local service areas. In either case, low-power stations will further stimulate demand for original programming.

TELEVISION PROGRAMMING POLICIES

The prevailing program goal for commercial television is to attract as many viewers as possible during every broadcast period. Program directors not only seek to attain dominant shares of the audience, but also to attract specific types of viewers who are most demographically desirable to advertisers. As a result, many programs are chosen because of their appeal to 18- to 49-year-old adults, the principal consumer demographic group in our society.

The TV networks, their affiliates, and most independent stations also maintain a varied schedule to satisfy all significant types of viewers at some time each week. This approach also enables broadcasters to serve many types of advertising clients. As mentioned previously, some nonnetwork stations provide specialty programming for minority races, ethnic groups, and viewers with other specialized interests.

To turn to *public* television, the noncommercial segment of US broadcasting is also characterized by a dominant programming philosophy. Simply stated, that philosophy is *alternative programming* which contrasts with that offered by commercial broadcasters. Alternative programs, as such, may be *any* type of broadcast that has insufficient appeal to warrant advertising support or the economic use of commercial stations. Examples include classical music (though there a few such commercial radio stations), serious drama, and minority and children's educational programs. Other examples include documentaries, financial analyses, and minor sports, although these are programmed to some extent by commercial outlets. Even classic motion pictures may fit the alternative category. Daytime hours on public TV stations, of course, are usually devoted to *educational* broadcasts for in-school teaching.

In practice, public television has moved in a direction toward more appealing programming than it formerly had in its "educational" period. Programming trends in public television are discussed in chapter 9.

RADIO BROADCASTING

Now more than 60 years old, radio broadcasting, like television, attracts large audiences. Listeners historically have favored AM radio, but FM's share increased so rapidly during the 1970s that it now exceeds that of the older AM service. In some of the nation's large markets, FM stations collectively attract more than 60 percent of the listenership. Among the reasons for this dramatic change in listening patterns are the adoption of new competitive formats by many FM stations, increased public awareness of FM's superior high-fidelity sound, its stereophonic capability, and its uniform day/night station coverage.

Much speculation has been advanced about the future of the AM service. Because FM especially excels with musical reproduction, many programming specialists expect it to maintain a dominant position with music formats. However, AM broadcasters hope to improve their competitiveness with FM through AM stereophonic broadcasting. AM stations also tend to emphasize news and talk programming more than most FM stations do.

CLASSIFICATION OF STATIONS

The AM band consists of 107 channels, each only 10 kilohertz wide, which severely limits the fidelity of the sounds transmitted. Each frequency is designated for a specific level of service, with power assignments ranging from 250 to 50,000 watts. The AM frequencies are classified as (1) *clear channel,* intended for broad area coverage, often extending across several states; (2) *regional channels,* used by stations that serve a principal city and a surrounding region; and (3) *local channels,* designated for service to small localities.

The FM band contains 100 channels, each 200 kilohertz wide, which facilitates high-fidelity broadcasting. Stations are divided into four categories, which reflect the extent of geographic coverage. *Class A* stations, which serve small communities, are approximately comparable to Class IV (local) AM stations. *Class B* and *Class C* stations serve larger cities and their surrounding regions. FCC limitations restrict the effective radiated power (ERP) of Class A stations to 3,000 watts, Class B outlets to 50,000 watts, and Class C stations to 100,000 watts.[3] In addition, the FCC authorizes *Class D* FM stations at 100 watts for broadcast training purposes.

In both AM and FM radio, coverage is very important in establishing a station's capability to compete in its market. In general, the greater its coverage, the better equipped a station is to compete, or perhaps even to dominate, with a popular mass-appeal format. The reverse also is true. The smaller its coverage area, the less likely a station is to be a successful competitor for the mass audience.

RADIO PROGRAMMING POLICIES

Program policies in both AM and FM broadcasting vary widely among radio stations. With large numbers of outlets operating in all cities (New York and Los Angeles newspaper logs list about 100 stations each), most licensees must be satisfied with relatively small shares of the total audience. Therefore, commercial stations tend to specialize in distinctive formats designed to appeal to specific target groups. However, in every market, a few stations—usually five to ten—attract significant shares with broad-based popular formats.

As with public television, educational or public radio stations tend to provide alternative programming. These stations range from low-power student stations to 100,000-watt public outlets. The latter type usually develops programming strength in serious music and public affairs broadcasts.

THE ORGANIZATION OF BROADCASTING STATIONS

Radio and TV stations vary considerably in size and number of employees. While a few large market television stations employ as many as 300 persons, the average station has a staff of about 60 employees. In contrast, radio stations are relatively small employers. One-half of all AM stations have fewer than 11 full-time workers, and only one station in ten has as many as 25 on its staff.[4]

Regardless of size, however, broadcast stations usually are organized into six major functional areas which are closely interrelated. A general manager typically coordinates the efforts of these departments, which include engineering, programming, news, sales, the business office, and promotion. A representative organizational chart is shown in Figure 1.5.

ENGINEERING DEPARTMENT

A station must have sound engineering to deliver a usable signal to its audience, as well as attractive programming to win their attention. This department, headed by a technical director or chief engineer, is responsible for both the station's physical plant and its broadcast facilities. Maintaining these facilities so as to provide the audience with the best possible broadcast service is a major engineering function. Engineers also provide production facilities needed to meet program requirements and operate technical facilities at both the studio and the transmitting plant.

PROGRAM DEPARTMENT

The program director, who heads this department, is expected to obtain and present programs that will satisfy the needs of the audience, sponsors, and management. Major program decisions at both radio and television stations usually involve station managers, program directors, and sales managers, though the program director is usually expected to serve as the principal resource person and catalyst in the decision-making process. The functions of the program department, which are central to the purposes of this book, are discussed in chapter 4.

NEWS DEPARTMENT

Headed by the news director, the news department prepares newscasts and other public affairs programs. Because of the importance of news on both radio and television, this activity has become a top-line department throughout much of the broadcasting industry.

SALES DEPARTMENT

While engineering and programming functions are essential if a station is to attract a substantial audience, the sales department generates the vitally im-

Figure 1.5 Television Station Organization Chart

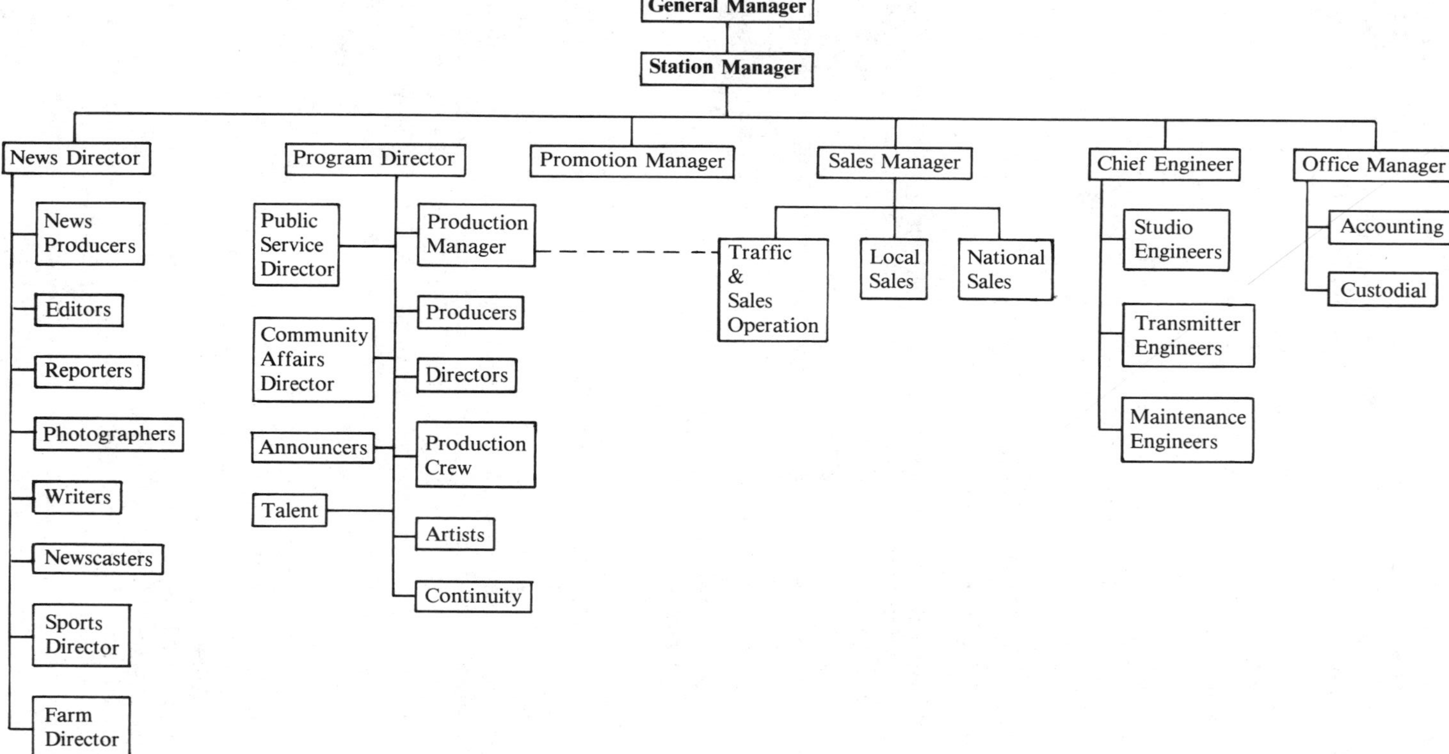

portant advertising revenue needed to defray costs of operation. This department usually is divided into national and local sales units. The national sales manager coordinates the solicitation of national advertising through the station's sales representatives in New York and other major advertising centers. The local sales effort is supervised by a local sales manager, and the number of local salespersons varies depending upon market size and competition.

BUSINESS OFFICE

This department of a broadcasting station handles such diverse activities as bookkeeping, billing, payroll, preparing tax and corporate forms, general secretarial duties, reception of guests, and custodial functions.

PROMOTION DEPARTMENT

Advancing the station's own interests is the function of the promotion department. This unit seeks to establish and maintain a large share of audience for the station's programs by promoting them through various media, including the station itself. Promotion personnel also assist the sales department by preparing sales presentation materials, both general and customized for specific prospective clients, and by planning advertisements for the trade press.

The promotion department has taken on a much more significant role in recent years as the radio and television industries have become more competitive.

OTHER DEPARTMENTS

In addition to the six principal departments, a number of lower ranking units perform other vital functions, such as copy preparation, traffic or scheduling, and research.

The *continuity department* assists advertisers, particularly nonagency clients, in the preparation of commercial messages. At many stations, this department also writes program material and public service announcements.

The *traffic unit* is responsible for preparing the station's operating schedules, which blueprint the day's on-air activities. The schedule lists each program, commercial, public service message, and any other type of material to be broadcast. It also must indicate the sources and times of broadcast for all items. Many television and large radio stations now produce their daily operating schedules with computer assistance. A typical schedule is reproduced in chapter 3.

Every station engages in some research pertaining to its audience and its marketing needs, though the studies may be informal and limited in scope. Usually only large stations and major groups have in-house *research departments*. However, when done well, a research project may produce results far greater than its cost by uncovering useful data on consumers and products as well as programs and audiences. In addition, formal ascertainment studies (now required only of television stations) can provide management with significant insight into program needs of a station's service area.

Because of the need for independent research, most stations in competitive markets subscribe to audience studies conducted in their markets by national research firms. The two most important research organizations in broadcasting are the Arbitron Company and the A.C. Nielsen Company.

RADIO AND TELEVISION NETWORKS

Networks have been integral to US broadcasting since 1923, when the American Telephone & Telegraph Company began linking distant radio stations with its New York outlet to rebroadcast the programs of WEAF. Today, TV networks occupy a commanding position in the industry, while radio networks play a lesser, but still important, role.

The nature of network operations involves a central control point from which programming is fed to distant stations for transmission through their local facilities. Programs may originate at a network production center or at a remote point (e.g., a football stadium), or they may be produced on film or tape, either video or audio, ready to be fed from the network control center to outlying stations. Network signals are distributed to affiliate stations principally through telephone company facilities; however, there is growing use of communication satellites for network interconnections.

In addition to *live* interconnected networks, there is a limited amount of *tape* networking in the United States. It is feasible, for example, to provide identical programming to large numbers of stations by shipping duplicate audio or video tapes to the respective stations. This form of networking, however, is not very different from the "bicycling" of syndicated programs from station to station.

NETWORKS AND THEIR CLASSIFICATION

A radio or TV network may be one of three types: (1) national, (2) regional, or (3) custom-made. Each has its own distinctive characteristics.

National Networks

The most important type of network, of course, is the national network, which provides a regular and continuous program service through affiliates in all or most parts of the country. In television, these networks provide a broad variety of programming, including entertainment, news, sports, and special events. The radio networks mainly offer their affiliates news and special events coverage.

Each of the national television networks—ABC, CBS, and NBC—has about 200 affiliated stations. These outlets vary in coverage and caliber of operation somewhat from city to city. Overall, however, the three commercial networks are comparable and highly competitive. In addition, as we have mentioned, the Spanish International Network (SIN) serves about 20 US television stations with Spanish-language programming; and Independent Network News, a service of WPIX-TV, New York, provides daily national newscasts via satellite to numerous independent TV stations.

Public television stations also are linked together, using the Public Broadcasting Service (PBS) designation. PBS, which obtains its principal support from the Corporation for Public Broadcasting and grants from corporations and foundations, distributes programs produced by public stations to other public outlets across the country. Even though PBS is not called a network, it maintains a regular program schedule that essentially complements those of the commercial networks.

Although cable television is not broadcasting as such, it is important that we note here the rapid growth of *cable networks* as the 1980s evolve. These networks involve satellite distribution of programming to local cable systems. A few of the more prominent ones include the Cable News Network (CNN), the Christian Broadcasting Network (CBN), the Cable Satellite Public Affairs Network (C-SPAN), the Entertainment and Sports Network (ESPN), Black Entertainment TV, and the USA Network. "Home Box Office" (HBO), "Showtime," and "The Movie Channel" are similar pay TV cable networks. And finally, such "super stations" as WTBS-TV, Atlanta, and WGN-TV, Chicago, have achieved national cable distribution and consequently resemble cable networks. The growth of cable networking in all of its forms has resulted from the development of satellite program delivery systems and the rapid growth of cable subscribership, which was estimated by broadcast economist Paul Kagan at 21,500,000 US homes on June 30, 1981.[5]

The four long-established radio networks—ABC, CBS, Mutual, and NBC—provided ten different program services as of January 1, 1982. At least one other service was planned by the CBS network during 1982. In addition, other networks have proliferated during recent years as America's radio stations have become more specialized demographically. These younger networks include the National Black Network (NBN) and the Sheridan Broadcasting Network, both Black-oriented services; RKO General, which operates three networks; and the CNN Radio Network, an all-news program service launched in 1982 by Turner Broadcasting, operators of the Cable News Network.

Public radio stations also are linked together to carry National Public Radio (NPR) programs, which are supported by the Corporation for Public Broadcasting. Some radio format syndicators also have turned to satellite distribution, which, in effect, has transformed their program services into a type of network operation. The Satellite Music Network (SMN) began a satellite-fed service in the late summer of 1981. Finally, both the Associated Press and United Press International operate news networks to which many radio stations subscribe.

Figure 1.6 lists each of the present (1982) radio network organizations, together with their complements of program services. The number of station outlets fluctuates frequently as the networks seek to improve the quality of their affiliate rosters. In fact, the radio network situation is in a state of constant change at this time, as new networks are established and, in some cases, survive for only brief periods.

With the exception of the national music format services and the CNN (All-News) Network, all of the present radio networks concentrate their programming efforts on hourly newscasts and short-form feature programs. Each program service available from a given network organization is intended for a different type of affiliate in terms of demographic appeal. CBS Radio, however, represents a variation from the typical pattern. The CBS Radio Network, as distinguished from its youth-oriented "RadioRadio," continues as a full-service network with hourly newscasts, commentaries, and short features related to consumer affairs, sports, homemaking, business, and other topics. CBS Radio also provides its affiliated stations with a nightly mystery drama and extensive play-by-play sports.

Figure 1.6 Radio Networks and Their Program Services

Network Organizations and Their Program Services	Demographic Appeal and/or Type of Service
ABC Radio	
1. ABC Contemporary Network	Top 40 AM and FM Stations (12-34)
2. ABC Directions Network	Adult Contemporary/MOR (25-44)
3. ABC Entertainment Network	Personality Oriented (18-54)
4. ABC FM Network	FM Contemporary Stations (12-34)
5. ABC Information Network	News-Talk and MOR Stations (18-54)
6. ABC Rock Radio	AOR/Top Tracks Stations (15-34)
CBS Radio	
1. CBS Radio Network	News/Variety/MOR Stations (18-54)
2. RadioRadio	AOR/Contemporary Stations (18-34)
CNN Radio Network	All-News Stations
Mutual Broadcasting System (MBS)	General Adult Stations (18-54)
National Black Network (NBN)	Black Formatted Stations
NBC Radio	
1. NBC Radio Network	General Adult Stations (18-54)
2. The Source	AOR/Contemporary Stations (15-34)
3. TalkNet	Talk Oriented Stations
RKO General	
1. RKO-1	Adult Contemporary Stations (25-34)
2. RKO-2	News/Talk and MOR (35-44)
3. RKO "Radio Shows"	Various Formats and Target Audiences
Satellite Music Network	
1. "Country Coast-to-Coast"	Country Music Stations
2. "Starstation"	Popular Adult Format
3. "Beautiful Music"	Bonneville "Easy" Format
Sheridan Broadcasting Network	Black Formatted Stations

Regional Networks

There are more than 100 regional radio networks in the United States. Ordinarily these chains function as state news networks, providing frequent newscasts oriented toward listeners in a given geographical area. Programs usually are distributed through a combination of telephone links and off-the-air pick-up from FM stations.

The largest regional network, the Texas State Network, has more than 100 affiliated stations located throughout the Lone Star state. A list of regional radio networks appears annually in *Broadcasting/Cable Yearbook*.

Custom-Made Networks

Other specialized networks are created from time to time to broadcast specific programs such as sports events, political speeches, and even occasional entertainment shows. A number of independent firms establish occasional networks to cover professional and collegiate sports contests that are not carried by the national television networks. Examples include the Hughes Television Network, Mis-Lou Productions, and TV Sports, Inc. Stations which use these broadcasts may be independent outlets or affiliates which preempt regular network programming for the special one-time broadcasts.

"Operation Prime Time," an organization owned jointly by several broadcast group owners, is another sporadic network operation. OPT produces occasional dramatic and general entertainment programs of network quality which are distributed simultaneously by communications satellite to participating stations. The possibility of a fourth regular TV network long has been discussed, including speculation that it might evolve from OPT.

In radio, there are many custom-made sports networks, including hookups for most major college and university football and basketball teams. One of the few custom-made radio networks beyond the realm of sports is the Texaco-Metropolitan Opera Network. Functioning annually during the opera season, this network carries live Saturday afternoon performances of the Metropolitan Opera from New York to radio listeners throughout the country. Although the program is sponsored by Texaco, Inc., many public radio stations carry the opera broadcasts without commercial announcements.

IS NETWORK AFFILIATION IMPORTANT?

Network affiliation is highly advantageous to television stations for several reasons. First, major portions of an affiliate's programming needs are met with network offerings; and, as noted earlier, affiliates obtain network TV programs with no direct outlay of funds. Independent stations, in contrast, must defray the cost of most of their programming. Second, attractive network programming enhances the appeal of a station, thus improving the station's viability as an advertising medium. Third, with a few exceptions, TV network affiliation is a revenue-producing arrangement, since affiliates receive payment (under a complicated formula related to audience reach and the local competitive situation) for carrying network commercial programs.

While network affiliations are generally useful to radio stations because of access to national news and special events coverage, some stations prefer to operate independently. Radio affiliates in large markets usually receive a modest amount of compensation for broadcasting network commercial programs. In contrast, most small market affiliates pay for the network service.

OTHER ENTITIES IN BROADCAST PROGRAMMING

Modern broadcast programming is a highly complex activity that depends upon a variety of different organizations. The following groups are prominent in the overall activity of radio and television programming.

PROGRAM PRODUCERS

Program producers are production organizations which create and produce programs for sale to networks and individual stations.

PROGRAM DISTRIBUTORS

The sale and distribution of syndicated programs to individual stations are handled by program distributors. Program types offered include movie programs, reruns of "off-network" programs, and new or "first-run" syndicated programs produced especially for TV or radio. Packaged radio formats, both taped and satellite-distributed, also are important items available from program producers/distributors.

TALENT AGENCIES

Agents represent the talent people who perform in programs and deliver or otherwise participate in commercials. Normally, talent agencies are located in major entertainment and media production cities such as New York, Hollywood, and Nashville.

PRODUCTION STUDIOS

Facilities and staffs for the production of both programs and commercials are maintained by production studio organizations. TV studios usually specialize either in film or video tape production. Radio programs and commercials as well as audio tracks for many TV commercials are produced at sound recording studios. Other production houses specialize in animation, special effects photography, and out-of-studio production.

LIBRARY SERVICES

These services make available stock production materials, such as recorded music, sound effects, and visual aids, suitable for use in programs and commercials.

WIRE SERVICES

Two principal newswire services—the Associated Press and United Press International—provide radio and TV stations with continuous national, international, and regional news copy. Other wire services for special types of material include those of the Dow-Jones Company (business news) and the National Weather Service.

RESEARCH ORGANIZATIONS

Research firms are used to determine audience size and demographic composition, to pretest programs and commercial messages, and to measure the overall effectiveness of advertising and station programming.

PROGRAM CONSULTANTS

Program and news consultants work with networks and stations to advise them on schedules, formats, and methods of presentation. Consultants usually base their advice on research studies in the marketplace, as well as their own expertise.

ADVERTISERS

Generally speaking, advertisers are business firms which use the communications media to persuade consumers to buy their products or services, support their activities, or approve their goals. Most important, they provide the funds that make programming possible.

ADVERTISING AGENCIES

These organizations are hired by advertisers to plan and execute advertising campaigns. Major responsibilities include media buying, preparation and production of commercial messages, and research.

BROADCAST SALES REPRESENTATIVE FIRMS

Advertising is sold by these firms to national and regional advertisers on behalf of their client stations. *National "rep" firms* handle stations on an exclusive basis in any given market area; therefore, stations handled by any given firm are not competitive with each other.

RADIO AND TELEVISION: A COMPARISON

Because radio and television belong to the same electronic media family, they are usually grouped together. But although they have much in common, the two broadcast media differ in a number of significant ways. This section explores the advantages and disadvantages of each as a communications medium and compares radio and television in terms of practical usage.

HOW RADIO AND TV ARE ALIKE

Radio and television broadcasting share certain attributes based upon their common electronic technology. These common characteristics are summarized next.

Universality

Few, if any, items are more universally present in the homes of the American public than TV and radio sets. The universality of broadcasting is revealed in the following data: (1) more than 98 percent of all US households have at least one television set in working order;[6] (2) 97 percent of all TV households can tune in signals from four or more stations, while 71 percent can receive seven or more stations and 43 percent pick up ten or more television signals;[7] and (3) half of the nation's television households own two or more TV sets, while 85 percent have at least one color set.[8] (All of these estimates were provided by the A.C. Nielsen Company.)

Turning to radio, the Radio Advertising Bureau (RAB) reports that 99 percent of all US homes are radio-equipped. If this statistic alone were not enough to equate with universality, RAB adds that the average household has 5.5 radio sets in working order.[9]

Popularity

Not only is ownership of TV and radio sets virtually universal in the United States, Americans spend more time using the broadcast media than in any other activity except working and sleeping. Total radio listening per person averages three hours per day, while radio's cumulative reach among persons over 12 years of age stands at 95 percent weekly and 81 percent daily.[10] For television, the Nielsen Company estimates that TV households, on average, watch about six and a half hours (6:36) of programming daily.[11] Translated into individual viewing, each person watches, on average, more than three hours of television fare each day. Indeed, broadcasting is a tremendously popular medium.

Immediacy and Timeliness

The instant a radio or TV program is broadcast, whether by network or by a local station, it's received by its audience. There is no delay in reception as there is in the space-oriented print media. Consequently, both of the broadcast media excel in presenting live broadcasts of news, sports, and other special events. Even in routine programming, the live component adds an aura of excitement and perception of being *with* the performers. Audiences generally perceive that they are up-to-date on anything important, and advertisers benefit because their messages can be fresh and timely.

Use of Sound

Sound transmission permits full utilization of the human voice for communication with the audience. This personal quality builds rapport between air talent and listeners, enhancing the credibility and interest levels in programming and commercial messages. In addition, music and sound effects may be used to augment production.

Although sound is present in both media, it is of utmost importance in radio, which relies upon sound alone to convey information.

Choice of Program Content

Although station licensees determine the programs they offer, management is guided primarily by audience response in its program decisions. The result of interstation competition is varied programming, permitting the public to choose from a broad range of content. Programming variety also allows advertisers to select commercial positions which best match their target audience needs.

Integration of Material

Advertisers also benefit because of the opportunity to integrate their messages into the fabric of broadcast programming. High attention levels are customary, particularly in television, because the audience receives only one message at a time (program, commercial, public service message, or whatever); and it is given in its entirety before another item begins. Lead-ins to commercials also may be provided by program personalities.

UNIQUE ATTRIBUTES OF TELEVISION

Television has certain distinct characteristics in addition to those shared with radio. The most important, of course, is its visual component, which permits the instantaneous transmission of sight, motion, and color. With both visual and aural capabilities, television comes closer to the ideal of person-to-person communication than any other mass medium. These attributes, coupled with modern production equipment, offer immense creative opportunities for program producers.

And, whether television is watched in groups or by individuals, it is a compelling medium. Involvement levels for different types of programs do vary, but on the whole they tend to be quite high.

UNIQUE ATTRIBUTES OF RADIO

Despite the fact that television has overshadowed radio as the most powerful of all mass media, radio broadcasting continues to enjoy several unique attributes of its own.

First, because there is no predetermined picture, radio stimulates the imagination. Furthermore, the type of listening most common with radio (a single individual tuned in for information, services, and companionship) is especially conducive to the power of persuasion inherent through the voices and *word-pictures* delivered by trusted announcers.

Radio is more pervasive than television because of its greater portability and mobility. Listeners may use radio at almost any time in almost any location. Automobile drive-time is a prime example of radio's out-of-home reach.

People may listen to radio while engaged in other activities. Although they enjoy the programming at a divided attention level at times, the attention they give rises and falls with the importance of the material being broadcast. Producers have learned that frequent repetition of messages can resolve much of the attention-level problem. Also helpful are messages (both commercials and public service) that incorporate catchy, highly recognizable music and those that closely resemble, and therefore reinforce, TV messages.

Radio is an extremely flexible medium. In many cities there are one or two general appeal stations that attract large heterogeneous audiences. However, most radio stations offer specialized programming intended for well-defined target groups. Advertisers and public service communicators may use radio stations in a multitude of combinations to reach their desired audiences.

PROBLEMS INHERENT IN RADIO AND TELEVISION

Despite the numerous advantages, certain handicaps are inherent in broadcasting. Probably the most significant is the lack of permanence and tangibility which characterize space-oriented media. Thus, the fleeting, intangible nature of broadcast programming which allows sponteneity and timeliness is also a limiting factor.

A second problem which inconveniences the audience is the fact that each program is broadcast only once—at a time selected by the broadcaster rather than the consumer. This problem is complicated by the fact that consumers sometimes would like to see or hear more than one program broadcast at a given hour. However, this problem has been resolved by some viewers who, using home video-taping systems, record programs for viewing at their own convenience.

Third, a problem for some radio advertisers and program producers lies in the low attention given to certain types of programming. Additional research is needed on the effectiveness of messages on stations with various formats. However, it is widely accepted that announcements placed within informative programs and other types of foreground radio achieve the highest levels of attention from listeners.

A WORD FROM THE SPONSOR

Because commercial radio and television stations thrive or starve economically in direct proportion to the public acceptance of their programming, program managers must be concerned with the advertising, as well as the creative, side of broadcasting. Radio and TV stations are quite different in terms of practical usage by advertisers, whose funds pay the cost of programming.

Television has emerged as the most important single medium for national advertisers. National network and national spot business combined now account for about 60 percent of all TV revenues. In contrast, radio's principal source of revenue is local advertising, which represents about 75 percent of its total income.

Television's involvement capabilities and audience reach give it major responsibilities for communicating advertising information. TV has risen to the forefront as a primary advertising vehicle for large national marketers, and it is being used increasingly by large retail firms.

Radio is an important secondary medium for national advertisers. Radio's flexibility and low cost permit its use as a reminder medium by those who use TV, magazines, and/or newspapers for primary advertising. At the same time, radio continues to be useful to many small business establishments as a primary means for communicating with the public.

TV is a large investment medium, a point which in itself may limit its use to businesses with large advertising budgets. However, the fact that TV advertising rates are comparatively high in no way suggests that television is expensive. On the contrary, television, when measured on the basis of the cost required to reach 1,000 households (CPM), is an extremely efficient advertising medium. Radio, as suggested earlier, is a lower cost medium that is also quite efficient on a cost-per-thousand basis.

Once strictly competitive, radio and television now function quite differently in terms of programming and advertising services. Their complementary nature makes them ideal media partners for countless communication purposes.

A LOOK AHEAD

Broadcasting has proven to be a dynamic industry, capable of rapid change. The radio industry went through the "television revolution" and emerged stronger than ever before. Now, radio is undergoing an "FM revolution," and television faces many changes prompted by technology that promise to bring much more competition for viewership.

The industry continues to grow internally through an increasing number of radio and TV stations, networks, and program sources. It is expanding technologically through new and improved communications equipment that stimulates innovation in program production. Perhaps the most important such development was the introduction of satellite technology for the distribution of network and other programming to radio and TV stations, and cable systems. In Figure 1.7, we see a typical satellite receiving antenna in use at WAGA-TV, an Atlanta television station.

Figure 1.7 New programming and advertising opportunities via satellite transmission will occur frequently and in increasing numbers during the 1980s. This satellite earth station is in service at WAGA-TV, Atlanta.

Photo courtesy of Scientific Atlanta, Inc., and WAGA-TV 5, Storer Communications, Inc., Atlanta, Ga.

Despite the progress, the future appears somewhat cloudy, but still basically optimistic for broadcasting. First, new technology and regulatory decisions may permit additional growth in the number of radio and television stations. Second, significant changes will likely occur in the distribution of listenership and viewership because of changes in media structure. Cable and pay cable television are attracting increasingly large audiences, particularly with specialized programming from nonbroadcast sources. Subscription TV stations also are increasing their share of audiences and competing vigorously for program material. AM radio stations face a special challenge with the dramatic rise in FM's popularity.

Third, further competition from nonbroadcast programming will result from videodisc playback systems and home video recorders. These devices also may alter, to some degree, the public's usage patterns of broadcast programs. Finally, and this is the ultimate concern, direct satellite transmission of broadcast programming to the public may become a reality.

Our final chapter takes a look at broadcast programming in the somewhat hazy media milieu of the future. To all who enter into this field, however, the challenge of creating programs for electronic media outlets will be immense whatever the future brings.

SUMMARY

In this first chapter of *Radio and Television Programming,* we began by noting that broadcasting, once a novelty, has become a marvelous means of mass communication. The public depends upon radio and television to a very great degree for entertainment, information, and service. And broadcast management looks to programming people to supply the material.

We examined the "ABC's" of broadcasting philosophy (authoritarianism, and the benevolent and competitive approaches), noting the strengths and weaknesses of each. Against this background, we examined the types, extent, and ownership characteristics of radio and television stations in the United States. We introduced the varied and usually mass appeal programming found in commercial television, format specialization of commercial radio, and the alternative programming concept of public broadcasting.

Moving further, we looked at the organization of typical broadcast stations, noting the functional departments of engineering, programming, news, sales, business, and promotion, and the interrelatedness of programming with each of the others. Then the characteristics of broadcast networks were discussed, including their recent proliferation. This discussion was followed by a listing of other program sources available to radio and TV programmers. Chapter 1 concluded with a brief look into broadcasting's future.

We turn now to a series of chapters that explore in detail the many facets of broadcast programming as it is currently practiced. But first, in chapter 2, we will examine the history of broadcast programming from which those current practices have evolved.

ENDNOTES

1. Multiple Ownership of Standard, FM, and Television Broadcast Stations, Second Report and Order (FCC), 40 F.R. 6449 (1975).
2. Herbert H. Howard, *Television Station Group Ownership and Cross-Media Ownership: 1982* (Knoxville: Communications Research Center of The University of Tennessee for the National Association of Broadcasters, 1982).
3. Although present FCC rules limit FM power to 100,000 watts, certain stations which had higher power before the limit was imposed were allowed to continue their operation with previously authorized signal strength. Examples of such "grandfathered" stations include WMC-FM, Memphis (300,000 watts); WRVQ-FM, Richmond (200,000 watts); and KQUE-FM, Houston (280,000 watts).
4. Ward L. Quaal and James A. Brown. *Broadcast Management,* 2d ed. (New York: Hastings House Publishers, Inc., 1976), p. 81.
5. "Cable TV Revenues to Hit $3.3 Billion" (News Release) (Carmel, Calif.: Paul Kagan Associates, Inc., July 31, 1981).
6. *Nielsen Report on Television 1981* (Northbrook, Ill.: A.C. Nielsen Co., 1981), p. 3.
7. *Ibid.*, p. 2.
8. *Ibid.*, p. 3.
9. *Radio Facts* (New York: Radio Advertising Bureau, 1981), p. 4.
10. *Ibid.*, p. 9, 12.
11. *Nielsen Report, op. cit.,* p. 1.

STUDY QUESTIONS

1. Select a country other than your own and examine its broadcast system in terms of the following:
   a. What form of media ownership prevails?
   b. How are the broadcast media supported economically?
   c. What are the programming goals of the system?
   d. What is the basic media philosophy—authoritarian, benevolent, or competitive?
2. Compare and contrast the programming of a local public TV station with that of a commercial network outlet.
3. Compare and contrast the programming of a local public radio station with one of the leading commercial radio stations.
4. Analyze the ownership of the major broadcast stations in your city or a nearby metropolitan center. Is there network ownership of any stations? What group ownerships are involved? Are any major stations individually or locally owned?
5. Compare and contrast the programming of a local network-affiliated TV station with that of an independent television operation.
6. Analyze the programming offered by any subscription TV or low-power TV stations present in your market.
7. What are the most prominent radio formats in your market? How do these formats reflect the tastes and culture of the area?
8. Based on a visit to a local station, discuss in detail the functions of one of the major departments of the station.
9. Make a list of the major TV and radio networks that have outlets in your market. Are any networks left out? Why?
10. Relate the advantages and disadvantages of radio and television to the use of these media in your community by (a) the public and (b) advertisers.
11. What recent developments in the field of telecommunications have affected the programming of radio and television stations?

SUGGESTED READINGS

Broadcasting Yearbook. Washington: Broadcasting Publications, Inc. 1935–present. Published annually.

Chester, Giraud, Garnet R. Garrison, and Edgar E. Willis. *Television and Radio*. 4th ed. New York: Appleton-Century-Crofts, 1971.

Foster, Eugene S. *Understanding Broadcasting*. 2d. ed. Reading, Mass.: Addison-Wesley Publishing, 1982.

Head, Sydney W. with Christopher H. Sterling. *Broadcasting in America: A Survey of Television and Radio and New Technologies*. 4th ed. Boston: Houghton Mifflin, 1982.

Smith, F. Leslie. *Prespectives on Radio and Television: An Introduction to Broadcasting in the United States*. New York: Harper & Row, Publishers, 1979.

Summers, Harrison B., Robert E. Summers, and John H. Pennybacker. *Broadcasting and the Public*. Belmont, Calif.: Wadsworth Publishing, 1978.

Television Factbook. Washington: Television Digest, Inc. Published annually.

2

BROADCAST PROGRAMMING: A HISTORICAL PERSPECTIVE

Radio and television broadcasting today represent a major source of entertainment, information, and service to hundreds of millions of people throughout the world. Practically every person in the United States, Canada, Europe, Japan, and most other advanced countries relies, at least in part, upon the broadcast media for daily communication.

Broadcasting as we know it today is the result not only of scientific advances begun in the 19th century but also of programming efforts that began with the earliest radio stations and evolved through well over half a century of practical broadcasting. Professional broadcasters of the final decades of the 20th century must understand these historical developments in order to appreciate more fully the capabilities of radio, television, and other developing media. This chapter, therefore, seeks to trace broadcast programming from its infancy to its present stage.

THE BEGINNINGS: THE "UNOFFICIAL" BROADCASTING ERA

Three stages mark the beginnings of radio broadcasting. The first broadcasts were made by scientific pioneers who transmitted voices and other sounds to limited audiences on their experimental stations. These isolated events were followed by sporadic broadcasts by experimentally licensed stations. The formal beginning of broadcasting, however, dates from 1920, when the first regularly licensed station began operation.

The first instance of wireless voice transmission remains in doubt. One early claim involves a sending of the message, "Hello, Rainey," by Nathan B. Stubblefield to a neighbor during a radio demonstration near Murray, Kentucky, in 1892.[1] Then, on Christmas Eve of 1906, Reginald A. Fessenden, while conducting a demonstration from Brant Rock, Massachusetts, transmitted an experimental program that was picked up by sailors on nearby ships. During the transmission, Fessenden played a violin solo, read verses from the Book of Luke, and played a phonograph recording of Handel's "Largo."[2] Both Stubblefield and Fessenden, however, used crude techniques for transmitting sound.

Lee De Forest, an American physicist, finally succeeded in developing a satisfactory means of transmitting sound in 1907. He used a triode or three-element vacuum tube that permitted the modulation of powerful radio signals by weaker energy patterns such as those generated by a microphone.

De Forest began experimental sound transmission during the summer of 1907, when he played phonograph music over his transmitter in New York. During the following year, he transmitted phonograph music from the Eiffel Tower in Paris. In 1910, De Forest staged the first live musical broadcast in history—an on-stage performance by Enrico Caruso, the famous Italian operatic tenor, at the Metropolitan Opera House in New York. In 1916, De Forest broadcast regular programs of phonograph records and announcements over his New York station. Credits to record suppliers and announcements about his own company's products may well have been radio's first commercial messages. De Forest also broadcast the 1916 election returns, four years before the celebrated inauguration of KDKA in Pittsburgh.

Two other important experimental stations operated during the same era. Charles David Herrold operated a facility at San Jose, California, as early as 1909. That station, which did not program continuously, is now KCBS, San Francisco. Another station was established in 1915 at the University of Wisconsin at Madison. That station (9XM), which specialized in weather and agricultural information, became the direct predecessor to WHA, Madison, the oldest operating educational radio station in the United States.[3]

The gradual emergence of radio as a public medium led to a prediction in 1916 by a young Marconi Company telegraph operator, David Sarnoff, that each home someday would be equipped with a "radio music box" capable of bringing listeners music, information, instruction, and entertainment. Sarnoff also suggested that the company which established this service could profit handsomely from it and reap important advertising benefits. Although the Marconi Company did not pursue the matter, Sarnoff's prediction ultimately came to pass. He eventually became chief executive of the Radio Corporation of America and perhaps the most powerful single figure in the development of broadcasting in the United States.

During the period of US involvement in World War I (1917–1918), the Wilson Administration placed all commercial wireless stations under government control and required the dismantling of all amateur stations. However, both experimental and amateur stations took to the air in many cities during 1919 and 1920. The University of Wisconsin's 9XM returned to the air, and two new and very significant stations began broadcasting. These outlets were 8MK, Detroit, established by the *Detroit News,* and 8XK, operated by Dr. Frank Conrad, a Westinghouse engineer, at East Pittsburgh. These two stations quickly attracted a public following among radio enthusiasts who built their own receiving sets.

A major turning point for radio broadcasting came at Pittsburgh's 8XK, where Dr. Conrad frequently played phonograph records requested by listeners. During the summer of 1920, a Pittsburgh department store took advantage of Conrad's programs to advertise a sale of radio receivers. These manufactured radios, priced at $10.95, were sold out shortly after the newspaper advertisement appeared.

The store's successful promotion caught the attention of Westinghouse officials, who suddenly realized that, instead of communicating from point to point, perhaps reaching the *largest* possible audience was the key to the future of radio. Westinghouse and Dr. Conrad then converted 8XK to a regular commercial radio station, with greater power and coverage than before. This new station, supported financially by Westinghouse, was operated in order to stimulate the sale of manufactured receivers built by the company.

BROADCASTING'S FORMAL BEGINNING IN 1920

After obtaining the first commercial license to operate a broadcast station, Westinghouse inaugurated KDKA's service on November 2, 1920. The occasion was the night of the presidential election between Warren G. Harding and James M. Cox, and the evening's program featured election returns interspersed with phonograph records and live music. The audience for the first licensed broadcast was made up primarily of amateur radio operators and others who had bought sets, as well as their guests and listeners in country clubs, bars, and other public places. Their response to KDKA's programming was phenomenal.

KDKA became an immediate success. The demand for receiving sets skyrocketed as the public became attracted to radio—first by its novelty, then by its programs. KDKA's program logs were printed by newspapers in many cities of North America. Shortly, inspired by its success, dozens of other stations were established throughout the country.

Like most early stations, KDKA transmitted only a few hours a day at first. Its initial schedule consisted of two hours of programs each night except Sunday. KDKA's Sunday night silence also was typical of early radio; it permitted listeners to use that evening to tune in distant stations—a favorite pastime of early listeners.

KDKA pioneered many types of programs that became standard for the young radio industry. Its early schedule consisted of phonograph records, orchestra music, news bulletins, public service messages, church services, political talks, sports, and occasional free entertainment from members of the audience who wanted to perform on the new medium.

In addition, KDKA established a reputation for "firsts" in broadcasting, such as the first remote church broadcast, first broadcast address by a national figure (Secretary of Commerce Herbert Hoover), first broadcast of stock market reports, and the first broadcast of baseball scores.

Other radio manufacturers, including the General Electric Company, the Crosley Corporation, the Stromberg-Carlson Company, and the Philco Corporation, followed the Westinghouse example, building stations to develop a market for their receiving sets. These licensees became known as the "Radio Group." Westinghouse itself established three additional stations.[4]

Early radio station licensees also included newspapers, educational institutions, churches, and department stores. In addition, dozens of small stations converted from amateur status to commercially licensed operations. Many were operated simply as hobbies by their owners. By May of 1922, more than 200 commercial station licenses had been issued, and the number reached a peak of 576 by early 1923.[5]

PROGRAMMING IN THE 1920s

Special events broadcasts overshadowed all other types of radio programming during the early 1920s. The dramatic live accounts of unfolding events, often broadcast from the scene, soon became the most exciting facet of radio.

A few examples of radio's early special events include the funeral of President Woodrow Wilson in 1921 and President Warren Harding's dedication of the Francis Scott Key monument at Fort McHenry in 1922. Harding's speech was the first formal address by a president on radio. Two years later, when there were 1,500,000 radio sets in use, millions of Americans heard both the Democratic and Republican national conventions and the election returns which sent Calvin Coolidge back to the White House.

In sports, both the Dempsey-Carpentier heavyweight championship fight and the World Series were broadcast in 1921. That four-game series between the Yankees and the Giants was reported from a last row seat at the old Polo Grounds in New York to the WJZ studios in Newark, where an announcer described the game into a microphone.

Radio's ability to reproduce sounds did not go unnoticed by its programmers, who constantly sought new program ideas. Among early special effects were such realistic and novel sounds as tugboat horns in New York's harbor, the noises of the subway, and the sound of an egg frying on a Manhattan sidewalk on a hot summer day.

As listeners tired of radio's novelty, stations responded with more discriminating material. Regular weekly shows soon replaced the informal, unstructured approach to programming. Free amateur talent was gradually replaced by paid entertainers, although talent fees were modest for many years. Barter arrangements to obtain professional talent also were common. Many stations, for example, presented dance music from hotel ballrooms throughout the 1920s. Typically, the stations gave both the hotel and its band a free plug in exchange for the programming.

One of the first hotel bands to broadcast was the Vincent Lopez orchestra, which started a long series of radio appearances over WJZ from Hotel Pennsylvania in 1921. Two other prototype programs begun during the same year at WJZ were a weekly comedy series by Ed Wynn and regular jazz shows by the Paul Whiteman orchestra. But not all live musical programs were of popular music. The Westinghouse station in Chicago, KYW, programmed complete live broadcasts by the Chicago Opera Company, beginning in 1921.

Because attractive programming became increasingly expensive, the subsidy approach for radio's economic support did not prove feasible. However, an alternative method of financial support was instituted in 1922, when the American Telephone and Telegraph Company established WEAF as a "toll" station in New York City. AT & T's concept, following the familiar long-distance pattern, called for a single powerful station to serve many senders of messages, rather than for each interested company to establish its own station. Therefore, from its beginning, WEAF offered to lease time to anyone who wished to broadcast a message.

WEAF failed to attract personal senders of messages, but it did begin to attract commercial sponsors. The first paid message was a ten-minute talk for the Queensboro Corporation, which paid WEAF $50.00 to advertise a real estate venture on Long Island. The message, broadcast on August 28, 1922, was quickly followed by sponsored entertainment programs that included commercial messages. WEAF required its clients to keep their advertisements subdued because radio was regarded as a guest invited into the homes of its listeners.

WEAF also availed itself of its parent company's long distance circuits to broadcast special news events and play-by-play sports from outside New York. The WEAF-AT & T combination quickly and inevitably led to the establishment of the country's first radio network. From 1924 through 1926, WEAF's programs were aired by stations in many of the large cities of the Northeast and Midwest. By 1924, the WEAF network could clear enough telephone lines to broadcast special events on a coast-to-coast basis. President Coolidge spoke to the American public on the first such hook-up in October, 1924.

Sponsored network programs in the early years usually carried the client's name as part of the title. A few examples included "The Lucky Strike Radio Show," "The A & P Gypsies," and the "Happiness Boys." The latter was a song and patter show with Billy Jones and Ernie Hare, who broadcast regularly for Happiness Candy Bars. Another popular song and comedy team, the "Gold Dust Twins," was sponsored by Gold Dust Soap Powders. Although WEAF's schedule emphasized light entertainment, the station's programming also included cultural fare. In 1924, for example, WEAF began a long-running series of music appreciation broadcasts conducted by Dr. Walter Damrosch.

With its network facilities and sponsored entertainment shows, WEAF soon began to eclipse the competitor "Radio Group" stations in audience appeal. Then, the "Radio Group" subsequently organized a network of its own, fed from WJZ, Newark. Because AT & T would not lease long distance lines to its competitor, the WJZ network was forced to use the less desirable circuits of Western Union. In addition, AT & T claimed sole rights to sell radio advertising under certain patent rights it held.

The stalemate in radio competition was broken in 1926 when the Federal Trade Commission initiated an inquiry into alleged monopolistic practices. Subsequently, a new agreement was reached between AT & T, RCA, General Electric, and Westinghouse, whereby (1) RCA, GE, and Westinghouse established a new company, to be known as the National Broadcasting Company, to handle their broadcasting activities, and (2) the telephone organization withdrew from broadcasting but provided long distance circuits to interconnect stations which then became network outlets. In addition, AT & T sold its New York station to NBC for $1,000,000, and WEAF became one of NBC's flagship stations.

With these agreements of 1926, most of the fundamental problems which had hindered radio's development were resolved. Broadcasting would be supported primarily by advertising income, and networks would originate and distribute quality mass-appeal and specialized programs for rebroadcast by their affiliated stations throughout the country. The only significant obstacle remaining was the unclear regulatory situation, which had allowed the technical aspects of broadcasting to deteriorate from an overcrowded broadcast band. In 1927, the 69th Congress enacted the Federal Radio Act, which helped immensely to restore technical order.

NATIONAL NETWORKS EMERGE

America's first nationwide network, the National Broadcasting Company, inaugurated its program service on November 15, 1926, with a gala coast-to-coast extravaganza. Nineteen stations scattered across the country carried NBC's debut.[6] The network's regular operational beginning, which took place early in 1927, signified the serious beginning of commercial broadcasting in the United States.

NBC actually inherited two established networks, the WEAF network and the second chain of stations associated with WJZ. It operated the two services as semi-independent entities. To distinguish between them, NBC called the WEAF hook-up the "Red" network and the WJZ feed the NBC "Blue" network. Many cities ultimately had an affiliate for each of the two systems.

Although NBC's two networks originated separate programs most of the time, they occasionally duplicated programming—particularly special events. The Red network, which always had the stronger roster of stations, carried the more popular mass-appeal entertainment shows, and consequently, more commercial advertising. The Blue network was oriented toward news, public affairs broadcasts, serious music, and other cultural programs; it often was used as a vehicle for experimentation with new program concepts. Once established, a new entertainment program was likely to be moved over to the more popular Red network. Thus, NBC's networks operated in a complementary rather than a fully competitive relationship with each other.

A second radio network was established soon after the debut of NBC. Arthur Judson, a musician and manager of artists, and a group of associates formed United Independent Broadcasters as a rival network for NBC. Although Judson lined up about a dozen affiliates, the venture was grossly underfinanced and its future doubtful. Only after Judson attracted the Columbia Phonograph Record Company as a part owner did the network—renamed the Columbia Phonograph Broadcasting System, Inc.—go into service on September 18, 1927.

In the following year, control of the network was purchased for about $400,000 by the William S. Paley family of Philadelphia. The Paleys, who had used the network successfully to advertise their La Paloma cigars, brought the network financial strength and, perhaps even more important, the native show business acumen of young William S. Paley, Jr., who became the network's president. Renamed the Columbia Broadcasting System, CBS bought its own flagship station, WABC (now WCBS), New York, in 1928.

With three radio networks in operation, the quality of radio programming improved vastly by the end of the 1920s. This improvement led to even greater popular acceptance of the new medium. The networks competed fiercely for programs, affiliates, and listeners. Because most of the powerful stations affiliated with one of the networks, radio broadcasting quickly was propelled to the status of a national mass medium. Since practically no one was beyond the range of radio's signals, especially at night, the new medium began to exert a homogenizing effect upon the American society by exposing people everywhere to the same cultural material, including commercials as well as entertainment programs and newscasts.

By 1929, almost all of the 600 stations accepted commercial advertising. The messages, however, were mostly institutional and almost always very low key. This approach reflected the common notion in early broadcasting that radio was an invited guest and could easily be invited to leave with a turn of a knob.

About one-third of the 600 radio stations operated on a full-time, 18-hour-a-day schedule by the end of the decade. The network affiliates, most of which were unable to produce quality programs on their own, generally used the network programming as much as possible. They filled the nonnetwork hours with phonograph records and electrical transcriptions, as well as occasional live talent broadcasts. Electrical transcriptions were high quality, durable recordings, used mainly to store music libraries and national product commercials. By selective use of music from transcription libraries, local stations could produce programs which rivaled the quality of network shows.

NETWORK PROGRAMS GAIN IMPORTANCE

During the period from 1927 to 1930, network programming became quite varied. Although hotel dance band broadcasts remained prominent, other types of musical programming emerged, including symphonic concerts, semi-classical and light popular music, and hillbilly and western material. Variety shows, which ordinarily contained both comedy and music, became a programming staple. Light drama, children's stories, talk programs, religious broadcasts, and news commentary also had prominence in the network

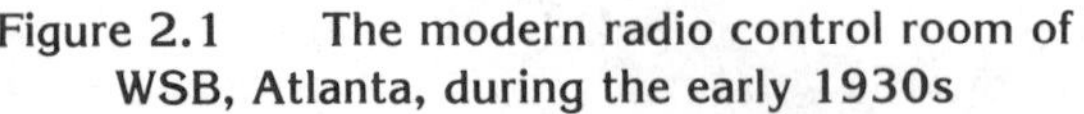
Figure 2.1 The modern radio control room of WSB, Atlanta, during the early 1930s

Photo courtesy of WSB, Cox Communications, Inc., Atlanta.

schedules. In addition, the networks used every opportunity to broadcast special news and sports events.

Unquestionably, the most popular single radio program to emerge during the late 1920s was the "Amos 'n' Andy Show," a serialized comedy-drama presented five nights each week. The program, derived from a vaudeville-type blackface act, was first produced locally in Chicago. The show gained immense national popularity, so much so that theaters across the country shut down their projectors and turned on radios so audiences could listen to the program.

Radio attracted other vaudeville acts. Comedians Ed Wynn, Eddie Cantor, and Will Rogers were appearing on network radio before the end of the 1920s.

Musical programming, important from radio's beginning, blossomed further during the early network era. Soloists and prominent musicians like Rudy Vallee, Al Jolson, Wayne King, and Paul Whiteman were attracted to radio. William S. Paley of CBS also began to display his ability to discover and promote talented unknowns. Three of his most notable early successes were Bing Crosby, Kate Smith, and Arthur Godfrey.

Special events covered by the young radio networks included the 1928 presidential campaign between Herbert Hoover and Al Smith, the arrival of Charles A. Lindbergh in Washington from his nonstop flight to Paris in 1927, and the Dempsey-Tunney championship fight from Chicago, also in 1927. This blow-by-blow report was carried on a network of 69 stations, a record number at the time.

The following is a partial list of prominent network shows, arranged by type, during the 1927–1929 seasons:

Musical Shows:	The Cities Service Orchestra Columbia Symphony Orchestra The Music Appreciation Hour The Voice of Firestone
Variety Shows:	Maxwell House Hour Palmolive Hour General Motors Family Hour The Ipana Troubadors
Children's Programs:	Let's Pretend Uncle Don's Children's Hour
Talk Programs:	Betty Crocker National Farm and Home Hour
Religious Programs:	National Radio Pulpit
News Commentary:	H.V. Kaltenborn

LOCAL RADIO PRODUCTION GAINS MOMENTUM

Meanwhile, around the country, a small number of local stations began to distinguish themselves as production stations. These stations were mostly high-power outlets that established reputations for creating quality programs using the writing and acting talent available in their communities. WLW, Cincinnati, and WTAM, Cleveland, produced excellent dramatic shows, as did WXYZ, Detroit, which originated "The Lone Ranger."

Others, particularly powerful stations in the South and Midwest, produced country music, or "hillbilly" shows. The two best known of the rural jamboree broadcasts were the "National Barn Dance," originated by WLS, Chicago, and the "Grand Ole Opry," started in 1925 by WSM, Nashville. Both were carried by the NBC network for several years. Today the "Grand Ole Opry" stands as one of radio's most successful and longest running programs.

A few stations gained fame by programming in unwise and inappropriate ways. The most notable of these maverick stations was KFKB, Milford, Kansas, whose call letters stood for "Kansas First—Kansas Best." The station's licensee was Dr. J.W. Brinkley, a Milford medical practitioner and druggist of questionable credentials.

Among KFKB's programs was a "Medical Question Box," to which listeners wrote seeking professional advice. Brinkley's sight-unseen, over-the-air diagnoses usually called for the doctor's own numbered prescriptions which could be obtained by mail from his pharmacy or from affiliated drug stores throughout the coverage area. In 1930, after several years fighting his detractors, Brinkley was forced to take KFKB off the air.

Figure 2.2 Billy Jones and Ernie Hare, the original "Happiness Boys," entertain with jokes and songs on a 1923 broadcast over pioneer station KDKA

Photo courtesy of KDKA Radio, Westinghouse Broadcasting Company, Inc., Pittsburgh.

As the 1920s ended, so did radio's formative period. Programming patterns, advertising support, and federal regulations "in the public interest" were firmly in place, ready for a new decade of significant growth for the medium.

THE 1930s: RADIO PROGRAMMING DURING THE DEPRESSION

Despite the Depression, the second decade of broadcasting was a very productive period in radio programming. With most of the fundamental issues resolved, radio quickly took its place with the newspaper and motion picture industries as a valuable medium for reaching mass audiences with entertainment, news, and advertising. Network radio actually thrived economically in the midst of economic chaos, largely because of its vast reach throughout the country and its broad appeal to listeners through entertaining programs.

By 1930, the radio networks—CBS and NBC's Red and Blue—had adopted the program structure that would be followed until the advent of television. The basic programming pattern consisted of drama, comedy, music, news, and variety programmed in 15-minute, half-hour, and full-hour segments.

To facilitate the level of production required, both NBC and CBS built modern studio facilities in New York. NBC's ultramodern studios were in the new 70-story RCA Building, the centerpiece of Rockefeller Center. The network's first broadcast from "Radio City" took place in 1933. CBS occupied a plush but less prestigious address at 485 Madison Avenue. Both networks also established studios in Hollywood, giving them access to performing talent in both of the nation's important entertainment centers. For many years, Chicago also was an important originating point for network programs.

Upgrading also took place at local stations as well as the networks. The decade began with about 600 local radio stations and ended with about 850. While the growth of new outlets was less robust than in the previous decade, it was more solidly based, more orderly, and more conducive to serving the public. By 1935, nine out of ten stations were licensed to operate full time, and most actually broadcast 16 hours or more each day.

By the end of the decade, nearly 90 percent of all American families owned radios. About 45 stations had boosted their power to the maximum of 50,000 watts to serve those listeners over large geographical areas. Another 150 operated with 5,000 watts. Most of the newer stations of the decade, however, were low-power outlets, often 250 watts, authorized for local coverage. These small stations proliferated in small cities across the country, initiating the trend toward localism that now prevails in radio broadcasting.

In 1934, a fourth network was added when four important stations joined together to form the Mutual Broadcasting System (MBS). The charter stations were WOR, New York; WGN, Chicago; WXYZ, Detroit; and WLW, Cincinnati. About 700 of the 850 radio stations in the United States were network affiliated by the end of the 1930s.

PROGRAMMING IN THE 1930s

Radio gained a great deal of professional quality during the 1930s as writers, producers, and talent came to understand how to use the unique sound-only medium. New types of programs were undertaken and older forms refined as both experience and confidence were gained by radio's craftsmen. While music remained important, comedy, drama, and variety shows came to the forefront in the 1930s. The concept of block programming emerged during the decade, with each network trying to establish a major program theme—such as variety night, music night, and mystery night—for each night. News and special events broadcasts also grew in importance during the Depression and the prewar years as millions of Americans came to depend upon radio for fast-breaking reports.

Network radio, the principal focus of broadcasting, steadily attracted well-known performers from both Hollywood and vaudeville, where unemployment among entertainers was common.

The first serious dramatic artist to perform on radio was Ethel Barrymore, whose presence gave radio an aura of legitimacy and broke the ice for many who followed her from the movies and the theater. Vaudeville stars attracted to radio early in the decade included Eddie Cantor, Jack Pearl, Ken Murray, Bob Hope, Jack Benny, and Fred Allen. The networks also continued to develop unknown talent, catapulting some to a fame equal to that of Hollywood's superstars.

The Rise of Radio Drama

The radio drama, a unique and imaginative art form, truly blossomed early in the 1930s. The tremendously successful "Amos 'n' Andy Show" proved conclusively that drama could be presented effectively and that listeners would tune in day after day as the plot unfolded. Soon the serial drama form was adopted for late afternoon children's adventure shows like "Jack Armstrong, the All-American Boy" and for daytime and early evening series focusing on the problems of ordinary people. Because so many serial drama programs attracted soap companies as their sponsors, they soon became known as "soap operas," a name that has stuck to the present day. By the end of the 1930s, serial drama was a major programming activity on both CBS and NBC's Red network. At one time, NBC's daily schedule included four continuous hours of 15-minute programs oriented toward women at home. NBC Blue and MBS carried a few soap operas, but they emphasized children's adventure serials in the late afternoon.

Not all drama, however, was serialized. During the prime evening hours, many types of episodic drama were offered, including Western stories, detective and crime drama, adventure stories, children's fairy stories, adaptations of theatrical and stage scripts, and, eventually, comedy drama, the forerunner of today's situation comedies.

The most successful of the adaptation genre was the "Lux Radio Theatre," which began in 1935 and continued until the late 1940s. Each week's program was hosted by Cecil B. De Mille, one of Hollywood's foremost producers, and featured a movie performer such as Helen Hayes, Barbara Stanwyck, Tyrone Power, and Clark Gable.

As radio drama grew in stature, serious writers began to use the form to deal with socially important subjects. Provocative drama was attempted by such writers as Norman Corwin, Arch Oboler, and Maxwell Anderson, on the "CBS Playhouse" and other series. Their radio plays often dealt with social injustice, patriotism, and historic subjects.

It was inevitable that someone would test the power of radio drama. That person was Orson Welles, who produced "War of the Worlds" by H.G. Wells on Halloween, 1938. Although identified as a drama on the "Mercury Theatre" anthology series, the broadcast produced mass hysteria, especially

A few program titles from the 1930s illustrate these categories:

Adventure Drama:	Sergeant Preston of the Yukon Jack Armstrong, All-American Boy
Detective Drama:	Charlie Chan Gangbusters Sherlock Holmes The Shadow
Movie/Stage Adaptations:	Lux Radio Theatre First Nighters
Western Drama:	The Lone Ranger

in the Northeast where the fictitious invasion from outer space supposedly was taking place. For radio and especially CBS, it was an embarrassment that has been long remembered.

Radio's Comedy Programs

The explosion in radio drama also spilled over into comedy with the emergence of the "comedy drama." As suggested earlier, nothing on radio ever has captivated listeners like "Amos 'n' Andy." Similarly, "Lum and Abner" serialized the lives of two country storekeepers in Pine Ridge, Arkansas. Both programs relied heavily upon misuse of words and harmless ineptitude for their humor.

The half-hour situation comedy emerged with "Fibber McGee and Molly" in 1931. Although each episode was complete, running gags, such as a weekly avalanche when McGee opened the hall closet, contributed to the week-to-week continuity of the show. Other prominent comedy dramas included "The Burns and Allen Show" and "The Jack Benny Show."

While the comedy drama became the ideal vehicle for many comedians, others preferred a format that allowed straight (monologue) humor or dialogue humor without a plot. Two comedians who worked best in the variety format were Eddie Cantor and Bob Hope, both of whom began their radio careers in 1933. Whether they preferred the dramatic or the monologue approach, radio comedians relied heavily on running gags, straight men, and pseudofeuds to aid in generating laughter. Reciprocal guest appearances, especially between "feuding" stars, was also a characteristic of the radio comedy shows.

In addition to comedy acts, radio's variety shows usually contained music, dramatic skits, interviews, and other features. These took many forms, as suggested by such titles as "The Cuckoo Hour," "The Nitwit Hour," "Major Bowes Original Amateur Hour," and "Rudy Vallee Varieties." A long-standing variety show, still presented as an occasional TV special, was the "Kraft Music Hall." During the 1930s, this series featured Bing Crosby and folk humorist Bob Burns. In daytime radio, the most successful variety show was "The Breakfast Club," a long-running program from Chicago, hosted by Don McNeil.

RADIO MUSIC PROGRAMMING

Music continued to play an important part in 1930s radio. Dance band broadcasts remained in favor, and both popular and country music were featured.

Not all musical programs, however, were light. During the decade, NBC maintained its own symphony orchestra, conducted by Arturo Toscanini, which gave weekly performances over the network. Although CBS did not have its own orchestra, it broadcast weekly concerts by the New York Philharmonic Orchestra. Other network musical programs included "The Voice of Firestone," which featured light classics, and the "Cities Service Band of America," a weekly program of march-style music.

A foretaste of present-day radio developed in 1935 when one of New York's independent stations sought to overcome network competition with recorded

Figure 2.3 Eddie Cantor poses before a makeshift microphone for his radio debut on KDKA in 1923, a few years before he became a regular performer

Photo courtesy of KDKA Radio, Westinghouse Broadcasting Company, Inc., Pittsburgh.

music and frequent newscasts. The station was WNEW and the concept was early format radio. Instead of broadcasting dance bands live from hotels, WNEW's Martin Block, an early disc jockey, created a "Make Believe Ballroom" in which bands played from recordings. Another contribution by WNEW was all-night radio; its schedule included a program called the "Milkman's Matinee." With popular music, news every hour on the hour, and disc jockeys stimulating the imagination, WNEW successfully competed in the 1930s and contributed the enduring concept of music-and-news programming.

Other Forms of Radio Programming

Other types of programming were undertaken on network radio, including audience participation programs and quiz shows, Broadway and Hollywood gossip programs, and human interest shows. Two popular network quiz shows were "Professor Quiz" and "Dr. I.Q." Gossip broadcasters included Walter Winchell and Louella Parsons. And two prominent human interest shows were "Alexander's Court of Human Relations" and "Mr. Keene, Tracer of Lost Persons."

Religious programming also had considerable appeal among radio listeners. NBC was in the forefront with three weekly series, one for each major faith. These broadcasts were "The Protestant Hour," "The Catholic

Hour," and "The Eternal Light" (Jewish). For several years, CBS carried daily broadcasts by Father Charles Coughlin, a Catholic priest from Michigan. Father Coughlin became a controversial spokesman on public issues and political candidates, resulting in the eventual cancellation of his program by CBS. However, this relatively obscure priest had demonstrated radio's power in the hands of a persuasive speaker. At the peak of his influence, Coughlin's audience was estimated at 30 to 45 million persons; his mail-count reached as high as 50,000 letters a week.

NEWS BROADCASTING GAINS IMPETUS

From its beginning in 1920, radio excelled in giving the public eyewitness accounts of special events and fast reports of breaking stories. Radio news continued its important role in the 1930s. However, for a time, its future as a news medium was in doubt because of growing concern by many newspaper publishers. Radio not only was delivering news faster, it also was gaining advertising revenues that traditionally had been placed in the print medium's coffers.

Following the 1932 presidential election, which was covered extensively by the networks, the American Newspaper Publishers Association demanded withdrawal of wire service privileges for radio. On March 1, 1933, the three services—the Associated Press, United Press, and the International News Service—discontinued delivery of news to their broadcast clients. It was a drastic move calculated by the powerful newspaper industry to restrict access to news to a competing medium.

The wire service ban failed because of three important factors. First, both CBS and NBC established news bureaus that, principally through adroit use of the telephone, successfully managed to obtain important national and international stories through direct contact with newsmakers. Second, newly elected President Franklin D. Roosevelt was inclinded to use radio to communicate directly with the American public. He did so 20 times during his first nine months in the White House. Third, each network's news commentators were able to continue their broadcasts without interruption, giving summaries and opinions on important events. Where they learned about the news was immaterial. The wire services were fully restored to the broadcasting industry in 1936. And, in fact, the wire service difficulty actually advanced the cause of radio news by forcing the networks to establish their own news-gathering units.

When World War II approached, the networks prepared for its coverage. Both CBS and NBC established extensive shortwave facilities to pick up signals from Europe for retransmission. H.V. Kaltenborn and Edward R. Murrow became prominent journalists because of their coverage of World War II.

Although radio began to excel in national and international coverage, few individual stations maintained local news departments until after World War II. However, from time to time, local stations devoted extensive coverage to local and regional emergencies. For example, during flooding of the Ohio and Mississippi rivers in 1937, major stations in the affected areas (particularly WLW, Cincinnati, and WHAS, Louisville) ceased regular programming to broadcast warnings and served as a clearing house of information.

Two other types of public affairs programs of the 1930s deserve mention. First, the news documentary emerged in 1931 with the "March of Time," a dramatization of the major news stories of the week from *Time* magazine. A second type was the public debate and discussion format, as typified by "America's Town Meeting of the Air." That series began in 1935 and lasted well into the 1950s. It was carried by NBC's Blue Network (which became ABC in 1943).

RADIO ADVERTISING BECOMES MORE STRIDENT

The nature of radio advertising changed noticeably during the Depression era. No longer were commercial messages restrained. Instead, with the need to move products during the "hard times," many advertisers resorted to hard-selling messages intended to impress brand names, slogans, and prices upon listeners. The radio networks accepted the relaxation of standards because they were anxious to retain sponsors.

Radio also entered into a new era of sponsor control of programming during the 1930s. Sponsors often owned their own shows, and the networks simply carried the shows produced by or for the advertisers. For this reason, the radio networks virtually lost control of their own schedules.

The 1930s eventually came to be known as radio's "golden era" because, during this decade, programming became professional and socially important. Radio reached into all parts of the country, sharing common experiences and a common culture. It brought laughter to a desperate nation. It also brought music, news, advertising, and public service. In the process, radio helped eliminate cultural isolation and brought a new degree of unity to the country. As the decade ended, radio faced new and uncertain competition while the nation faced the prospect of war.

1940–1945: BROADCASTING IN THE WAR YEARS

Radio became deeply involved in the war from the first bulletin of the Japanese attack until the broadcast of Japan's surrender on the deck of the U.S.S. Missouri in 1945.

With the all-out war effort, all new broadcast station construction, including TV and FM radio, was stopped. Thus, the industry was held at pre-1940 levels until 1945. At that point, there were about 940 AM stations, approximately 30 FM outlets, and half a dozen TV stations in the United States. The threat of newly developing TV and FM competition was thus delayed until the end of the war. With fewer than 10,000 receiving sets in use, the few television stations operated only on a token basis. However, the New York TV stations produced a surprising amount of live drama during the war.[7]

Radio prospered as never before. Listening levels were high because the public, deprived of ample gasoline, relied upon radio and the movies for diversion. Because of fast reporting, radio newscasts commanded large audiences. Much advertising was diverted from newspapers to radio because newsprint was scarce.

Figure 2.4 H.V. Kaltenborn delivers a news commentary on network radio following his return to the United States from an assignment to cover the Spanish Civil War

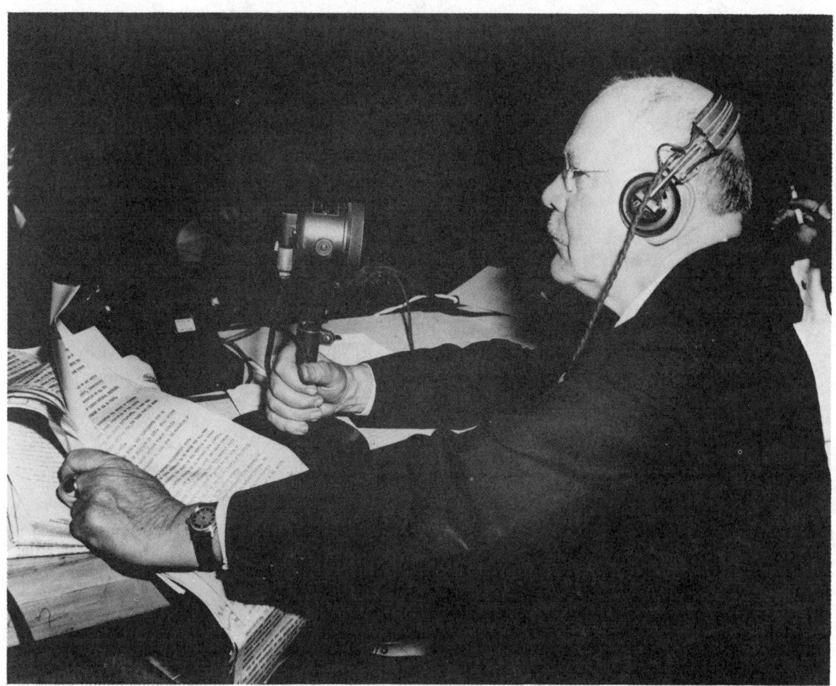

Photo from The National Archives, Washington, D.C.

Perhaps the greatest fear of broadcasters—that they would be silenced as they had been in World War I—was averted when broadcasters agreed to voluntary self-censorship. The Roosevelt administration established the Office of War Information, headed by former CBS newsman Elmer Davis, to work with the media to prevent any transmission of information that could assist the enemy. Such open microphone broadcasts as live man-on-the-street interviews were taken off the air because of the inability to screen participants. Weather broadcasts also were limited on coastal stations since enemy submarines might make use of the information. The transmitters of high-powered stations near the two coasts and the Gulf of Mexico also were guarded by military police to prevent the possibility of their being taken over by the enemy.

PROGRAMMING DURING WAR TIME

During the difficult war years, radio helped unify and mobilize the public to support the war effort, while also continuing its role as entertainer and informer. President Roosevelt continued to deliver his persuasive "fireside

Figure 2.5 President Franklin D. Roosevelt delivering one of his famous fireside chats to the American public

Photo from The National Archives, Washington, D.C.

chats" to the public, a task made much easier because of radio's national coverage. Regular programs were subject to delay, preemption, and interruption for emergency messages and news bulletins.

The World War II era truly established radio as an important news medium. Newscasts and commentaries were frequent throughout the day, and the networks broadcast daily reports from overseas throughout the war. Among the most poignant of these were Edward R. Murrow's live broadcasts from London, some of which had in the background the sirens of the British capital during German air attacks. Prominent commentators, usually in New York, explained and analyzed each day's events to keep the public informed as the war progressed.

Radio also became an important force for mobilizing public support of the war effort. Entertainment programs were permeated with messages, songs, drama, and comic bits that reminded civilians of the war, the fighting men away from home, and ways in which they could help bring victory to the nation.

Situation comedies, for example, reminded housewives to save and turn in ordinary items such as toothpaste tubes, lard, and junk—all of which were recycled for war needs. In one episode, Fibber McGee toyed with Molly's idea of keeping a horse in their home to save gasoline. Many variety shows featured interviews with servicemen and -women, focusing attention on the military effort. Programs produced by military personnel for civilian consumption also were common. One soldier-oriented show was "Stage Door Canteen," which opened each week with the line, "Curtain up for victory!" Music during the war often reflected war themes, such as nostalgia, loneliness, patriotism, and anticipation of victory.

One of the most popular network musical programs during the 1940s was "Your Hit Parade," sponsored by Lucky Strike cigarettes. Each week, the program surveyed record and sheet-music sales and ranked the ten top tunes. The show's star in 1943 was a young singer named Frank Sinatra, whose career was just beginning to take off.

Drama programs served to boost morale while keeping the public focused on the war. These broadcasts ranged from serialized adventure stories for children ("Hop Harrigan, Air Ace") to spy dramas ("David Harding, Counterspy") to serious dramatic shows which dealt with war-related themes. A classic example was "The Man Behind the Gun," which portrayed American soldiers doing their jobs on the battlefronts of the world. This program was highly acclaimed for its sensitive writing and innovative use of sound effects. Also, radio writers occasionally were called upon to deal with social themes such as race prejudice, which sometimes disrupted communities and impeded the manufacture of war supplies.

Figure 2.6 Actor Charles Laughton took time out in the early 1940s to examine the original KDKA microphone and some of its successors. These are quite different from today's highly specialized equipment.

Photo courtesy of KDKA Radio, Westinghouse Broadcasting Company, Inc., Pittsburgh.

Figure 2.7 CBS correspondent Edward R. Murrow giving a news report from London during World War II

Photo from the Broadcast Pioneers Library, courtesy of the National Association of Broadcasters, Washington, D.C.

Perhaps the most significant single dramatic production of the era was broadcast on May 8, 1945, when CBS produced "On a Note of Triumph" by Norman Corwin. It was an inspiring tribute to those who had brought victory in Europe, coupled with poignant motivation for continuation of the fight for a complete victory and a better society. Such dramatic productions, appealing to the listener's imagination, brought radio to perhaps a pinnacle of creativity.

1946–1952: TRANSITIONAL YEARS IN BROADCASTING

The end of World War II marked a major turning point in the history of radio programming. Two developments contributed to the new environment in broadcasting: (1) a great increase in the number of radio stations, and (2) the beginning of commercial television as a mass medium.

NEW MEDIA EMERGE: TELEVISION AND FM RADIO

Two new broadcast media—television and frequency modulation (FM) radio—actually had their beginnings during the 1930s. England began a national television service in 1936, and TV was publicly demonstrated for the first time in America at the 1939 New York World's Fair. Scientists and engineers who had worked diligently for more than a decade on picture transmission predicted that TV was just around the corner as a mass medium. Regular television service in the United States formally began in 1939 on the General Electric Company's experimental station (now WRGB) in Schenectady, New York. Both NBC and CBS began regular programming on their experimental stations in New York in 1941.

The coming of television was only one of the complications for the existing standard broadcast system. A second was a new form of radio transmission known as frequency modulation, which was tested during the 1930s and approved in 1940 by the FCC. Heralded by its developer, Major Edwin H. Armstrong, as a much better system of sound transmission than AM (amplitude modulation), FM was to occupy channels in the 42 to 50 megahertz portion of the spectrum.

The increase in radio broadcasting resulted primarily from a lowering of technical restrictions on AM transmission, as well as the permanent launching of FM radio in the VHF band. From 1945 to 1952, the number of AM stations grew from 940 to nearly 2,400. Most were low-power and many were daytime-only outlets. The new FM stations usually became extensions of their sister AM stations by duplicating their programming. However, most large AM stations and the Radio Corporation of America, the principal developer of television, did little to encourage the expansion of a second radio service.

The increase in the number of stations took local broadcasting to small towns across the country for the first time. While some became network affiliates, usually with MBS, these small, local outlets tended to emphasize news, sports, personalities, and advertisers in their hometown communities. The number of stations in many cities doubled during the same period. New urban stations usually featured music and news programming as a means of competing against network affiliates.

For a few brief years, network radio continued its varied pattern of elaborate evening shows, daytime serials, and morning variety programs. However, many sponsors gradually removed their programs from nighttime schedules because the audience increasingly watched television. Variety and musical shows especially declined in number by 1952. They were replaced with less costly productions like quiz shows and "thriller" drama. The latter were especially prominent at the end of this period, when more than 50 thrillers were presented each week during evening network schedules. The number of newscasts and commentary programs also declined after the war ended.

The live network radio era also ended in 1951 with the development of quality audio tape recording. Up to that time, the radio networks rigidly forbade the use of recorded material. However, the convenience of pretaping appealed to radio's performers. In 1951, Bing Crosby first convinced network executives to allow him to pretape his weekly "Kraft Music Hall" shows.

Network daytime programming continued to emphasize serial dramas, but this genre was clearly in decline by 1952. Two daytime variety shows stand out—Don McNeil's "Breakfast Club" from Chicago on ABC, and "Arthur Godfrey Time," originated by CBS in New York.

TELEVISION'S FIRST STEPS

Televison became a strong competitor to radio during this period; however, its effect was far from universal, because TV licenses were held by only 108 stations in 50 scattered markets. Only after 1952, when the FCC lifted a freeze on construction permits, did TV truly become a national service.

As a new venture, television represented a financial risk. Early stations suffered heavy losses, and sales of TV sets were slow. However, as programming improved, the public responded by purchasing sets, which usually cost more than $300 each. By the end of 1952, most of the "prefreeze" TV stations were earning modest profits.

By 1947, four television networks were in operation. Three were extensions of radio chains: ABC-TV, CBS-TV, and NBC-TV. A fourth was the DuMont Television Network, operated by DuMont Laboratories. Mutual was the only radio network to avoid televison. In 1948, the TV networks were capable of broadcasting from the East coast westward to Chicago and, on a delayed (kinescope recording) basis, to the West coast.

The two keys to successful network television were to gain a large number of strong affiliate stations and to obtain popular programming. NBC and CBS almost always obtained the choice affiliates, while ABC and DuMont, because of weaker programming, had to fight for the remaining station—usually there were only three—in each market. Because it never achieved a solid line-up of stations and also because it had no profitable radio network to carry its losses, DuMont ceased operation in 1955.

From a programming standpoint, CBS excelled in popular entertainment from TV's beginning. This resulted from an aggressive talent hunt by William Paley, the network president, who attracted numerous creative and highly popular performers from Hollywood, Broadway, and especially from NBC's radio network. In a dramatic "talent raid" in 1948, Paley convinced such NBC performers as Jack Benny, Burns and Allen, Red Skelton, Fred Allen, Edgar Bergen, and "Amos 'n' Andy" to move to CBS. Thus, many of radio's most popular shows changed networks just before the television era. While the price was enormous for CBS Radio, Paley's shrewdness paid off handsomely by placing CBS-TV in a strong programming position.

In addition, CBS obtained Hollywood's leading comedienne, Lucille Ball, and New York entertainment columnist Ed Sullivan, whose show business contacts were probably unequalled. The "I Love Lucy" comedy show began its long run on CBS in 1951, while "Toast of the Town" (later the "Ed Sullivan Show") brought an incredible variety of entertainment into American homes from 1948 until 1971.

NBC's most successful programs were Milton Berle's "Texaco Star Theatre" and "Your Show of Shows," which featured Sid Caesar and Imogene Coca. Berle was often called "Mr. Television" because of his rapid rise as a TV star through his vaudeville-type show. NBC also had early television's most popular children's show in "Kukla, Fran & Ollie," a daily puppet program produced in Chicago.

ABC and DuMont had few truly popular programs in the early TV era. Both leaned heavily on inexpensive boxing and wrestling matches and, during the 1949–1950 seasons, ABC telecast two hours of "Rollerderby" each Saturday night. One of ABC's more popular shows was a television adaptation of "Stop the Music," which had attracted a large radio following by offering prize money to listeners who could name musical selections.

Lack of experience in visual production was a particular problem in early television. As an offshoot of radio, TV owed the older medium a great debt

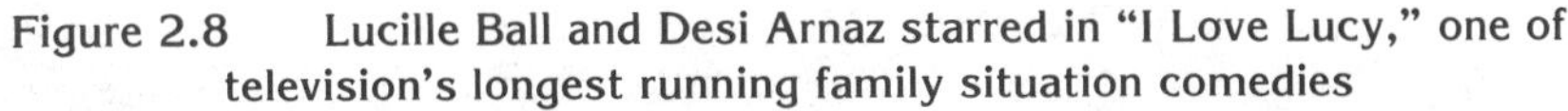

Figure 2.8 Lucille Ball and Desi Arnaz starred in "I Love Lucy," one of television's longest running family situation comedies

for programs, program concepts, and even for initial economic subsidy. However, television was a different medium, and its producers had to learn to work with it. Some radio shows, especially audience participation and quiz programs, transferred well, but others failed. Comedy, drama, and variety shows presented special problems, because in radio they had been based on imagery rather than visual treatment. Ultimately, however, film, stage, and vaudeville techniques, which are essentially visual, were adopted.

Live TV drama became quite popular during the early 1950s. Whereas radio drama worked well in half-hour formats, longer periods were needed in television to develop plots and characters adequately. Presentations included both anthologies and original plays, often produced by top-flight casts. One of the early dramatic showcases was Westinghouse's "Studio One" on CBS. A cadre of creative TV playwrights whose works were performed on "Studio One" and other similar shows soon began to emerge. A few of the more prominent TV dramatists were Rod Serling, Tad Mosel, and Gore Vidal.

A second problem for early television was production cost. Advertising revenues were low, while production costs were high in comparison with radio. Thus, the search for low-cost programming became a major consideration. Lavish budgets were allowed such programs as "The Milton Berle Show" ($8,000 a week) and "The Ed Sullivan Show" ($5,000 a week), but these expensive shows were offset with old movies, especially Westerns, puppet shows for children, and inexpensive sports pickups.

At first, most local TV stations operated only from late afternoon until about midnight; but they gradually expanded their hours as network programming became available in the daytime. Most stations quickly learned to ride the network and filled nonnetwork hours with locally produced programs, very old movies, and other syndicated material. Interestingly enough, they actually produced more live programming then than most local stations do today because of limited availability of syndicated shows and the low level of competition between stations. Local TV productions usually included cooking shows, news-weather-sports roundups, children's programs, and musical broadcasts.

THE UBIQUITOUS DISC JOCKEY

As TV gradually gained strength, radio entered into a period of decline, then began to change its programming drastically. The primary trend was the rise of the local personality disc jockey, which occurred simultaneously with the decline of network radio. Independent stations increasingly used personalities and records to compete inexpensively against network programming. Many affiliated radio stations adopted the DJ approach during nonnetwork hours. Finally, by 1952, disc jockey programming even permeated the network level when both ABC and Mutual introduced daytime record shows. ABC's record spinners included Paul Whiteman, the famous band leader; Martin Block, creator of WNEW's original "Make Believe Ballroom"; and Tennessee Ernie Ford, who had recently gone to Hollywood from station WOPI in Bristol, Tennessee. As competition from television intensified, the music-and-news approach, pioneered by large independent stations, became radio's salvation.

In 1952, the FCC adopted a new nationwide TV allocation plan and lifted its four-year freeze on new station construction. The allocations table—which included 12 VHF and 70 UHF channels—designated specific channels to each city, using mileage separation as the criterion to prevent interference between stations. The table provided for more than 2,000 stations, including 242 noncommercial outlets on channels reserved for educational use.

As the transitional period from 1946 to 1952 ended, new patterns were forming in radio programming, and television was finding its niche as a service that soon would replace old-style radio.

1953-1960: TV AND THE RISE OF FORMAT RADIO

Beginning in 1953, television rapidly became the dominant home entertainment medium. As hundreds of new TV stations were built across the country, the public became captivated with the new sight-and-sound medium. By 1960, ownership of black-and-white TV sets had climbed to 87 percent, and the average viewing per household reached five hours a day.

Radio set ownership stood at 98 percent of all homes, with 156,000,000 receivers in use, an average of about three units per household. While radio's reach was universal, overall listening dropped sharply. However, the public continued buying radios, and each year about 200 new radio stations were built. It was truly a paradox—an expanding industry facing dreary predictions and a tremendous challenge.

Radio met its challenge successfully by transforming itself into a companion medium for individuals in an increasingly mobile society. More than one-fourth of all working radios were in automobiles, while new, lightweight portable receivers gave listeners access to radio wherever they went. Clock radios became popular in bedrooms, and sets began to proliferate in dens, kitchens, basements, and every other conceivable place. While TV took charge as the family medium, radio had found an untapped audience beyond television's reach, an audience that radio had never directly attempted to serve, even in its heyday.

The four networks were reduced to three in 1955, when the DuMont operation folded. The economy simply could not support four services at that time. ABC-TV, CBS-TV, and NBC-TV soon expanded their networks to live, instantaneous coast-to-coast service. In radio, the four networks remained in operation, but they carried only remnants of their former entertainment schedules. Instead, they substituted low-cost programming and began to assume a larger role as a national news source.

As the television audience grew, advertisers—particularly large, national companies—confidently placed greater budgets in the new medium which allowed both visualization and demonstration of their products. In turn, radio stations became increasingly local in their advertising emphasis and programming.

TV PROGRAMMING DEVELOPMENTS

During this period, network television programming evolved considerably from the radio model to more innovative concepts that more effectively used the visual capabilities of the medium. In other words, TV became "tele*vision*" instead of "radio with pictures." Even so, nighttime network schedules resembled those of the preceding period in their programming variety.

Popular program types included Westerns, detective shows, comedies, serious drama, quiz shows, and musical programs. Special events also represented an important area of programming throughout the 1950s. Replacing simple game shows, TV was invaded by prime-time, big-money quiz shows in 1955. This trend proved to be short-lived, however, when some shows were found to be rigged. Other innovations included magazine-talk programs and jazz detective dramas. Finally, increased competence marked the beginning of a more serious effort in news programming by the end of the decade.

During the second half of the 1950s, program ratings became quite important as advertisers faced the escalating costs of TV time. This led to a constant search for larger audiences through new program ideas, fresh material, new talent, better production, and gimmicks. After 1957, film and video tape were used heavily, virtually eliminating live network shows in favor of flawless "canned" broadcasts. Local live productions also declined as video-tape equipment was acquired throughout the industry. Still another factor that contributed to the decline of live TV was the release of hundreds of pre-1948 movies for television by Hollywood studios in 1956.

TV Drama in the 1950s

Serious drama held an important place in network television during the early 1950s, but it began to disappear as the decade ended. Important prestige dramatic showcases included "Studio One," "Theatre Guild on the Air," and the "CBS Television Playhouse," all produced live. Two notable plays written for the "TV Playhouse" were "Marty" by Paddy Chayefsky in 1953 and "Twelve Angry Men" by Reginald Rose in 1954. The "CBS Television Playhouse" was replaced by "Playhouse 90," a 90-minute weekly dramatic program, in 1956.

An important filmed dramatic series during the decade was "The General Electric Theatre," whose host was a future US president, Ronald Reagan. Another dramatic program that outlasted all of the above was the "Hallmark Hall of Fame," which presented original TV dramas, adaptations of musical comedies, and Broadway successes. Except for occasional specials, however, the era of serious drama on commercial television ended with the 1950s, as TV turned to other dramatic forms which had broader public appeal.

Western stories became prominent on 1950s television and continued to be popular for nearly two decades. TV's earliest Westerns were edited cowboy movies, such as "Hopalong Cassidy," the "Lone Ranger," and "The Gene Autry Show."

A new era of Westerns began with "Gunsmoke" on CBS Radio in 1952 and on network television starting in 1955. This long-running series (1955–1975) inaugurated the "adult Western" concept, which substituted emphasis on character development for mere action adventure. "Gunsmoke" was joined in 1956 by "Cheyenne," produced by Warner Brothers. An avalanche of new TV Westerns, including "Maverick" and "Bonanza," followed. By the 1959 season, more than 30 different Western dramas were carried each week by the three networks as the public's thirst for this genre was seemingly unquenchable.

The 1950s also witnessed a surge in popularity for detective and adventure shows. In 1952, producer Jack Webb established a new trend for realistic crime programs with "Dragnet," based on actual cases of the Los Angeles Police Department. Like "Gunsmoke," "Dragnet" also had been a successful radio drama. The most successful police series in TV history, "Dragnet" inspired many other police and detective programs, including "77 Sunset Strip," "Naked City," "I Led Three Lives," and "The Untouchables."

A more cerebral approach to crime was undertaken by the "Perry Mason" series, which began in 1957. The show, TV's longest running lawyer series, featured Erle Stanley Gardner's famous defense attorney, as portrayed by Raymond Burr. Another crime show variation, the "jazz detective," also began in 1957. "M Squad" and "Peter Gunn" were the two principal shows of this type, which incorporated urban detective plots accompanied by original jazz music.

Finally, during the 1950s, afternoon television began to take over one of radio's last strongholds, the daytime serial drama. In 1952, "Guiding Light," a long-time radio serial, became one of the first soap operas to be shown on TV. It still retains its place on the CBS-TV schedule three decades later. Before the end of the decade, the afternoon TV schedules were filled with serialized stories, and the radio versions were doomed. Radio soap operas finally

Figure 2.9 "Gunsmoke" introduced the adult western to television in 1955. Shown here is James Arness as Marshall Matt Dillon with other members of the regular cast.

disappeared altogether in 1960, when "Ma Perkins" left the air after running continuously for more than 25 years.

Comedy Shows

Comedy remained a favorite on TV during the 1950s. The two big vaudeville-type shows of the previous era, "Texaco Star Theatre" and "Your Show of Shows," continued to attract large audiences. They were joined by three

Figure 2.10 Three TV "Superstars" appear together as the "Three B's": Bing Crosby, Jack Benny, and George Burns

Photo courtesy of the National Association of Broadcasters.

other important comedy-variety shows and numerous situation comedy programs.

The "Colgate Comedy Hour," which NBC introduced in 1950, became the first commercial TV program to originate in Hollywood and, in 1953, the first network color telecast. "Colgate," which was programmed directly opposite the "Ed Sullivan Show," was a high-cost showcase for leading comedians. Its guests included such performers as Ray Bolger, Eddie Cantor, Fred Allen, and Abbott and Costello.

Red Skelton had been successful as a radio performer for 10 years before CBS launched "The Red Skelton Show" on television in 1951. Perhaps the greatest clown on the tube, Skelton used comic routines that were largely visual, which insured success on TV. The Skelton show was one of the longest running programs in television's history, ending in 1971.

The third of the new comedy-variety shows of the 1950s was "The Jackie Gleason Show." In 1952, Gleason, who previously had performed on DuMont's "Cavalcade of Stars," began a Saturday night variety format, which included songs, dances, and comic sketches. One of the most memorable routines, "The Honeymooners," became a fullblown situation comedy during the 1955–56 season. Except for a two-year hiatus, Gleason's program was a regular network feature until 1970.

Radio's success with comedy-drama in earlier years prompted adaptations as well as new situation shows on TV in the 1950s. The first radio sitcom to succeed on television was "The Life of Riley," which ran from 1949 through 1958. Other radio situation comedies that did well on TV include "The George Burns and Gracie Allen Show" (1950–1958), "The Jack Benny Show" (1950–1964), "Our Miss Brooks" (1952–1956), and "Father Knows Best" (1954–1962). The latter, which starred Robert Young, was regarded as the classic wholesome family situation comedy.

Ironically, two of the most popular radio programs of all time had short TV existences. "Amos 'n' Andy," though popular on television, lasted only two years (1951–1953) because of opposition to its stereotyping of Blacks. "Fibber McGee and Molly," a highly successful radio show (1935–1957), did so poorly on TV that it lasted only four months during the 1959–1960 season.

A group of new situation comedies with no previous radio connections began to appear during the decade. One of the first and certainly the most popular show of the 1950s was "I Love Lucy," starring Lucille Ball and Desi Arnaz. For the six seasons from 1951 through 1957, this antic-oriented series ranked first in national ratings four years, second one year, and third one year. After the series ended in 1961, Lucille Ball continued to do specials for a number of years, while reruns of "Lucy" retained popularity through syndication on local stations.

Second only to "Lucy" in popularity among situation comedies was "December Bride" (1954–1961). Other notable sitcoms of the era include "Mama" (1949–1956), "Make Room for Daddy" (1953–1971), and "The Phil Silvers Show" (1955–1959).

Quiz and Game Shows

The quiz show involving participants from the studio audience was another program form borrowed from radio. The first notable TV quiz program, "Break the Bank," made its radio debut in 1945 and was simulcast on television in 1948. "Break the Bank," hosted by Bert Parks, was considered a lavish broadcast since its prizes sometimes exceeded $10,000 in cash. However, even bigger prizes emerged in 1955 when radio's "$64 Question" moved to TV as "The $64,000 Question."

"The $64,000 Question," which ushered in the big-money era for quiz shows, became an enormous hit. The prize money then escalated further in 1956 when "Break the Bank" became "Break the $250,000 Bank." The popularity of these two high-stakes programs prompted still more shows with a quiz format.

In 1958, the famous quiz show scandals broke after a few contestants disclosed that they had been given answers by the producers. In turn, the producers pleaded that this was merely another form of entertainment and, like a play, did not need to be authentic. In effect, the producers admitted helping contestants who drew favorable viewer response.

The Justice Department disagreed. After a request from an outraged President Eisenhower, that department launched an intensive investigation. A self-examination by the networks soon produced policy changes in which CBS banned quiz shows altogether and the other two networks imposed strict regulations. By 1959, all of the big money shows were off the air. Only three contestants ever won more than $200,000 during the heyday of those broadcasts.

Two other quiz shows deserve mention because of their uniqueness. Identifying song titles was the participant's task on "Name That Tune," which lasted from 1953 until 1959 on network television. A second show, "You Bet Your Life," actually was a vehicle for the sarcastic wit of comedian Groucho Marx. It was carried by NBC from 1950 until 1961.

While audience participation quiz shows have retained a place in daytime TV, this form ceased to exist as a prime-time feature after the 1958–1959 scandal.

Other Regular Programming

Although this listing of 1950s television shows cannot be complete, two other weekly programs belong in our review. The first is "Omnibus," the longest running cultural series in the history of television.

A second unique network program was a half-hour religious talk broadcast entitled "Life Is Worth Living," featuring Catholic Bishop Fulton J. Sheen. Sheen assumed an anecdotal approach in dealing with morality and problems of living. The program was immensely popular.

Television "Spectaculars"

As TV's screens grew larger, so did the lavishness of its productions. One of the finest, one-time shows of the 1950s was the "Ford 50th Anniversary Show," which was broadcast simultaneously on both NBC and CBS in 1953. This "spectacular" featured Mary Martin and Ethel Merman and was produced by Leland Hayward.

The success of the Ford special so impressed NBC's executives, particularly Sylvester L. (Pat) Weaver and Robert Sarnoff, that they established the largest budgets in broadcasting history to underwrite a schedule of big, special shows starting in 1954. The "spectacular" was particularly suitable for NBC because (1) it did not have as much strength in regular series programming as CBS and (2) NBC's parent organization, the Radio Corporation of America, needed a vehicle which could be used to promote color television.

NBC's specials were primarily musical variety and/or comedy shows which required elaborate stage sets and high-budget talent. All three networks soon began to include some specials each season. ABC accomplished a magnificent coup when it contracted for "The Disneyland Show," the predecessor of "The Wonderful World of Disney." CBS, more content to lead from the strength of its weekly programming, carried infrequent specials.

News, Special Events, and Public Affairs

The daily newscast had been important since the TV networks began operation in 1947. Until 1964, network news programs were only 15 minutes long.

Affiliated stations usually produced an additional quarter-hour, typically a news-weather-sports package, to round out an early evening half-hour.

A typical network newscast from 1947 until 1953 consisted of stories read by a newscaster, plus footage from a newsreel service. NBC's nightly "Camel News Caravan" was announced by John Cameron Swayze, with visual material from Fox Movietone newsreels. The CBS newscast, "Television News with Douglas Edwards," followed the same pattern. ABC used dual anchors in its version, called "News and Views." Within a few years, each network expanded its news-gathering capabilities so that outside sources of film stories no longer were required.

Among the first public events broadcast on network TV were the Senate Crime Hearings of 1951. In those hearings, Senator Estes Kefauver of Tennessee questioned underworld agents, and Americans suddenly realized how organized crime affects their daily lives.

Although the Democratic and Republican political conventions were televised in 1948, 1952 was the first year that large national audiences had an opportunity to witness the two events via television. On January 20, 1953, another TV "first" was accomplished when the inauguration of President Dwight Eisenhower was telecast to the nation.

An important innovation in informational programming was developed by NBC in 1952. Sylvester L. (Pat) Weaver, the network's president, conceived the TV "magazine" concept based on the idea that television should resemble a magazine with commercials sold individually like pages. The result was three shows—"Today," "Tonight," and "Home"—which combined news, interviews, features, and humor pieces. "Today" and "Tonight" remain even now as important legacies left at NBC by Weaver, who also was responsible for the long-running weekend radio magazine, "Monitor."

The year 1953 marked the start of "Person to Person," a weekly series of celebrity interviews by Edward R. Murrow. However, Murrow's chief accomplishment in television related to the documentary series, "See It Now," which he coproduced with Fred W. Friendly. This series (1952–1955) is best remembered for a famous expose of Senator Joseph McCarthy, whose tactics were viewed by Murrow as a threat to freedom in the American society. That broadcast, on March 9, 1954, pioneered a new style of TV journalism, presenting on-scene visual reports documenting important current issues. Eventually Senator McCarthy became the central figure in the nationally televised "Army-McCarthy Hearings," during which the Senate, in 1954, probed the senator's activities.

Another first for television came in 1955, when President Eisenhower permitted the filming of his press conferences for TV. Live telecasting of presidential press conferences began in 1961 under President John F. Kennedy.

Again in 1956 and 1960, television covered the national political campaigns. By this time, however, the conventions were adapting to television. No longer were they loosely organized events. Instead, they became TV platforms used by the two parties to reach the American public. Consequently, highlights were scheduled to occur when television audiences would be large, and dull proceedings were buried at inconspicuous hours.

Another outcome of the 1956 conventions was the teaming of the NBC reporters as coanchors of that network's nightly newscasts, an arrangement that would last for 14 years. The public so liked the repartee between Chet Huntley and David Brinkley at the conventions that, starting in October 1956, NBC assigned them to report the evening news jointly. "The Huntley-Brinkley Report" remained the most-watched network newscast for a number of years.

Finally, the powerful influence of television was felt in the 1960 presidential election, when Congress relaxed the "equal time" restrictions to allow television debates between the two principal candidates. Four televised debates were held between Vice-President Richard Nixon and Senator John F. Kennedy. Both Kennedy and Nixon stated that the TV debates determined the winner in 1960.

Television began carrying major football bowl games and baseball's World Series in the late 1940s. The most significant development of the 1950s in sports broadcasting was the addition of color to telecasts. The first instances were NBC's color telecasts of the Cotton and Rose Bowl games on January 1, 1954.

RADIO PROGRAMMING DEVELOPMENTS

Despite the success of the local disc jockey and the newly discovered companion function of radio, the US radio industry was far from healthy in 1954. Forecasts varied from guarded optimism to outright despair. Broadcaster Todd Storz described the situation this way: "The break from traditional network concepts into the early localized music-and-news pattern was simply a direction, not the promised land."[8] It was Storz himself who would lead radio to the "promised land" by creating what came to be called "formula radio."

Modern format radio was conceived in a bar in Omaha, Nebraska. Todd Storz and fellow broadcaster Bill Stewart were drinking beer when they noticed the same few songs being played repeatedly on the jukebox. Perhaps the public would like to hear the top tunes over and over on the radio, they concluded. Storz then tried his revolutionary idea on his station. Within three months, KOWH had skyrocketed from also-ran status to a strong number one in the Omaha market. Storz quickly acquired three other stations—in Minneapolis, Miami, and New Orleans—and all three moved to the top in audience ratings with his repetitive top-tune programming.

About the same time, a Texas broadcaster named Gordon McLendon was trying a similar approach on KLIF in Dallas and KELP in El Paso. McLendon, who had operated the Liberty Broadcasting System radio network from 1950 to 1952, played the top tunes in high rotation; but he also promoted his station in ways previously unheard of in the industry. For example, KLIF gave away $50,000 cash in a window sticker promotion in 1954. Listeners won cash prizes simply by calling the station if they heard their sticker number mentioned on the air. Thus, McLendon added audience participation to enhance the play-the-hits formula. With his use of fast-paced, loud DJ's and frantic production to increase the excitement, his stations matched the success of Storz.

Industry acceptance of formula radio was surprisingly slow because many broadcasters resisted the new strategy. The majority of the established personality disc jockeys vehemently opposed the formula approach because it usurped the power of the DJ to be his own programmer. Second, the formula plan was a brash, boastful method of programming since the high energy levels needed for its successful execution were not conducive to modesty. The larger, more professional stations usually executed the format without excessive negative reaction, but imitators did not always use the format tastefully. Third, formula radio coincided with the advent of rock and roll music. As a result of this coincidence, formula stations often became synonymous with "rock and roll radio." During its early years, rock music was almost universally disliked by middle and upper income whites over 30 years of age—the demographic group into which most station managers fell.

Despite the opposition, audience surveys from markets all over the United States convinced an ever-increasing number of broadcasters to try formula radio. Also, between 1954 and 1960, radio programming gradually became continuous rather than segmented into blocks, as total station personality took precedence over individual personalities.

Three dominant radio station types emerged by 1960. First, many stations became "Top 40" outlets, playing the top hits only or the top hits with a light sprinkling of old and new tunes. Another category played albums and mood music with a strict ban on rock and roll. A third group played selected hit songs, plus album cuts and oldies. These became known as "Middle-of-the-Road" (MOR) stations.

In addition, in many markets, certain stations carved special niches for themselves by appealing to ethnic or special interest audiences. Foreign language programming had long been successful in large cosmopolitan cities. The new wave of specialty service was directed to Blacks, Spanish-Americans, and persons interested in religious programming.

The development of specific radio formats to express a distinct station personality was the beginning of vertical programming. It is this form of programming—continuous and specialized rather than diverse and segmented—that prevails in present-day radio broadcasting.

1961–1970: A MATURING PERIOD

The 1960s were turbulent years in the United States, with war, tragic assassinations, and problems related to civil rights. Great strides also were made, particularly in the nation's space program. It was only natural that news and public affairs would become the major thrust in broadcasting, while entertainment programming forms remained basically the same.

In 1961, young John F. Kennedy became president of the United States. Kennedy, who had benefitted greatly from TV exposure in his 1960 campaign, quickly initiated live telecasts of his press conferences. He also encouraged broadcasters to upgrade their programming by emphasizing documentary forms and public affairs broadasts. Such series as NBC's "White Papers," "CBS Reports," and ABC's "Close-Up" soon followed. Through these programs, the public learned about Soviet-US competition in space, troubles in the Congo, migrant farm laborers, and anti-American attitudes abroad.

Figure 2.11 "The Andy Griffith Show," a typical situation comedy of the 1960s, continues to enjoy success in syndication. Shown are Andy Griffith as Sheriff Andy Taylor and Don Knotts as Barney Fife.

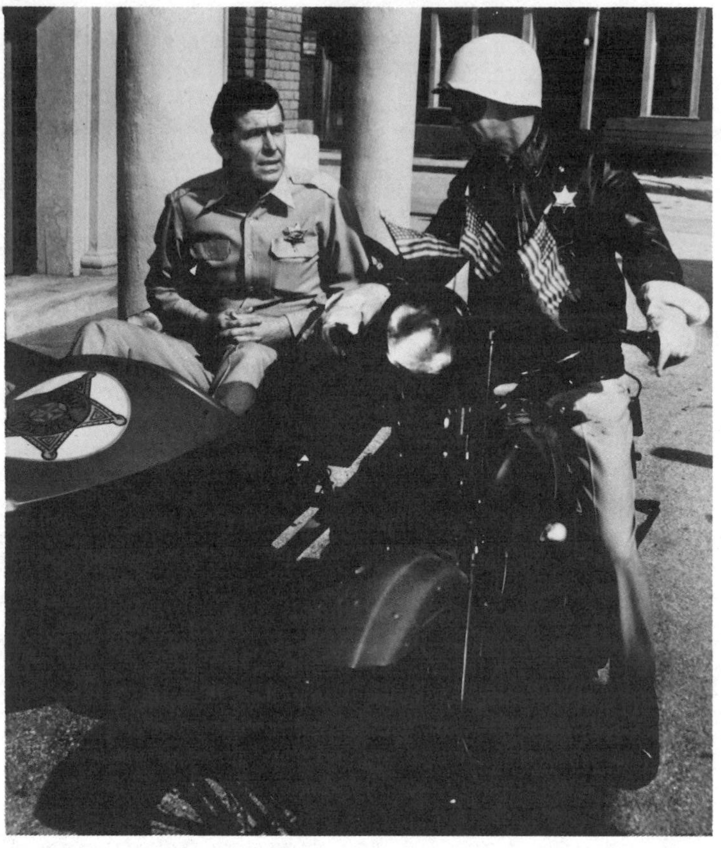

Photo courtesy of the National Association of Broadcasters.

While the President encouraged broadcasters to strive for quality programming, his appointed FCC chairman, Newton S. Minow, chastized and challenged them. At the National Association of Broadcasters convention in 1961, Minow compared contemporary television to a "vast wasteland" and urged TV executives to watch their own stations.

> You will see a procession of game shows, violence, audience participation shows, formula comedies about totally unbelievable families, blood and thunder, mayhem, violence, sadism, murder, Western badmen, Western good men, private eyes, gangsters, more violence, and cartoons. And, endlessly, commercials—many screaming, cajoling, and offending. And most of all, boredom.

> True, you will see a few things you will enjoy. But they will be very, very few. And if you think I exaggerate, try it.[9]

Broadcasters responded angrily, but perhaps because of the attack, they aired an increasing number of special events, documentaries, and quality one-time entertainment specials. In 1961 a tour of the White House conducted by the First Lady Jacqueline Kennedy was televised. Another documentary, "The Tunnel," based on the digging of a tunnel by a group of East Berliners to help their friends and relatives escape to the West, raised concern at the State Department about possible effects on international relations.

The year 1962 brought new achievements in the US space program and in satellite communications technology. Astronauts John Glenn, later a US Senator from Ohio, and Scott Carpenter took flights into space during the year, and both launches were extensively covered by network television.

During the summer of 1962, the communications satellite "Telstar" was launched, making possible the first live trans-Atlantic TV transmissions. Satellite technology improved rapidly with the development of synchronous, or "fixed position," satellites, which permit continous transmissions from continent to continent.

In 1963, the Communications Satellite Corporation, or Comsat, was formed to develop a global system of satellite communication links. In 1965, Comsat launched its first commercial satellite, "Early Bird," or Intelsat I, to feed television material between the United States and Europe. Although novel in the 1960s, communications satellites now are used routinely by the TV networks to transmit news stories and international special events to their New York operating centers from points throughout the world.[10]

In November 1962, President Kennedy informed the nation of the Cuban missile crisis over television, and the public depended upon radio and TV for information throughout the crisis period. The president also requested and was granted the use of a number of powerful clear-channel radio stations to beam messages to the Cuban people.[11]

The most significant industry development during the 1960s was the rise of color television. Color TV sets sold very slowly at first. However, with NBC leading the way, the amount of color programming increased greatly by the middle of the decade. In 1965, for example, NBC's nighttime schedule was 96 percent color, while CBS and ABC had 50 percent and 40 percent color programs, respectively. By 1970, with nighttime programming virtually 100 percent in color, the percentage of color-TV homes rose to 39 percent (from only 5 percent in 1965). In a related development, as color sets replaced older, but still useable, monochrome receivers, the percentage of households with two or more TV sets grew to 33 percent by 1970.

Other significant industry developments during the 1960s included passage of the all-channel receiver legislation, which required new TV sets to have UHF tuners after April 30, 1964; the greater use of film for television production; and the breakthrough by Black performers on network programming. The first situation comedy to feature a Black heroine was NBC's "Julia," starring Diahann Carroll, in 1968. The most important Black TV personality, however, was Flip Wilson, who began a popular NBC variety show in 1970. One additional development, begun as a device to rejuvenate a floundering schedule, was the introduction of the "second season" by ABC in 1966.

BROADCAST JOURNALISM IN THE SIXTIES

Television news was expanded in 1963, when both CBS and NBC lengthened their evening newscasts from 15 to 30 minutes. The "CBS Evening News" was anchored by Walter Cronkite, who had taken over from Douglas Edwards in 1962. NBC's dominance of news ratings continued with "The Huntley-Brinkley Report," which remained that network's news entry until Chet Huntley's retirement in 1970. ABC retained its 15-minute news format until 1967.

The year 1963 became a landmark for TV news. Civil rights disturbances and Martin Luther King's "March on Washington" were among the highlights. Then, on November 22, President Kennedy was shot in Dallas. Network coverage continued uninterrupted for three and a half days, including a live broadcast of the transfer of Lee Harvey Oswald, the assassin, from the Dallas County Jail. During the transfer, he, too, was shot and killed. This TV first was seen live by millions and was repeated moments later in one of television's first instant replays.

As TV news became increasingly important to the nation, the networks continued to upgrade their technical capabilities and their budgets and personnel. Three major events dominated the news in 1964—race-related prob-

Figure 2.12 Walter Cronkite anchored the "CBS Evening News" from 1962 until 1981. Cronkite also covered the space program and numerous other special events during his long career in TV news.

Photo courtesy of the National Association of Broadcasters.

lems, the Viet Nam war, and the presidential election. Total costs of network coverage for the two conventions were estimated at roughly $16,000,000, only a fraction of present-day convention budgets.

The chief newsmaker during the middle 1960s was President Lyndon Johnson. He and his family owned TV stations themselves, and the president was a friend of high network officials. During a two-year period (1965–1966), Johnson appeared on live television 58 times for press conferences and policy speeches.

During 1965, the three TV networks established news bureaus in Saigon as the Viet Nam conflict intensified. In the same year, the networks began regularly telecasting their newscasts in color. The result was the first war ever seen in the homes of the public in living color. While film coverage was generally restrained and carefully edited, there was little direct censorship. Viet Nam continued to dominate TV news until 1973.

Television news during 1968 was characterized by extraordinary special events coverage, including the conventions and the election campaign. The total expenditure for news by the TV networks reached an all-time high of $150,000,000, primarily because of the election and extended coverage required by several dramatic events. The first such event was the Apollo Eight mission, during which the first live television pictures of outer space were beamed down to earth and then fed over the three networks. Each network programmed continuous coverage of Apollo Eight during most of the flight. Extensive coverage also was necessitated by the assassinations of Martin Luther King and Senator Robert Kennedy.

In 1968, Richard Nixon was elected president, and the Tet offensive was launched by the Viet Cong. CBS and NBC also began magazine-type documentary programs in public affairs. CBS's "Sixty Minutes" gradually developed into a highly popular Sunday night program based largely on investigative reporting. In radio, the most important development in 1968 was the splitting of ABC Radio into four separate networks. Each tailored its newscast delivery and story selection to match a different type station format. The multiple-service approach was adopted later by the other radio networks.

In 1969, criticism of television came from a new source, as Vice-President Spiro Agnew accused TV news of having a "liberal bias." However, the decade ended on a high note when the first steps by a human being on the moon were seen by a vast worldwide audience. Astronaut Neil Armstrong's remarks to his distant earthly audience ("One small step for a man, one giant leap for mankind") reached the largest audience (550,000,000) of all time. The sending of Armstrong's image live from the moon to earth was almost as significant an event as the moon landing itself.

GROWTH IN SPORTS BROADCASTING

Sports broadcasting not only retained its prominence but actually increased markedly during the 1960s. This was especially evident on Saturday and Sunday afternoons as the networks competed for rights to broadcast major league baseball, college and professional football, basketball, and professional golf and bowling tournaments.

Professional football, popularized by television, reached new heights in 1967 with the first annual "Super Bowl." The game brought together the winning teams from the American and National Football Leagues. The annual Super Bowl telecasts almost always command the highest network advertising rates because of the vast audience they attract. Other important sports telecasts during the decade included the Olympic games of 1960, 1964, and 1968, as well as baseball's annual World Series.

Another innovation, the "instant replay," was instituted in 1964. This video-recording technique permits instant rebroadcast and examination of crucial or otherwise interesting plays in any game.

TELEVISION ENTERTAINMENT PROGRAMMING

Regular series TV programming during the 1960s reflected the new interests and concerns of the times, including spies, space, and war themes. Other new programs were based on activities of doctors and lawyers. Variety shows, crime drama, and situation comedies thrived, but new approaches evolved. There was also a new wave of animal programs. However, TV Westerns and game shows lost much of their popularity by the end of the decade.

TV Perennials: Westerns, Crime, Comedy, and Variety Shows

As the decade began, Westerns and situation comedies enjoyed high ratings. Crime dramas and variety shows also were popular with the public. The most-viewed Westerns included "Wagon Train," "Bonanza," and "Gunsmoke," all holdovers from the 1950s. The latter two retained their slots in prime-time network schedules well into the 1970s.

Two new Western dramas also left their marks on 1960s television—"Rawhide," which starred Clint Eastwood, and "The Richard Boone Show," an anthology of Western drama.

As the Western era began to subside, the new vogue in adventure programming came from detective dramas. Early in the decade, such programs as "Hawaiian Eye" and "Naked City" carried the crime banner on TV. Some violence-prone dramas, such as "The Untouchables," prompted Senate hearings in 1961 on television violence. New crime dramas, such as "The F.B.I." and "Hawaii Five-O" then launched a strong trend for the genre in the 1970s.

While "The Lucy Show" continued to enjoy high ratings in the 1960s, the most promising new situation comedy was "The Andy Griffith Show" (1960–1968). Griffith, a successful Broadway actor ("No Time for Sergeants"), played the leading role as Sheriff Andy Taylor in the mythical small town of Mayberry, North Carolina. The show also helped launch the careers of Don Knotts, Jim Nabors, and Ron Howard.

In 1962, a new comedy form emerged—based on implausible and/or ludicrous situations. "The Beverly Hillbillies," based on the highly improbable premise that a group of mountain people discovered oil on their land and then moved to Hollywood, became an instant and long-running success. Other improbable situation comedies of the decade included "Green Acres," "Bewitched," "The Flying Nun," and "Gilligan's Island."

A third new type of situation comedy, based on war themes, also emerged during the decade. These will be discussed later in the chapter.

The 1960s represented the last big decade for TV variety shows. Certainly the most popular variety program was "The Red Skelton Show," which ranked among the top ten shows nationally for seven of the ten seasons in the decade.

The most important new comedy-variety show of the decade was "Rowan and Martin's Laugh-In," which led off NBC's Monday night schedule from 1968 to 1973. Characterized by innovative comic approaches, including blackouts, cameo appearances, and quick-cuts, "Laugh-In" was interspersed with political satire and occasional "blue" lines. The show introduced many new performers and influenced almost every comedy show that followed.

Another new show, "The Smothers Brothers Comedy Hour," broke with tradition in 1967 to poke fun at many traditionally dear subjects. Its stars, Tom and Dick Smothers, brought both high ratings and public relations problems to CBS with their satire. The show, known for its antiestablishment slant, finally was cancelled in 1969 because of a script conflict. Its replacement was "Hee Haw," a country replica of "Laugh-In" produced in Nashville.

Several musical variety programs were popular in the 1960s, including "The Dean Martin Show" (1965–1974), "The Andy Williams Show" (1958–1971), and "Sing Along with Mitch" (1961–1966). However, "The Carol Burnett Show" (1967–1978) was the last major variety show on regular network television.

Although variety shows were in decline, the networks offered numerous "specials" to liven their schedules. Such one-time programs reached a high of 300 hours in the 1968–69 season.

The scheduling of full-length feature movies in nighttime network schedules became pronounced during the decade. NBC began the trend in 1961 with its weekly "Saturday Night at the Movies." The ultimate in movie scheduling, however, occurred in 1968 when a major movie was shown every night of the week on network television. Furthermore, when it became obvious that TV soon might run out of Hollywood movies, the networks began contracting for the production of their own to supplement the dwindling supply.

New Program Content: Espionage, Space, and War Themes

A new wave of espionage shows emerged in the mid-1960s, apparently inspired by the success of James Bond and other spy movies. The violence, however, was usually discreet, unlike that in the "Untouchables" era.

First, "The Man from U.N.C.L.E." (1964–1968) featured two superagents whose charge was to conquer an international crime syndicate. In contrast to the spoofing "U.N.C.L.E." shows, "I Spy" (1965–1968) was a more serious and believable espionage series. Featuring Bill Cosby, "I Spy" also was the first regular dramatic program on network TV to have a Black performer in a starring role. Another success among the intrigue shows was "Mission: Impossible" (1966–1973).

Several space-oriented drama shows also focused on supremely evil, world-threatening infiltrators who had to be overcome at any cost. The most enduring was "Star Trek" (1966–1969), which developed a fanatic following and is still seen via syndication. "Star Trek," a meticulous production, regularly featured conflicts in space. Other science fiction/space series included "The

Invaders" (1967–1968), "Outer Limits" (1963–1965), and "Lost in Space" (1965–1968), a less serious serial. Even cartoon shows such as "The Jetsons" reflected interest in space adventure.

Viet Nam was the war of the 1960s, but as a controversial conflict, it was not a fitting subject for TV dramatization. However, to cater to the interest in war themes, shows were developed about other military engagements. Such war-oriented dramas included "Combat," "Twelve O'Clock High," "Convoy," and "Garrison's Gorillas."

A group of military-based situation comedies also arose. Again, the stories related to other military conflicts. Already mentioned is "Gomer Pyle, U.S.M.C." (1964–1970), a spinoff from "The Andy Griffith Show." Another war sitcom, "Hogan's Heroes" (1965–1971), depicted the comic side of a prisoner of war camp in Germany during World War II. "McHale's Navy" (1962–1966) dealt with the antics of a PT boat commander and his crew in the Pacific during World War II.

Other New Forms: Doctors, Lawyers, and Animals

Two early '60s medical shows, "Ben Casey" and "Dr. Kildare," brought the drama of hospital life to nighttime television. The Casey series (1961–1966) scored very high ratings and became the most popular show on ABC-TV. "Dr. Kildare," an NBC show (1961–1966), was a continuation of the Kildare character presented earlier in movies and on network radio.

In the last year of the decade, CBS introduced the hour-long "Medical Center" series. It, too, focused on a large hospital and the interaction between doctors and patients. A ratings success, "Medical Center" continued on the network schedule until 1976. Finally, in 1969, ABC launched probably the most successful medical show of all times in "Marcus Welby, M.D." with veteran actor Robert Young.

Programmers took a new approach to attorney dramas with "The Defenders" (1961–1965). In this courtroom series, a father and son legal team represented their accused clients.

The perennial animal series, "Lassie," was on television throughout the 1960s. This children's adventure story, which has its roots in the movies, presented the warm story of a brave and loyal collie and its remarkable feats under several sets of owners. While "Lassie" (1954–1971) rarely achieved unusually high ratings, the show was a favorite of its loyal audience for many seasons. Other animal stories, usually of the situation comedy genre, included "Flipper," about a pet dolphin; "Mr. Ed," about a talking horse; and "Gentle Ben," about a black bear.

Daytime TV Programming

Network daytime programming changed very little through the 1960s. Serial dramas continued to rule the afternoons, with old favorites such as "The Edge of Night" and "As the World Turns" retaining popularity. Game shows also were popular, but their turnover rate was much higher. Consistent favorites, however, included "Jeopardy," "Let's Make a Deal," and "Password."

Saturday mornings, once a "throw-away" time, became lucrative during the 1960s with cartoon shows and advertising directed to children. Both, however, came under frequent attack—the cartoon shows for their violence and advertising for its too frequent interrruptions, as well as its appeal to an unsophisticated audience. Gradually, however, the networks deemphasized the violent content, limited the advertising, and inserted educational vignettes. "In the News" and "Multiplication Rock" became two of the most popular such inserts.

Public Television Programming

In 1967, following a Carnegie Commission study, Congress passed the Public Broadcasting Act. This legislation created the quasigovernmental Corporation for Public Broadcasting (CPB), which became responsible for fostering quality noncommercial broadcasting in the United States. From 1967 on, noncommercial stations, both TV and radio, became known as "public" rather than "educational" stations. CPB also established the Public Broadcasting Service (PBS) to coordinate national program production and distribution.

From a modest beginning, PBS has come to offer an important programming alternative. With corporate underwriting and governmental grants, PBS offered quality programs such as "Firing Line," "The Great American Dream Machine," and "Civilisation." And beginning with "Forsyte Saga" in 1969, the PBS "Masterpiece Theatre" brought British-produced drama, including "Elizabeth R" and "The Six Wives of Henry the Eighth," to American TV screens.

The most important children's program in television's history also was introduced by PBS in 1969. "Sesame Street," a well-researched, high-budget show, used TV's unique capabilities to teach basic concepts to preschool children. Almost overnight, "Sesame Street," produced by the Children's Television Workshop, made stars of Big Bird, Ernie and Bert, and the Cookie Monster. Subsequently, PBS introduced a similar program for older children, "The Electric Company," with similar acclaim. These two public television programs have strongly influenced children's television programming throughout the world.

RADIO PROGRAMMING

Radio programming during the 1960s was characterized by an ever-increasing trend to vertical programming and specialization. The three major formats of the late 1950s proliferated into no less than 12 distinct formats. These formats included contemporary (Top 40, "Solid Gold," and album-oriented rock), middle-of-the-road, beautiful music, country-and-western, news/information/talk, soul, Spanish, religious, classical, and jazz.

Improved technology in FM transmission, especially advances in stereo broadcasting, produced a boom in FM listenership. Competitive formats also began to emerge in FM radio after a 1965 FCC ruling that limited the duplication of AM and FM programming, bringing new popularity to formerly nondescript stations. By the end of the decade, FM was actually challenging AM for supremacy in a few of the larger US markets.

1971–1982: PROGRAMMING IN THE MODERN ERA

Broadcasting continued to expand during the 1970s, though at a slower pace than during the two previous decades. Each of the electronic media was now accustomed to its distinctive role—TV as a mass-appeal family medium and radio as a specialized companion service. Each forged ahead, expanding programming services and audience reach in what must be described as a period of mature growth.

TELEVISION INDUSTRY DEVELOPMENTS

From almost any standpoint, broadcast television had matured by the start of the 1980s. First, set penetration was almost universal, and color-set ownership was at an all-time high of 85 percent in the United States. Second, programming had matured so that almost any subject, including ones formerly taboo, could be presented. Third, for the first time, it became commonplace for Blacks and other racial minorities to perform on regular network shows. Fourth, networks and stations alike were prospering, based on high audience levels and heavy demand for TV advertising time. And fifth, new competitors were emerging.

With the public's desire for more viewing choices, new UHF stations were opened in many markets during the 1970s. Most were independent outlets, which tended to show movies, reruns of former network series, and sports. Other new stations adopted religious or ethnic, especially Spanish and Black, specialty formats. In addition, over-the-air subscription television (STV) was launched.

During the 1970s, new technology contributed to television's improvement. The use of satellite transponders for sending and receiving program materials was a very promising development. Local and network TV news benefitted from the introduction of portable electronic cameras and microwave transmission. The increased availability of quality mass-appeal programming enabled independent stations to compete effectively for the first time.

While most of these developments may be regarded as positive for broadcast television, a number of issues were building up to threaten the industry. First, public criticism became a sensitive problem during the decade. There were charges of news bias, particularly during the era of the Nixon administration. A second major criticism related to violence in children's programs and on those programs shown during hours in which children usually watch TV. Criticism came from Action for Children's Television (ACT), a national organization of concerned parents, as well as from such distinguished organizations as the Parent-Teacher Association, the American Legion, and church entities. Reducing violence in TV programs, many producers substituted sexually explicit material and innuendo, thus prompting further protests.

Other adverse developments included growing competition from cable television, especially distant "superstations," special cable networks, and pay TV programming, both via cable and from STV stations. Still other developments that threaten to reduce television's audience include home video recording/playback systems and direct broadcast satellites (DBS). All of these developments, coupled with the growing number of broadcast TV outlets, presage a more fragmented industry competing for both mass audiences and specialized demographic viewership.

BROADCAST JOURNALISM: 1971–1982

The public's reliance on broadcast news continued to grow during this period as a number of dramatic events occurred. The winding down of the Viet Nam conflict soon gave way to one of the nation's most convulsive historical developments—the Watergate story. Large audiences watched the Senate Watergate hearings and the House Judiciary Committee's impeachment hearings, which culminated in the resignation of President Richard Nixon. On a happier note, broadcasting covered the pageantry and celebration of the nation's 200th birthday in 1976, as well as the election campaigns of that year and 1980.

Two major special events were covered simultaneously on January 20, 1981—the inauguration of President Ronald Reagan and the dramatic release of US hostages held captive for more than 14 months by Iran. On that day, the TV networks provided continuous news programming for more than 12 hours. Extended coverage again was required on March 30, 1981, when President Reagan was wounded in an assassination attempt.

The daily newscast took on greater importance as television became the single most important source of news for most Americans. Station licensees also realized—perhaps for the first time—the tremendous potential that news holds for profits and for enhancement of a station's image. This realization led owners across the country to provide increased funding for their news operations. Many TV stations also turned to consultants for advice. Some innovative concepts, including midevening newsbreaks and "happy talk" formats, emerged. As the period ended, however, the extreme approaches had declined and local TV newscasts were generally upgraded, but were certainly less formal than in earlier decades.

Network newscasts remained at the half-hour length despite pleas for longer air time by prominent anchormen. Unable to clear additional early evening time, the networks began adding news to other parts of the day, especially Sunday morning and late night. One of the strongest advocates of a longer nightly newscast was Walter Cronkite, the long-time CBS anchorman, who retired from that assignment in 1981. His "CBS Evening News" was consistently the most heavily viewed network news program throughout the 1971 to 1981 period. By 1980, however, ABC, traditionally third ranked in news, mounted a strong challenge to CBS and NBC for viewership of its newscasts as well as its entertainment programs.

News and information programming also increased on radio, particularly on AM stations, which generally lost music audiences to FM. An all-news network was attempted briefly by NBC from 1975 into 1977.

TELEVISION ENTERTAINMENT PROGRAMMING

In entertainment programming, the most notable fact of the period was the enduring appeal of the situation comedy. Movies also retained popularity, but variety shows and Western dramas declined sharply. These two types often were replaced by sitcoms and crime-detective dramas, both of which underwent structural changes.

Many long-time favorite shows disappeared from the network schedules during the 1970s. Prominent casualties included "Gunsmoke," the "Ed Sullivan Show," and the "Lucy" series. A number of other successful shows such as "Hee Haw," "Lawrence Welk," and the "Beverly Hillbillies" were removed from network schedules because they appealed mainly to older and often rural viewers rather than younger urbanites, the preferred target audience of consumer goods advertisers.

Program syndication activities notably increased, including both new productions and reruns of former network shows. In some instances, popular network reruns brought $60,000 or more per episode from large market stations. Other new sources of TV material included several "occasional" networks. The most notable were the Hughes TV Network, which emphasized sports, and "Operation Prime Time" (OPT), which produced network-quality entertainment programs for a prominent group of supporting stations. Finally, the Independent News Network (INN) was established by WPIX-TV, New York, in 1980, to feed a nightly national newscast to other independent stations across the country.

Comedy Programs

Situation comedy shows dominated the audience ratings of the 1970s. However, there was a radical departure from the traditional but often unrealistic family comedies in favor of a new and bolder approach dealing with contemporary and sometimes controversial subject matter. The two leading producers of the new-style sitcoms were Norman Lear's Tandem Productions and MTM Productions. The two, however, followed different approaches with the new comedy form.

Lear's shows, particularly "All in the Family," broke new ground by presenting topics and vocabulary that had long been taboo in broadcasting. Introduced in 1971, "All in the Family" featured Carroll O'Connor as Archie Bunker and Jean Stapleton as his wife, Edith. Bunker was portrayed as a bigoted working-class husband who disliked all racial minorities and religious groups other than his own. Lear's purpose was to show the absurdity of bigotry through the medium of comedy.

Not only was "All in the Family" one of the decade's most popular shows, it also became the most influential series program of the 1970s. It paved the way for frankness and opened the television medium to the realistic treatment of such subjects as rape, abortion, and homosexuality. While some later shows adopted the same technique purely for exploitation, Lear's comedies always focused on a social message.

Two important shows were spun off from "All in the Family"—"Maude" (1972–1978) and "The Jeffersons" (1975–   ). The second was centered around a Black family that had been neighbors of the Bunkers in Queens. George Jefferson, a central character, became a successful businessman. George also was bigoted and arrogant, something of a Black replica of Archie Bunker. However, his success seemed to say that Black Americans could also be successful.

Figure 2.13 One of the top hits of the 1970s, Norman Lear's "All in the Family" broke new ground for the situation comedy genre. Shown are Jean Stapleton as Edith Bunker and Carroll O'Connor, who played the "uneducated prejudiced, and blatantly outspoken" central figure of Archie Bunker.

MTM's situation comedies, in contrast, dealt with contemporary themes in a more sympathetic manner. "The Mary Tyler Moore Show," which captivated a large, loyal audience during its six seasons (1970–1977), basically made the point that a bright, single young woman could succeed in a professional career. The show's theme song, "You're Going to Make It After All," highlighted that message week after week.

The setting of "The Mary Tyler Moore Show" was a low-rated Minneapolis television station, in which Mary Richards landed a job as news producer. Her boss was a blustery but kind news director named Lou Grant. He and other newsroom employees, as well as Mary's outside friends, figured in the plots. In addition to the principal theme, occasional episodes also highlighted the importance of news, accuracy in reporting, and issues related to freedom of the press.

Spin-offs from the Moore show included "Rhoda" (1974–1979), "Phyllis" (1975–1977), and "Lou Grant" (1977–1982). Like the original, both "Rhoda" and "Phyllis" were situation comedies. However, "Lou Grant" was a more serious hour drama in which the former TV news director continued his journalistic career as city editor of a major newspaper.

Although it is impossible to cite every successful sitcom of the decade, a few others deserve special mention. One of these is "M*A*S*H," the story

Figure 2.14 "The Mary Tyler Moore Show," a situation comedy based in a mythical Minneapolis TV newsroom, was one of the most enduring shows of the 1970s. Shown are Mary Tyler Moore, Ted Knight as Ted Baxter, the anchorman of WJM-TV, and Gavin McLeod as Murray Slaughter, a writer.

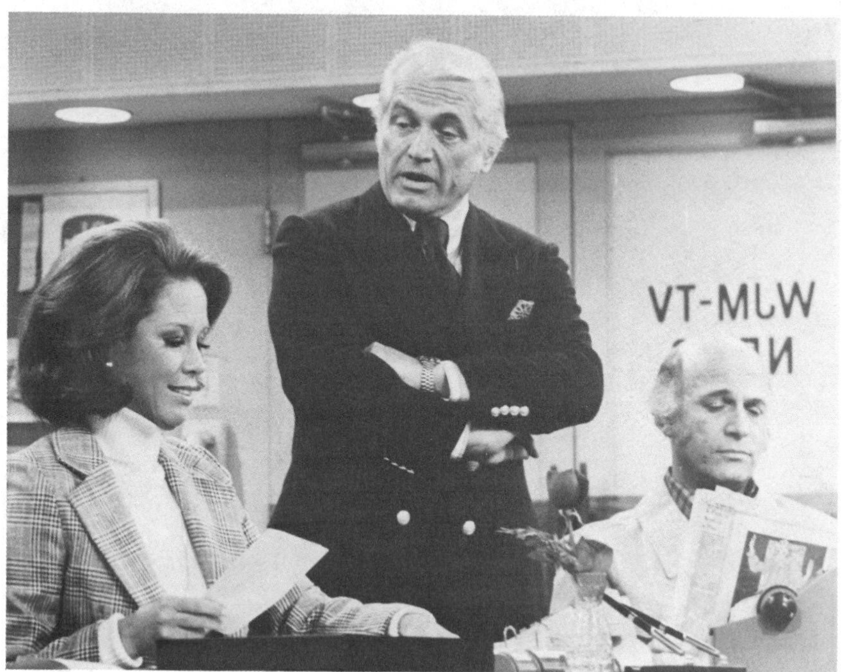

of a mobile hospital company during the Korean War. Begun in 1972, it presented an underlying antiwar and probrotherhood message during the years immediately after the Viet Nam War. An unusual blend of comic interplay among the regular characters and serious moments related to the medical mission contributed to the show's longevity.

"Alice," one of the first sitcoms to be based in a typical, interior city, depicted a young widow's attempt to survive and rear a precocious 12-year-old son. Other successful situation comedies of this period include "The Odd Couple" (1970–1975), "Room 222" (1969–1974), "Sanford and Son" (1972–1977), "Happy Days" (1974–), "Barney Miller" (1975–1982), "One Day at a Time" (1975–), and "WKRP in Cincinnati" (1978–1982).

Crime Dramas

Next in popularity to situation comedies were crime programs featuring police detectives and private investigators. With a few exceptions, most of the detective dramas of this period used suggestion rather than overt violence in portraying their stories.

Among the popular carry-over dramas were "Hawaii Five-O," "Ironside," "Mannix," and "Mod Squad." "Ironside" (1967-1975) was unique in that its central figure was confined to a wheelchair—paralyzed from an assassin's attempt on his life. "Mannix" (1967-1975) was a Los Angeles private detective. And "Mod Squad" (1968-1973) reflected its era through a trio of young "hippie" cops who worked as undercover police agents in Los Angeles.

The popularity of existing detective dramas, coupled with the demise of the Western stories, resulted in a proliferation of new crime shows, each with a unique central figure. "Cannon" (1971-1976), played by William Conrad, was an atypical bald and fat investigator who was inclined toward expensive tastes. "Kojak" (1973-1978), also bald, was a lollipop-licking police detective in New York, played by Telly Savalas. Buddy Ebsen portrayed "Barnaby Jones" (1973-1980), who came out of retirement to take over the detective agency left by his murdered son. And "The Rockford Files" (1974-1980) was built around a private eye who served time in prison but later was exonerated when the true circumstances came to light. In the story, Jim Rockford was played by James Garner.

Finally, since public opinion forced crime-show violence to be subdued, the networks attempted to replace that commodity with sex. In "Charlie's Angels" (1976-1981), three stunningly beautiful young women worked as private detectives for their never-seen boss, "Charlie."

General Drama

Although less popular than the sitcoms and crime dramas, general dramatic programs continued to play an important role on television. Three major themes predominated during the period: professions, nostalgia, and adventure.

Two important medical dramas retained popularity into the 1970s: "Marcus Welby, M.D." (1969-1976) and "Medical Center" (1969-1976). Another carry-over, "The Bold Ones" (1969-1976), rotated its spotlight on doctors, lawyers, and "protectors." In 1972, NBC launched "Emergency," an adventure drama based on the work of a paramedical team in Los Angeles.

Near the end of the 1970s, the dedicated journalist emerged as the principal character in an hour-long newspaper drama. As city editor of the *Los Angeles Tribune,* "Lou Grant" revealed the problems of covering a large city, while also depicting the human side of an editorial staff at work in a large metropolitan newspaper.

Two nostalgic dramas achieved popularity during the mid-1970s in "The Waltons" (1972-1981) and "Little House on the Prairie" (1974-). Both were moralistic stories in which ordinary people of strong will and independence struggled to survive against the elements. "The Waltons" depicted life in the Virginia mountains during the Great Depression, while "Little House" went further back to the homesteading era of the 1870s in the West.

In contrast, a new superhero concept emerged in a series of "bionic" fantasy characters who used their strength to battle criminals. In ABC's "Six Million Dollar Man" (1974-1978), the first of this genre, a critically injured former astronaut was given superhuman strength through the replacement of his ailing parts with powerful electromechanical devices. Other superhuman TV characters inspired by this series included "The Bionic Woman" (1976-1978) and "The Incredible Hulk" (1978-1981).

Two other important dramatic series during this period were "Love Boat" (1977-) and "Dallas" (1978-). The first depicts three stories of love and romance interwoven into each week's episode. Each program takes place on a cruise ship and includes both guest performers and a regular cast (the ship's crew). Although not the first nighttime serial drama, "Dallas" became the most popular by far. Its weekly story revolves around an immensely rich, but corrupt, Texas family of oil and cattle wealth. The Ewings, especially their contemptible oldest son, J.R., engage in unethical business dealings, civic affairs, and personal life problems.

Finally, historical drama became prominent, often in "mini-series" form, during the period. One of the first docudramas was Taylor Caldwell's "The Captain and the Kings" (1976), a historical novel in the post-Civil War era. It dealt largely with a fictional Irish Catholic who wanted his son to become President. However, the docudrama that received the greatest acclaim was "Roots," a 1977 mini-series based on Alex Haley's search into Africa for his own ancestry. Other notable TV docudramas included "Holocaust," a mini-series on the extermination of Jews in Nazi Germany, "The Missiles of October," which recreated the 1962 Cuban missile crisis, "Shogun" in 1980, and "Marco Polo" in 1982.

OTHER TELEVISION PROGRAMMING

A harbinger of the demise of variety programming was the cancellation of "The Ed Sullivan Show" by CBS in 1971. Thus, as the period began, this longest running of all variety programs ended its 24-year schedule. However, several new variety shows made their appearance during the early 1970s and some lasted until as late as 1978. These included "The Flip Wilson Show" (1970–1974), "The Sonny and Cher [Bono] Comedy Hour" (1971–1977), "Tony Orlando and Dawn" (1974–1976), and "Donny and Marie," which featured members of the Osmond family, whose youth-oriented variety show lasted from 1976 until 1978. "The Carol Burnett Show" (1967–1978) was also one of the last weekly variety shows on evening television. However, variety specials continued to be offered frequently, including occasional shows by the veteran comedian Bob Hope.

Undoubtedly the outstanding children's program on evening TV was "The Wonderful World of Disney" (1954–1981). It accommodated a variety of types of presentation—cartoons, animations, and adventure shows being most prominent. Another long-running children's show was "Captain Kangaroo," a daytime favorite with its third generation of viewers. ABC's main entry for children was a series of occasional "After School Specials." On PBS, such children's programs as "Sesame Street," "The Electric Company," and "Zoom" continue to educate as well as entertain young children.

Sports remained one of network television's greatest attractions. Not only are vast audiences attracted to such spectacular events as the Super Bowl, the World Series, and the Olympic Games, but each network also developed a weekly sports magazine show which permits it to cover exciting events on a weekly basis. The most successful is ABC's "Wide World of Sports," which is scheduled during late Saturday afternoons.

The basic pattern for weekday daytime programming remains virtually unchanged from previous periods—with reruns, game shows, and serial dramas predominating. The lengthening of several of the most popular soap operas from one-half to a full hour was a major development in the late 1970s. Another significant move was to reorient daytime serials toward a younger female audience, which now includes large numbers of college students as well as their mothers and grandmothers. Among the more popular serial dramas in 1982 are "As the World Turns" and "The Guiding Light" on CBS; "One Life to Live" and "General Hospital" on ABC; and "Another World" and "Days of Our Lives" on NBC.

Three other TV time blocks have evolved into important viewing periods and, consequently, profitable times for stations and networks. First, early morning network television, historically dominated by NBC's "Today" show, became a battleground in the late 1970s when ABC launched its "Good Morning, America." This program, much akin to "Today," emphasizes news about the entertainment industry, as well as general news, sports, and weather. In 1982, CBS also expanded its straightforward "CBS Morning News" to two hours.

Second, in 1972, the FCC moved to reduce the amount of network evening time to stimulate local live and first-run syndication programming. The "Prime Time Access Rule" limited the networks to three hours of time per evening (four hours on Sunday); however, cheaply produced game shows and network reruns often were used by local stations to fill the extra time awarded them. As the 1970s ended, though, the prime-time access period began to blossom with public affairs/informational programs. The most promising was an innovative, cooperatively produced, syndicated/local series known as "PM Magazine." This series, developed by Group W (Westinghouse Broadcasting), has achieved remarkable audience success in a large number of markets.

Finally, the three networks have become very competitive for late-night viewers. Again, with its early start in 1952, NBC was the entrenched network with "Tonight." Both ABC and CBS attempted to compete early in the 1970s with similar talk shows, but lost the battle to the durable "Tonight" show and its popular host, Johnny Carson. By the end of the period, CBS had returned to movie and crime/adventure programming, while ABC had introduced its late evening "Nightline" newscast, followed by movies.

RADIO PROGRAMMING

Growth in radio during the 1970s occurred mainly on the FM band because new stations had practically nowhere else to go. And FM, with its better quality sound reproduction, had finally caught on with the public. By the end of this last period, FM listening had surpassed that of AM in practically every important market in the country.

Several factors contributed to the upsurge in FM radio. These include the rapidly growing penetration of FM receivers in automobiles, greater appreciation for FM's stereophonic and high fidelity sound, and new and separate programming by most FM stations.

Another significant development of the 1970s and 1980s was National Public Radio's development of "All Things Considered," a daily evening radio newscast that won awards and developed a loyal following. In 1980, NPR also developed "Morning Edition," a morning news program which also gained rapid listenership. Many public stations nationwide carried one or both of the programs, offering a serious alternative to network television news programming.

Increased listening to FM posed an increasing problem for all AM stations, but especially lower power outlets. Even some long-dominant AM powerhouse stations had lost significant audience shares to FM stations as the period ended. One possible solution was the proposed introduction of AM stereo broadcasting. However, the emerging pattern seemed to be what industry observers had predicted a decade earlier: FM was becoming the principal source for music programming, while AM stations were retaining audiences with news, talk, and information.

As to specific format trends, radio continued to become increasingly specialized as all but a few hold-outs went to vertical programming. Formats proliferated. High-power AM and FM stations generally preempted the most popular formats, leaving smaller stations to find narrow niches to serve.

As the 1980s began, the most popular radio formats included adult contemporary, easy listening, contemporary hits, album-oriented rock, and all-news. Others which did well, depending on market demographics, included country music, talk radio, and ethnic specialties. Small-town stations continued to serve varied segments of their communities, relying on either block programming or an integrated mixture approach to their music programming.

SUMMARY

In this chapter, we have traced the historical evolution of broadcast programming from radio's unofficial beginning early in the 20th century to the space-age telecommunications era of the 1980s. The 60-plus years that have elapsed since the first regular radio station began its programming from a factory penthouse in Pittsburgh have been fascinating, to say the least. Certainly the novelty of wireless transmission has developed into a monumental communications institution, depended upon almost universally for entertainment, information, and service.

As broadcasting enters the next-to-last decade of the 20th century, the industry faces the possibility of sweeping structural changes, including new media outlets, nonbroadcast competitors, and significant audience fragmentation. The news emerging from this picture for the young people embarked on careers in the telecommunications industry is good. The message that comes through loud and clear is that there will be a much greater need than ever for program ideas, effective writing, and capable production and performing talents to supply the programs needed by the expanding industry. The chapters which follow are intended to help those individuals who plan careers in the programming side of broadcasting. Next is an examination of regulation as it relates to programming.

ENDNOTES

1. Erick Barnouw, *A Tower in Babel* (New York: Oxford University Press, 1966), p. 18.
2. Lynn S. Gross, *SEE/HEAR: An Introduction to Broadcasting* (Dubuque, Iowa: W.C. Brown Co., 1979), p. 5.
3. Joseph E. Baudine and John M. Kittross, "Broadcasting's Oldest Station: An Examination of Four Claimants," *Journal of Broadcasting,* 21:61-83 (Winter 1977), p. 73.
4. WBZ is now located in Boston, KYW is in Philadelphia, and the former WJZ is now WABC-AM, New York. Westinghouse still holds the licenses for KDKA, WBZ, and KYW. It also uses the WJZ call for its Baltimore TV station.
5. Sydney W. Head, *Broadcasting in America,* 3d. ed. (Boston: Houghton Mifflin Co., 1976), p. 113.
6. Irving Settel, *A Pictorial History of Radio* (New York: Bonanza Books, 1960), p. 55.
7. Grayson William Meredith, *Opening Night in Your Living Room: History and Criticism of the Live Television Drama, 1928–1948* (Unpublished Master's thesis, The University of Tennessee, 1977).
8. *Sponsor,* May 28, 1962, p. 54.
9. From a speech delivered by FCC Chairman Newton S. Minow at The National Association of Broadcasters convention in 1961.
10. Such internationally televised events have included Olympic Games, trips abroad by US Presidents and other world leaders, and funerals of important public figures.
11. Stations donating their nighttime hours to carry Spanish-language broadcasts originated by the Voice of America during the Cuban crisis included WSB, Atlanta; WWL, New Orleans; WCKY, Cincinnati; WGBS, WMIE, and WCKR, Miami; WKWF, Key West; plus shortwave stations WRUL, New York, and KGEI, San Carlos, California.

STUDY QUESTIONS

1. List the five individuals who, in your opinion, have been most influential in broadcast programming since 1920. This list may include entertainers and news personalities, as well as executives and other professionals. Explain your choices.
2. Which decade do you consider the most important period in the development of broadcasting in the United States? Explain and support your answer in a two-page essay.
3. Radio broadcasting emerged as a mass medium during the 1920s. In terms of socioeconomic conditions, was this an opportune time for radio to develop? If not, what decade might have been more suitable? Explain your answer.
4. Television was ready to be launched in 1940, but it was delayed until the late 1940s because of the war. Taking socioeconomic conditions into account, would television have developed as successfully had its start been earlier? How might it have been different? Explain your answers.
5. What do you consider to be the single most important show or series program in the history of radio broadcasting? Explain your answer.
6. What has been the single most important show or series program in the history of television? Explain your answer.
7. Why did radio change its principal orientation from national to local? To what extent would this have occurred had television not emerged?

SUGGESTED READINGS

Andrews, Bart. *Lucy & Ricky & Fred & Ethel: The Story of I Love Lucy.* New York: E.P. Dutton, 1976.

Archer, Gleason L. *History of Radio to 1926.* New York: American Historical Society, 1938; Arno Press, 1971.

Barnouw, Erik. *A Tower in Babel: A History of Broadcasting in the United States.* Vol. I—to 1933. New York: Oxford University Press, 1966.

___________. *The Golden Web: A History of Broadcasting in the United States.* Vol. II—1933-1953. New York: Oxford University Press, 1968.

___________. *The Image Empire: A History of Broadcasting in the United States.* Vol. III—from 1953. New York: Oxford University Press, 1970.

___________. *Tube of Plenty: The Evolution of American Television.* New York: Oxford University Press, 1975.

Bogart, Leo. *The Age of Television.* New York: Frederick Unger, 1972.

Brooks, Time, and Earle Marsh. *The Complete Directory of Prime Time Network TV Shows: 1946–present.* New York: Ballantine, 1979.

Brown, Les. *The New York Times Encyclopedia of Television.* New York: The New York Times Book Company, 1977.

___________. *Television: The Business Behind the Box.* New York: Harcourt Brace Jovanovich, 1971.

Campbell, Robert. *The Golden Years of Broadcasting.* New York: Charles Scribner's Sons, 1976.

Foster, Eugene S. *Understanding Broadcasting.* Reading, Mass.: Addison-Wesley Publishing Co., 1978.

Glut, Donald, and Jim Harmon. *The Great Television Heroes.* New York: Doubleday, 1975.

Gross, Lynne S. *SEE/HEAR: An Introduction to Broadcasting.* Dubuque, Iowa: W.C. Brown Co., 1979.

Halberstam, David. *The Powers That Be.* New York: Alfred A. Knopf, 1979.

Hammond, Charles M. *The Image Decade: Television Documentary: 1965–1975.* New York: Hastings House, 1981.

Lichty, Lawrence W., and Malachi C. Topping. *American Broadcasting: A Sourcebook on The History of Radio and Televison.* New York: Hastings House, 1975.

MacFarland, David T. *The Development of the Top 40 Radio Format.* New York: Arno Press, 1979.

Metz, Robert. *CBS: Reflections in a Bloodshot Eye.* Chicago: Playboy Press, 1975.

Mitchell, Curtis. *Cavalcade of Broadcasting.* Chicago: Follett Publishing Company, 1970.

Paley, William S. *As It Happened.* New York: Doubleday, 1979.

Settel, Irving. *A Pictorial History of Radio.* New York: Bonanza Books, 1960.

Settel, Irving, and William Laas. *A Pictorial History of Television.* New York: Grosset & Dunlap, Inc., Publishers, 1969.

Sterling, Christopher H., and John M. Kittross. *Stay Tuned: A Concise History of American Broadcasting.* Belmont, Calif.: Wadsworth Publishing, 1978.

Summers, Harrison B. *A Thirty Year History of Programs Carried on National Radio Networks in the United States, 1926–1956.* New York: Arno Press, 1972.

3

THE ROLE OF REGULATION IN PROGRAMMING

Although federal regulation of broadcasting mainly relates to technical matters, certain aspects of radio and TV programming also are affected. This governmental influence on programming has been both active and quiescent during various periods of regulatory history. This chapter will explore the role of federal regulation as it currently relates to the programming of broadcast stations. It also will examine regulatory history, as well as self-regulation as practiced by the broadcasting industry.

THE DEVELOPMENT OF BROADCAST REGULATION

Two wireless communications acts were passed by Congress before the beginning of radio broadcasting in the United States. Neither, however, was appropriate for the new industry. First, the Wireless Ship Act of 1910 required ocean-going vessels carrying as many as 50 passengers to be equipped with transmitters and receivers to handle distress calls.[1] The Radio Act of 1912 further regulated the wireless transmission of sporadic point-to-point messages.[2] It was this unsuitable legislation under which broadcasting was governed until 1927.

Because continuous programming for the general public was not anticipated in 1912, the regulation of radio broadcasting was minimal during the first years of the new industry. Technical interference between stations soon became common, as hundreds of radio stations took to the airwaves.

Although Secretary of Commerce Herbert Hoover attempted to establish order within the new industry, his efforts repeatedly were thwarted when the courts held that the Radio Act of 1912 provided no authority for the regulation of broadcasting.[3] Several different bills were introduced in Congress between 1921 and 1927 to improve radio's regulation. Finally, Congress passed the Radio Act of 1927, which became the basis of US broadcast legislation to the present.[4]

THE RADIO ACT OF 1927

The Radio Act of 1927 recognized the important distinction that radio broadcasting is a unique service, one that is quite different from earlier forms of point-to-point wireless transmission. It also created the Federal Radio Commission (FRC), an agency of Congress, to regulate the broadcasting industry. The FRC was given specific licensing powers, including the authority to establish licensee criteria and to select from among applicants for the same facility, as well as the authority to assign stations to specific frequencies, hours of operation, and power output.

Congress also adopted the basic concept advanced by Herbert Hoover and other radio advocates that a broadcast licensee holds a trust to the public airwaves and that those entrusted with licenses must serve the public interest. Another significant point contained in the 1927 Act was a specific prohibition against censorship of programming by the Commission.

While Congress granted the Federal Radio Commission certain discretionary regulatory powers, it also specified that any rules, regulations, or decisions made by the agency are subject to judicial review.

THE FEDERAL RADIO COMMISSION GOES TO WORK

The first few years of the FRC's authority were devoted largely to cleaning up the airwaves of practices that were patently contrary to the public interest. For example, the FRC sought to eliminate stations that would not conform to its new technical rules and those that abused their licenses with programming regarded by the Commission as detrimental to the public. Thus, from the outset, the agency assumed that its responsibilities included consideration of the program service as well as the technical aspects of the stations it licensed.

The Commission significantly concluded that, while the anticensorship provision prohibited direct control of programming, the public interest mandate required it to judge each station's service to the public. Therefore, the FRC held each licensee responsible for its program service and periodically reviewed its past programming to determine if the station deserved the renewal of its license on the merits of its service.[5]

It was not the Commission's intention, therefore, to pass judgment on individual programs in advance of their presentation, but rather to review the overall past performance of a station in determining whether or not to renew a license. This approach has been retained to the present. Another early action of the FRC was to require stations to keep logs as a means of documenting their program performance.

Two early cases tested the Federal Radio Commission's authority to review a station's past programming at the time designated for its license renewal. These two rulings, known as the *Brinkley* and *Shuler* cases, strengthened and clarified the Commission's powers. The courts upheld the FRC in both cases.

The Brinkley Case

Dr. John W. Brinkley, a physician and pharmacist, operated radio station KFKB in Milford, Kansas, from 1923 until 1931. Although KFKB's programming was quite varied, its licensee used the station daily as a vehicle for prescribing medication to persons whom he had not seen. Three times a day Brinkley broadcast his "Medical Question Box," in which he answered questions sent by listeners. The doctor usually responded by prescribing remedies prepared in his own drug store.

Eventually, Brinkley's unorthodox approach to sight-unseen diagnosis caught the attention of the American Medical Association. Upon finding that Brinkley did not hold a recognized medical degree, the society appealed to the FRC to revoke KFKB's license. Then, in 1930, after a newspaper exposé of Brinkley's operation, the Kansas Medical Society announced hearings to consider revoking Brinkley's license to practice medicine in the state. Shortly afterwards, the Commission instituted revocation hearings on KFKB's license. The FRC charged that the licensee had illegally engaged in point-to-point communication over his broadcast station and that he had also perpetrated a fraud upon his listeners.[6]

In his defense, Brinkley accused the Commission of attempting to censor his broadcasts in violation of the Federal Radio Act and the First Amendment. Although KFKB's license technically was not revoked, the Commission denied its renewal in June, 1930. Brinkley then took his case to the US Court of Appeals in Washington. However, the appellate court upheld the Commission's authority to deny the station's license.[7] In its decision of February 2, 1931, the Court stated:

> In considering the question whether the public interest convenience or necessity will be served by a renewal of appellant's license, the Commission has merely exercised its undoubted right to take note of appellant's past conduct, which is not censorship.[8]

Thus, in the *Brinkley* case, the court clearly established the Commission's authority to examine a licensee's past programming as a means of evaluating its probable future service to the public. Although procedures have been changed, broadcast stations still are evaluated on this same basis by the Federal Communications Commission.

The KFKB decision also restricted broadcast stations to general communication rather than point-to-point messages except during emergency situations. Exceptions include occurrences of tornadoes, hurricanes, floods, tidal waves, earthquakes, heavy snows, icing conditions, widespread fires, discharge of toxic gases, widespread power failures, industrial explosions, civil disorders, and school closings and changes in school bus schedules resulting from such conditions.

The Shuler Case

Another landmark case relative to broadcast programming involved station KGEF, Los Angeles. This station, owned by the Rev. Robert "Fighting Bob" Shuler, was licensed to Trinity Methodist Church of which Shuler was pastor. KGEF was supported mainly by contributions from its listeners.

Shuler, formerly a prohibitionist preacher in Texas, became noted for his efforts to clean up corruption in the California city. For example, he used KGEF during the 1920s in an effort to expose sin and vice. Shuler was so successful, in fact, that he brought about the dismissal of a Los Angeles police chief through an exposé of the officer's association with racketeers.[9]

In 1931, the Federal Radio Commission received numerous protests of Shuler's crusading broadcasts, especially his personal but unsubstantiated attacks against prominent individuals and his anti-Catholic and anti-Jewish pronouncements. After holding public hearings in Los Angeles, the Commission, on November 13, 1931, ordered KGEF off the air. The agency based its decision on Shuler's broadcasts, which included unproven charges against public officials and the courts, as well as his provocation of religious strife in the community.

In his appeal, Shuler claimed the Commission sought to deprive him of his constitutional rights, specifically freedom of speech under the First Amendment and protection against deprivation of property without due process under the Fifth Amendment. However, the Court of Appeals fully upheld the FRC decision, stating:

> In the case under consideration, the evidence abundantly sustains the conclusion of the Commission that the continuance of the broadcasting programs of the appellant is not in the public interest.[10]

The Court also emphasized that broadcast licensees voluntarily subject themselves to certain restrictions on their freedom of speech:

> Appellant (Shuler) may continue to indulge his strictures upon the characters of men in public office. He may just as freely as ever criticize religious practices of which he does not approve. He may even indulge private malice or personal slander—subject, of course, to be required to answer to the abuse thereof—but he may not, as we think, demand, of right, the continued use of an instrumentality of commerce for such purposes, or any other, except in the subordination to all reasonable rules and regulations Congress, acting through the Commission, may prescribe.[11]

In the Shuler decision, the Court also held that the broadcast frequencies are public property that are only entrusted to station licensees. On this premise, the Court upheld the FRC's authority to take away broadcast rights when it believes such action is required by the public interest. Doing so, the Court added, is not "an unconstitutional taking of property without due process of law."[12] Shuler's subsequent appeal was rejected by the US Supreme Court in 1932.

The Shuler case established three bedrock principles upon which the Commission could build its public interest regulatory structure. First, the Court reaffirmed the Commission's power to examine a station's past programming when considering whether or not to renew its license. Second, by refusing to consider an appeal in the Shuler case, the Supreme Court sanctioned limitations on freedom of speech by broadcasters. To the present, the Courts have held that, although the First Amendment applies to broadcasting, it does not apply in exactly the same way or to the same extent that it does in the publishing industry. And, third, the Court judicially established public, rather than private, ownership of the frequency spectrum. As a consequence, licensees are granted only temporary trusteeships to the airwaves for the purpose of serving the public.

THE COMMUNICATIONS ACT OF 1934

After a recommendation from President Franklin D. Roosevelt, Congress passed the new Communications Act of 1934 to consolidate the regulation of all electronic communication. This Act, as amended, remains in effect as the legal foundation of present-day broadcasting. The new act retained the basic philosophy of the 1927 legislation; however, it replaced the FRC with an enlarged Federal Communications Commission (FCC) to deal with telephone, telegraph, and other forms of electronic communication, as well as broadcasting.

The Communications Act of 1934 essentially accomplished four things in regard to broadcasting. First, it created the FCC as a permanent regulatory agency. Second, the Act specifically denied the Commission the power to censor programs or to dictate program policies to its licensees. Third, Congress imposed several specific programming prohibitions and requirements, which will be discussed later in this chapter. And fourth, the Act empowered the FCC to issue rules and regulations as needed to assure the public of the caliber of service to which it is entitled.

The FRC's dilemma—a mandate to regulate broadcasting in the public interest while being forbidden any *direct* control over program content—essentially was resolved by the Brinkley and Shuler cases. However, the NBC case of 1943 further clarified the Commission's role in programming. On May 10, 1943, the US Supreme Court affirmed the FCC's regulations governing network affiliation matters and, in addition, legally shattered the "traffic cop only" philosophy of regulation. The Court declared:

> The Act itself establishes that the Commission's powers are not limited to the engineering and technical aspects of radio communication. Yet we are asked to regard the Commission as a kind of traffic officer, policing the wave lengths to prevent stations from interfering with each other. But the Act does not restrict the Commission merely to supervision of the traffic. It puts upon the Commission the burden of determining the composition of that traffic.[13]

The Court's "traffic composition" ruling has been interpreted by the Commission to mean that it has the right and the responsibility to insist upon "balanced" programming. This position was explained during hearings of the Senate Committee on Interstate Commerce in 1943 by FCC Commissioner Ray C. Wakefield:

> This is similar to the power the I.C.C. has to say to a railroad that it shall not haul farm products to the exclusion of manufactured products, or vice versa. It does not mean, however, that the I.C.C. could properly concern itself with whether a particular car, or even a certain train, is loaded with apples, livestock, or Grand Rapids furniture. Similarly, in my opinion, the Commission can require of a radio station that it offer a balanced diet and that it not carry entertainment to the exclusion of public-service programs, or network programs to the exclusion of local programs if some of the latter are in the public interest. It, however, does not mean that the F.C.C. can interfere with the content of individual programs or require that a licensee either put on or delete a particular program.[14]

In summary, under various court decisions, the FCC holds the power to influence indirectly the programming of broadcast stations by requiring applicants to submit detailed program proposals when they seek a license. Furthermore, the Commission may examine a licensee's past programming as a means of evaluating its past and probable future service to the public. Such a review of past programming thus may be used in determining the advisability of granting a renewal of the station's license.

In addition to the Commission's impact on broadcast programming, public opinion and industry self-regulation are two other strong forces which influence the program content of radio and TV stations. These items will be explored later in the book.

THE FEDERAL COMMUNICATIONS COMMISSION

The Federal Communications Commission, an independent government agency directly responsible to Congress, has a mandate to direct the orderly development of both foreign and interstate electronic communication "in the public interest, convenience, and necessity."[15] Both wire and wireless communications systems, including satellite transmissions, come under its jurisdiction.

The FCC is headed by seven commissioners, who are appointed to seven-year terms by the president. Commissioners also must receive Senate confirmation. However, the president designates the chairman, who determines the policy matters brought before the Commission. More than 2,000 persons are employed in the various bureaus and branches of the FCC. Most are engineers, attorneys, and clerical workers.

The FCC consists of five major bureaus, as follows:

1. *The Broadcast Bureau,* which is responsible for allocating spectrum space, granting licenses, and reviewing the service of AM, FM, TV, and shortwave broadcasting stations.
2. *The Cable Television Bureau,* which handles CATV and related matters.
3. *The Common Carrier Bureau,* which deals with telephone, telegraph, and domestic satellite services.
4. *The Private Radio Bureau,* which handles aviation, industrial, and amateur radio services.
5. *The Field Operations Bureau,* which monitors and inspects broadcast stations and their equipment.

Only the Broadcast Bureau and the Field Operations Bureau directly affect radio and television station licensees.

The Commission administers the laws of Congress pertaining to the telecommunications industries and also issues its own rules and regulations. It may levy penalties against licensees who violate these laws and rules, including fines up to $20,000 per violation, license revocation, and short-term licenses. FCC also issues *cease-and-desist* orders to halt the violation of its rules.

PROGRAM RESTRICTIONS IN THE COMMUNICATIONS ACT

As noted above, the Communications Act contains several specific programming prohibitions enforced by the FCC. The following are among those prohibitions specified by the Act.

Political Advertising

One of the most important requirements of broadcast licensees is that they treat all candidates for political office on an equal basis. Thus, Section 315 compels stations that accept political advertising to make the time available on an *equal and comparable* basis to all candidates for the same public office. Practically speaking, if a station decides, for example, to sell (or donate) political advertising to one candidate in a mayoral election, it also must sell (or give) up to the same amount of time to all other bona fide candidates who request it. Furthermore, the time made available must be *comparable*. Thus, a station legally could not offer a schedule of political spots during substandard listening periods to a candidate when the opponent had better time placement even though the same number of commercials were accommodated.

Although Section 315 does not force a station to make time available for all elections, it does require licensees to offer a reasonable amount of time to candidates for federal elective offices. In addition to availablility, charges for political time must be not greater than the lowest (discounted) rate available to any advertiser. Each station is expected to maintain a file, available for public and FCC inspection, containing all requests for political time and the disposition of those requests.

Finally, station licensees may not censor political broadcasts by legally qualified candidates even though the messages may be patently offensive. On the other hand, stations are not held liable for any defamatory material broadcast as political advertising.

Section 315 issues also have arisen in regard to news and public affairs programming. The Communications Act, which originally required equal time for opposing candidates in all situations, has been amended to waive those requirements when candidates appear on certain types of informational broadcasts. These exceptions include (1) bona fide newscasts, (2) bona fide news interviews, (3) bona fide documentary programs when a candidate's appearance is incidental to the program, and (4) on-the-spot news coverage of bona fide news events, including but not restricted to the political conventions. In all of these cases, news judgment may dictate the extent and type of coverage given to each candidate.

The question of broadcast debates between candidates also relates to Section 315. Since most presidential races involve many candidates, broadcasters were unable before 1976 to offer debates between the two leading candidates without special legislation by Congress. Thus, the famous Kennedy-Nixon TV debates of 1960 were the only such face-to-face confrontations to materialize before 1976. Political debates now may be broadcast without regard for equal time concerns for minor party nominees provided the debate itself is arranged by a third party which is not a licensee. The 1976 and 1980 presidential debates, therefore, were sanctioned by the League of Women Voters. Third-party sponsorship also permits stations to broadcast debates involving state and local elections.

It is very important that all station employees who handle political broadcasts and advertising be familiar with the provisions of the Communications Act dealing with political broadcasting. A detailed study of these rules is contained in the FCC's public notice entitled "The Law of Political Broadcasting and Cablecasting," issued July 20, 1978.

The Fairness Doctrine

The complexities involved in broadcast presentation of controversial public issues are covered in the FCC's Fairness Doctrine, which is a further implementation of Section 315, as amended. In eliminating the equal-time requirements for bona fide newscasts, Congress reminded broadcasters of their public interest obligations as follows:

> Nothing in the foregoing sentence shall be construed as relieving broadcasters ... from the obligation imposed upon them under this Act to operate in the public interest and to afford reasonable opportunity for the discussion of conflicting views on issues of public importance.[16]

Both Congressional action and FCC policy making seem to agree that licensees should deal with controversial public issues in their programming and that, in doing so, they must present *all opposing viewpoints.* The Fairness Doctrine particularly applies when a station takes editorial positions on controversial issues. In such cases, the FCC has held that licensees have an affirmative responsibility to seek out a responsible spokesperson from the other side to present that viewpoint.

The Fairness Doctrine also applies to documentary programs that deal with controversial issues, in which case a licensee is obligated to maintain a balanced presentation or to provide comparable time for the opposing side to reply. Other special applications relate to political endorsements and personal attacks. In both, the persons involved must be given ample time to reply to statements broadcast by the station.

The advertising of cigarettes raised Fairness Doctrine questions about broadcast advertising in 1967 when the FCC upheld a complaint by New York attorney John Banzhaf III, who wanted cigarette commercials to be balanced with antismoking messages. The Commission stated in the Banzhaf case that its concurrence would be a one-time application of the Doctrine in regard to advertising. However, many other advertising-related complaints were brought to the FCC.

The Commission subsequently upheld broadcast licensees who had denied reply time to (1) environmentalists who sought to refute certain oil company commercials and (2) anti-Viet Nam war groups that wished to express their editorial viewpoints. Although the Court of Appeals reversed the FCC's action, the US Supreme Court ultimately agreed with the Commission that licensees have a right to exercise editorial judgment and may not be forced to sell time for editorial advertising merely because they sell time for commercial messages. Nothing, however, forbids a licensee from accepting editorial advertising.

For complete details of the Fairness Doctrine, see the FCC's public notice, "Fairness Doctrine and the Public Interest Standards."[17]

Sponsorship Identification

Section 317 requires commercial messages and sponsored programs to carry clear sponsorship identification. This rule also applies to noncommercial public service announcements. It is intended to safeguard the public from anonymously sponsored messages. Since advertisers are interested mainly in registering their names with the audience, problems seldom arise with commercial advertisers.

In certain circumstances, however, special statements must be made to indicate the names of sponsors whose payment—regardless of its form—is used to purchase time or to defray the cost of programming. The following are the principal examples:

1. Sponsorship of political broadcasts must be stated clearly.
2. Advertiser identification must be revealed for any "teaser" announcement.
3. Disclosure must be made of all payola/plugola types of payment used in support of program production (for example, payment for incidental mention or usage of a firm's products in a TV show).
4. Names of donor organizations must be given when prizes or other promotional materials or services are contributed to a program.

Rebroadcast Authorization

Under Section 325 of the Communications Act, no radio or TV station may pick up and rebroadcast any program or portion of a program without the express permission of the originating station. It is customary to seek such permission in advance and in writing whenever it is desired. Such documents granting rebroadcast permission should be kept on file in the program director's office and should be readily available should an FCC field inspector request them.

Censorship

Section 326 protects the broadcaster from direct program control by the FCC. *Censorship,* usually defined in the communications field as prior restraint of media content, specifically is forbidden in these words of the Communications Act:

> Nothing in this Act shall be understood or construed to give the Commission the power of censorship over the radio communications or signals transmitted by any radio station, and no regulation or condition shall be promulgated or fixed by the Commission which shall interfere with the right of free speech by means of radio communication.[18]

Section 326 also contains the original prohibition against broadcasting obscene, indecent, or profane material. That section, however, was incorporated later into the US Criminal Code in order to enforce penalties against individuals who might violate the statute without the knowledge of the licensee.

In regard to protection of free speech over the broadcast media, the US Supreme Court held in the Red Lion decision of 1969 that it is the "right of the viewers and listeners, not the right of broadcasters which is paramount."[19] Thus, though freedom of speech for the broadcaster is maintained, licensees must share those rights to free expression with the general public they serve.

The Red Lion decision has stimulated the expansion of discussion and talk programming on both radio and TV, as well as the airing of all sides of controversial issues stemming from station editorials.

Payola and Rigged Contests

After the payola and quiz show scandals of the late 1950s, Congress added two new sections to the Communications Act. Sections 508 and 509 deal respectively with payola and deception through rigged quiz shows.

Section 508 requires any station employee who accepts money or other valuable consideration from an outside source for promoting any item (e.g., a phonograph record) over the station to make full disclosure to the licensee. Station program managers usually are charged with the responsibility of preventing the practice of payola at their stations.

Section 509 makes it illegal for anyone to deceive the listening or viewing public by supplying information to contestants in quiz shows or by prearranging the outcome of such programs.

Violators of Sections 508 and 509 are subject to potential fines of $10,000 and imprisonment up to one year, or both.

PROGRAM RESTRICTIONS IN THE US CRIMINAL CODE

In addition to enforcing the Communications Act and its own rules and regulations, the FCC also enforces certain statutes of the US Criminal Code relating to broadcast programming. Prohibitions against lottery broadcasting, obscenity, and schemes to defraud are the principal items.

Lottery

Secton 1304 of the US Criminal Code forbids the broadcasting of all types of lottery advertising or information other than state-operated legal lotteries. Thus, with this one exception, stations must refuse to present information about contests or promotions which constitute a lottery, whether the sponsor is a commercial advertiser, a benevolent nonprofit organization, or the station itself.

Because of the insidious nature of lottery promotions, all staff members responsible for the content of advertising, promotion, and public service materials should watch for the three elements that *together* constitute a lottery: (1) a prize, (2) the element of chance, and (3) consideration. The latter is usually defined as a monetary exchange. Violation of the lottery statute may result in a $1,000 fine and/or a year's imprisonment.

To avoid legal problems, most contests and promotional campaigns omit one of the three lottery ingredients. Thus, a "no purchase necessary" statement usually circumvents the question of lottery. Or if a purchase is *required* before a *free* gift is given, everyone who buys becomes a winner and, therefore, there is no element of chance.

Despite the traditionally tough regulatory stance taken on lotteries, as mentioned above, the law permits state-operated lotteries to advertise on broadcast stations in the home state and contiguous states. Winners may also be announced. However, according to law, such broadcasts must not unduly encourage the public to engage in betting.

Indecent Language

Section 1464 of the US Criminal Code, originally part of Section 326 of the Communications Act, forbids the broadcast of material which contains "obscenity, profanity, or vulgarity." The stated penalty for an individual violator is a $10,000 fine or imprisonment up to two years. The FCC is responsible for enforcing this statute, as well as other applicable sections of the Criminal Code.

Station licenses have been revoked for gross violations of the antiobscenity statute. Perhaps the most famous case involved station WDKD of Kingstree, South Carolina. In that 1961 case, a disc jockey was found guilty of using foul and suggestive language regularly during his daily broadcasts. The Commission revoked the station's license because WDKD's management had not properly supervised the operation of the station.[20]

With changing attitudes and mores, society's definition of what is obscene, profane, or vulgar has been altered. Media regulators and the courts have also become more tolerant toward the broadcasting of once-taboo material, particularly when young children are not likely to be in the audience. The Supreme Court has held that what constitutes obscenity varies from one locale to another and that the media must be guided by community standards. Those standards, unfortunately, are extremely difficult to discern. Despite some liberalization in official attitudes, the courts still hold that any material that describes "in terms patently offensive as measured by contemporary standards for the broadcast medium, sexual or excretory activities and organs" is considered indecent and may not be aired when large numbers of children are likely to be in the audience.[21]

The George Carlin case comes to mind here. In that instance, Carlin's album, "Seven Dirty Words That Can Never Be Broadcast," was broadcast during the afternoon when many children could listen. The FCC found the material indecent, and the Supreme Court upheld the Commission's decision. However, a broadcast of the same record at a more judicious time would probably not be questioned by the FCC.[22] Further discussion on the topic of obscenity appears in chapter 10.

Electronic Fraud

Section 1343 of the Criminal Code makes it illegal to devise any scheme to defraud the public, or to obtain money or property through "false or fraudulent pretenses, representations, or promises" involving radio, television, or wire communication systems. Individuals convicted of using writings, signs, signals, pictures, or sounds on the electronic media to defraud may be fined up to $1,000 or imprisoned up to five years, or both. In addition, station licenses may be revoked when management is a party to fraud.

Two cases come to mind. First, a St. Louis radio station lost its license in the 1950s because it promoted a fraudulent hidden treasure contest. In that case, clues for finding the treasure were broadcast daily for nearly a month *before* the loot was actually hidden. In the second case, a New York TV station once broadcast old news film of the Soviet invasion of Hungary to represent the later invasion of Czechoslovakia. Although WPIX did not lose its license, the station was severely reprimanded by the Commission.

THE FCC AND PROGRAMMING GUIDELINES

In March, 1946, the FCC took its first major step toward influencing programming when it published a policy guide known as "Public Service Responsibility of Broadcast Licensees."[23] This document, popularly known as the "Blue Book" because of its cover, was never adopted as official Commission policy. However, the Blue Book has had a lasting influence on programming and license-renewal procedures.

A second policy statement, issued in 1960, again revealed the Commission's thinking on public interest programming. Although the basic attitude of the FCC has not changed drastically since then, the Commission's methods of evaluating public interest programming have undergone some changes.

The Blue Book

In its 1946 policy document, the FCC identified four specific practices by radio stations which it considered contrary to the public interest. Those practices were (1) overcommercialization, (2) excessive reliance on networks, (3) too few discussion programs of public affairs subjects, and (4) a general imbalance among program types presented. After presenting these concerns, the Commission announced plans to scrutinize renewal applications closely in regard to four "good practices" it endorsed. These included the broadcasting of (1) sustaining, or nonsponsored, programs, (2) local live programs, (3) discussion programs dealing with controversial issues, and (4) the avoidance of excesses in advertising.

The FCC advocated that each station air a significant proportion of *sustaining* programming as a means of reducing advertising excesses and balancing the schedule. Other positive functions of sustaining programs were said to be:

1. To enable a station to carry types of programs that are not suitable for commercial sponsorship,
2. To promote the discussion of public issues,
3. To satisfy minority tastes,
4. To provide service to nonprofit organizations, and
5. To encourage experimentation in new types of programs.

Local live programs were encouraged as an antidote for excessive reliance on networks and transcription services. The FCC thus encouraged stations to originate their own productions, particularly as outlets for developing local talent and for the presentation of local sports and public affairs broadcasts.

Before the Blue Book, few radio stations originated regular local broadcasts dealing with public issues. Radio's strong national orientation was a factor; however, the FCC believed the reluctance also stemmed from fears of antagonizing vested interests in local communities. The Commission contended that if a station promoted the discussion of public issues through its broadcasts, being sure to carry all points of view, no one should be offended and stations should reestablish favor with public-minded listeners.

In regard to *advertising,* the Commission acknowledged that the broadcasting industry must depend upon this source for revenue and that informative advertising "is itself of direct benefit to the listener in his role as a consumer." However, the Blue Book cited examples of heavy advertising among stations and called upon the industry to avoid excesses. Interestingly, though, the Commission has never specified what constitutes excessive advertising.

The Blue Book aroused a great deal of controversy both within and outside the broadcast industry. The National Association of Broadcasters and other industry groups vigorously opposed the concept of the FCC suggesting, or prescribing, the type of programming a licensee should provide. To most broadcasters, the issue was *censorship.* Despite the concern, the Blue Book proposals never were incorporated into the FCC's rules. However, the effect of the document was very significant, making "Public Service Responsibility of Broadcast Licensees" perhaps the most influential programming proposal ever issued by the Commission.

Three short-term results occurred. First, the NAB Code of Good Practices was strengthened in 1948, particularly in regard to public affairs broadcasts and commercial levels. Second, the Commission adopted revised station application and license renewal forms that called for specific promises regarding an applicant's proposed programming. A licensee's performance, therefore, could be measured against his *own* program proposals at the time of the next license renewal. And third, however reluctantly, broadcasters began to implement programming that complied with the FCC's suggestions.

The FCC shortly established uniform program definitions to be used by all stations in their program logs as well as in all filings with the Commission. The Commission's new forms then required applicants to specify percentages of their weekly broadcast schedules to be devoted to each of eight program categories, as well as the estimated number of announcements, both commercial and public service, to be aired during specific hours of the week. Interestingly, the program categories established by the FCC related to *sources* (network, recorded, wire, and live) rather than to *types* of broadcasts.

The final step in the new procedure required applicants for license renewal to perform a content analysis of their programming during the period of the expiring license. These analyses were based on program logs drawn from a *composite week,* with specific dates announced by the FCC at the time of license renewal. Thus, the Commission instituted the procedure commonly known as *promise vs. performance,* which compared the licensee's programming during a license period with promises made when the license was sought. Rather than establishing standards or requiring certain percentages of specific programming, in effect, the Commission prodded applicants into setting their own criteria. Therefore, once a license was granted, the FCC held the licensee accountable for fulfilling his *own* pledges. This approach proved to be a masterful way for the Commission to achieve its goals by means *other than prior restraint.*

The Programming Policy Statement of 1960

Fourteen years after issuing its first program guidelines, the Federal Communications Commission again outlined its concept of public interest programming. The 1960 Programming Policy Statement, in contrast with the Blue Book, emphasized *types* rather than *sources* of programs.[24]

This report acknowledged first that all specific program choices must be made by licensees, thereby defusing possible questions of censorship by the Commission. It also recognized the practical necessity for television stations to rely upon the networks for much of their programming. The document then spoke of the obligation of the broadcast licensee to determine the programming needs of its service area:

> In the fulfillment of his obligation the broadcaster should consider the tastes, needs and desires of the public he is licensed to serve in developing his programming and should exercise conscientious efforts not only to ascertain them but also to carry them out as well as he reasonably can. He should reasonably attempt to meet all such needs and interests on an equitable basis.[25]

The Commission then enunciated 14 specific program elements "usually necessary" to meet a licensee's public interest obligations. The list, which was drawn by the Commission from the NAB Code of Good Practices, included the following:

1. Opportunity for local self-expression
2. The development and use of local talent
3. Programs for children
4. Religious programs
5. Educational programs
6. Public affairs programs
7. Editorialization by licensees
8. Political broadcasts
9. Agricultural programs
10. News programs

11. Weather and market reports
12. Sports programs
13. Service to minority groups
14. Entertainment programs.

Having re-emphasized the licensee's obligation to provide a balanced program service appropriate to local needs, the FCC again revised its application forms. Henceforth, all applicants for new stations, transfers of ownership, and license renewal had to specify percentages of their proposed programming to be devoted to each of the 14 categories. Applicants for license renewal also were required to analyze their program logs for a composite week (designated by the FCC) and to report the percentages of that week's schedule actually programmed for each of the categories. Log-keeping requirements again were modified to reflect the new categories.

Ultimately, the FCC simplified its application and renewal forms by reducing the 14 items to three nonentertainment categories: (1) news, (2) public affairs, and (3) all other programs, exclusive of entertainment and sports. The third category ("other") became a catch-all for such diverse types of broadcasts as agricultural, educational, instructional, and religious programs. See Figure 3.1 for current program log requirements. As we shall discuss later in the chapter, these became applicable only to television stations after the FCC's radio deregulatory actions of 1981.

In its 1960 log revisions, the FCC carried its promise vs. performance practice a step further by requiring licensees to pledge specific percentages of time to *content,* as opposed to *source,* categories. Approval of licenses based on *promises* made by applicants compared with subsequent *performance* became further entrenched as the FCC's mode of operation. A sample program log for a large market television station is shown in Figure 3.2.

Figure 3.1 Program Log Requirements

1. Identification of each program by title, with beginning and ending times.
2. Classification of each program as to type, using the FCC's standard program definitions.
3. Classification of each program as to source, using the FCC's definitions.
4. Sponsorship identification indicating (a) the sponsor of each program; (b) the person or persons who paid for each announcement; and (c) the person or persons who furnished materials for a program.
5. Sponsorship identification of political advertising, including the candidate's name and political affiliation.
6. An entry showing the total duration of commercial matter in each hourly time segment or the duration of each commercial message in each hour.
7. An entry indicating that appropriate announcements have been made to identify the sponsorship and/or donorship of each program.
8. An entry for each commercial and public service annoncement.
9. An entry for each required station identification announcement.
10. An entry for each local notice announcement. (These announcements are required at designated intervals before and after license renewal to provide the public with information about the licensee, its public inspection file, and the public's right to file comments about the station's performance with the FCC.)
11. An entry to indicate that mechanical reproduction announcements have been made whenever required.

Under its radio deregulation actions of 1981, the FCC removed AM and FM radio stations from the log-keeping requirement. The Commission continues to require television stations to keep standardized logs.

Figure 3.2 A typical operational program log for a major television station

WSB TV 2 ATLANTA
PROGRAM LOG

ANNOUNCEMENT CODES	PROGRAM TYPE: MAJOR (MA)	MINOR (MI)	PROGRAM SOURCE	ORIGIN		TIME
C-NON-NETWORK COMMERCIAL MATTER	1. AGRICULTURAL	0. UNSPECIFIED	1. LOCAL	A-ABC	R-REMOTE	1. EST-EASTERN STANDARD NON-ADVANCED
ID-STATION IDENTIFICATION	2. ENTERTAINMENT	1. EDITORIALS	2. NETWORK	B-BOOTH	S-STUDIO	2. EDT-EASTERN DAYLIGHT ADVANCED
MG-MAKE GOOD COMMERCIAL MATTER	3. NEWS	2. POLITICAL	3. RECORDED	C-COLOR	SI-SPECIAL INSTRUCTION	
NC-NETWORK COMMERCIAL MATTER	4. PUBLIC AFFAIRS	3. EDUCATIONAL INSTITUTION		CH-CHIRON	SL-SLIDE	
PR-PROMOTIONAL ANNOUNCEMENT	5. RELIGIOUS	4. EDITORIALS/POLITICAL		CT-AUDIO CARTRIDGE	SLF-SUPER SLIDE/FILM	
PS-PUBLIC SERVICE ANNOUNCEMENT	6. INSTRUCTIONAL	5. POLITICAL/EDUCATIONAL INSTITUTION		CV-VIDEO TAPE CARTRIDGE	SLN-SUPER SLIDE/NETWORK	
	7. SPORTS			ET-ELECTRICAL TRANS.	SLS-SUPER SLIDE/STUDIO	
	8. OTHER			F-FILM	SLV-SUPER SLIDE/VIDEO TAPE	
				MCR-MASTER CONTROL ROOM	SN-SPECIAL NETWORK	
				O-TONE OSC.	SP-SPORTS NETWORK INC.	
					VR-VIDEO TAPE REEL	

DATE	OPERATOR	TIME ON	TIME OFF	OPERATOR	TIME ON	TIME OFF		PAGE
MON 06/29/81							1034A EDT	29

LINE NUMBER	TIME PROGRAMMED ON	TIME PROGRAMMED OFF	SCHED. TIME HR.	MIN.	SEC.	A/P	PROGRAM - ADVERTISER - PRODUCT	ORIGIN VIDEO	ORIGIN AUDIO	ANN. CODE	PROGRAM S	PROGRAM TYPE	LENGTH	PROJECTION ROOM DATA AND SPECIAL INSTRUCTIONS	INT. #
C1014S13870							GODFATHER'S PIZZA 1 PIZZA	CV	V	C			0:30	EG-102-30	2934
C1030S 9375							WSB-TV PROMOTION 1 MASH-COMING UP N	CV	V	PR			0:10	MASH-MON-10	3550
							PARADE VOC								
E 30 P 393			05	28	57	P	------WSB NEWS CAPSULE ------	CS	CS		1	30	0:30		
E 30 R1048			05	29	27	P	STATION BREAK						1:00		
C 342S 5025							GENERAL FOODS 1 KOOL AID MOTHERS	CV	V	C			0:30	GFKD1084	3632
C1594S17533							WESTERN SIZZLIN 1 RESTAURANT	CV	V	C			0:30	WS-5-13	848
S2151 R 260			05	30	27	P	SHARED ID/PARADE ID-2-03	CV	V	PR			0:03	ID-2-03	
E 30 P 484			05	30	30	P	------M.A.S.H ------	CV	V		3	20	28:27	#G-515 (21:51)	
							"Dear Ma"								
E 30 R1039							1ST BREAK						2:00		
C1223S25596							PET, INC 1 DAIRY PRODUCTS	CV	V	C			0:30	PTFD0380	3033
C 272S 4193							GENERAL FOODS 1 CNTRY TIME LEMON	CV	V	C			0:30	GFCL0529	3494
C 4S 1868							BURGER KING 1 ADULT "EVERYBODY	CV	V	C			0:30	PBBK1307	3418
							****BREAK CONTINUED ON NEXT PAGE****								

Courtesy of WSB-TV, Cox Communications, Inc., Atlanta.

Ascertainment of Community Needs

The Program Policy Statement of 1960 also introduced broadcasters to the practice of systematically ascertaining how best they might serve the needs of their potential audience. The revised application forms thereafter required applicants for radio and TV stations to state (1) how they determined the tastes, needs, and desires of their service area, and (2) how they proposed to meet those needs and desires. Ascertainment procedures thus became an integral part of the application process, with the emphasis placed on nonentertainment needs.

The rationale for ascertainment was explained by the Commission as follows:

> Particular areas of interest and types of appropriate service may, of course, differ from community to community, and from time to time. However, the Commission does expect its broadcast licensees to take the necessary steps to inform themselves of the real needs and interests of the areas they serve and to provide programming which in fact constitutes a diligent effort, in good faith, to provide for those needs and interests,[26]

Although ascertainment was first introduced in the Program Policy Statement of 1960, the FCC formally required broadcast applicants to conduct such studies in 1966. Specific procedures called for interviews with community leaders and a general public survey to determine the concerns and needs of the community. Policy guidelines were issued in 1971 and 1976 to assist applicants in conducting research. In 1981, the Commission exempted radio stations from formal ascertainment requirements. However, radio licensees still must program to the needs of their communities.

In its 1976 primer,[27] the FCC suggested that a licensee's contacts with community leaders should be continuous throughout a license period and insisted that leaders from all segments of the community be contacted. On the other hand, the public survey should be a one-time undertaking during each license period to maintain randomness. From a methodological standpoint, the Commission requires that at least half of the leader interviews be conducted by management-level employees. Therefore, the TV program director usually becomes deeply involved in this aspect of ascertainment. The public survey, however, may be conducted by station employees or by an outside entity.

Having determined the needs of its community, a licensee is expected to present programming "to meet some of the community problems."[28] In addition, the Commission requires all licensees to list annually up to ten problems they have discovered and the programs broadcast to meet these needs. This "problems-programs" list must be placed in the station's public inspection file (at its principal business address) annually on the anniversary date on which the station's renewal application is due for filing with the FCC.

Bringing ascertainment more up-to-date, in 1981 the Commission relieved AM and FM radio stations from the responsibility of *formally* ascertaining the problems of their communities. In its order,[29] however, the FCC emphasized that radio station licensees must continue to be alert to the problems of their service areas even though they no longer must follow the formalized ascertainment procedures. Radio licensees remain obligated to maintain the annual problems-programs list in their public file as before and must indicate how they identified the issues they chose to cover.

Although at first ascertainment studies were considered an imposition, many licensees today regard them as a valuable means for identifying public concerns and for providing their audiences with a more meaningful form of service. Any broadcaster charged with the responsibility of directing an ascertainment study should become familiar with the FCC's latest primer on "Ascertainment of Community Problems by Broadcast Applicants."

What About Programming Promises?

Earlier in the chapter, we mentioned that the FCC required applicants to make pledges in terms of their proposed news, public affairs, and other nonentertainment programming. This requirement naturally led many licensees to ask, "How much is enough to satisfy the Commission?" Although the FCC never formally adopted specific percentage requirements for nonentertainment programming, unofficial guidelines subtly were revealed.

By delegating authority to the license renewal division of the Broadcast Bureau to approve renewal applications meeting minimum criteria, the FCC indicated the benchmark levels of service programming necessary for speedy license renewal without the need for a hearing. Specifically, the Broadcast Bureau was given the power to approve renewals of television stations that propose at least 10 percent of their weekly schedules on an aggregate basis to news, public affairs, and other nonentertainment programs.[30] In addition, TV stations must specify their maximum hourly commercial limits and explain any excesses over 16 minutes.[31]

Communications attorneys usually recommend that applicants assign some figure to each of the three nonentertainment categories. Most applicants also promise more than the stated minimum figures to avoid delays such as required explanations and possibly formal hearings in the processing of their applications. Obviously, however, promises made to the Commission need to be both reasonable and attainable since they become obligatory after approval is granted.

RADIO DEREGULATION

In a major reversal of policy in February, 1981, the FCC eliminated the programming percentage guidelines, formal ascertainment requirements, commercial guidelines, and program logging requirements that had been required previously of AM and FM radio licensees. The deregulatory action was taken after the Commission determined that significant changes in the radio marketplace had occurred over the past 45 years so that detailed regulation of radio programming practices was no longer appropriate.[32] Thus, with the number of radio outlets having risen to about 8,000 overall and to 25 stations or more in most large cities, the FCC concluded that market forces should guide the industry and that its own role should be reduced.

Although radio licensees were freed from numerous specific requirements, they remain under a strong public interest obligation. Instead of proposing percentages of schedules to be devoted to specific categories, applicants now must provide the FCC with a narrative statement of their proposed programming service. Whenever major changes are undertaken either in the entertainment format or in the nonentertainment segment, the licensee is obligated to inform the Commission in writing.

As discussed previously, radio stations no longer need to engage in formal ascertainment studies. Some will continue to do so, however, because of their demonstrated value in helping to build community acceptance. Nevertheless, radio stations must maintain contact with their communities and respond to community problems and needs in their programming. Although log-keeping is a necessary *business* function for radio broadcasters, the only programming record required by the Commission of radio licensees is an annual listing of five to ten public issues covered by the station, together with examples of programming provided in response to those concerns and needs.

License Renewals Simplified in 1981

Although the traditional license-renewal procedures worked well, they became burdensome on both the Commission and its licensees. Following an extensive review of its procedures, the FCC adopted a new and different license-renewal approach on June 10, 1981. The plan requires all licensees to file a brief renewal, which will be discussed shortly. License-renewal enforcement shifted from a review of all applicants to a random sample of audits and field inspections at a small percentage of the television and noncommercial radio stations. Commercial AM and FM stations are exempt from such audits and inspections. Although this change relaxed many *procedures,* nothing about the plan lessened the public interest *obligations* of broadcast licensees.

The most striking change was the adoption by the FCC of a simplified license-renewal form (SRA), sometimes called a "postcard renewal," which calls for basic information about the licensee. From those answers, the Commission determines if there are problems that preclude the renewal of a station's license. Should a question arise, a station will be audited or inspected and possibly designated for a hearing. As mentioned above, the SRA is accompanied by a new series of enforcement measures, including a new long-form audit, field audits, and on-site inspections. Each of these will be discussed in detail. See Figure 3.3 for their applicability to commercial TV, commercial radio, and noncommercial radio/television stations.

The Simplified Renewal Form The simplified renewal form (SRA) is a postcard size questionnaire that all broadcast licensees must file at each renewal date. This form (#303-S) is shown in Figure 3.4. It includes five basic questions that are essential to the renewal process.

Question 1 identifies the licensee and the station's location.

Question 2 (a) calls for verification that the licensee has filed the required Annual Employment Reports which facilitate the Commission's review of licensee compliance with its nondiscrimination and affirmative action requirements.

Question 2 (b) verifies that a current ownership report is on file at the FCC.

Question 3 verifies that the licensee remains in compliance with Section 310 of the Communications Act, which relates to ownership interests held by aliens.

Figure 3.3 Applicability of License-Renewal Procedures

	Commercial Television	Noncommercial Radio and TV	Commercial Radio
Simplified Renewal Application (SRA)	Yes	Yes	Yes
Long-Term Audit Renewal	Yes (Minimum of 5% of all licensees, randomly selected)	Yes (Minimum of 5% of all licensees, randomly selected)	No
Random FOB Audit	Yes (Minimum of 10% of all licensees, randomly selected)	Yes (Minimum of 10% of all licensees, randomly selected)	Yes (Minimum of 10% of all licensees, randomly selected)
Random Broadcast Bureau Field Inspection	Yes (Problem cases)	Yes (Problem cases)	No
Pre- and Post- Filing Announcements	Yes	Yes	Yes
Formal Ascertainment of Community Needs	Yes	Yes	No

Question 4 confirms the applicant's continued good character, a requisite for holding a broadcast license. Convictions involving felonies, lotteries, or unfair business practices contraindicate the required character qualifications.

Question 5 asks whether the applicant placed the required documentation, including composite week logs for TV stations, in the station's public inspection file at the appropriate time.

How Does the Commission Enforce Renewal Procedures?

In adopting simplified renewal procedures, the FCC introduced three new measures to assure continued broadcast service in the public interest. These enforcement tools include the long form audit, field audits, and on-site inspections.

Long Form Audit Instead of the short renewal, at least 5 percent of all TV licensees and noncommercial radio stations are required to complete an extended audit renewal form. These forms are similar to the previous renewal forms (#303) used by all licensees. They require, among other items, a content analysis of a composite week's program logs as well as promises for news, public affairs, and other nonentertainment programming in the new license period. Sample "promise vs. performance" questions are shown in Figure 3.5.

Because all affected stations (commercial radio stations are excepted) are subject to use of the audit form, the FCC requires those licensees to keep composite week program logs in their public inspection files.

Because of the importance attached to promise vs. performance, it is advisable that program managers establish procedures for periodic content analyses of their logs to determine how closely the program promises are being kept. Periodic log analysis, such as one week every three months, represents excellent insurance against unfavorable surprises with the FCC-selected composite week. Such a planned approach also allows ample time to make

Figure 3.4 The new short renewal application (SRA) form, adopted by the FCC in 1981

Appendix C

FCC Form 303-S
March 1980

United States of America
Federal Communications Commission
Washington, D C 20554

Approved by GAO
B-180227(R0)

Application for Renewal of License for Commercial and Non-Commercial AM, FM or TV Broadcast Station

1 Name of Applicant	Call Letters	Street Address	City	State	Zip Code

2. Are the following reports on file at the Commission:

(a) The three most recent Annual Employment Reports (FCC Form 395)
□ Yes □ No
If No, attach as Exhibit No.__ an explanation

(b) The applicant's Ownership report (FCC Form 323 or 323-E)
□ Yes □ No
If No, give the following information.
Date last ownership report was filed:
Call letters of the renewal application with which it was filed:

3. Is the applicant in compliance with the provisions of Section 310 of the Communications Act of 1934, as amended, relating to interests of aliens and foreign governments?

□ Yes □ No If No, attach as Exhibit No. an explanation.

4. Since the filing of the applicant's last renewal application for this station or other major application, has an adverse finding been made, a consent decree been entered, or final action been approved by any court or administrative body with respect to the applicant or parties to the application concerning any civil or criminal suit, action, or proceeding, brought under the provisions of any federal, state, territorial or local law relating to the following: any felony, lotteries, unlawful restraints or monopolies, unlawful combinations, contracts or agreements in restraint of trade, the use of unfair methods of competition; fraud, unfair labor practices, or discrimination?

□ Yes □ No If Yes, attach as Exhibit No.__ a full description, including identification of the court or administrative body, proceeding by file number, the person and matters involved, and the disposition of litigation.

5. Has the applicant placed in its public inspection file at the appropriate times the documentation required by Section 73.3526 and 73.3527 of the Commission's rules?

□ Yes □ No If No, attach as Exhibit No __ a complete statement of explanation

THE APPLICANT hereby waives any claim to the use of any particular frequency or of the ether as against the regulatory power of the United States, because of the previous use of the same, whether by license or otherwise, and requests an authorization in accordance with this application. (See Section 304 of the Communications Act.)
THE APPLICANT acknowledges that all the statements made in this application and attached exhibits are considered material representations and that all the exhibits are a material part hereof and are incorporated herein as set out in full in the application.

CERTIFICATION

I certify that the statements in this application are true, complete and correct to the best of my knowledge and belief, and are made in good faith.

Signed and dated this _____ day of ________ 19___

Name of Applicant __________

By Signature __________

Title __________

WILLFUL FALSE STATEMENTS MADE ON THIS FORM ARE PUNISHABLE BY FINE AND IMPRISONMENT, U.S. CODE, TITLE 18, SECTION 1001

BILLING CODE 6712-01-C

Source: Federal Communications Commission.

Figure 3.5 The FCC's principal means for evaluating the past programming service of its television licensees is through a comparison of station "promises versus performance." (*a*) The 1982 commercial TV program proposal form; (*b*) the performance, or follow-up, form.

Federal Register / Vol. 46, No. 90 / Monday, May 11, 1981 / Rules and Regulations 26255

Section III STATEMENT OF TV PROGRAM SERVICE

9. Indicate the minimum amount of time the applicant proposes to devote normally each week to the categories below. Commercial time should be *excluded* in all computations except for the entries in columns 2, 6 and 10 of the total time operating line (line a).

ANTICIPATED TYPICAL WEEK DATA	FROM 6AM TO MIDNIGHT				FROM 6PM TO 11PM (5PM to 10PM CENTRAL AND MOUNTAIN TIME)				FROM MIDNIGHT TO 6AM			
	ALL PROGRAMS		LOCAL PROGRAMS ONLY		ALL PROGRAMS		LOCAL PROGRAMS ONLY		ALL PROGRAMS		LOCAL PROGRAMS ONLY	
	MINUTES OF OPERATION	PERCENTAGE OF TOTAL TIME OPERATING	MINUTES OF OPERATION	PERCENTAGE OF TOTAL TIME OPERATING	MINUTES OF OPERATION	PERCENTAGE OF TOTAL TIME OPERATING	MINUTES OF OPERATION	PERCENTAGE OF TOTAL TIME OPERATING	MINUTES OF OPERATION	PERCENTAGE OF TOTAL TIME OPERATING	MINUTES OF OPERATION	PERCENTAGE OF TOTAL TIME OPERATING
(1)	(2)	(3) 2/	(4) 1/	(5) 2/	(6)	(7) 3/	(8) 1/	(9) 3/	(10)	(11) 4/	(12) 1/	(13) 4/
a. TOTAL TIME OPERATING		100%				100%				100%		
b. NEWS 1/												
c. PUBLIC AFFAIRS 1/												
d. ALL OTHERS (*Exclusive of entertainment and sports*) 1/												

1/ Excluding Commercials
2/ Percentages are of the total minutes of operation reported at the top of column 2.
3/ Percentages are of the total minutes of operation reported at the top of column 6.
4/ Percentages are of the total minutes of operation reported at the top of column 10.

BILLING CODE 6712-01-C

Section III

PROGRAMMING

COMMERCIAL TV

Call letters____________

8. Indicate the minimum amount of time the applicant has devoted to the categories below during the composite week of the past license term. Commercial time should be excluded in all computations except for the entries in columns 2, 6 and 10 of the "TOTAL TIME OPERATING" line (line a).

WEEK DATA	FROM 6AM TO MIDNIGHT				FROM 6PM TO 11PM (5PM to 10PM CENTRAL AND MOUNTAIN TIME)				FROM MIDNIGHT TO 6AM			
	ALL PROGRAMS		LOCAL PROGRAMS ONLY		ALL PROGRAMS		LOCAL PROGRAMS ONLY		ALL PROGRAMS		LOCAL PROGRAMS ONLY	
	MINUTES OF OPERATION	PERCENTAGE OF TOTAL TIME OPERATING	MINUTES OF OPERATION	PERCENTAGE OF TOTAL TIME OPERATING	MINUTES OF OPERATION	PERCENTAGE OF TOTAL TIME OPERATING	MINUTES OF OPERATION	PERCENTAGE OF TOTAL TIME OPERATING	MINUTES OF OPERATION	PERCENTAGE OF TOTAL TIME OPERATING	MINUTES OF OPERATION	PERCENTAGE OF TOTAL TIME OPERATING
(1)	(2)	(3) 2/	(4) 1/	(5) 2/	(6)	(7) 3/	(8) 1/	(9) 3/	(10)	(11) 4/	(12) 1/	(13) 4/
a. TOTAL TIME OPERATING		100%				100%				100%		
b. NEWS 1/												
c. PUBLIC AFFAIRS 1/												
d. ALL OTHERS (*Exclusive of entertainment and sports*) 1/												

1/ Excluding Commercials
2/ Percentages are of the total minutes of operation reported at the top of column 2.
3/ Percentages are of the total minutes of operation reported at the top of column 6.
4/ Percentages are of the total minutes of operation reported at the top of column 10.

8b. If the applicant's composite week programming varied substantially from the relevant programming representations made to the Commission, attach as Exhibit III-8b a statement explaining the variation(s) and reasons therefor.

Source: Federal Communications Commission.

needed programming corrections *during* the license period, thus eliminating crisis behavior should the composite week logs reveal a discrepancy.

Field Inspections A second enforcement procedure established by the FCC in 1981 is the random field inspection conducted by the Commission's Field Operations Bureaus. At least 10 percent of all licensees, including commercial radio stations, are subject to field inspections. Samples are drawn using a computer or manual random number generator, the same as with the selection of stations to complete the long form audit renewals.

Field inspections consist of examinations of the technical facilities and public files of the selected stations. The purpose of the latter is to assure the Commission that licensees keep the documentation on programming required for filing the audit renewal forms.

On-Site Broadcast Bureau Inspections The third enforcement procedure, on-site inspections by Broadcast Bureau staff personnel, are used to investigate licensees that have submitted "problem SRA's" and long-term audit renewal forms. Other licensees also may be included on a random basis.

The purpose of on-site inspections is to verify the information supplied by stations, using documents contained in their public files. This procedure, which is limited to commercial TV stations and noncommercial radio and television outlets, is an important element in the FCC's enforcement process.

A checklist of items required in a broadcast station's public file, prepared by the National Association of Broadcasters, is shown in Figure 3.6.

PUBLIC NOTICE OBLIGATIONS

Every broadcast licensee must inform its listeners and viewers of their right to express themselves regarding the station's performance during a license period. This requirement is fulfilled through the broadcast of on-air announcements as specified by the Commission. At the time of writing, the FCC required the broadcast of on-air "public notice announcements" on the first and sixteenth days of each calendar month during the period from six months prior to the expiration of the license through the last full month prior to the expiration. Additional announcements also are required during the second week following the tendering for filing of the application.

Complete details of the licensee's public notice obligations may be found in Section 73.1202 of the FCC's Rules.

OTHER FCC PROGRAMMING MATTERS

The Federal Communications Commission has established a number of specific rules which affect programming operations in addition to its broad guidelines and the statutory requirements of the Communications Act. Since Congress authorized the FCC to issue necessary rules for the on-going regulation of broadcasting, these rules and regulations, unless rejected by the Courts, have the same force as the law itself.

The most significant of these additional FCC regulations are discussed next.

Figure 3.6 The National Association of Broadcasters checklist of items that should be included in a station's public file

Field Operations Bureau Public File Checklist

	Commercial Television	Noncommercial Radio & TV	Commercial Radio
a. Construction permit or program test authority application if filed within the last seven years	•	•	•
b. Two latest renewal applications	•	•	•
c. Ownership reports covering last seven years	•	•	•
d. Annual employment reports for the last seven years	•	•	•
e. Two latest equal employment opportunity model programs	•	•	•
f. "The Public and Broadcasting — A Procedure Manual"	•	•	•
g. File for time requests by political candidates (according to the FCC, this file may be empty)	•	•	•
h. Letters received from members of the public for the last three years	•		•
i. Statement of TV program service	•		
j. Composite week logs for the last seven years	•		
k. Annual problems-programs lists for the last seven years	•	•	
l. Leader interview documentation for the last seven years	•	•	
m. Two most recent community leader checklists	•	•	
n. General public survey (if non-commercial, documentation required for last seven years)	•	•	
o. Statement of sources consulted and ascertainment methodology		•	
p. Community composition documentation		•	
q. Issues-programs lists			•

June 8, 1981 Supplement to **HIGHLIGHTS** d.

Courtesy of the National Association of Broadcasters.

Network Programming Restrictions

The national TV and radio networks—the most powerful elements in the broadcasting industry—are not licensed by the FCC. However, the Commission does enforce several rules related to network business and programming practices through its power to regulate *stations* that may affiliate with a network. Thus, the FCC has indirectly achieved certain public interest goals by issuing rules governing the acceptance of network programs by licensed affiliated stations. Two items, the Prime Time Access Rule and program rejection rights, are of particular interest.

The Prime Time Access Rule During the early 1970s, the Commission concluded that the three television networks were using a disproportionate amount of TV's heaviest viewing period, the evening hours from 7:00 to 11:00 PM, which we call "prime time." To deal with this problem, the FCC issued a rule prohibiting any TV station in a top 50 market from carrying more than three hours of *network* or *off-network* programming per night during the prime-time hours.

The three networks implemented the Prime Time Access Rule (Sec. 73.658 (k)) by giving up the half-hour period from 7:30 to 8:00 PM (EST). Thus, the evening prime-time schedule begins at 8:00 in all time zones except Central, where it starts at 7:00 PM.

Certain exceptions are permitted. First, the Prime Time Access Rule does not apply to Sunday as long as the 7:00 to 8:00 hour is used for children's and public affairs programming. Second, exceptions are permitted when special broadcasts, such as sports events or election coverage, impede the implementation of the rule.

The Prime Time Access Rule, originally intended to stimulate local public affairs and first-run syndicated productions, has become a financial boon for many local TV stations since they do not have to share advertising revenues for the period with the networks. However, the rule has been only moderately successful from a creative standpoint. With some exceptions, such as Group W's "PM Magazine," the access period has been filled largely with game shows and other modest cost programming rather than with innovative productions and public affairs.

Stations located in markets outside the top 50 are not covered by the Rule. Although the networks cannot economically provide programming for those secondary market outlets, such stations are free to use network reruns between 7:00 and 8:00 PM.

Rejection of Network Programs An historic FCC position has been that its licensees are accountable for the programs they broadcast. Any shifting of responsibility for programming decisions represents an abdication of licensee responsibility. While the FCC also recognizes the practical necessity for many stations to rely on networks for much of their programming, the Commission also guarantees licensees the right to reject any network program "which the station reasonably believes to be unsatisfactory or unsuitable or contrary to the public interest" and to substitute another program "which in the station's opinion, is of greater local or national importance."[33]

In practice, most TV stations do preempt network programs occasionally. A frequent cause is the need to broadcast an important local event. A second reason is to replace weak network programs with other shows which management believes will attract more viewers. A third reason is that sometimes a network program may be considered too controversial or perhaps inappropriate for the station's coverage area. While the elimination of such a program may be regarded as censorship by disappointed viewers, the right to determine its own programming is fundamental with a broadcast licensee.

Identification Announcements

Three other specific requirements must be covered because of their prominence in station operation. These include station identification announcements, mechanical identification, and the rebroadcast of telephone conversations.

Station Identification Requirements Although most radio and TV stations promote their identity frequently, the FCC requires an "official" station identification announcement at the beginning and ending of each period of operation and each hour, as close to the hour as feasible. However, during long broadcasts in which a station ID would interrupt program continuity, the FCC permits official station identifications to be given at natural breaks in programming, but still as close to the hour as feasible.

A station, for example, is not required to interrupt an opera broadcast or a religious service to give a station ID announcement at the top of the hour. Instead, the station should give its identification at the first opportunity that is not obtrusive to the programming.

An official station ID, as defined in Section 73.1201 of the FCC's rules, consists of the *call letters, immediately followed by the name of the city of license.* However, *it is permissible to insert between the call letters and the city the name of the licensee or the frequency or channel number.* However, no other information may be inserted in an official station identification. Other "promotional" station ID announcements, of course, may differ from the official break.

These examples illustrate correct and incorrect official (top of the hour) station identification:

Correct: KOA-TV, General Electric Broadcasting, Denver.
Incorrect: KOA-TV, your NBC affiliate, Denver.

Correct: KCBS, 740 on your dial, San Francisco.
Incorrect: KCBS, your all-news station, San Francisco.

Correct: WBAP, *Fort Worth*-Dallas.
Incorrect: WBAP, Clear Channel Modern Country Radio, Dallas-Fort Worth.

The last example illustrates a station having dual or multiple-city licensing which must identify its *primary city of license* first, even though another city is larger. Indeed, WBAP is licensed primarily to Fort Worth.

Mechanical Identification Just as the FCC requires proper station identification, the Commission also requires clear identification of any program or program material as "recorded" or "mechanically reproduced" when time is of special significance and the listener or viewer might believe such a delayed broadcast to be live.

For example, a taped, filmed, or recorded speech by the president, which would appear to be live, must be clearly identified visually or aurally as recorded. A "mock up" which simulates an instantaneously occurring event also must be labeled as simulated.

In contrast, there is no requirement to tell listeners that phonographic music or announcements, either commercial or public service, are recorded because time is unimportant in the airing of such items.

Section 73.1208 of the FCC's rules and regulations details the requirement on identification of taped, filmed, or recorded material.

Broadcasting Telephone Conversations Increasingly the telephone is used as a news-gathering instrument by radio and television stations. However, a special FCC rule (Sec. 73.1206) requires licensees to inform any party to a telephone call of the station's plans to broadcast the conversation.

Calls placed by a station's own personnel, such as on-the-spot news reports, and calls that have been invited by the station, such as those on telephone talk programs, are exempted from this rule.

SELF-REGULATION, PUBLIC OPINION, AND PROGRAMMING

Two other powerful forces that influence radio and TV programming are public opinion and industry self-regulation. Only in recent times have powerful citizens organizations been formed to promote reform in broadcasting. Two notable movements deserve mention because of the effectiveness of their efforts. First, the Association for Children's Television (ACT) has spearheaded the movement for improved children's programming, including a reduction of violence and reforms in advertising messages directed to children. A second movement, led by the Parent-Teachers Association and numerous religious groups, has sought a reduction in sexual material on television. Both lobbying and pressure tactics have been used by these groups.

The principal response from the broadcasting industry to its critics usually has emanated from the National Association of Broadcasters, which sponsors codes of good practice for both radio and television. In addition, the networks also maintain continuity acceptance departments to screen and approve all program material before it is broadcast.

Admittedly, some of the impetus for self-regulation stems from the fact that it likely deters increased governmental control, which broadcasters abhor. However, enlightened self-regulation by responsible broadcasters also results in higher standards and better service for the public.

THE NATIONAL ASSOCIATION OF BROADCASTERS

The National Association of Broadcasters (NAB) is the principal trade association of US commercial broadcasting. Headquartered in Washington, D.C., the NAB represents the industry before congressional committees, the FCC, and other governmental agencies. Beyond its lobbying function, the association provides member stations with information useful to station management, including economic studies, interpretation of governmental rules and regulations, and industry guidelines. However, for our purposes here, a most important activity is the sponsorship and administration of the self-regulatory codes of good practices.

NAB Radio and Television Codes

Members of the National Association of Broadcasters formulated their first radio code in 1928. The original TV code, which was based on the radio version but also influenced by the motion picture code, was established in 1952. Each code deals specifically with programming and advertising standards, including prohibitions and recommendations which subscribing stations are expected to follow.

Since 1961, both codes have been administered and enforced by the NAB Code Authority under general oversight of the Radio Code Board and the Television Code Review Board. All stations, regardless of membership status in the association, may become code subscribers. In practice, about 52 percent of all US commercial radio stations and 65 percent of all commercial TV stations are dues-paying code members. These members usually display the NAB code seal in their printed material and on the air.

Although a substantial number of stations do not subscribe, code standards are followed widely by both subscriber and nonsubscriber stations. It is significant, too, that the three national television and four major radio networks subscribe to the NAB codes.

Administration of these two broadcast codes has been delegated to the NAB Code Authority, which is supported by fees from subscribing stations. With offices in New York, Hollywood, and Washington, the Authority reviews advertising materials and specific programming questions to determine broadcast acceptability. Recommendations are made to subscribing stations through the monthly publication, *Code News,* shown in Figure 3.7.

Other responsibilities of the Code Authority include (1) investigating complaints about programming and advertising and informing subscriber stations, (2) monitoring program logs to determine whether or not a station is in compliance with the code's advertising and time standards, and (3) making recommendations to the Code Boards concerning violations. In addition, the Code Authority maintains liaison with governmental agencies, such as the Federal Trade Commission and the FCC. The code boards, which meet at least twice annually to review the status of the codes, may recommend

Figure 3.7 Radio and TV stations which subscribe to the NAB Codes of Good Practice receive this monthly publication, which provides current information on actions of the Code boards

CODE NEWS

THE CODE AUTHORITY OF THE NATIONAL ASSOCIATION OF BROADCASTERS/VOLUME 14/NUMBER 1/JANUARY 1981

Radio Code Board Hears Subscription Is at All-Time High; Hears Reports on Wide Range of Issues

At its November 7 meeting in Scottsdale, Ariz., the Radio Code Board of the National Association of Broadcasters heard the results of a commercial time quantum survey compiled by the Code Authority. The survey covered the period of April 1978 through June 1980 and involved 52 states and territories, as well as the District of Columbia. Results of this study show that over 98 percent of the hours surveyed were found to adhere to the Radio Code's advertising guideline of 18 minutes per hour.

The Board also was advised that subscription to the Radio Code is at an all-time high. As of November 1, 1980, some 4,026 commercial radio stations subscribed to the Code. This represents 51.9 percent of all on-air and licensed commercial radio stations.The results of a Radio Code subscription campaign conducted by the Code Authority with the assistance of NAB Radio Board Chairman Eddie Fritts and Radio Code Board Chairman H. Wayne Hudson were also reported on to the Board.

Following discussion of the relationship of a commercial technique to the Radio Code's "news simulation" standard (I-I,2), the Board directed the Code Authority to draft a proposed revision of the standard.

In another action, the Board directed its Gambling-Related Advertising Committee to conduct a review of Code policy on gambling-related radio advertising. Members of the Committee are: Enzo DeDominicis, general manager, WRCQ(AM)-WRCH-FM Farmington, Conn.; Philip T. Kelly, president, Communications Properties, Inc., Dubuque, Iowa, and Hal Kormann, director, program practices, CBS Radio, New York, N.Y.

During the course of its meeting, the Code Board discussed the Broadcast Town Meetings held on October 7 in Milwaukee, Wis., and on October 20 in Tucson, Ariz. They endorsed the continuation of the meetings that are designed to give the public an opportunity to direct questions and comments regarding the radio and television industry's voluntary program of self-regulation to industry representatives. The Radio and Television Code Boards have sponsored two Broadcast Town Meetings each year since 1977.

Additionally, the Board heard reports on: The Code Authority's commercial review service; non-prescription medications advertising; non-tobacco smokes advertising; personal products advertising, and professional advertising.

Members of the Radio Code Board are: H. Wayne Hudson (chairman), president, Plough Broadcasting Company, Inc., Memphis, Tenn.; Mr. DeDominicis; Ron Gomez, president and general manager, KPEL(AM)-KTDY(FM) Lafayette, La.; Sally V. Hawkins, president and general manager, WILM(AM) Wilmington, Del.; Richard Kale, president, radio division, Golden West Broadcasters, Los Angeles, Calif.; Mr.

(continues on next page)

Holiday Season for Some Children Made Merrier By Gift of Toys

As part of their review process for children's toy commercials, the New York and Hollywood offices of the Code Authority receive toys and games for examination from advertisers and their agencies.

After the toys have been used in the toy commercial review process, they become part of a collection which several times each year is donated to local children's hospital, orphanage or school facilities.

At any time of the year, but especially during the recent holiday season, the gift of toys takes on added meaning for the children who receive them.

This year the toys from the New York office were sent to St. Dominick's Home, Blauvelt, N.Y., and the ones from the Hollywood office were given to Children's Hospital, Los Angeles, Calif.

In past years, toys have been sent to such organizations as the New York Foundling Hospital, the Jewish Child Care Association, Cardinal McClosky Home, the Astor Home and Abbott House, all of New York From the Hollywood office, toys have been sent to the Orange County Indian Center and the Valley Presbyterian Hospital, Van Nuys, Calif., among others.

Courtesy of The Code Authority of the National Association of Broadcasters.

amendments, which then must be ratified by the NAB Board of Directors before they become effective.

Finally, the code boards may (1) initiate formal charges against stations which have been accused of violating the codes, (2) consider appeals stemming from any decision made by the Code Authority, and (3) consult with the director of the Authority on matters affecting code administration.

As noted earlier, NAB code standards are widely accepted throughout the broadcasting industry. However, since subscription is voluntary, penalties are levied only against subscribers. When violations occur, action may include the suspension of a station's membership in the code and revocation of its right to display the NAB code "seal of good practice."

Contents of the Codes

The NAB radio and television codes bear a strong resemblance to each other. Both consist of (1) a prefacing statement which presents the philosophy and purpose of self-regulation, (2) program standards, and (3) advertising standards. Philosophically, the codes recognize the need for thoughtful attention to the content of material broadcast by radio and TV stations and suggest that advertisers and viewers also share in the responsibility for upholding high standards.

> The purpose of this Code is cooperatively to maintain a level of television programming which gives full consideration to the educational, informational, cultural, economic, moral and entertainment needs of the American public to the end that more and more people will be better served.[34]

> The viewer also has a responsibility to help broadcasters serve the public. All viewers should make their criticism and positive suggestions about programming and advertising known to the broadcast licensee. Parents particularly should oversee the viewing habits of their children, encouraging them to watch programs that will enrich their experience and broaden their intellectual horizons.[35]

With respect to programming, the codes acknowledge that broadcasters have a special obligation to children, which, among other things, calls for restraint in regard to the presentation of violence and sexual themes during hours in which children constitute a substantial segment of the audience. When depictions of conflict are present during hours when children normally view television, it is the broadcaster's responsibility to be certain they are handled with sensitivity.

Although the two codes recognize the great need for artistic freedom, they call for the responsible exercise of creative talent in regard to a number of sensitive items. Thus, special programming standards govern the handling of (1) violence and conflict; (2) crime and antisocial behavior; (3) drugs, gambling, and alcohol; (4) sports programs; (5) mental and physical handicaps; (6) human relationships and sex; (7) minorities (sex, race, color, age, creed, and ethnic origin); (8) obscenity and profanity; (9) hypnosis; (10) superstition and pseudosciences (fortune telling, occultism, astrology, etc.); (11) professional advice, diagnosis, and treatment; (12) subliminal perception; (13) use of animals in programming; (14) game programs and contests; (15) prizes, credits, and acknowledgements; and (16) deception or misrepresentation.[36]

In addition, the codes encourage licensees to exercise constructive responsibility in their communities through, among other things, the presentation of news and public affairs broadcasts of high standards of integrity.

THE NETWORKS

Although the TV and radio codes of the National Association of Broadcasters represent the major undertaking in industry self-regulation, significant self-policing also is done by the networks. Each of these organizations maintains a continuity acceptance department which examines and must approve all program and commercial materials before they are aired.

As many as thirty or forty thousand commercial announcements are scrutinized each year for product acceptability, method of presentation, and substantiation of advertising claims. Program scripts are examined in detail and tapes of extemporaneous shows are screened before broadcast. Even material which passes inspection often does so only after repeated screenings, detailed discussion, and numerous headaches.

SUMMARY

In conclusion, the programming efforts put forth by America's radio and TV stations come under varying degrees of scrutiny from government and the public. Program executives must follow FCC procedures scrupulously, even though the Commission does not force any programming upon its licensees. License renewal, political broadcasting, fairness issues, and potential lottery advertising are a few of these concerns that demand meticulous care.

Not only does the FCC fulfill its role as guardian of the public interest, but also numerous special interest groups bring pressure to bear upon licensees and their advertisers. Individual listeners and viewers, however, are the most effective force upon programming through their right to turn the channel. The industry and its employees must and do respond to public opinion. Significantly, most well-intentioned broadcasters abide by and support the self-regulatory codes of the industry as perhaps the best available means of protecting the cherished right to free speech on the airwaves.

Now that we have examined the regulatory aspects of broadcast programming, we can turn to the activity of programming. Our next chapter focuses on the program department.

ENDNOTES

1. The Wireless Ship Act of 1910. Public Law 61-262, June 24, 1910. Reprinted in Frank J. Kahn, ed., *Documents of American Broadcasting,* 2d. ed. (New York: Appleton-Century-Crofts, 1972), pp. 6-7.
2. The Radio Act of 1912. Public Law 62-264, August 13, 1912. Reprinted in Kahn, *op. cit.,* pp. 8-16.
3. In the Intercity Radio Co. case of 1923, the Supreme Court held that the Secretary of Commerce could not refuse a radio license to anyone. Then in 1926, the Supreme Court held in the Zenith case that the Radio Act of 1912 did not give the Secretary the power to establish regulations to assign stations to specific wavelengths. With these two actions, Hoover's efforts to promote order on the airwaves virtually collapsed, necessitating new legislation by Congress.

4. The Radio Act of 1927. Public Law 69-632, February 23, 1927. Reprinted in Kahn, *op. cit.*, pp. 35-51.
5. Federal Radio Commission, *Third Annual Report* (Washington, D.C.: U.S. Government Printing Office, 1929), p. 3.
6. Lawrence W. Lichty and Malachi C. Topping, *A Source Book on the History of Radio and Television* (New York: Hastings House, Publishers, 1975), p. 565.
7. KFKB Broadcasting v. Federal Radio Commission, 47 F 2d 670 (D.C. Cir. 1931).
8. KFKB v. F.R.C., 47 F 2d 670 at 671.
9. Charley Orbison, "'Fighting Bob' Shuler: Early Radio Crusader," *Journal of Broadcasting* (Fall, 1977), *21,* 461.
10. Trinity Methodist Church, South v. Federal Radio Commission, 62 F 2d 850 (D.C. Cir., 1932). Reprinted in Kahn, *op. cit.*, p. 121.
11. *Ibid.*, p. 853.
12. *Ibid.*
13. National Broadcasting Co., Inc. et al. v. United States et al., 319 U.S. 190 at 215-16 (1943).
14. U.S. Senate, Hearings before the Committee on Interstate Commerce, 78th Cong., 1st Sess., on S 814 (1943).
15. The Communications Act of 1934, 47 U.S.C., Ch. 5, Sub. 1, Pgh. 151 *et seq.* This Act, Public Law 73-416, June 19, 1934, is reprinted in Kahn, *op. cit.*
16. The Communications Act of 1934, Sec. 315(a) (4), as amended.
17. For complete details, see the FCC public notice, "Fairness Doctrine and the Public Interest Standards," 39 F.R. 26372. Copies are available upon request from the F.C.C.
18. The Communications Act of 1934, Sec. 326.
19. Red Lion Broadcasting Co., Inc., et al. v. F.C.C. et al. 395 U.S. 367 (1969).
20. In re Palmetto Broadcasting Company (WDKD), 33 FCC 265 (1961). A detailed discussion of this case is given in "The Charlie Walker Case," *Journal of Broadcasting* (Spring 1979), *23,* 137-151.
21. Although broadcast stations are expected to exert caution in the presentation of sexual material, pay TV services do not operate under such strict measures because their programming may be seen only by subscribers who have specifically sought it out.
22. *Perry's Broadcasting and the Law* (Knoxville, Tenn.: Larry Perry and Associates, September 15, 1979), p. 2.
23. *Public Service Responsibility of Broadcast Licensees,* FCC Mimeograph No. 81575, March 7, 1946. This document also was published by the U.S. Government Printing Office in 1946 and reprinted in Kahn, *op. cit.*, p. 207.
24. Report and Statement of Policy re: Commission en banc Programming Inquiry, FCC 60-970, July 29, 1960; 25 F.R. 7295 (1960). Reprinted in Kahn, *op. cit.*, p. 207.
25. Kahn, *op. cit.*, p. 219.
26. *Ibid.*
27. Federal Communications Commission. "Ascertainment of Community Problems by Broadcast Applicants," 41 F.R. 1372 (1976).
28. *Ibid.*
29. Federal Communications Commission, "Deregulation of Radio," 46 F.R. 13888 (1981).
30. 47 C.F.R. Sec. 0.281.
31. Until 1981, AM and FM radio applications were measured by 8 percent and 6 percent benchmark levels and a maximum commercial load of 18 minutes per hour.
32. Federal Communications Commission, "Deregulation of Radio," 46 F.R. 13888 (1981).
33. Federal Communications Commission, Rules and Regulations. Section 73.658 (e).
34. *The Television Code* (Washington, D.C.: National Association of Broadcasters, January 1980), p. 24.
35. *Ibid.*, p.1.
36. The legality of the advertising guidelines contained in the NAB Radio and Television Codes has been challenged by the antitrust division of the Department of Justice. Therefore, at least temporarily, the NAB has suspended enforcement of those guidelines.

STUDY QUESTIONS

1. Take a position for or against Section 315 and defend it logically. Be sure to include your position on such specific points as:

   a. The equal-time concept itself;
   b. The minimum rate for political advertising;
   c. The exceptions which apply to bona fide news programs; and
   d. The rules governing political debates.
2. Take a position for or against the Fairness Doctrine and defend it logically.
3. Take a position for or against the FCC's 1981 deregulatory policy which eliminated program percentage promises by radio station licensees. Defend your position logically in a written brief.
4. Make a list of 10 important problems or concerns for the community in which you live. What types of programs are presented by local stations in response to these problems?
5. How is the Prime Time Access period used by stations in your area? Can you offer any suggestions for better usage of the time?
6. Study a copy of the NAB's radio and TV codes. Then make a list of any practices that appear questionable as you watch and listen to stations in your area. Are any of the practices in violation of the code?
7. Discuss the ethical questions that relate to organized public groups that seek to reform broadcast programming. You should be concerned specifically with questions of censorship and responsibility.

SUGGESTED READINGS

Bittner, John R. *Broadcasting Law and Regulation.* Englewood Cliffs, N.J.: Prentice-Hall, 1982.

Broadcasting and the Law [newsletter]. Knoxville, Tenn.: Perry Publications, 1972–present.

Cole, Barry G., and Mal Oettinger. *Reluctant Regulators: The FCC and the Broadcast Audience.* 2d ed. Reading, Mass.: Addison-Wesley, 1978.

Emery, Walter B. *Broadcasting and Government: Responsibilities and Regulation.* Rev. ed. East Lansing: Michigan State University Press, 1971.

Francois, William E. *Mass Media Law and Regulation.* Columbus, Ohio: Grid Publishing, 1975.

Geller, Henry. *Fairness Doctrine in Broadcasting: Problems and Suggested Courses of Action.* Santa Monica, Calif.: RAND Corporation, 1973.

Krasnow, Erwin G., and Laurence D. Longley. *The Politics of Broadcast Regulation.* New York: St. Martin's Press, 1973.

Lewis, F.F. *Literature, Obscenity, and Law.* Carbondale: Southern Illinois University Press, 1976.

NAB Legal Guide to FCC Broadcast Rules, Regulations, and Policies. Washington, D.C.: National Association of Broadcasters, 1977.

Toohey, Daniel W., Richard D. Marks, and Arnold P. Leitzker. *Legal Problems in Broadcasting: Identification and Analysis of Selected Issues.* Lincoln, Neb.: Great Plains National Instructional Television Library, 1974.

4

MANAGING THE PROGRAM DEPARTMENT

Which is the most important department to the success of a radio or television station? Indeed, a case can be made for *programming,* since this department's entire efforts are directed toward attracting and holding an audience for the station. And, without that audience, how could the sales department function? Furthermore, what need would there be for the business office if the sales unit couldn't land clients because of lackluster programming?

But wait! How can a station reach its audience if there's no engineering department to provide technical facilities? And what about sales? It brings in the revenue that makes programming possible. Then the promotion department lets the public know about up-coming specials, new programs, and format changes. Yes, even though programming is vitally important, we are constantly reminded that broadcasting is a team effort! Each department—engineering, programming, news, sales, promotion, and the business office—makes such a vital contribution to a station's success that no unit can function effectively without *all of the others.*

In this chapter, we will explore the program department in depth, looking at its organization, personnel, and major functions. Distinctions will also be made between TV and radio departments whenever they are appropriate.

HOW IS THE PROGRAM DEPARTMENT ORGANIZED?

The program department usually is headed by a *program director*—sometimes called *program manager*—who is responsible for supervising the staion's programming efforts, including the selection, production, and scheduling of programs to meet the public's needs and interests. This person reports to the station manager and usually holds the same rank as the heads of other major departments in the station.

The program director or "PD" must understand people and have a strong insight into the public's needs for information, entertainment, and service. He/she also must be capable of creating successful locally originated programs as well as evaluating program products available from outside sources. As the administrative head, the program director also manages the department's internal affairs and coordinates the station's programming activities with those of the other departments.

The program director's specific duties will be discussed in considerable detail in this chapter. However, it should be noted here in the beginning that the job of program director combines the detail work of administration with the more exciting creative aspects of station programming.

Although there are certain similarities, program departments in radio and TV stations differ somewhat because of inherent differences between the two media. They also vary in size and complexity, depending upon a station's economic situation and its programming needs. However, certain essential functions must be performed regardless of size. In a large station, for example, the work load is shared by several persons. However, in most small stations, only a few people are available to perform the same functions. Now let's look at the organization of program departments of both radio and television stations.

THE RADIO PROGRAM DEPARTMENT

Program departments of medium and large radio stations usually include, in addition to the program director, a music director, music librarian, production manager, sports director, and a community affairs or public service coordinator. Continuity writers and the traffic persons, who schedule all programs and announcements, are often shared between the program and sales units. In addition, there may be an administrative assistant or an assistant program director, as well as producers and the talent staff.

Figure 4.1 shows a graphic depiction of a large radio program department at WGN Radio, Chicago, while Figure 4.2 presents an organization chart for the same department in a much smaller station. In the smaller station, the program director often assumes many additional responsibilities, including on-air announcing duties.

THE TV PROGRAM DEPARTMENT

Like radio, television is a collective art in that the program product results from the efforts of staff members who possess various skills. However, TV production is much more complex than radio. Thus, a larger and more diversified staff is needed.

In addition to the program director, a typical television program department includes a programming assistant, a community affairs and/or public

Figure 4.1 Organizational Chart: Large Radio Program Department

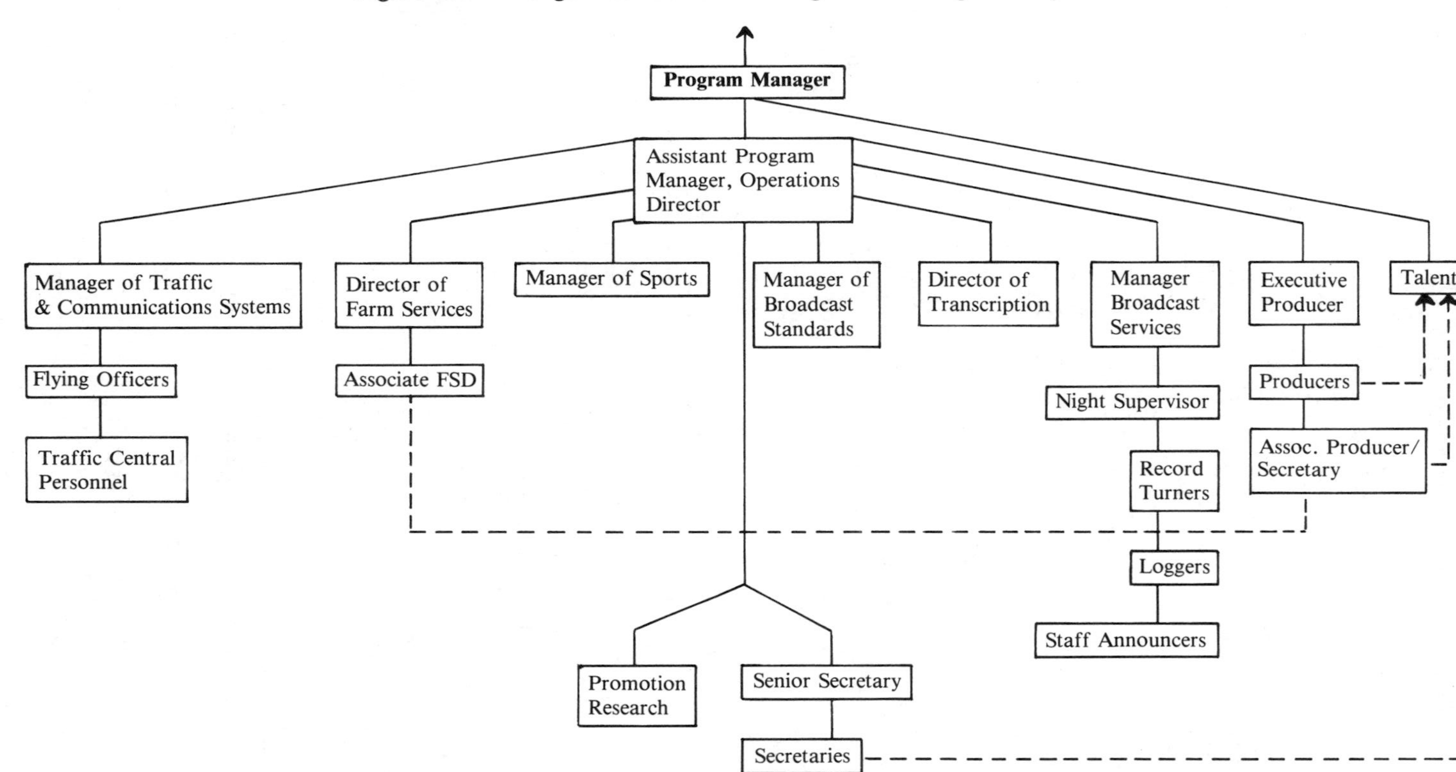

Courtesy of WGN Radio, WGN Continental Broadcasting Company, Chicago.

Figure 4.2 Organizational Chart: Small Radio Program Department

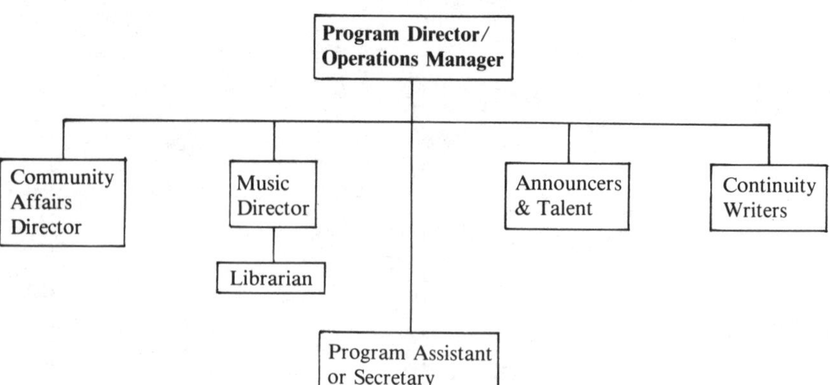

service director, and a production manager to whom numerous production employees report. Among this production complement, there usually are producers, directors, cinematographers, artists, carpenters, video tape and film editors, and performing talent. Figure 4.3 shows the organizational plan for the program department of WSB-TV, Atlanta, a large pioneer television station.

THE PROGRAM DIRECTOR

The program director is the key decision maker for programming in the broadcast station. But, as we shall see, he/she does not function alone in this respect. The program director's responsibilities begin with administrative functions as head of the department and as a member of the station's management team.[1] Second, and no less important, is the duty to guard the station's broadcast license. Without its license from the Federal Communications Commission, everything else becomes purely academic. Third comes the actual programming of the television or radio station—identifying and scheduling viable programs and formats to attract as large a share of the audience as possible. Fourth, the program director must see that the programming is executed in such a way as to be both commercially attractive and artistically successful. Fifth, the program director coordinates the department's activities with those of the other units of the station. And, sixth, the PD seeks to cultivate good relationships with the community and area served by the station.

Accomplishing these varied responsibilities requires a person who possesses administrative ability; an understanding of the applicable FCC rules and regulations, as well as other governmental regulations; expertise in both show business and journalism; a sense of public relations; and an understanding of people from a behavioral and motivational perspective. The job also entails

Figure 4.3 A Television Station Program Department

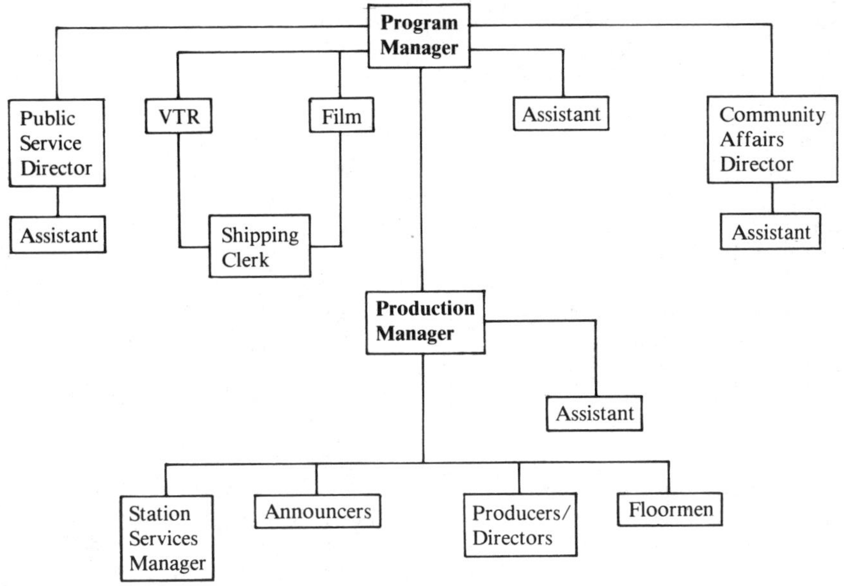

Courtesy of WSB-TV, Cox Communications, Inc., Atlanta.

numerous specific activities which vary from station to station. Now let's explore the details of the program director's job.

AN EXCESS OF ADMINISTRATION

In the role of administrator, the program director recruits, hires, and supervises the program staff. The PD also negotiates talent contracts, plans and controls the departmental budget, buys programs and program materials, handles correspondence, and coordinates all interdepartmental activities involving programming. In large stations, an assistant program director may be present to help the department head with these matters. In contrast, for many small radio stations, the program director is usually the best announcer on the staff. As such, his/her responsibilities generally include making up the announcers' work schedules, handling requests for public service time, and supervising local production activities. The administrative authority, in fact, may be quite limited, since the station manager in many small operations reserves that right.

Hiring and Supervising the Staff

Large stations often maintain personnel departments to assist in staffing their operating departments. Nevertheless, the program director must play a prominent role in obtaining a staff of talented, professional broadcasters and (if the program director also acts as production manager, as most radio and some TV PD's do) production personnel as well. It is also the program director's duty to coach the staff in its on-air performance and to maintain a healthy, creative environment so they not only will stay with the station for a reasonable time, but also give their best efforts while in its employ.

Knowing the details of the federal government's Equal Employment Opportunity Program also is required of the program director when filling staff vacancies or adding new personnel. In addition, when applicable, the PD must prepare for and assist with negotiation of union contracts as they apply to the program department. Among the labor unions which may be involved are the American Federation of Television and Radio Artists (AFTRA), which represents talent and announcers; the International Alliance of Theatrical Stage Employees and Moving Picture Machine Operators (IATSE), representing studio production crew members; and the International Brotherhood of Electrical Workers (IBEW), representing film editors, cinematographers, and artists.

Finally, the program director reviews all time cards for members of the department, approves all vacations, approves all overtime, and, in general, supervises the day-to-day personnel matters of the department.

Handling the Budget

The program director who truly is assigned an administrative role prepares the annual operating and capital budgets for the department. Then, after the budget document has been reviewed and approved by management, the program director must operate the department within the cost guidelines of the yearly budget. This task requires a regular review of expenditures, probably each month, to determine how much variance there has been and to take any needed corrective measures.

Preparing and living within the budget calls for an intimate knowledge of programming costs and the ability to make wise decisions that result in the greatest possible benefit from each expenditure. Justification and cost efficiency are the major guidelines as the program director operates the department on a budget basis.

Purchasing Program Materials

The program director administers the department on a day-to-day basis and also initiates major programming decisions, which are subject to approval by the station manager. Both activities require negotiating for and purchasing programs and materials. These purchases include syndicated material and other program items, broadcast rights to sports and special events, music performance agreements, and miscellaneous supplies. The PD usually reviews all requets for purchases, prepares purchase orders, and approves invoices.

Correspondence

Much of the program director's time will be spent handling communications with the audience. Any opportunity to respond to a listener's or a viewer's comments should be regarded as a chance to win the good will of that person for the station. Therefore, the program director should answer all mail from the audience promptly and helpfully. In addition, as a public relations gesture, he/she usually sends a congratulatory letter with any contest prize the station awards to a listener.

There is also a considerable amount of business correspondence between the program director and program syndicators, networks, people with program ideas, and job applicants. This, too, should be handled with dispatch.

LICENSE RESPONSIBILITIES AND PROGRAM STANDARDS

The responsibility to maintain a station's license is of paramount importance. Although the general manager and each department head must give this item high priority, the program director is the chief "guardian of the license." As such, the PD must have a thorough working knowledge of all applicable FCC rules and regulations, as well as the NAB code and policies of the licensee. In particular, the program director of a television station must know what percentages of its weekly schedule the licensee has committed to news, public affairs, and other nonentertainment programming, as well as the number of public service announcements promised per week. Although radio stations no longer make specific programming commitments, radio program managers nevertheless should pay close attention to the quality and extent of the station's service to the public.

Once the program schedule or format has been structured to attract the station's target audience and to conform with promises made to the Commission, the TV program director must see that the station's actual operation routinely meets or surpasses the licensee's promises. The operating logs should be analyzed periodically to be sure those minimum promises were fulfilled. Examination of program logs at regular intervals, such as one week every three months, alerts the astute program director to any deviation from the original promises and provides ample time to make corrections long before a formal accounting must be made. This on-going surveillance of station performance is an appropriate assignment for the program director since, in many cases, he/she is expected to recommend the specific percentages to be included in license renewal applications.

In addition to periodic log checks, the program director or an assisistant should check the program logs on the day after broadcast to make sure the log keepers have completed the forms correctly and that all items—programs, announcements (commercial, public service, and political), promotion messages, and contests—have been logged properly as to source, type, and time of broadcast. Although radio stations no longer are required by the FCC to keep such program logs, good business practice dictates that accurate on-air performance records by kept.

The program director or an assistant must take responsibility for the station's public service material. This task involves making certain the station broadcasts at least the minimum number of PSA's promised in the license and that specific messages used are meaningful to the station's audience. (Radio stations no longer are required to make such promises, but they must be able to demonstrate that they serve the public interest.) In addition, the PD must be on guard against lottery (see chapter 3), even in public service copy, and make sure each PSA is truly sponsored by a nonprofit organization. However, it is usually the duty of the *creative director* or *production manager* to produce these messages and keep them fresh.

In regard to public affairs, the program director must be alert to the significant problems of the station's service area. Then the PD must see to it that the station focuses attention on some of these problems or needs. At this writing, television stations are still required to conduct formal ascertainment studies; however, radio stations were exempted from such formal studies in 1981. Although ascertaining the general public's concerns usually is assigned to an outside research organization, the TV program director and other department heads often become involved in interviewing community leaders. The program director also may be expected to prepare and file the required Annual Report of Ascertained Problems and programming produced to meet those concerns. Other FCC forms usually assigned to the program director include the Annual Report on TV Station Programming and the program sections of license renewal applications.

At some stations, the program director is responsible for maintenance of the local Public Inspection File as required by the FCC. If so, he/she receives and reviews all material placed in the file and checks regularly to be sure all required items are in place, including the mandatory documentation for political broadcasts.

Finally, the program manager is expected to communicate the station's programming standards to the staff and to enforce those standards in the production operation. Radio disc jockeys, for example, customarily are required to sign payola affidavits to signify that they have not received any form of extra compensation for promoting records on the air. These affidavits must be updated periodically. The news staff and talk show hosts must be instructed in the Fairness Doctrine and its implications on broadcasts of controversial issues and attacks on individuals. The on-air staff also must be instructed and reviewed periodically on procedures for broadcasting during emergency conditions.

Many stations subscribe to "The Radio Code" or "The Television Code" of the National Association of Broadcasters as their guide to broadcast standards. Even many stations which are not members of the NAB follow these codes because of their wide acceptance in the industry. In addition, special policies of the ownership must be implemented. Thus, seeing that the station's adopted standards are followed has become another important duty of the program director.

PROGRAM PLANNING: THE GREAT CHALLENGE!

Lest the reader conclude that the program director's job is only administrative, we turn now to the real job of program planning. The radio or TV program director holds the prime responsibility for developing the station's schedule or format. This is a challenging activity, much more exciting than the administrative side of the job because it's competitive and it's also "show business."

The program director is expected to be the expert on program selection and scheduling. For television, this means being highly knowledgeable about syndicated shows, network offerings, and local creative talent available for the station's own productions. The radio program director similarly must understand the strengths and weaknesses of various formats that might be used, as well as have a working knowledge of network and syndicated material and local programming resources.

As the station's programming specialist, the program manager must keep abreast of the interests and tastes of the public in the area served by the station. The PD also must be alert to programming moves by competitive stations in the same market, as well as to national programming trends.

Although the program director is the key resource person for program decision making, he rarely acts alone in making major programming changes. Those decisions usually are made on a management team basis, with input from the general manager, the sales manager, the promotion manager, and the news director, as well as the program manager. Certainly promotional considerations and the commercial potential of programming must weigh heavily in the major program decisions, since the station's economic success depends upon its ability to attract both listeners/viewers and advertisers. At the same time, however, the program director should be a staunch defender of good taste and quality in whatever programming is selected. The final decision regarding format direction or any significant change in the program schedule always rests with the general manager.

It often takes a great deal of time for a format or schedule to develop to its full potential. Therefore, once basic programming decisions have been reached and implemented, wholesale changes are out of place. (Some radio stations actually have changed formats just after a rating sweep and before the arrival of the results only to discover too late that they were doing well.) However, constant refinements are made to enable a station to reach and serve the target audience better. This on-going process, which may involve numerous day-to-day details, consists of fine tuning the basic program plan to achieve an improved sound or better audience flow, or to rejuvenate programs or personalities that have lost some of their former luster.

Because the success of programming is measured by audience response, the PD must know how to read and analyze ratings reports. Although audience measurement studies primarily serve as a sales aid, they are also a most useful programming tool, especially when audience turnover and long-term trends can be analyzed.

Many program directors also attempt to conduct their own monitoring of audience preferences through in-house research as well as through the standard market sweeps and special contract studies. Thus, being able to design reliable and useful research studies is a desirable skill for program managers.

WHAT ABOUT PRODUCTION?

With the probable exception of news, the program director is responsible for everything that is aired on the station. In most TV stations, however, the details of program implementation are delegated to the *production manager.* There also may be a production manager or *operations manager* in charge of format execution in a radio station. However, many radio PD's, especially those in medium and smaller stations, must assume the added responsibility of day-to-day program implementation. Moreover, at many radio stations, the title of program director is dropped altogether in favor of the operations manager designation.

A later section of this chapter will explore program and format execution in detail.

INTERDEPARTMENTAL COORDINATION

In today's highly competitive broadcasting industry, all units of a radio or TV station must work well together to put the best possible product on the air. Furthermore, because of the interrelatedness of station departments, close coordination is essential. This cooperation ideally is fostered through a management-team approach in which the department heads participate with the general manager in decisions affecting the entire station.

It is in this context that the program director serves as a key resource person and program initiator, whose major recommendations are subject to debate. Basic programming decisions, therefore, are reached only after all the department heads have made their own recommendations to the general manager, usually in a management conference. As we have said before, the wise program director in a commercial station will forthrightly advocate artistic quality and public service, while also recognizing the fact that major programming decisions must be based upon the need to attract a commercially viable audience. After basic programming choices have been made, the department heads and their staffs must continue to work together on a daily basis to implement the decisions. Some examples will suggest ways in which programming and other departments can cooperate for the long-term enhancement of a station.

Programming and Sales

A program director usually is expected to assist the sales department in implementing its goals. This generally means striving for maximum numbers of the target audience and developing commercial availabilities and program vehicles suitable for specific advertising clients. Thus, the program director should attempt to develop a continuous flow of new and salable ideas to offer prospective clients.

In turn, it is important that the sales personnel understand and respect the basic programming philosophy of the station. A problem can arise, for example, when a salesperson has a client ready to go on the air, but the commercials or program violate good taste or are incompatible with the station's sound or image. A wise sales manager, like the program director, will be more concerned about the station's long-term image than about the immediate account. However, there is an ever-present danger that a station's image may be compromised under these circumstances, particularly among marginal stations. The program director should defend the integrity of the station's programming as much as possible under the circumstances.

Few sophisticated advertisers, of course, choose the wrong stations for their messages. Why, for example, would a promoter for a hard rock concert attempt to advertise on a beautiful music station? Similarly, why would an agency for a geriatric product buy time on a rock music station? A more likely problem is the scheduling of commercial announcements that are incompatible with the station's programming style. Whenever this occurs, the program director, as the quality control expert and principal guardian of the station's image, should exercise the authority to redo the commercial to fit the station's style, or reject it outright.

In addition to these considerations, both the programming and sales departments must work very closely with the traffic director, who schedules all programs and announcements. Orderly procedures must be instituted, such as time-order forms to begin and end any program or announcement schedule. The traffic director also must keep sales informed of upcoming availabilities so they may be sold to advertisers, while also carefully following the advertising time limitations adopted by the station.

Programming and sales also work closely with the continuity department, which is responsible for written copy to be delivered over the station. This copy includes locally produced commercial and public service announcements, as well as other program scripts.

Programming and Promotion

Decisions as to what programs need promotion and how this should be done bring the program director and persons in the promotion department together on a regular basis. Most stations use their own facility to promote up-coming programs and features. In addition, audience promotion may involve *TV Guide,* Sunday supplements and other newspaper ads, outdoor billboards, radio spots for TV shows, and television announcements for radio stations.

Competitive radio stations usually engage in audience participation contests and other on-air promotions to increase their audience share. Because these activities involve the on-air sound and image of the station, the program director usually takes a prominent role in designing and executing them. In this regard, the program director and the promotion manager must understand fully the purpose of the promotion. Is the station saying "thank you" to its audience? Or is it generating excitement? They must recognize that only a small percentage of a station's audience will participate actively in a contest, but if the activity is structured to be entertaining, nonparticipants may also enjoy it.

The program director, along with others involved in building station promotions, should be constantly on the lookout for ways to give away prizes entertainingly. They must also make sure that any promotion campaign involving prizes conforms to federal lottery statutes and the stipulations of the audience measurement services. Generally speaking, the latter require published disclosure of any unusual audience promotion contests broadcast during ratings periods. The lottery laws forbid the broadcasting of any contest, advertising, or other kind of message which involves three specific elements—prize, chance, and consideration. Thus, a promotion that awards a prize and involves a drawing or some other form of chance is legal only if the participants are not required to make a purchase or engage in any other activity that might be defined as "consideration."

The program director also must make sure any contest is compatible with the station's image and format and that it is compatible with the prize offered.

Programming and Engineering

The program director and the engineering staff must cooperate effectively because of the importance of the technical sound of the radio station and the sound and visual quality of the TV signal. When listeners choose between radio stations of the same generic format, for example, the technical superiority of one station's sound over the other may play a major role in determining their share of listenership. Other matters to be coordinated include jurisdiction over and responsibility for equipment, ordering of remote lines, and setting up schedules for maintenance and performance checks.

The program director needs to develop a strong and positive relationship with the station's chief engineer so their two units can provide the audience with quality program production and transmission. This relationship can be enhanced if the PD insists that all programming personnel treat the technical and recording equipment with respect.

In stations which employ members of labor unions, the job divisions between production, talent, and engineering staffs are usually very clearly delineated. At the networks and among most large market stations, only members of the engineering union may operate a station's control equipment. Production members, under a union contract, usually handle the studio equipment, such as cameras, lights, and microphones. Only stagehands move props and sets, and lighting engineers manipulate TV lighting instruments. In highly unionized radio stations, announcers seldom operate any equipment.

In some unionized stations, however, there is greater staff flexibility. For example, while engineers operate the control equipment, announcers may be permitted to handle turntables and cartridge tape decks, as well as to turn their own microphones on and off. Disc jockeys usually prefer this approach because they are able to achieve tighter production on their shows.

Total flexibility for the use of staff, of course, prevails among nonunionized stations. These include the vast majority of secondary and small market radio and television outlets in the United States.

Regardless of the arrangement, it is vital that the program director and the chief engineer have an understanding as to how job responsibilities are divided and that both strive together to utilize their staffs as effectively and efficiently as possible.

Programming and News/Public Affairs

Although news and public affairs frequently are handled by a separate department, this unit (or these units) is a major supplier of program material. Included are regular newscasts, public affairs programs, and special events. Whether news is an independent unit or part of the program department, a close working relationship is necessary. For example, every station should have a policy in force to indicate when, and under what conditions, the news director may authorize an interruption or preemption of regular programming for bulletins, newsbreaks, or special events coverage.

COMMUNITY RELATIONSHIPS

The program director occupies a unique position in a station in that his/her department most prominently represents the station to the community. Through its programming, the station attracts and holds its audience and projects its image or personality. Thus, the loyalty a station enjoys in its community results almost directly from the caliber of its program service.

To succeed in building public acceptance for a station, the program director should attempt diligently to *know the community.* Knowledge of its people, their demographics, their interests, tastes, habits, and mores, all give the PD a needed insight into the public for whom he/she programs and for whom the programming decisions are made. While statistical data are available from various sources, nothing can replace personal involvement as a means of understanding a community. Many program directors, therefore, make it a special point to become involved through community activities and civic and religious organizations.

Practically every station has at least an occasional local live broadcast, and the trend is growing as competition for audience increases. This is especially apparent in television, where new technologies have made additional services possible. Furthermore, every community, large or small, contains some talented people who could be attracted for appearances in local programs. These persons may be discovered in such places as schools and colleges and from among local musical and theatrical groups. An alert program director tries to become aware of the community's talent resources which can be tapped for programming needs.

Being aware of one's competition is another facet of understanding the local broadcast market. The program director should monitor and analyze the competitive stations regularly. The competitive situation changes frequently, particularly as changes are made in response to audience measurement studies. The PD should be alert to the strengths and weaknesses of each competitor and even role play the programming of each. This kind of competitive analysis can be conducted through monitoring, either live or on a taped basis, as well as by studying the audience rating reports.

Finally, the program director must remember that a broadcast station is licensed to *serve* its community. In a broad sense, everything transmitted should serve the public in some way. However, in a narrow sense, the licensee is obligated to help the community by focusing attention on its problems and needs, by publicizing worthwhile activities of noncommercial organizations, and by supporting projects that promise to benefit the community to which the station is licensed. In summary, a station should be a positive force for the betterment of its service area.

Broadcasting is truly a service business. While public service programming is obligatory, we must also remember that profits usually relate closely to the level of service a station performs. Any opportunity to assist the community, therefore, should be regarded by management as an opportunity to demonstrate the persuasive power of the station. And that opportunity can facilitate greater use of the station as an advertising medium, which is important in fulfilling a second legitimate station goal—earning a profit on the stockholders' investment.

THE PROGRAM DIRECTOR: AN OVERVIEW

Being a program director, in a sense, is much like holding several jobs at the same time. It is a multifaceted job which calls for a mature person with such traits as good judgment, common sense, an insight into the behavior of people, an understanding of show business, and a sense of humor. Program directors must be effective as administrators, coordinators, problem solvers, production supervisors, creative originators, public relations representatives, promoters, and as team members. Program directors usually are on call 24 hours a day. And, occasionally, they have an opportunity to advance to the top management position in a station. Needless to say, the program director's job is always challenging.

Students interested in the remunerative aspects of broadcast jobs should note that program directors usually rank third in compensation among station executives, based upon national salary studies of broadcast executives. In 1982, for example, typical TV program directors earned about $40,000 annually. Radio PD's earn considerably less on the average. It is encouraging, however, that program directors rank only behind general managers and sales managers, both of whom are directly involved with the revenue and fiscal aspects of the station. Thus, the ever-demanding job of program director brings moderately high financial rewards, at least by broadcast industry standards, as well as job satisfaction, to its holder.

RADIO PROGRAMMING IMPLEMENTATION

In many broadcast stations, especially in small radio operations, the program director's job includes *implementing* as well as *planning* the programming. However, the usual pattern in medium and large stations involves delegation of the daily operational details to a production or operations manager. Because this division of responsibilities is typical among the more sophisticated stations, our discussion will follow the plan of delegated production management.

THE PRODUCTION MANAGER

The radio production manager is the station's expert producer, or presentation specialist, whose duties usually include scheduling air personalitites, producing commercials and other announcements, and orchestrating the station's on-air sound. This person is assisted mainly by a music director and the announcing staff. In most radio stations, news and public affairs programs are produced in a separate department.

The production manager must be totally familiar with the station's programming, its production facilities, and its production and talent staff. He/she must understand management's goals and attitudes and how they relate to the station's expected sound. Production details must be mastered, including timing specifications of network schedules, syndicated shows, and play-by-play sports which originate outside the station. Cost analysis of proposed productions takes the production manager into the financial side of broadcasting. Finally, the operations chief must see that all production personnel are trained in the proper operation of equipment, that the on-air talent follow station guidelines, and that the on-air product closely corresponds with the sound and image desired by management. A modern automated radio production facility is shown in Figure 4.4.

Radio format execution begins with an understanding of the target audience the station's management wishes to attract—both demographically and in terms of psychographics or "lifestyle." It also must take into account the "tools" available to create the station's sound, including personalities, music, features, network schedules, and current events. The production manager also must understand the methodologies of the various audience measurement services and how to positively affect their research findings through music rotation strategies and other programming techniques.

Among the numerous duties involved in implementing a radio format are (1) talent coaching and direction; (2) music selection and controls, which are usually coordinated between the production manager and the music director; (3) continuity preparation, including commercial, public service, and promotion announcements and talk material for disc jockeys and talk show hosts; (4) preproduction of on-air material; and (5) acting as a "first sergeant" to maintain quality control over the station's sound.

Talent Coaching

Coaching the announcing staff—the disc jockeys and newscasters—is essential if a station is to have a cohesive sound bonded to the image management wishes to impart to the public in general and its regular listeners in particular. No announcer should ever be allowed to go on the air until he/she understands the desired sound and the intricacies of the station's format. Frequent performance reviews by the production manager with each individual performer help to maintain the desired style of presentation.

Alan W. Anderson of WIOD/WAIA, Miami, Florida, described his approach for critiqueing the on-air staff as follows:

> At least once every two months (more frequently directly before and during a rating period), I schedule a meeting with each of our on-air talents and review a

Figure 4.4 A modern automated radio production system, used in the on-air operation of WSB-FM, Atlanta

Courtesy of Cox Communications, Inc.

> recent hour of their show. I will have taped it (without their knowledge), and we will listen to it together. This scheduled critique session is not intended to be solely a fault-finding meeting. Again, the good elements within the hour are recognized as positives. The negatives are discussed (at times "explained" by the talent), and an alternate approach is suggested. It is a give-and-take session, concluded by a brief discussion of just where we're at as a station, and what we have upcoming.
>
> I listen to suggestions not only about their individual shows, but the station as a whole, and indeed will act upon them if I feel them to be valid. If not, I'll tell them why. A written summary of the meeting is then prepared and furnished the talent. In the case of the WIOD personalities, these critique sessions are held directly *after* the personality's show, and not before. For A1A talent (WAIA), we listen to an entire day's prerecorded "bits," at a mutually convenient time.[2]

Since log keeping is usually assigned to the on-air announcing staff, the production manager also must make sure all operating personnel can keep program logs properly in accordance with FCC rules and station policy. As a follow-up he/she must establish a system for checking each daily program log for possible corrections or omissions. When corrections or additions are necessary, the signed-on operator must make them. If program logs are kept by automation, the production manager must make sure all prerecorded programming broadcast by automation is properly and accurately encoded.

Music Selection and Control

Production responsibilities relative to musical programming will be discussed in the next section under the music director's responsibilities. Keep in mind, though, that the production manager also may be the music director and that, in any case, close liaison must be maintained between these two persons.

Continuity Preparation

The term *continuity* refers to the written material prepared for delivery in a broadcast station. It includes commercial messages, as well as public service announcements for nonprofit organizations and promotion spots for the station itself.

Many advertising and public service messages reach local stations fully produced by their sponsors or agencies. In these instances, the recorded messages only need to be scheduled. In some cases, however, the continuity department may add an announcer's tagline to indicate where the product may be purchased or to localize a public service announcement to achieve greater impact. Similarly, network affiliates may use preproduced promotion announcements about network shows they carry. Despite the trend toward outside preparation of continuity materials, radio stations usually maintain a copy department to write local nonagency commercials and to assist in promotion and public service efforts.

In addition, some stations provide their air talent—both disc jockeys and talk show hosts—with daily "prep sheets" from which they may select subject matter for each day's broadcasts. Such "prep" materials, which may require considerable research, often include informative features, humorous items, and other topical content. The use of such original incidental material, however, may give the station a unique and more professional sound. This approach also helps maintain a unified point of view or focus in the station's programming.

Because advertising copy is the principal written product (outside of news) in a radio station, the continuity department sometimes is attached to the sales unit rather than to production or programming. Nevertheless, because of the overlapping of responsibilities, a close relationship must exist between the continuity writing staff and both sales and production personnel.

Preproduction of On-Air Material

At most stations, it is common practice to produce much of the commercial material in advance to reduce the demand for live copy announcing and to insure quality delivery of each message. This preproduction work requires expertise in tape editing as well as the capability to work with music and sound effects. The production manager, as suggested previously, must work closely with the writer who prepared a commercial to produce the most suitable final product for the client.

The production manager also assists local public service organizations in producing their PSA messages. In addition, the production manager must produce the station's own promotion announcements and decide which station jingles, sounders, and production music will be used. The production manager also may work closely with the program director in the creation of on-air promotional contests.

On-Air Quality Control

The quality of a station's sound is a constant concern of the production manager. In this regard, alertness to the smoothness of production by the on-air staff, as well as to possible problems of distortion and frequency response, and methods of enhancing the station's sound through audio processing techniques, is a must. The production manager's task in this area becomes easier with a strong, positive relationship with the station's chief engineer.

Both the production manager and the program director in today's highly competitive radio industry must constantly be aware of the quality of the on-air product. Thus, as part of the station's quality control procedures, they must monitor the station critically to provide the talent and production staff with proper guidance and direction.

One program/production manager, Alan W. Anderson of WIOD/WAIA (FM), Miami, explained his monitoring approach as follows.

> I listen to the station(s) as much as possible during a given week, both while at work and at home. I do make it a point to *listen to everyone* within the course of a week. Rarely will I go running into the Control Room to complain about a specific incident, unless we are in violation of some legal mandate, or there is a chance of the same "negative" occurring immediately. Typically I will make note of my negative criticism, and following a personality's shift, talk with him or her about it. At the same time, I will make mention of the "positives" as well. In that way, we amplify and rely more on our strengths, while at the same time [we] eliminate the weaknesses.[3]

Listening to one's own programming product without either becoming too critical or too blasé is very difficult. A second operations director, B.C. Davis of WHIO Radio, Dayton, Ohio, suggests listening with "intelligence" for tone, content, and error trends, even though this is difficult to do.

> Announcers are human and, like all of us, make mistakes. Those little things aren't the problem. What you should listen for is gradual sloppiness across the broadcast day, or one particular announcer who always makes mistakes. These are mechanical things which are easily corrected. What I listen for is content and not so much technique. Anyone can run a tight board, but only a good communicator can put together a package that has meaningful content that makes sense and is listenable.[4]

Davis continued with specific criteria to help in monitoring one's station:

> Humor in the right places, and not humor for humor sake. Is the pace too up or too down? Should the pace always be the same? Is our news, talk and information really meaningful? Is the flow disjointed or do we sound slick? Do we cross promo ourselves too much or not enough? And above all, are we "comfortable"? These are the questions I always ask myself. But the last question, I

> believe, is the bottom line, the missing ingredient of a good station being a great station. "Comfortable" flows from your air personalities, the content, and from the audio chain. "Uncomfortable" from any one of these parts and you have a problem.[5]

Stations that use automation devices for their on-air production present a special case of quality control that is quite different from a "live" operation. Automation systems in present use range from home-made units to ultrasophisticated production models. These systems vary widely in their complexity and their capabilities. Whatever the system, it is usually one of the production manager's responsibilities to coordinate the production and encoding cues with basic program scheduling and logging systems and to maintain quality control of all cartridge tape materials.

Finally, the production manager should strive for close, professional relationships among all members of the production and talent staffs. Successful production operations generally result from a collective team effort in which the various individuals work professionally together.

THE MUSIC DIRECTOR

Music occupies more radio time than any other single programming element. Consequently, except for the limited number of all-news and all-talk stations, music represents a very significant portion of a station's programming effort. It is the program director's responsibilitiy to conceive the station's sound and, with management's concurrence, to have it implemented on the air. In addition to selecting and developing a format, the music responsibility involves establishing a universe of music, which may consist of only one or of several categories of selections, the evaluation of new selections from which additions to the universe are made, and the development of a music rotation plan.

Although the program director is deeply involved in format decisions, many stations have a *music director* to coordinate the station's music. This person usually serves as the first-line contact with record promoters, securing the needed music product for the station. The music director also auditions and screens all selections before accepting them for air presentation and works closely with the program director in determining the station's music emphases and its rotation plan.

Music trends and the popularity of individual selections are very important programming criteria. The music director must determine often what new music should be added as well as what selections are to be deleted from a station's music universe. That decision usually is based on trade press information on how well a particular title or artist is doing nationally, local station research on the appeal of a particular selection being considered, and information on whether the proposed selection has been exposed in the market and, if so, how well it has been received as measured by record sales and telephone requests. The final determining factor as to exactly what new product is added is its "texture." Specifically, does the selection fit with and enhance the station's on-air sound? It must have the right feel about it, which is an artistic judgment to be made by the music director or program director.

Such publications as *Billboard, Variety,* the *Gavin Report, Broadcasting,* and *Radio and Records* devote sections to current music to assist stations with their music programming. As suggested above, additional insight into local music preferences also can prove rewarding to stations that try to lead rather than follow the trends. For this reason, the ability to design and conduct music research has become an increasingly important consideration in hiring music directors.

Although some successful radio stations allow their announcers a great amount of latitude in choosing and sequencing music, the trend is toward greater control of the music by management to maintain the desired station sound.

There are many systems for music control throughout the radio industry. Typically, however, once the music universe has been established in a "controlled playlist" (music discipline) station, a programming assistant schedules the selections for the on-air talent to play each day. (In other stations, rotating card systems and other control variations have been devised.) Scheduling of music is done in such a way as to achieve the desired variety of artists and tempos, as well as to achieve optimum rotation of selections.

The amount of rotation, or repeat performance of a given selection, varies greatly with the type of format. A popular music station builds its listenership because of frequent repetition of current hits, while a classical or easy-listening station usually minimizes repetition in favor of playing a broad spectrum of their types of music.

With respect to rotation on a popular music station, some selections, particularly the most popular ones, are usually rotated much more frequently than others in the universe. A rotation plan also may be modified during different hours of the day to emphasize the type of music that is most appealing to the demographically available audience.

The music director should review the station's music list daily and also should monitor the station closely to be sure the announcers adhere to the playlist and the rotation plan. One method used to control the music is to transfer records to cartridge tapes. Under this plan, turntables usually are removed from the control room so only preselected "cart" tapes can be broadcast on the station.

The typical music director also supervises the record storage and filing system as well as the music control system used to minimize error in airplay by station personalities.

Further details on music programming, including format development, will be given in chapter 8 on radio programming.

TV PROGRAMMING IMPLEMENTATION

Program implementation in television is much more complicated than in radio because of the simultaneous coordination of sight and sound production. A TV production necessarily involves such elements as live talent, camera operation in the studio, set design, graphics and other art work, film/video tape material, and sound. While radio production often is a simple one-person effort, television requires teamwork by a larger group of talent and production people. However, live or taped production represents only a small percentage of the air time of most TV stations.

Some TV program directors actively direct their production operations as well as their departmental duties. They do so usually because of a desire to maintain personal control of programming until it leaves the station or because of budget restraints. However, because production details are so time consuming, most PD's delegate the operational details to a production manager. His/her supporting personnel usually include the film/VTR director, an art director, and possibly a studio manager.

In Figure 4.5, we see a TV control and editing facility at Metromedia Square, a major television production center in Hollywood. Many network shows are produced at this facility.

Figure 4.5 A computerized television control room at Metromedia Square, Hollywood, used for editing network productions

Courtesy of Metromedia, Inc.

THE TV PRODUCTION MANAGER

The typical television production manager's duties are quite broad, including responsibility for all on-air and studio activity, as well as for staff, props, sets, and supplies. In short, the production manager is responsible for getting all of the station's programs on the air attractively and smoothly produced and within the allocated production budget.

The following are among the production manager's principal duties:

1. Responsibility for managing the production staff. Specific duties include recruiting, hiring, training, and scheduling personnel, based on the station's production requirements.
2. Responsibility for the on-air appearance of the station. The principal focus is the station's master control room, where switching takes place between network, syndicated, and prerecorded programs and announcements—just as the program signal is sent to the transmitter for broadcast to the public. The production manager must monitor the on-air operation regularly to insure a polished performance with a minimum of errors. He/she also follows up all discrepancy reports (notations of operational problems and mistakes) to prevent recurring errors.
3. Responsibility for studio management, including the scheduling of live and video-taped sessions. This duty also includes responsibility for the operation and appearance of the studios, announcer's booth, and other production facilities. The production manager also handles billing and other paperwork details related to studio and production services.
4. Supervision of the studio crew. The production manager administers the schedule and work assignments of the floor manager, studio camera operators, lighting technicians, utility men, and other crew members.
5. Supervision of all directors and producers in the organization, scripting, formatting, and production of local programs and announcements. This duty usually includes overall responsibility for creating commercials and copy for the local sales department and public service announcements for nonprofit agencies.
6. Supervision of the film department, which handles all filmed and taped program materials. The film/VTR director's duties are outlined in the next section of this chapter.
7. Supervision of the art department, which designs and paints all sets and produces graphics for local programs and announcements. This department also provides a wide range of on-air and print media graphics for the news, sales, and promotion departments. (In some larger stations, the art department may come under a creative services department.)
8. Responsibility for keeping the general manager aware of technical advances in production equipment and for making recommendations regarding new equipment to keep the station competitive in its production capabilities.

In summary, the TV production manager is an administrator of people and other resources. As in radio, this person should be an expert producer who is thoroughly familiar with the station's production facilities and talent resources. The production manager works with the program director in developing cost analyses of programs, as well as with the sales and promotion departments in producing commercial material and creative on-air messages for the station itself. It should be obvious that the creative success of a TV station, both in the aesthetic and commercial contexts, depends greatly upon how well the production manager's duties are carried out.

THE FILM/VTR DIRECTOR

The film/video tape operation is a crucial and busy center in a television station. This unit, headed by the Film Director or Film/VTR Director, is responsible for handling all film and video-taped program and announcement materials, including movies, syndicated shows, and commercial and public service announcements.

These are among the specific responsibilities of the Film/VTR Director and the staff of editors and librarians.

1. Booking, scheduling, and record keeping to keep track of the film/VTR programs, their runs, and the expiration date for each item purchased.
2. Screening movies to see that they meet the station's standards, then marking appropriate cuts for commercials and other breaks.
3. Maintaining a standby library for emergency film purposes as well as a current library of promotion excerpts for movies under contract.
4. Shipping and receiving films and tapes and necessary related record keeping. Typically, many film products are forwarded after their use to the next station on a routing list. Such a "bicycle" system reduces shipping costs, but its success depends upon careful expediting at each station involved. Increasingly, delivery of commercial material and syndicated shows is being accomplished via communication satellites which transmit the material from its point of origin to receiving equipment at local stations for video taping.
5. Responsibility for other film/VTR reports as the station requires. Examples include a film product inventory report, a film cost report, a monthly film schedule, and a usage report for program distributors.
6. Finally, authenticating the film billing records prior to approval for payment to program distributors. This form generally must be approved by the production manager and/or the PD also before it is sent to the accounting office for payment.

OTHER PRODUCTION UNIT MANAGERS

In addition to the Film/VTR Director, there may be other unit managers who schedule and supervise personnel in the production area. These second-level managers usually include the art department head, continuity director, studio manager, and chief announcer.

SPECIAL COMMUNITY LIAISON

The importance of strong ties with a station's community cannot be overemphasized. We have noted previously the desirability of close relationships between the program director and community groups. However, limited hours and extensive demands often preclude the optimum level of involvement by the program director. This problem has been handled by many large stations through the addition to their staffs of community affairs and/or public service directors. Because of their potential contributions, both to their stations and their communitites, we shall include here a brief description of the two relatively new positions.

THE DIRECTOR OF COMMUNITY AFFAIRS

Community affairs directors usually are delegated considerable, but not complete, responsibility for coordinating the station's activities in and for the community. The purpose is to maintain and strengthen the station's total community involvement.

Typical duties of a community affairs director include the following.

1. Participating in community activities and reporting community attitudes to station management. Special attention usually is given to minority and grass-roots activities.
2. Coordinating educational and religious programming.
3. Contributing ideas for news coverage and general interest programming.
4. Developing, producing, and/or directing special interest programming.
5. Making speeches to civic and community groups and assisting groups that request help in disseminating information through the media. However, all department heads are usually involved in these activities.
6. Assisting in the preparation of license-renewal applications and supervising the ascertainment of community needs and interests.

THE PUBLIC SERVICE DIRECTOR

While community affairs directors work with and for community groups on behalf of a station, many stations also designate someone specifically to handle their public service activities. Admittedly, public service and community affairs activities may overlap. However, a slight distinction should be noted: the community affairs director is primarily a conduit between the station and the community, while the public service director concentrates directly on the station's public service programming.

As discussed in our chapter on FCC regulation, each broadcast licensee is expected to support the worthwhile service activities of its community with public service announcements and other free programming. Consequently, there are heavy demands for the time which can be allocated for public service. Thus, the public service director becomes the arbitrator of public service time and the facilitator of its effective use.

Duties of a public service director, then, include the following.

1. Representing the station in all matters pertaining to local public service—such as attending regular or called meetings of nonprofit agencies that seek media exposure for their activities.
2. Developing PSA campaigns for service-oriented community organizations. This often involves preproduction meetings with representatives of the groups, advising them on ways to communicate their messages effectively, and producing the announcements accordingly. The public service director, of course, refers situations requiring decisions beyond his/her authority to the station's management.
3. Determining the allotment of time granted to the various campaigns and agencies, since few stations can accommodate all public service requests. Complete records are kept on all such activities on behalf of public service organizations.
4. Seeking adequate opportunities for public service programming/announcements to satisfy the station's responsibility under its broadcast license.
5. Supervising the screening and scheduling of all PSA material received from outside the station. A large amount of local and national public service material comes to an average station without any prior contact. It is the public service director's job to analyze each such campaign to determine if it merits air time. In some cases, unsolicited announcements are too general and lack appeal to a station's local audience. These materials sometimes may be localized or otherwise improved in presentation if they are to be used on the air.

SUMMARY

The success of a radio or TV station depends greatly upon how effectively the program department functions in meeting its responsibilitites. These responsibilities, all of which are fulfilled through the station's programming activities, fall into four basic categories: (1) attracting an audience, (2) serving the audience's needs as perceived by management and as pledged to the FCC, (3) creating a positive station image, and (4) creating, through programming, an effective advertising medium. These four objectives are truly inseparable; however, the first three are essential if the fourth goal is to be attained.

Putting all of the program elements together in a way that will achieve commercial as well as artistic success is one of the most challenging, as well as rewarding, responsibilities of the program director. To create an artistic success without being commercially successful is relatively easy, but commercial success without artistic integrity is difficult. However, to create and maintain an artistically as well as a commercially successful station operation is the most difficult of all. That, of course, is the prime goal of broadcasting. It is a challenge that taxes the capabilities of any dedicated program director. And that's also where an effective working relationship with the station's other department heads, especially sales, is vitally important.

Our next chapter will take us into audience considerations, where we will examine recent audience trends, usage patterns of radio and television, audience composition, attention levels, program selection patterns, and audience research. Stay tuned!

ENDNOTES

1. The management team, in addition to the general manager, includes the sales manager, program director, chief engineer, and business manager. Other key staff members who may be part of this team include the promotion manager, production manager, and the news director.
2. Personal correspondence between Alan W. Anderson, WIOD/WAIA Program/Production Manager, and Michael S. Kievman, February 8, 1980.
3. *Ibid.*
4. Personal correspondence between B.C. Davis, WHIO Radio Operations Director, and Michael S. Kievman. Undated.
5. *Ibid.*

STUDY QUESTIONS

1. Contact the program director of a nearby radio or television station for an appointment to conduct an interview. During the interview, you should try to learn (a) how the station is organized, (b) the extent of the program director's administrative duties, (c) the extent of his/her operational duties, and (d) his/her approach to competitive programming, public service, and community relations. Your instructor may wish to assign some class members to radio program directors and others to television program personnel.
2. Discuss the similarities and differences between the jobs of program director and production manager in television and between program director and operations manager in radio.
3. Contact local radio stations to determine who chooses the music played on the station and how this is done.
4. We have learned that the program department functions closely with several other station departments. Which of these other departments do you think involves the greatest amount of coordination with programming? You might attempt to confirm your answer by contacting a local program director.
5. The means of delivery of program material from networks, syndication sources, and advertising agencies has undergone several changes during recent years. Find out how and why these changes have taken place.

SUGGESTED READINGS

Coleman, Howard W. *Case Studies in Broadcast Management: Radio and Television.* Rev. ed. New York: Hastings House, 1978.

Dessart, George. *Television in the Real World: A Case Study Course in Broadcast Management.* New York: Hastings House, 1978.

Fisher, Michael G. *A Survey of Selected Television Station Program Managers: Their Backgrounds and Perceptions of Role.* M.A. thesis. Temple University, 1978.

Johnson, Joseph S., and Kenneth Jones. *Modern Radio Station Practices.* Belmont, Calif.: Wadsworth Publishing, 1972.

Koenig, A.E., ed. *Broadcasting and Bargaining*. Madison: University of Wisconsin Press, 1970.

Quaal, Ward L., and James A. Brown. *Broadcast Management: Radio, Television*. 2d ed. New York: Hastings House, 1976.

Radio Program Department Handbook: A Basic Guide for the Program Director of a Smaller Operation. Washington, D.C.: National Association of Broadcasters.

The Radio Code. Washington, D.C.: National Association of Broadcasters, January 1980.

The Television Code. Washington, D.C.: National Association of Broadcasters, January 1980.

5

BROADCASTING'S NEAR UNIVERSAL AUDIENCE

The two broadcast media—radio and television—attract vast audiences through their programming efforts. Many decades ago this attraction propelled both of the electronic media to near universal acceptance by the US public. While radio and TV exert a powerful audience appeal, the audience itself is very complex. It is both a mass audience and a mosaic of audience subsets. Understanding the characteristics of the broadcast audience from a behavioral perspective is necessary if one is to program a station or network successfully.

Overall listening and viewing levels usually follow very predictable daily and seasonal patterns. However, the popularity of specific programs constantly fluctuates because of vigorous efforts by competing stations and networks to win large audience shares. Because reliable audience data are needed to guide in program decision making, a vast amount of expensive research is conducted annually. The same research also is used widely by advertisers and agencies in buying media.

In this chapter, you will find a discussion of the general characteristics of the radio and television audience—the potential audience for which broadcasters compete. The chapter also will explore the topic of audience research, which is vital today in developing schedules and formats appropriate for attracting target audiences.

THE UNIVERSALITY OF BROADCASTING

The potential audience of the broadcast media is virtually the entire population of the United States. At the beginning of 1981, the Radio Advertising Bureau (RAB) estimated that 99 percent of all US households owned at least one radio set in working order and that 77 percent have four or more working sets.[1] On the same date, television's household penetration stood at 98 percent.[2] Few, if any, other items are as universal in our society as are radio and TV sets.

Let's explore the set-ownership figures further. The RAB reports that in 1981 Americans owned an estimated 457,000,000 radio receivers of all types, including 114,000,000 sets in automobiles.[3] With annual radio set sales averaging nearly 50,000,000, the average American household owns an astounding 5.5 radio receivers.

In addition to the dramatic increase in set ownership overall, perhaps the most significant trend has been made in the sale of FM receivers. RAB now estimates that 84 percent of all radios sold each year are equipped with FM as well as AM tuners.[4] A significant increase in FM-equipped automobiles represented a major breakthrough for the frequency modulation service during the 1970s. It was certainly one reason that FM made significant gains in total listenership during that decade.

With the proliferation of receivers per household and the adoption of a more personal style of programming, radio listening patterns have changed dramatically. No longer the principal home entertainment medium, radio has evolved into a companion, used almost entirely by individuals as opposed to groups of listeners. Figure 5.1 shows the location of America's 339,000,000 in-home radios, based on RAB projections.

In addition to the home market, radio has emerged strongly in offices and business establishments, barns and fields (via farm tractors), in resort areas, and most important of all, in 95 percent of all of the automobiles in the country.[5] The slogan, "Wherever you go, there's radio," aptly describes the reach of the aural medium to which millions listen in every imaginable location. The pervasiveness and mobility of radio have opened vast opportunities for service, programming, and advertising. For example, timely traffic reports during morning and afternoon drive time represent a valuable service that only radio can provide.

Returning to television now, there has been steady growth in both color and multiple-set households during the past decade. The latter development undoubtedly has enlarged the total amount of viewing by permitting individual selection of programming by different family members. Although this

Figure 5.1 Where Home Radios Are Located

Bedroom	159,135,000
Living Room	60,946,000
Kitchen	47,402,000
Den/Playroom	20,315,000
All Other Rooms	50,788,000
TOTAL	338,586,000

Source: Radio Advertising Bureau, 1981.

trend parallels the companionship use of radio, television still attracts large numbers of family groups. As of January 1, 1981, the A.C. Nielsen Co. estimated that 85 percent of all US homes had at least one color receiver and that 51 percent had two or more TV sets.[6] Figure 5.2 shows graphically the growth of TV set ownership from 1950 to 1980.

Television ownership, which was nearly 82,000,000 households at the begining of 1982, is at a near universal level in all sections of the United States and at all economic levels in society. Indeed, the nation's TV households mirror the characteristics of American society. Set *usage,* however, does vary somewhat with economic status. Figure 5.3 shows the hourly patterns of television viewing per week by household characteristics. Note also that cable-subscribing households, which numbered more than 22,000,000 at the beginning of 1982, view about seven hours a week more than the noncable homes.

RADIO AND TELEVISION SET USAGE

The previous section depicted the potential audience for the broadcast media in terms of its universality. In practical programming, however, the program manager and program producers must understand the complexities of audience behavior in much greater detail. To what extent, for example, is the vast *potential* audience converted into *actual* listenership and viewership? What are the *characteristics* of the actual audience? And how can specific target groups be reached? In this section we will attempt to answer these questions through a discussion of overall listening and viewing levels, including average daily set usage, daily audience patterns, seasonal variations, AM and FM shares, and audience composition.

DAILY LISTENING/VIEWING LEVELS

Americans spend a suprisingly large amount of time each day with radio and television. The A.C. Nielsen Company, the Arbitron Company, and other audience research services confirm that the level of viewing by an average family has risen steadily since 1950, when television began to emerge as the principal home entertainment source. Today, on an average throughout the year, a typical family watches TV about six and one-half hours each day.[7]

With the growth of television in the 1950s, the public began to devote less of its leisure time to radio. However, by the end of that decade, in-home listening stabilized at slightly under two hours per day per family. While that level of in-home listening has persisted to the present, out-of-home listening has increased dramatically. In 1981, according to the RAB, adults 18 years of age and older tuned in an average of three hours and 27 minutes per day, including both in-home and out-of-home listening.[8]

It's quite obvious that few activities occupy as much of the time of contemporary Americans as do television and radio. The programmer's challenge, of course, is to capture as much of that time as possible for his/her station through imaginative programming concepts and techniques.

Figure 5.2 The Growth of Television Receivership: 1950–1980

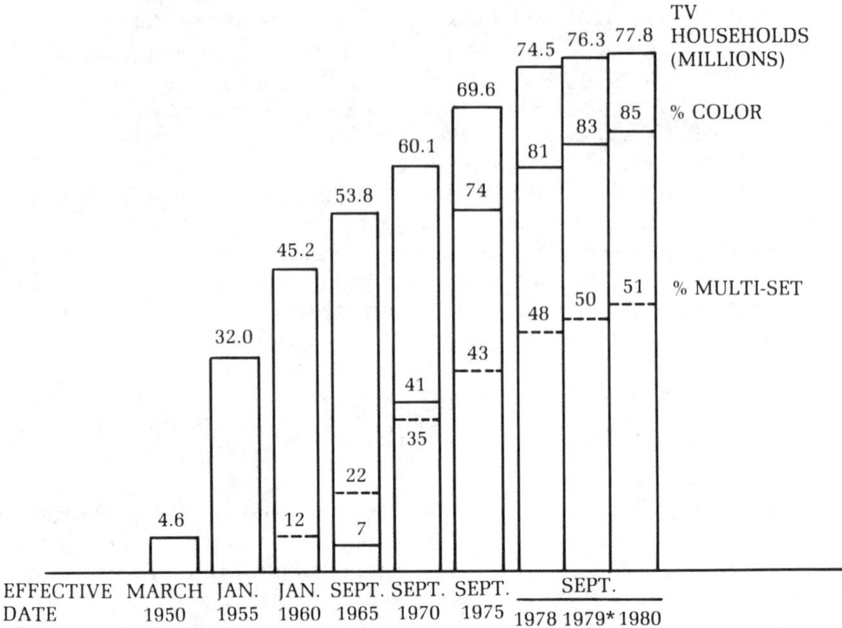

TV OWNERSHIP: U.S. CENSUS 1950–70; NIELSEN ESTIMATES 1975–80
COLOR: ARF CENSUS 1965; NIELSEN ESTIMATES 1970–80
MULTI-SET: U.S. CENSUS 1960–65; NIELSEN ESTIMATES 1970–80
*AS OF 1979, ESTIMATES BASED ON JAN. 1 OF FOLLOWING YEAR, EFFECTIVE IN SEPTEMBER
Courtesy of The A.C. Nielsen Co.

HIGH PREDICTABILITY IN DAILY AUDIENCE PATTERNS

Highly predictable patterns of daily radio and TV usage prevail, reflecting the composite lifestyles of the public. These patterns indicate extensive use of both media, with the amount of usage per person determined by accessibility to each medium, as well as the attractiveness of TV and radio as competitors with each other and with other leisure-time pursuits. Listening and viewing patterns now strongly suggest a complementary relationship between the two electronic media, with each having both high and low audience periods daily.

Figure 5.4 shows the daily audience patterns for both radio and television. The chart clearly reveals television's dominance during the evening hours and radio's strength during the daytime. Radio achieves its highest audience levels between 6:00 and 10:00 AM, after which in-home listening drops off. The decline progresses slowly through the afternoon, then falls off sharply following the afternoon "drive time." Afterwards, radio's audience declines to its lowest level during the evening (prime-time television) hours.

Although TV's audience trails that of radio until early afternoon, viewership increases throughout the day. It rises sharply in the late afternoon when students and workers return home. Television enjoys substantial viewing dur-

Figure 5.3 Hours of TV Usage Per Week By Household Characteristics Monday–Sunday 24-Hour Total

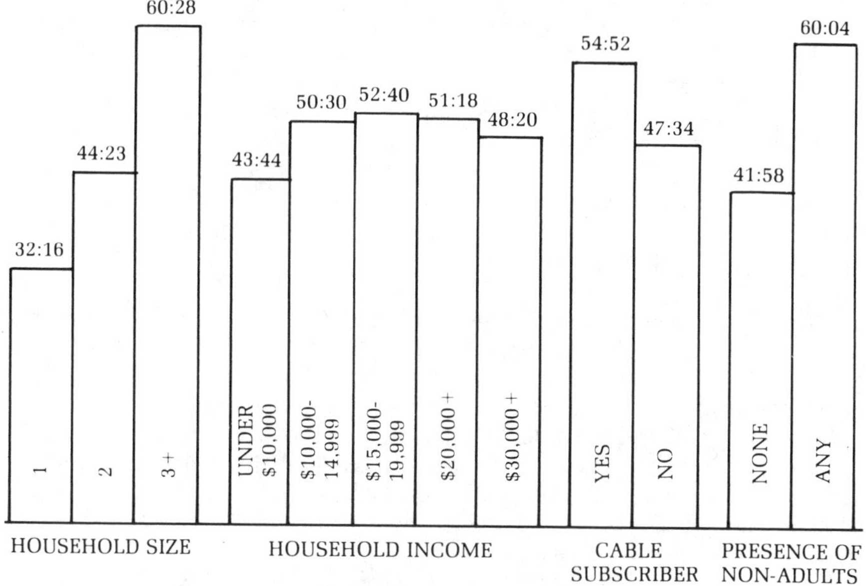

NEILSEN ESTIMATES: NATIONAL AUDIENCE DEMOGRAPHICS REPORT, NOVEMBER 1980

Courtesy of The A.C. Nielsen Co.

Figure 5.4 Daily Radio and TV Audience Patterns

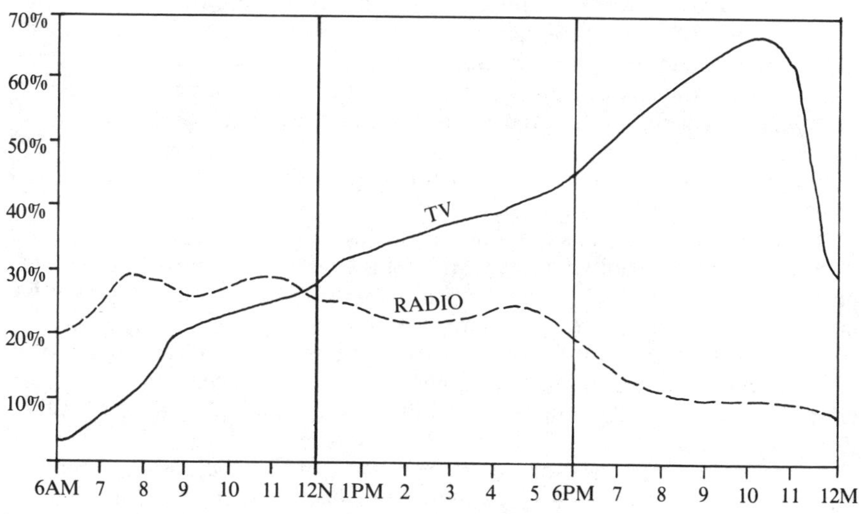

Sources: A.C. Nielsen Co. and the Radio Advertising Bureau.

ing the early evening when most stations offer network and local newscasts. However, TV attracts its greatest audience, often 60 percent or more of all households, during the evening prime-time period, when the networks provide three hours of high-budget programming. As viewers retire, television's audience levels gradually decline, then drop off sharply by 11:30 PM, following the late newscasts.

Despite the fact that both TV and radio have their respective prime hours, an audience is always present. For this reason, most stations attempt to identify the available audience and serve it as effectively as possible, even during hours of low media usage.

SEASONAL VARIATIONS

The amount of viewing per household cited previously (six and one-half hours daily) reflects the year-round average for TV households throughout the United States. In practice, however, the time devoted to television varies considerably on a seasonal basis and to some degree on a regional basis.

Did you ever stop to think about what is TV's strongest competitor? It isn't radio, nor is it the movies or newspapers. In reality, television gets its stiffest competition from out-of-door activities such as golf, tennis, picnicking, camping, and driving! Therefore, both the weather and the seasons influence the amount of viewing each of us does.

Viewing of television programs is at its highest during the winter, when daylight hours are short and outside activities are curtailed by darkness and poor weather. On the other hand, viewing is lightest during the spring and summer months, when the longer daylight hours and usually pleasant weather permit us to enjoy the outdoors until 9:00 or 10:00 in the evening.

The peak months for TV viewing are November through March, with viewing levels at their annual zenith during January. Then average household viewing declines steadily through the spring season, reaching the annual low during July. In general, the summer viewing audience is only about three-fourths as large as it is in the winter. During the low season, the networks and local stations typically program reruns and other less costly replacement shows to compensate for the smaller potential audience and advertising revenue. With the end of summer and the beginning of the new TV season in September, viewing levels reverse again, rising toward the peak fall-winter season.

Not only is seasonality evident in total viewing hours, its effect also is reflected in the level of viewing during various parts of the day. As Figure 5.5 reveals, seasonal variations are minimal during the morning and early afternoon hours, but are quite noticeable during the late afternoon and in the evening. It is very significant that the peak viewing hours occur progressively later in the evening as summer approaches.

In addition to seasonal factors, television usage levels are influenced to a lesser degree by local and regional climatic conditions. During the winter, for example, viewing tends to be heaviest in northern regions and lightest in the deep South.

Although seasonal variations are characteristic of television usage, in-home radio listening remains relatively stable throughout the year. Radio listenership actually increases, however, during the summer season, when millions of

Figure 5.5 Seasonal Variation In Percentage of TV Households Using Television

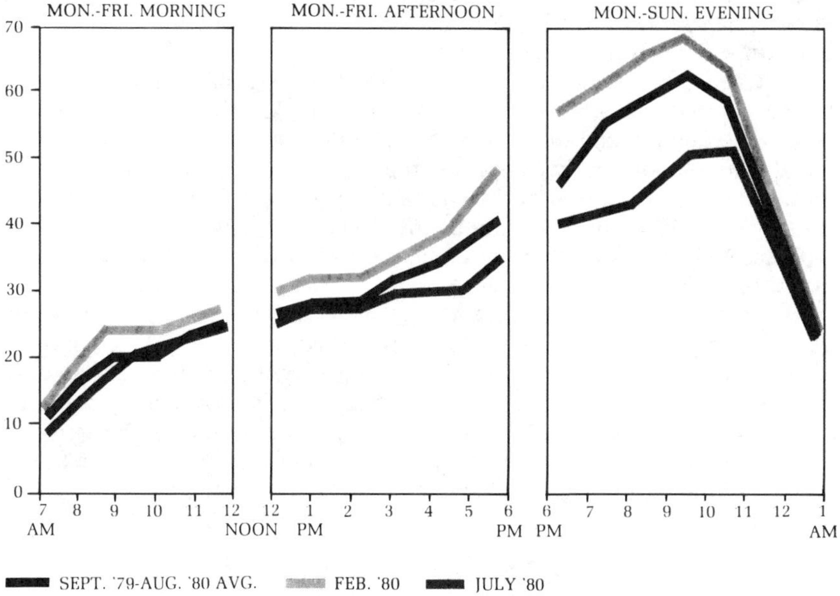

SEPT. '79-AUG. '80 AVG. FEB. '80 JULY '80

NIELSEN ESTIMATES–TOTAL U.S. N.Y. TIME, EXCEPT N.Y.T. + 3 HOURS IN PACIFIC TERRITORY

Courtesy of The A.C. Nielsen Co.

automobile radios and portable sets are used extensively by out-of-home listeners.

FROM AM TO FM: A MAJOR LISTENING SHIFT

Traditionally, AM has been the dominant radio service. However, a significant shift toward FM appeared in the late 1970s. By 1980, FM's share of audience surpassed that of AM radio in the nation's combined metropolitan communities. According to Arbitron data published in *American Radio* by James Duncan, Jr., FM accounted for 57.35 percent of all radio listening in the measured metropolitan (SMSA) markets of the United States during the spring of 1981.[9] That figure represents a whopping gain of 40.6 percent over FM's share (40.8 percent) five years earlier.

According to the same source, FM radio attracts more than 66 percent of the listening in 25 metropolitan markets. The highest was registered in Greenville-New Bern, North Carolina, at 85.6 percent. On the ADI market basis, the 60 percent figure is exceeded in 20 markets. Interestingly, the nation's capitol led all ADI markets in FM listening at 74.6 percent. Furthermore, eight of the top ten stations in Washington were FM outlets. FM percentages for spring 1981 in other selected markets were as follows: Charlotte, 71.7 percent; Atlanta and Houston, 70.0 percent; Indianapolis, 67.9 percent; Detroit,

66.8 percent; Philadelphia, 66.5 percent; Boston, New Orleans, and Cleveland, 62.3 percent; and San Diego, 61.6 percent. In contrast, some of the largest cities barely exceeded 50 percent. These included Los Angeles, 55.0 percent; San Francisco, 54.2 percent; New York and Chicago, 53.0 percent; and Minneapolis-St.Paul, 51.6 percent.[10]

The recent gains made by FM reflect a fundamental change in radio broadcasting. The once-laggard medium has benefitted greatly from increased set sales, especially in automobiles; superior sound quality; and stereophonic sound transmission. Perhaps equally important was the FCC's action to discourage the duplication of AM programming on commonly owned FM outlets. As a result, many FM stations introduced attractive and often unique programming. As its listenership grew, the FM service blossomed into a full spectrum of formats.

As the growth of FM continues, AM broadcasters must seek innovative ways to compete. One which has been advocated widely is AM stereophonic broadcasting. Greater emphasis on talk and information is another approach taken by many AM outlets. Although there is cause for some pessimism, especially for low-power urban AM stations, few industry leaders write off the AM service. High-powered outlets, especially those on clear channels, should continue to provide a valuable service well into the future.

AUDIENCE COMPOSITION

Audience composition refers to the demographic make-up of the television or radio audience at any given time or for any particular program. Audience composition data tell us the proportions of men, women, and children within the audience, as well as their age characteristics. Since each program is unique in its audience attraction, the program manager would be well advised to study the data available from various research organizations for an understanding of individual programs or formats under consideration. Obviously, the type of program chosen should match well with the available audience and/or the target audience at each point in a station's schedule.

In turn, the program manager must understand that the demographic make-up of the audience at any given time is influenced greatly by the nature of the *available audience.* This audience is limited largely by work and school schedules and competing leisure pursuits. For television, it represents those persons who are at home or in public places where sets are located. For radio, the available audience is greater, since it includes those persons who are in radio-equipped automobiles and those with portable receivers, as well as individuals at home. In addition, many persons listen to radio at work; however, few can enjoy television under working conditions. Both radio and TV, of course, can reach large heterogeneous audiences during evening hours and on weekends, while the available daytime audience is heavily weighted toward homemakers, preschool children, and retireees.

THE TELEVISION AUDIENCE: LADIES FIRST

As a general rule, adult women watch television more than men, and older women tend to do more viewing than younger ones. As shown in Figure 5.6,

Figure 5.6 Television Viewing By Demographic Groups

HOURS: MINUTES PER WEEK	DISTRIBUTION OF HOURS IN WEEK	TOTAL PERSONS 2+	WOMEN 18-34	WOMEN 35-54	WOMEN 55+	MEN 18-34	MEN 35-54	MEN 55+	TEENS FEMALE	TEENS MALE	CHILDREN 6-11	CHILDREN 2-5
	168:00	29:46	29:44	33:31	38:26	25:24	27:28	35:39	22:19	23:40	25:44	29:14
REMAINDER	36%	12%	12%	12%	12%	12%	12%	11%	8%	10%	11%	17%
MON.-SUN. 11PM-1AM	8%	8%	9%	10%	8%	12%	11%	9%	7%	9%	2%	1%
SAT. 1-8PM SUN. 1-7PM	8%	12%	10%	10%	10%	15%	16%	14%	11%	14%	13%	10%
SAT. & SUN. 7AM-1PM	7%	5%	4%	3%	3%	5%	4%	3%	5%	7%	12%	12%
MON.-FRI. 10AM-4:30PM	19%	14%	19%	18%	19%	8%	6%	11%	16%	7%	10%	20%
MON.-FRI. 4:30-7:30PM	9%	16%	13%	14%	17%	13%	14%	18%	18%	15%	21%	21%
MON.-SAT. 8-11PM SUN. 7-11PM	13%	33%	33%	33%	31%	35%	37%	34%	35%	38%	31%	19%

NIELSEN ESTIMATES, NATIONAL AUDIENCE DEMOGRAPHICS REPORT, NOVEMBER 1980

Courtesy of The A.C. Nielsen Co.

women over the age of 55 watch TV the most, while female teens are the lightest viewing group. Not only do women dominate the daytime audience, they also outnumber men as viewers of nighttime programs of all types except sports. Young women, the most prized target audience of consumer advertisers, are attracted by TV programming in large numbers, both during the daytime and evening hours.

During the evening hours, TV's viewership comes closest to being a representative cross-section of society. According to Nielsen data, more than 92,000,000 people watched television during an average prime-time minute during the fall of 1980. As Figure 5.7 shows, Sunday evening wins the largest audience of the week, while Thursday represents the low point. In terms of specific time periods, the 8:30 to 9:00 PM slot attains the highest prime-time audience level, with 10:30 to 11:00 being the lowest.

Not only does TV reach a large mass audience during prime time, it also reaches selected target groups effectively during certain time periods. Daytime hours are especially useful for reaching homemakers. Similarly, children tune in on a large scale on Saturday mornings and during late weekday afternoons. Finally, the adult male, TV's most elusive audience, may be reached as part of prime time's mass viewership, but in more concentrated numbers during news and sports programs. Both programming decision makers and advertising media buyers are guided in their scheduling activities by these viewership patterns.

Figure 5.7 Viewing Patterns During Prime Time (Average Minute)

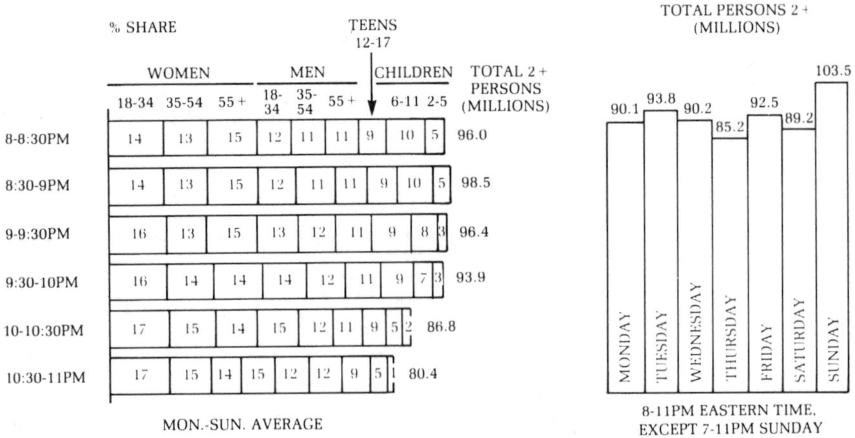

NOVEMBER 1980, EXCLUDING UNUSUAL DAYS

Courtesy of The A.C. Nielsen Co.

THE RADIO AUDIENCE: A DIFFERENT MIXTURE

In contrast to television, radio listening is much more evenly balanced between men and women. However, listening patterns often differ markedly among various individual stations. According to the Radio Advertising Bureau, men above the age of 18 listen an average of 3 hours and 26 minutes daily, while women tune in for 3 hours and 28 minutes. Listening levels also are higher among young adults (18 to 34 years of age) of both sexes than among persons over age 50. And in another contrast with television, radio is used extensively by teenagers, who represent a significant segment of the total audience. During the school year, of course, teens listen most during afterschool hours and on weekends.

During the daytime, when radio's audience is at its highest, adult women outnumber men by an approximate ratio of 1.5 to 1. The ratio approaches 1 to 1 during afternoon drive time, when commuting men, as well as working women, have greater access to radio. Males generally outnumber females in radio's audience during the evening hours. This results, in part, from the heavy programming of sports by many stations and the strong appeal of rock music to young men.

AUDIENCE CONCENTRATION VS. FRAGMENTATION

In another comparison, let's note that fewer TV stations vie for the viewing audience than radio stations for the listening audience. According to the A.C. Nielsen Co., an estimated 97 percent of all US households can pick up at least four usable television signals, and 71 percent can get at least seven stations.[11] However, the number of radio signals available in markets of all sizes far exceeds the number of TV sources.

This situation, however, may not hold true by the arrival of the 1990s. The number of TV stations continues to grow, particularly independent and subscription outlets. Super stations and nonbroadcast networks are rapidly filling the capacities of cable systems—even those with 40 or more channels. Some research studies during 1981-82 indeed show significant audience shares being registered by certain pay cable programming services. Furthermore, nonbroadcast programming available on video tapes and disc records also is proliferating. At this time, however, relatively little fragmentation takes place within the TV audience *as compared with radio*. Achieving a 50 percent or greater share of audience, therefore, sometimes occurs among major TV stations during their weekly schedules.

In contrast, because of the proliferation of licensees, few radio stations in the entire United States attract audience shares above 25 percent. Only nine did so during April-May 1981, and only 37 stations in all of the SMSA areas achieved shares of 20 percent or more during the same survey period.[12] In fact, the leading stations in most large cities rarely attain shares higher than 12 percent. This high fragmentation of the audience has forced radio broadcasters to choose niches in their markets and to program directly to those demographic or other special interest audiences.

WHAT ABOUT ATTENTION LEVELS?

Advertisers justifiably are concerned about the amount of attention viewers and listeners give to their commercial messages. Television's power to compel attention is well documented. However, additional research is needed to understand the degree to which various types of programs command attention. It is widely accepted, for example, that viewers pay more attention to evening programs than those in the daytime because of different viewing circumstances. Housewives who watch daytime TV often engage simultaneously in their housework or other activities. Therefore, some daytime "viewing" consists of listening to TV's audio, much like a radio, while glancing occasionally toward the television set. Evening viewing, in contrast, tends to involve people more fully because they are less likely to be preoccupied.

One of the advantages promoted on behalf of radio is the fact that listeners can use this medium while performing other activities. By its very nature, therefore, radio's attention levels are lower than those of television. However, since radio programming varies from background music to foreground information, it's obvious that attention levels vary, perhaps significantly, between types of formats.

THE CONSTANTLY CHANGING AUDIENCE

Although it may sound self-contradictory, change is constant within the broadcast audience. The reason? The society to which broadcasters program is *dynamic*. Population trends always develop slowly, but long-term implications must be contemplated.

Each 10 years, the federal census is taken to determine the official population count for states, counties, and cities. These tabulations yield a vast amount of socioeconomic and demographic data that should be considered by program managers as they determine what to broadcast and what audience or audiences they should seek.

Among long-term national trends at this writing is the decline of the youth market and the corresponding increase in the adult and elderly population groups. These overall trends, however, may be accelerated in certain markets, while the opposite trend may prevail in others. Demographic changes within the available audience, whether national network or local station, must be considered. In short, successful broadcasters seek to know the characteristics of their potential audience and attempt to identify significant trends in their early stages so as to position the stations for maximum service and commercial potential.

WHAT INFLUENCES AUDIENCE SIZE?

A number of factors influence the size of audience attracted to any given station or program. Among these factors are:

1. The number of stations competing for audience in the market;

2. The strength and reliability of the broadcast signals;
3. The strength of the appeals provided by the specific program or format in comparison with those on competing stations;
4. The general popularity of the station carrying the program;
5. The popularity of the preceding program and the extent of audience carry-over; and
6. Which member of the family is likely to select the program in most homes at the time of broadcast.

Concepts of program building and scheduling, fundamentally based on several of these factors, will be discussed in chapters 6, 7, and 8. However, it's appropriate at this point to note *how* individuals select programs and formats and that both psychological insight and intuition are needed by those who schedule programs for the public's choosing.

In general, individuals select programs in three distinct ways, which we shall call (1) carry-over, (2) dial twisting, and (3) deliberate choice.

CARRY-OVER SELECTION

Many people, once they have chosen their initial program during a viewing session, leave the set tuned to the same channel for an extended period of time. These "carry-over" viewers are easily retained as long as the successive programs satisfy them. Thus, if there is no compelling reason (a tune-out factor) to change the dial, subsequent programs benefit from the lead-in provided by the preceding show. Audience carry-over is the principal rationale for "block" programming.

DIAL-TWISTING BEHAVIOR

The selection process of turning the dial occurs when the key selector in a household is not especially interested in any program known to be scheduled at a given hour. It also occurs when a program following one that has just been watched does not "grab" sufficient interest. The selector typically tunes across different channels in search of an interesting program. The sampling process continues until one of three events takes place: (1) an attractive program is discovered; (2) the least objectionable program (LOP) is chosen; or (3) the set is turned off.

Because dial twisting typically occurs most frequently at the beginning of program periods, program producers are keenly aware that the first three to five minutes of any program are crucial. As we shall discuss in chapter 6, a strong start is an important factor in developing a successful program.

DELIBERATE SELECTION

This third form of program selection, which is the most sophisticated approach, occurs when a viewer has made a mental note to watch or listen to a particular program at a specific time. It may be a special that has been touted through on-air promotion, newspaper advertising, or a favorable mention in

TV Guide or a newspaper's program log. It also may be a favored program whose scheduled time has become fixed in the person's mind. Testifying to broadcasting's impact on the public, millions of individual viewers and listeners habitually plan their daily routines so they will not miss their favorite programs.

In radio, listeners typically choose stations deliberately through their past knowledge of station formats. Listening habits are reinforced as individuals continue to be satisfied with a radio program service.

For both radio and televison, consistent scheduling and promotion are very important in developing deliberate choice viewing or listening behavior.

RESEARCHING THE AUDIENCE: IT'S BIG BUSINESS!

The American broadcasting system provides the public with daily entertainment, information, and service of immense value. In turn, the vast audience that tunes in represents billions of dollars worth of sales opportunities for advertisers, their agencies, networks and stations, program producers, and other groups that participate in these electronic media. As the broadcasting industry has expanded and as expenditures for programming and advertising have risen dramatically, pressure has grown for sophisticated audience measurement.

Today's audience studies bear little resemblance to the earliest attempts at analyzing radio listening, which consisted mainly of counting fan mail attracted by various programs during the 1920s. Audience measurement since then has been elevated to a science, relying upon widely accepted statistical procedures and computerized data processing.

A later section of this chapter will focus on the major research organizations currently serving the broadcasting industry. However, the two most prominent firms must be noted here. The A.C. Nielsen Company provides both national network and local market TV audience studies on a regular basis. The Arbitron Company concentrates on market-by-market studies for both television and radio. Nielsen is particularly well known for its weekly network ratings and "overnight" studies in New York, Chicago, and Los Angeles. Moreover, both Nielsen and Arbitron conduct concurrent market-by-market national "sweeps" to measure viewing behavior throughout the country.

The fact that ratings play such a prominent role in the selection and scheduling of programs attests to the acceptance of audience research. However, program ratings should be regarded as only one of several helpful indicators for analyzing programming. When used correctly, audience measurement studies are valuable tools for both program managers and advertisers.

HOW IS AUDIENCE MEASUREMENT DONE?

Modern audience research essentially relies on the concept of statistical inference, which permits the estimation of characteristics of a population (such as all TV households in an area) from data obtained by sampling a cross-section of the population being measured. When a sample is carefully selected, following valid statistical procedures, the information gained may be projected confidently to the total population.

Although methods vary somewhat among research organizations, all audience measurement involves three distinct steps: (1) selecting the sample, (2) gathering the data, and (3) processing the data.

SAMPLING PROCEDURES

The ideal form of audience research would include information on viewing or listening behavior for every household in the market. However, economic and logistical constraints prohibit such a universal *census*. Instead, audience researchers obtain data on audience behavior from *sample* households selected systematically to represent the whole of the population being measured.

Although broadcast ratings are sometimes criticized because of their relatively small samples, there is ample evidence to support the usefulness and reliability of sampling techniques. For example, statistical projections on voting intentions usually compare favorably with actual vote tabulations. And in many less sophisticated ways, individuals base everyday decisions on sampling techniques. What housewife, for example, has not tasted the food she prepared to determine if more seasoning is needed? Likewise, farmers test the nutrients in their fields through soil sampling, and physicians take samples of body fluids for diagnostic purposes.

Obviously, to permit the projection of sample data to larger populations, a sample must accurately reflect the universe or population it represents. Such representativeness of samples used in audience research is determined by two factors: (1) sources of information on populations and (2) the method used to draw samples from such listings.

Commonly used population listings include telephone directories, the US census data on housing, and household mailing lists prepared by direct mail firms. Naturally, the adequacy of any population catalog depends upon how accurately and completely it lists and locates the population it purports to include. Because it excludes both nonphone homes and nonlisted telephone households, the telephone directory has obvious limitations. These may be overcome, however, by selection through "random digit dialing" rather than from the directory itself. Tables of random numbers are frequently used to gain access to all telephone households rather than only those whose numbers are published.

The selection of respondents for an audience survey may be accomplished by random choice or by means of a structured "quota" sample approach. In random sampling, each household within a universe has an equal chance of being selected, which, on an overall basis, tends to produce a highly representative sample. In contrast, quota samples prescribe representative proportions of persons in such categories as age, sex, education, urban/rural residency, and socioeconomic status. Specific respondents within such quotas, however, still may be selected through random processes. The principal advantage of the quota system is the assurance that all significant elements within a population are represented in proportion to their numbers.

Sample Size

Whereas representation of a sample is mainly a function of sampling procedure, the precision of results largely depends upon sample size. The more precision one needs, the larger the sample should be. However, below a certain size, the results become too subject to error; above a certain point, it becomes unproductive to increase the number. Researchers must decide how much sampling error they are willing to tolerate in view of the costs for conducting research surveys.

Audience research organizations generally seek to maintain sample bases which produce credible information, subject to acceptable error tolerance. This practical decision results in a sound economic balance in terms of the purpose of the research and the cost involved. Although there are exceptions, most individual market audience studies are based on samples involving 500 to 1,500 respondents.

DATA GATHERING

Methods used to obtain listening and viewing data from sample households are among the most critical factors in producing reliable audience data. Four techniques commonly employed include (1) metering devices, (2) the diary method, (3) personal interviews, and (4) telephone surveys. A fifth approach, mail surveys, is used in rare instances. Each of these methods has both advantages and disadvantages. Since no technique is perfect, sometimes two or more are combined to produce more reliable research.

Metering Devices

Metering devices are monitoring instruments that can be attached to a receiving set to record its usage. Typified by the Nielsen Company's "Audimeter," such devices silently and automatically measure all set usage in a constant sample of homes. Information stored in electronic memory banks consists of exact times when each receiver is turned on and off, how long it stays on the channel first tuned, and all subsequent channel switching.

Modern metering devices are usually connected via special telephone lines to a central computer which dials each unit periodically, retrieves the stored information, and tabulates the results. By placing recorders in a cross-section of homes, detailed and highly accurate information on all set usage may be obtained. This provides the basis for sets-in-use data, program ratings, share-of-audience, and homes reached.

Despite their accuracy, metering devices have certain inherent limitations. First, this method is very costly. For this reason, meters are used exclusively for network audience research and for "overnight" TV ratings in a few large cities.

Second, since such devices measure only *tuning,* rather than viewership, a question arises as to validity. How many sets are turned on, but not watched? Third, such devices are incapable of providing audience composition data. Therefore, to compensate for this deficiency, research services generally supplement recorder data with audience composition information obtained by another method.

The Diary Method

Research organizations frequently obtain basic audience behavioral and composition data by placing diaries (viewing or listening logs) in a sample of cooperating households in which family members agree to keep a record of all their television or radio usage. Diaries are especially useful in obtaining data on audience composition, as well as raw information needed to compute program ratings, shares, and total size. The diary method also is reasonably fast and economical.

On the negative side, diary research is only as reliable as the respondents who list their set usage. A second problem is that family members may become extremely conscious of their viewing and listening and, consequently, not follow their usual behavioral patterns. One diary keeper, for example, told this writer that she watched the news more than usual during the logging period because it was important to show her interest in current events. In such cases, program selections may become artificial and viewing/listening levels may become inflated. Some research firms disregard the first week of a diary to reduce this possiblity, using only data from later weeks when respondents have become more accustomed to keeping the logs.

The A.C. Nielsen Company uses the diary method to obtain data for its network ratings as a supplement to its metered households, Nielsen also employs the diary system for its local TV market studies. Arbitron uses the diary system for both radio and television studies. In Figure 5.8, you will see a sample Arbitron radio diary form.

The Personal Interview

The personal interview is another acceptable technique for gathering audience data. Face-to-face interviews, usually conducted in the homes of respondents, are especially valuable for obtaining detailed information on viewing and listening, including use of out-of-home receivers. This method offers the greatest flexibility among survey methods and, unlike the metered systems and the diary approach, permits interviewers to probe in depth for opinions and other qualitative information on program choices.

Typically, personal interviews rely upon recalled information. Respondents usually are asked to recall their viewing and/or listening within the past 24 hours. To assist respondents, research firms may provide listings of shows broadcast during the period under study. Thus, "aided recall" has become a standard item in personal interviewing.

The Pulse, Inc., a long-time radio measurement service, was the principal user of this technique until the firm ceased operation in the late 1970s. One reason for its demise was the growing difficulty of persuading interviewers to work in certain urban neighborhoods because of fear and prejudice.

The Telephone Survey

The telephone survey method, pioneered during the early 1930s by the C.E. Hooper Co., is particularly useful for gathering data on viewing and listening

Figure 5.8 A Sample Arbitron Radio Diary Page

PLEASE START RECORDING YOUR LISTENING ON THE DATE SHOWN ON THE FRONT COVER.

THURSDAY								
TIME				**STATION**			**PLACE**	
CHECK (✓) AM or PM				FILL IN STATION "CALL LETTERS" (IF YOU DON'T KNOW THEM, FILL IN PROGRAM NAME OR DIAL SETTING)	CHECK ONE (✓)		CHECK ONE (✓)	
FROM —		TO —			AM	FM	AT HOME	AWAY FROM HOME (INCLUDING IN A CAR)
6:40	AM ✓ PM	7:30	AM ✓ PM	WWTM		✓	✓	
10:10	AM ✓ PM	NOW	AM PM ✓	PIERCE SHOW	✓			✓
4:45	AM PM ✓	6:30	AM PM ✓	WREF	✓			✓
6:30	AM PM ✓	8:30	AM PM ✓	WWAC	✓		✓	
10:50	AM PM ✓	MID	AM ✓ PM	88.1 ON THE DIAL		✓	✓	
	AM PM		AM PM					
	AM PM		AM PM					
	AM PM		AM PM					
	AM PM		AM PM					
	AM PM		AM PM					
	AM PM		AM PM					
	AM PM		AM PM					
	AM PM		AM PM					
	AM PM		AM PM					
PLEASE CHECK HERE ○ IF YOU DID NOT LISTEN TO RADIO TODAY.								

Each time you listen to the radio, please be sure to use a new line, and write in the station "call letters".

Courtesy of The Arbitron Company.

at the time calls are made. It is presumed that such "coincidental" data are less likely to contain errors than information produced on a recalled basis. Telephone surveys, however, may be used to obtain past information just as can personal interviews.

Since telephone interviewing may be done easily from one central location, this technique is faster and less expensive than face-to-face interviewing. Even when long-distance calling is involved, costs can be minimized through use of WATS (wide area telephone service) lines. Subject to certain limitations, therefore, telephone surveys can be used as a substitute for face-to-face questioning.

The telephone survey, however, has certain weaknesses. First, many individuals hesitate to answer questions asked over the telephone by an unknown interviewer. This hesitancy may become increasingly acute if the interviewer probes into family characteristics and program preferences. Also, the telephone method cannot be used for obtaining coincidental listening or viewing data during the early morning and late evening hours.

Unquestionably, however, the most serious problem lies in the fact that not everyone has a telephone. Even when random digit dialing is used to gain access to unlisted numbers, the sampling may underreport certain types of families, especially lower income urban dwellers. Thus, at best, telephone surveys measure only those households that subscribe to telephone service. Despite these limitations, telephone surveys may be used to advantage unless telephone ownership itself is a significant consideration.

DATA PROCESSING

The final step in producing quality audience research involves careful processing and tabulation of the raw audience data. With a flow of reliable information from carefully drawn sample households, the next step is processing the data through to its final, usually printed, form.

Data contained in diaries and interview forms first must be scrutinized for authenticity and procedural accuracy. The information then is coded by editors for computer processing. Data obtained by metering devices must be checked for technical malfunctions before entry into the computer for tabulation. Once data have been entered into the research computer, this information may be tabulated and analyzed in many different ways to reveal the patterns of audience behavior.

The major audience research services work with industry representatives on a continuing basis to improve their methodology. Minimum standards for broadcast research have been established by the Broadcast Rating Council, the agency which audits and accredits rating services. The BRC maintains offices at 420 Lexington Avenue, New York 10017.

TERMS USED IN AUDIENCE MEASUREMENT

Although each audience research service defines its own terms, and slight variations do exist, this section will present audience measurement definitions as they are generally used in the broadcast industry. We can divide the terminology into three categories: (1) terms that define survey areas geographically; (2) terms that express audience size; and (3) analytical terms.

SURVEY AREA TERMINOLOGY

Audience studies are conducted both on the national level and within individual markets. National program ratings, such as those produced for network TV programs by the Nielsen Television Index, reflect sampling throughout the 48 contiguous states. For local market studies, three designations are commonly used: (1) metropolitan areas (SMSA); (2) television market areas (ADI/DMA); and (3) total survey areas (TSA).

The Metropolitan ("Metro") Area

As defined by the US government's Office of Management and Budget, a metropolitan area consists of a central city and the urban area that surrounds it. Officially known as a Standard Metropolitan Statistical Area (SMSA), such an urban concentration consists of at least one city of 50,000 population or more, or two nearby cities with at least 50,000 population combined. The SMSA specifically includes the entire county in which the urban center is located, as well as adjacent counties which are integrated socially and economically with the central community into an urban complex.

In broadcast audience measurement, SMSA data are particularly useful when one is interested in audience patterns in the urban community, as opposed to the broader market areas which include additional rural counties beyond the SMSA.

The Television Market Area

Television stations normally provide regional coverage, transmitting signals that can be received at distances approaching 100 airline miles distant. Since TV signals often reach far beyond an urban area, the metro is inherently an inadequate definition for most television markets.

Although they differ slightly in their criteria, Nielsen and Arbitron have developed methods for delineating television market areas. In essence, both firms have identified each of the country's television markets geographically and exclusively on the basis of *preponderance of viewing*. What this means simply is that each county is attributed to the television city to which most of its viewing is directed. Thus, we have Nielsen's "Designated Market Areas" (DMA) and Arbitron's "Areas of Dominant Influence" (ADI). This concept is illustrated in Figure 5.9, showing the "Eastville" market, in which some 16 counties are included. In all of the designated counties, the Eastville stations are viewed more heavily than those from any other television city.

Since each county in the 48 contiguous states is designated as part of some TV market, the continental United States has been divided into about 240 geographical market areas. Interestingly, Arbitron uses its television ADI markets as geographical areas for measuring radio listening as well as television viewing. This standardization of radio markets with television facilitates market planning by advertisers. Arbitron also publishes radio audience reports on the metro basis.

The Total Survey Area

Under the ADI and DMA concepts, each county goes into one specific TV market. But what of the viewing within any given county to stations of *other* cities? While Arbitron and Nielsen have satisfactorily delineated arbitrary boundaries between TV communities, should stations not receive credit for

Figure 5.9 A Typical Television (DMA) Market Area

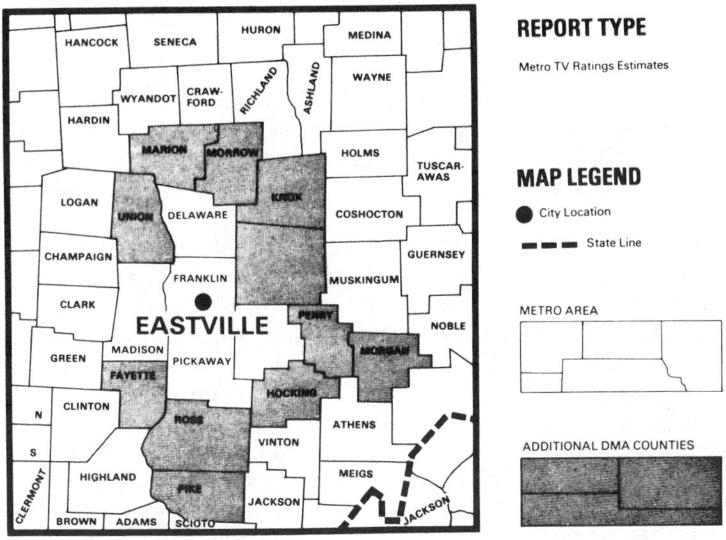

Courtesy of The A.C. Nielsen Co.

all of their viewership—even in counties where the audiences are small? Obviously, the answer is yes.

To provide total viewership information, these rating services also include numerical estimates of total station viewership regardless of where the viewing takes place. This total viewing information becomes increasingly important with the development of "super stations" such as WTBS-TV, Atlanta, and WGN-TV, Chicago. Total Survey Area (TSA) data include total households reached, total persons reached, and estimates of viewers for each program on the basis of the demographic categories of age and sex.

AUDIENCE DATA TERMINOLOGY

A second group of audience measurement terms is used to indicate the size of audiences for various stations and programs. These terms include *potential audience, households-using-television* and *sets-in-use* (radio), *share-of-audience,* and *program rating.* In addition, program and station audiences frequently are estimated in terms of their composition and their cumulative or unduplicated reach.

Potential Audience

The *potential audience* for any program, station, or network consists of all households equipped with receiving sets in the sampling area. Estimates of the potential audience for national network television are revised annually. For the 1981–1982 season, the A.C. Nielsen Company estimates the national audience potential at 81,937,250 households. Potential audiences for local TV markets vary with their populations and extent of set penetration.

Households-Using-Television

Households-Using-Television (HUT) is an estimate of the number of different households with at least one TV set turned on during any specific time period. Thus, HUT represents the total *available audience* at any given time. Conversely, those households not using television sets are automatically excluded from the HUT.

HUT is expressed as percentage of the total number of television households (TV HH) in a survey area, which may be the nation, an SMSA area, or an ADI or DMA television market. The concept of households-using-television is illustrated in Figure 5.10. In this example, with 500 of a possible 1,000 receivers in use, the HUT figure is 50 percent.

Sets-in-Use

The term *sets-in-use* (SIU) as used in radio surveys means precisely the same thing for radio that HUT designates for television. Sets-in-use represents the percentage of radio-equipped homes with one or more receivers turned on.

Share-of-Audience

In understanding share-of-audience, it is important first to remember that, at any given time, the *audience* consists of precisely those homes (or persons)

Figure 5.10 Audience Measurement Concepts: HUT, Share, and Rating

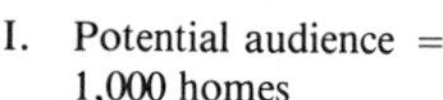
I. Potential audience = 1,000 homes

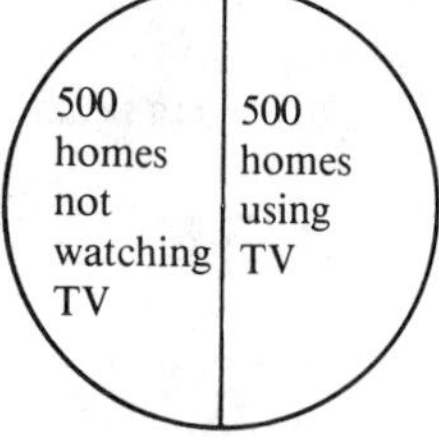

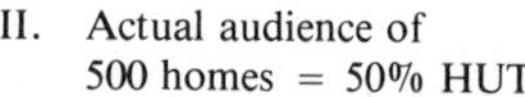
II. Actual audience of 500 homes = 50% HUT

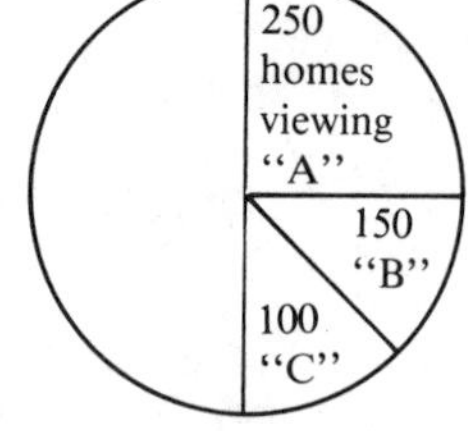

III. Station "A" is being watched in 250 homes, which = a 50% share of audience and a rating of 25

Station "B," watched in 150 homes, has a share of 30% and a rating of 15

Station "C," watched in 100 homes, has a share of 20% and a rating of 10 that are *using* their TV or radio receivers. Consequently, share-of-audience simply represents the percentage of those homes (HUT or SIU) that are tuned to a given program or station.

Referring again to Figure 5.10, if one-half of the households using television (½ × 500) are tuned to Station A, that station has a 50 percent share of the audience. Stations B and C have 30 percent and 20 percent shares respectively.

Share-of-audience percentages permit a comparison of the popularity of all programs broadcast at the *same* time. However, share data for programs broadcast at *different* times are not comparable because the size of the available audience (HUT or SIU) fluctuates widely throughout the day.

Program Ratings

By definition, a *rating* is the estimated percentage of the total potential audience which is tuned to a specific program or station. Since the potential audience remains constant (all homes equipped with TV or radio receivers in the market area), ratings for different programs can be compared regardless of time of broadcast, so long as the ratings are taken from the same audience survey.

Suppose two network shows have reported ratings of 20 each. It follows that an estimated 20 of every 100 homes nationwide viewed both programs. While their respective shares and demographic composition may differ, the estimated audience reach is identical.

A convenient formula for computing program ratings is RATING = SHARE × HUT. To illustrate, a program with a 50 percent share of audience during a 50 percent HUT period has a rating of 25.

RATING = 50% × 50%   RATING = 25

Although we speak of ratings in terms of "points," a rating is always *a percentage of the total potential audience.*

Each rating point has a stated value in numbers of households, always equalling one percent of the potential audience. Since there were about 82,000,000 TV households nationally during the 1981–1982 season, one rating point was valued at 820,000 homes (1% × 82,000,000). Similarly, in a local market having 600,000 TV households, one rating point represents 6,000 homes.

Cumulative Audience

Cumulative audience data ("cumes") indicate the number of different households or persons who tuned to a program at least once during a stated period of time. TV cumes, for example, are estimates of the number of different households that may have watched a five-day-a-week program *at least once* during the week. In radio, *cumulative persons* is used to indicate the number of different individuals who listened to a station at least once during a stated time frame. *Cume ratings* express the number of *different* persons (unduplicated audience) as a percentage of the population in the surveyed area.

"Cumes," which indicate the *reach* of TV programs and radio stations, are particularly useful when reach and frequency are important considerations in an advertiser's strategy.

ANALYTICAL TERMS

In addition to the terms discussed above, other concepts are employed to measure the extent and efficiency of advertising exposure across a campaign. Since programming is the foundation for developing a station into a successful advertising medium, we include here the analytical terms of *gross audience, gross rating points,* and *reach* and *frequency.*

Gross Audience

The *gross audience* of a program represents the total number of households (or persons) reached over a period of time, counting each household every time it chooses to watch/listen to the program. Whereas cumulative audience counts each viewing or listening unit only once (*unduplicated* audience reach), the gross audience figure indicates the total number of homes reached regardless of duplication.

The gross audience of a TV campaign may be tabulated by adding the estimated audience for each program used in the schedule. For example, if a client's schedule includes one message each day in a Monday-through-Friday newscast, the gross audience equals five times the *average* audience.

Gross Rating Points

With each rating point representing one percent of the potential audience, *gross rating points* (GRP) indicate the extent of reach of a campaign in rating terminology. A schedule that consists of 100 GRP's delivers an audience that is *equivalent to the population of the area surveyed.* However, the audience delivered is *not* 100 percent of the population because some persons were reached more than once, while others were not reached at all.

Gross rating points may be calculated on the same basis as gross audience. The number of rating points for each program on a client's schedule are counted each time the program appears in the schedule.

Reach and Frequency

The term *reach* usually indicates the number of *different* households (or persons) exposed to a particular program or message. A viewer needs to watch/listen only once to be counted in this number. Thus, *reach* is synonymous with cumulative audience.

Frequency refers to the average number of times each viewer or listener is reached by a particular program or message during a given period of time.

Some stations achieve broad reach through heavy turnover of listenership. Others, whose listeners stay tuned for longer listening spans, meet the needs of advertisers that need a high frequency of message repetition to the same audience.

Two types of radio formats which usually involve heavy audience turnover are all-news and top-40 music. In contrast, easy listening music and album rock stations tend to retain their audiences through longer periods of time. Certainly, audience turnover and listening span are important factors to be considered when format deliberations are underway.

AUDIENCE MEASUREMENT SERVICES

Radio audience measurement was undertaken on a systematic basis during the 1930s by an organization called Cooperative Analysis of Broadcasting and by Clark-Hooper, Inc. (later C.E. Hooper, Inc.). The CAB was formed by the Americal Association of Advertising Agencies and the Association of National Advertisers as an industry-supported organization. The famed "Hooperatings," which employed the telephone coincidental technique, were widely used in the radio industry during the 1930s and 1940s.

At present, two major and a number of lesser important research organizations produce audience studies for the broadcast industry. The A.C. Nielsen Company and the Arbitron Company are the major groups. Each provides data on a regular basis for a large number of markets, and Nielsen also specializes in network ratings. A third service known as "TvQ," produced by Marketing Evaluations, Inc., measures the degree of viewer enthusiasm for network programs.

Trendex, Inc. is one of several research companies that may be engaged for customized studies of viewing behavior. Other organizations which offer custom rather than routine audience research include (1) Media Statistics, Inc.; (2) Videodex, Inc.; (3) Burke Research, Inc.; and (4) Birch Research, Inc.

This section will explore the current services of the major research organizations.

A.C. NIELSEN COMPANY

The broadcast division of the A.C. Nielsen Company, Northbrook, Illinois, conducts national and local TV audience studies on a continuing basis. Nielsen's operation includes two units, the Nielsen Television Index (NTI) and the Nielsen Station Index (NSI). The former produces network program ratings and a variety of other national audience data, while the NSI supplies audience data (ratings, shares, and demographics) on local television markets, using diaries for data collection.

Data for NTI studies are gathered by means of the "Storage Instantaneous Audimeter"® (SIA), a monitoring instrument which silently records all TV set usage in sample homes on a minute-by-minute basis. The Audimeter stores information on set usage in its electronic memory. Each SIA unit is connected to a special telephone line which is dialed at least twice a day by Nielsen's computer. This computer retrieves the stored data, which are then correlated with program schedules to produce program ratings. The entire process is automatic and requires no work on the part of the sample households.

Because monitoring devices cannot obtain demographic data, Nielsen uses a diary system to obtain further information on audience composition. This specially designed diary is placed in a separate panel of households in which cooperating families log the programs watched. NTI's Audimeter draws information from a sample of about 1,170 households, while the diary sample includes more than 2,100 households. These households are selected through an area probability sampling technique, using the US census listings of all households in the country as a base. Each of the cooperating households is replaced over a five-year period, remaining in the sample long enough to provide continuity of information.

The Nielsen Station Index utilizes random selection of sample households from telephone directories except in the 14 largest markets, where the "total telephone frame" is used. In addition, NSI uses the NTI area probability samples in the three largest cities (where sample bases are large), in which data gathering is accomplished by a combination of monitoring device and diary.

After basic information from sample homes reaches Nielsen's central office, diaries and Audimeter recordings are examined closely to preserve the accuracy of the data in the processing and production operation. After passing inspection, the diary data are keyed directly into computers (which already contain Audimeter data). The final inspection involves checking completed data for internal consistency and verification of any unusual trends. The entire process from receipt of raw data to finished tabulations and reports is almost completely automatic.

Nielsen Television Index (NTI)

The Nielsen Television Index's best known publication is the "Nielsen National TV Ratings," usually called "The Pocketpiece" in the industry. This biweekly publication, which fits neatly into the vestpocket, provides the following information about the national TV audience:

1. Household audience estimates and rankings for sponsored network programs;
2. Audience composition estimates for a large array of age/sex characteristics;
3. Season-to-date averages of program audiences;
4. Average audience estimates for major types of programs;
5. Overall TV set usage data on a comparison basis with the previous year;
6. Television set usage by time periods.

Figure 5.11 reproduces sample information from "The Pocketpiece."

The Nielsen Television Index also provides a number of other, more specialized reports. These studies include: (1) Daily National Ratings; (2) Fast Weekly Household Ratings for all sponsored network programs; (3) Daily 70-Market Ratings, providing audience data for each network in some 70 markets where there is full competition among the three networks; and (4) Households and Persons Ranking Report, which shows the ranking, rating, and estimated audience of each network in terms of households and 15 demo-

Figure 5.11 Sample Nielsen National TV Ratings From The "Pocketpiece"

28 PROGRAM AUDIENCE ESTIMATES (Alphabetic) 2ND APR. 1981 REPORT

PROGRAM NAME / WK # / DAY / START TIME / DUR / NET / PROG. TYPE	T/C THIS SEASON	NO. OF STATIONS & PROGRAM COVERAGE WK 1	WK 2	KEY	HOUSEHOLD AUDIENCES AVG. AUD. %	SHARE %	AVG. AUD. (0,000)	TOTAL PERSONS (2+)	LADY OF HOUSE	WORKING WOM.	WOMEN TOTAL	WOMEN 18-34	WOMEN 18-49	WOMEN 25-54	WOMEN 35-64	WOMEN 55+	MEN TOTAL	MEN 18-34	MEN 18-49	MEN 25-54	MEN 35-64	MEN 55+	TEENS (12-17) TOTAL	TEENS FEM.	CHILDREN (2-11) TOTAL	CHILDREN 6-11
EVENING CONT'D																										
WALKING TALL	1		200	A	13.2	25	1027	1929	729	313	797	185^	432	439	453	296	727	252	401	342	375	243	230	97^	175^	108^
2 SAT. 10.00P 60 NBC OP			99	B	13.2	25	1027	1929	729	313	797	185	432	439	453	296	727	252	401	342	375	243	230	97	175	108
10.00 - 10.30				A	13.1	24	1019	1947	735	309	812	209^	446	436	445	302	738	247	403	358	395	250	207^	82^	190^	120^
10.30 - 11.00				A	13.4	26	1043	1882	712	311	769	158^	410	434	453	288	705	256	393	320	344	233	250	112^	158^	90^
WKRP IN CINCINNATI	23	189	168	A	12.3	23	957	1797	705	311	749	266	404	390	331	264	715	318	480	458	304	183	168	49^	165	82^
SAT. 8.00P 30 CBS CS		98	94	B	16.8	28	1307	1903	727	283	797	289	445	408	348	281	659	255	396	381	301	200	168	73	279	176
•LATE FRINGE																										
ABC NEWS:NIGHTLINE	61	190	191	A	7.6	24	591	1365	543	203	602	183	341	350	323	191	697	247	412	431	366	180	43^	25v	23v	17v
M-F 11.30P 30 ABC N		97	97	B	7.8	24	607	1376	594	205	642	178	338	341	358	233	671	228	374	354	340	224	51	18	12	LT
ABC WEEKEND REPORT-SAT.	27	173	172	A	8.0	17	622	1305	579	240	673	201	430	452	382	180^	481	104^	267	306	291	130^	103^	23v	48v	48v
SAT. 11.00P 15 ABC N		93	92	B	8.0	17	622	1488	640	258	700	255	436	399	353	209	596	228	369	327	286	182	111	59	81	65
ABC WEEKEND REPORT-SUN.	28	170	167	A	4.5	14	350	1343	575	249^	586	183^	394	371	357	141^	532	180^	388	306^	271^	112^	54v	LT	171^	115^
1 SUN. 11.00P 15 ABC N		93	93	B	5.4	13	420	1446	616	245	662	235	409	382	359	178	665	274	422	396	320	174	88	37	31	27
2 SUN. 12.31A 15																										
CBS SUNDAY NEWS-BRADLEY	30	129	130	A	7.1	15	552	1337	692	197^	733	150^	281	373	394	344	529	101^	188^	235	297	265	62^	62^	13v	13v
SUN. 11.00P 15 CBS N		71	71	B	8.1	17	630	1476	721	246	794	212	384	381	418	332	593	186	305	278	301	245	60	36	29	16
CHARLIE'S ANGELS-12.00	14	178	177	A	3.6	17	280	1150	579	158^	647	219^	301^	327^	310^	233^	418^	196^	261^	207^	168^	125^	60v	53v	25v	LT
THU. 12.00M 68 ABC PD		96	95	B	4.1	19	319	1059	459	163	509	204	283	259	250	161	460	166	273	252	228	154	77	46	LT	LT

WEEK 2		1	2	3	4	5	6	7	8	9	10	11	12	13	14	15	16
ABC TV	TOTAL AUDIENCE (Households (000) & %)			4,750 6.1				5,060 6.5									
	Program	← GOOD MORNING, AMERICA-730 (CO-OP) (PARTICIPATING) (S)(OP) →				← GOOD MORNING, AMERICA-830 (CO-OP) (PARTICIPATING) →											
	AVERAGE AUDIENCE (Households (000) & %)			3,730 4.8				4,200 5.4									
	SHARE OF AUDIENCE %			25				25									
	AVG. AUD. BY ¼ HR. %			4.8	4.7			5.4	5.4								
CBS TV	TOTAL AUDIENCE (Households (000) & %)	3,890 5.0				4,280 5.5								5,210 6.7		5,520 7.1	
	Program	← MORNING-CHARLES KURALT →				← CAPTAIN KANGAROO →								JEFFERSONS M-F		ALICE-M-F	
	AVERAGE AUDIENCE (Households (000) & %)	2,410 3.1	2.9*		3.3*	2,880 3.7	3.4*		4.0*					4,280 5.5		4,900 6.3	
	SHARE OF AUDIENCE %	18	19 *		17 *	17	16 *		18 *					25		29	
	AVG. AUD. BY ¼ HR %	2.7	3.2	3.3	3.4	3.2	3.7	3.9	4.0					5.3	5.7	6.1	6.5
NBC TV	TOTAL AUDIENCE (Households (000) & %)			4,980 6.4				5,210 6.7						2,880 3.7		3,660 4.7	
	Program	← TODAY SHOW-7.30AM (CO-OP) (PARTICIPATING) →				← TODAY SHOW-8.30AM (CO-OP) (PARTICIPATING) →								LAS VEGAS GAMBIT		BLOCKBUSTERS	
	AVERAGE AUDIENCE (Households (000) & %)			3,810 4.9				4,360 5.6						2,410 3.1		3,110 4.0	
	SHARE OF AUDIENCE %			26				25						14		19	
	AVG. AUD. BY ¼ HR. %			4.9	4.9			5.7	5.6					3.0	3.2	3.9	4.1
TV HOUSEHOLDS USING TV (See Def. 1)	WK. 1	13.7	16.4	18.4	19.6	21.2	22.1	22.4	22.1	21.3	20.9	20.8	20.6	19.9	19.5	19.0	18.8
	WK. 2	10.0	13.0	14.8	16.5	19.0	20.8	21.6	21.7	21.7	21.9	21.9	22.2	21.9	22.2	21.5	21.5

U.S. TV Households: 77,800,000

For explanation of symbols, See page A.

A-21

DAY MON.-FRI. APR.13-17, 1981

Courtesy of The A.C. Nielsen Co.

graphic categories. NTI also offers a number of nonscheduled reports and specialized custom services.

Nielsen Station Index (NSI)

The Nielsen Station Index provides individual stations and media buyers with a local measurement service comparable to NTI's national service. Currently NSI surveys TV audiences in more than 150 markets, providing at least three and up to eight audience studies (based on four-week periods) per year, depending upon the needs of the research clientele in the specific market. These reports, called "Viewers in Profile," include both metro and Designated Market Area ratings, total audiences, cumulative reach, and estimates of viewing over a wide range of demographic groups. Information is tabulated for each time period and program during the week, as well as summarized by parts of the day. A sample page from a local market "Viewers in Profile" is reproduced in Figure 5.12. Special customized studies also may be ordered for local markets from NSI.

THE ARBITRON COMPANY

The Arbitron Company, a subsidiary of the Control Data Corporation, engages in network and local research for both TV and radio. This organiza-

Figure 5.12 Sample Local Market TV Audience Report

FT. WAYNE, IN

WK1 2/05-2/11 WK2 2/12-2/18 WK3 2/19-2/25 WK4 2/26-3/4

TUESDAY 6.45PM-11.00PM

TIME PERIOD	METRO HH RTG	METRO HH SHR	STATION	PROGRAM	DMA HH RATINGS WEEKS 1	2	3	4	MULTI-WEEK AVG. RTG	SHR	SHARE TREND NOV '80	MAY '80	FEB '80	DMA RATINGS PERSONS 2+	18+	12-34	WOMEN 18+	18-34	18-49	25-49	25-54	WKG	FEM 12-24	PER 12-24	MEN 18+	18-34	18-49	25-49	25-54	TNS 12-17	CHILD 2-11	6-11
	1	2			3	4	5	6	7	8	10	11	12	14	15	16	17	18	19	20	21	22	23	24	25	26	27	28	29	30	31	32
	7		R.S.E. THRESHOLDS 25+%		14	14	14	14	4					3	3	5	4	11	7	7	6	10	13	8	5	10	7	8	7	13	12	16
	2		(1 S.E.) 4 WK AVG 50+%		4	4	4	4	1					1	1	1	1	3	2	2	2	3	4	2	1	3	2	2	2	4	3	4
6.45PM	12	23	WANE	CBS EVE NWS	21	10	10	11	13	24	26X	37	31	9	12	4	13	5	8	9	9	10	6	5	10	4	7	9	9	3		1
	14	27	WFFT	HOGANS HEROES	17	15	9	14	14	25	23X	11	20	9	8	12	7	11	9	6	6	9	12	12	10	16	13	13	12	8	15	18
	9	16	WKJG	NBC NITELY NWS	8	5	8	11	8	14	12X	19	15	5	6	4	6	3	4	5	6	3	3	4	5	4	4	4	4	6	4	5
	14	25	WPTA	TIC TAC DOUGH	17	12	12	16	15	26	30X	26	23	8	10	5	11	7	6	7	7	7	5	4	8	4	4	4	5	2	5	6
	53			HUT/PUT/TOTALS *	69	47	47	59	55		60	36	57	35	39	28	41	29	32	32	33	32	28	26	36	30	31	32	32	22	29	34
7.00PM	8	13	WANE	MATCH GAME	15	11	8	7	10	17	21	32	23	7	9	3	10	4	7	9	9	6	2	2	7	3	6	6	7	2	5	5
	11	20	WFFT	HOUR MAGAZINE	14	9	9	12	11	18	11X	16	9	6	8	5	9	8	7	5	6	10	7	5	7	4	3	3	4	1	4	4
	11	19	WKJG	FAMILY FEUD PM	12	10	10	9	10	16	16	14	15	7	7	3	9	4	5	6	7	7	2	2	6	2	3	4	4	3	7	7
	24	42	WPTA	MASH EARLY	22	23	19	27	23	38	41X	26	40	17	16	22	16	21	19	19	18	15	19	21	17	23	22	21	19	22	16	19
	57			HUT/PUT/TOTALS *	68	59	53	60	60		59	41	60	42	45	36	48	41	43	47	46	42	33	32	41	36	36	38	38	31	37	42
7.15PM	7	12	WANE	MATCH GAME	14	10	7	6	9	16	20	31	23	7	8	3	9	3	6	7	7	5	2	2	7	3	5	5	6	2	5	5
	11	19	WFFT	HOUR MAGAZINE	14	9	9	11	11	18	11X	17	9	6	8	4	9	8	7	6	6	11	6	4	7	3	3	2	4	1	4	4
	11	20	WKJG	FAMILY FEUD PM	12	10	10	10	10	17	17	14	15	7	8	4	10	5	6	7	8	7	3	2	6	3	3	4	5	3	7	7
	25	44	WPTA	MASH EARLY	23	25	19	27	23	39	41X	27	40	17	17	23	16	22	20	19	18	16	21	23	18	24	22	21	19	22	16	19
	56			HUT/PUT/TOTALS *	67	60	52	59	60		58	41	60	42	44	37	48	42	42	45	45	43	34	33	40	36	36	36	37	31	37	41
7.30PM	17	29	WANE	PM MAGAZINE	27	17	16	10	18	29	25	32	26	12	15	9	17	9	11	11	10	10	8	9	12	12	11	9	9	5	6	5
	9	16	WFFT	HOUR MAGAZINE	12	9	9	7	9	16	10X	15	9	5	7	4	8	7	6	6	6	9	4	3	5	2	2	2	3	1	4	5
	10	17	WKJG	WELCOME-KOTTER	10	11	10	11	10	17	26	17	19	8	6	9	7	8	8	10	9	8	10	9	5	7	6	6	6	14	13	18
	20	34	WPTA	ALL IN FAMILY	18	20	9	20	17	28	27X	26	33	11	12	12	12	13	12	12	12	12	14	12	12	13	12	11	12	11	9	10
	57			HUT/PUT/TOTALS *	72	61	52	56	60		62	38	58	41	43	37	47	41	42	44	42	45	37	36	39	36	34	31	33	33	36	41
8.00PM	14	23	WANE	#THAT'S MY LINE					13	21	24	14	20	8	11	6	14	7	6	6	6	8	4	5	7	6	5	4	4	4	2	2
	18	28		THAT'S MY LINE	19	14	16		16	24				10	13	7	16	8	8	7	7	11	6	7	9	8	6	5	5	6	2	3
	<			CONVERSTN-PRES				6	6	10				3	4	1	7								2							
	5	8	WFFT	#PRIME TIME MOV					5	8	9	10	10	3	4	3	3	3	3	2	2	4	5	4	4	3	4	3	3	1		
	<			NOTRE DM BKBL	5				5	7				2	3	1	3								4							
	4	7		PRIME TIME MOV		6	2	7	5	8				3	4	3	3	3	4	3	2	6	6	5	4	4	5	3	3	2		
	14	23	WKJG	LOBO	19	16	19	13	17	26	25	34	24	13	12	10	13	11	12	13	14	13	10	9	12	8	9	10	11	11	17	19
	25	40	WPTA	HAPPY DAYS	25	25	15	23	22	34	31	29	38	18	14	20	15	22	20	21	19	17	23	20	14	17	17	18	16	24	27	31
	62			HUT/PUT/TOTALS *	73	66	58	59	64		65	48	63	48	47	45	49	47	46	46	46	47	46	46	44	41	41	40	41	48	51	59
8.30PM	13	22	WANE	#THAT'S MY LINE					13	20	23	13	24	8	10	6	13	7	6	6	5	7	5	5	7	6	5	4	4	4		
	16	26		THAT'S MY LINE	19	12	14		15	23				9	12	7	15	8	8	7	6	9	6	7	9	8	6	5	5	5		1
	<			CONVERSTN-PRES				5	5	9				3	4	1	6								2							
	5	8	WFFT	#PRIME TIME MOV					5	8	10	10	9	2	3	2	3	2	3	2	2	5	3	3	4	3	4	3	3			
	<			NOTRE DM BKBL	5				5	7				2	3		2								4							
	4	8		PRIME TIME MOV		6	3	6	5	8				3	4	3	3	3	4	2	2	6	4	4	4	4	5	3	3			
	14	25	WKJG	LOBO	19	17	20	12	17	27	27	34	25	13	12	10	13	12	12	14	14	14	10	9	12	8	10	10	11	10	18	20
	22	38	WPTA	LAVERNE&SHIRLY	23	23	14	22	21	33	30	28	34	17	14	20	15	21	20	20	18	15	24	19	13	16	16	18	16	25	25	29
	59			HUT/PUT/TOTALS *	72	65	56	57	62		65	49	64	46	46	45	48	47	45	45	44	44	46	44	43	42	41	42	42	46	48	56
9.00PM	17	28	WANE	#CBS TUE-MOV					17	28	24	19	20	12	14	12	16	15	15	13	13	13	15	13	11	11	11	10	11	8	4	6
	15	25		CBS TUE-MOV	12	14	22		16	26				11	13	12	15	16	14	12	13	12	16	12	10	9	10	10	10	10	3	4
	<			JESSE HALLAM				20	20	33				14	17	12	20								15							
	5	8	WFFT	#PRIME TIME MOV					4	7	11	10	7	2	3	2	3	1	2	2	2	5	1	2	3	2	2	2	2	2		1
	<			NOTRE DM BKBL	6				6	9				3	3	2	3								3							
	4	6		PRIME TIME MOV		3	3	5	4	6				2	3	1	3	1	2	2	2	5	2	2	3	3	2	2	1			
	14	23	WKJG	#BJ&THE BEAR					14	23	24	24	25	10	11	10	12	12	12	14	13	8	10	9	11	10	10	10	9	8	5	6
	10	17		BJ&THE BEAR	13	13		11	12	20				9	10	9	10	11	11	11	11	5	11	10	10	8	9	9	8	9	7	9
	<			NBC TUE-MOV			18		18	31				11	14	11	16								12							
	21	35	WPTA	3'S COMPANY	22	28	12	18	20	32	28	37	38	14	15	16	15	16	16	18	17	15	16	14	14	14	15	16	15	17	10	11
	61			HUT/PUT/TOTALS *	62	64	59	61	62		63	56	67	43	49	44	51	49	49	52	51	46	43	42	47	42	44	44	44	41	21	24
9.30PM	19	33	WANE	#CBS TUE-MOV					18	32	27	23	21	12	14	12	17	16	16	15	15	14	15	13	11	11	11	10	11	10	3	4
	17	29		CBS TUE-MOV	12	18	21		17	30				12	13	13	16	17	15	14	14	13	17	13	10	9	10	10	10	12	3	4
	<			JESSE HALLAM				21	21	38				14	18	12	20								15							
	4	6	WFFT	#PRIME TIME MOV					4	6	10	10	7	2	3	1	3	1	2	2	2	4	1	2	3	2	2	2	2	1		1
	<			NOTRE DM BKBL	4				4	7				2	2	1	2								2							
	3	6		PRIME TIME MOV		3	3	5	4	6				2	3	1	3	1	2	2	2	5	2	2	3	2	2	2	1			
	14	25	WKJG	#BJ&THE BEAR					14	24	26	26	25	10	12	10	12	12	13	15	14	9	10	9	11	9	11	11	10	10	5	6
	11	19		BJ&THE BEAR	13	14		10	12	22				10	11	10	10	12	12	13	12	7	12	10	11	8	10	10	9	11	6	8
	<			NBC TUE-MOV			18		18	33				11	14	11	17								12							
	17	30	WPTA	2 CLOSE-COMFRT	15	22	10	15	15	27	22	33	36	10	11	11	11	13	11	14	13	11	9	8	11	11	12	14	13	9	7	6
	57			HUT/PUT/TOTALS *	55	62	55	55	57		61	57	65	39	45	39	48	46	47	51	49	43	38	35	43	37	40	41	41	33	17	17
10.00PM	16	32	WANE	#CBS TUE-MOV					16	33	31	25	22	11	13	12	16	15	15	13	13	13	16	13	11	11	10	9	10	9	2	2
	14	27		CBS TUE-MOV	10	15	20		15	30				10	12	11	15	15	13	11	12	12	17	12	9	8	8	9	9	10	1	2
	<			JESSE HALLAM				20	20	42				13	17	13	19								15							
	5	9	WFFT	INN NW+PRIME					4	8	5	12	6	2	3		3	1	3	3	3	3			3		2	3	2			
	5	11		INDEP NET NWS	5			3	4	8				3	4	1	3	2	3	4	4	2	1	1	4		3	4	3	1		
	4	7		PRIME TIME MOV		4	4		4	7				2	2		3		2	3	2	5			1		1	2	1			
	11	23	WKJG	#FLAMINGO ROAD					10	21	24	24	26	7	9	6	10	7	9	12	12	9	4	3	8	6	6	8	7	4	1	1
	8	15		FLAMINGO ROAD	7	12		6	8	17				6	8	4	8	5	7	9	8	7	4	3	7	3	4	6	6	4	2	1
	<			NBC TUE-MOV			17		17	33				10	13	11	16								10							
	15	30	WPTA	HART TO HART	15	19	9	15	14	28	28	30	33	9	11	11	11	15	14	16	14	11	9	9	10	11	12	12	11	6	1	2
	50			HUT/PUT/TOTALS *	47	55	52	49	50		52	55	58	33	41	34	45	43	45	48	46	41	33	30	37	32	35	35	35	23	5	5
10.30PM	15	33	WANE	#CBS TUE-MOV					16	34	32	26	24	11	13	11	15	14	14	12	12	12	15	12	10	10	10	9	10	8	2	2
	13	27		CBS TUE-MOV	10	13	20		15	31				10	12	10	14	13	12	10	11	11	16	11	9	8	8	9	9	10	1	2
	<			JESSE HALLAM				20	20	44				13	17	12	19								14							
	3	7	WFFT	LOV AM+IND-LT					2	5	3	12	4	1	2		2		1	1	1	2	1	1	1		1	1	1			
	4	9		LOVE AMER STYL	2			3	2	5				1	2	1	1	1	2	2	2	2	1	1	2		1	2	1	1		
	3	5		IND NET NWS LT		3	2		2	5				1	2		2		1	1	1	2			1		1	1	1			
	11	24	WKJG	#FLAMINGO ROAD					10	22	24	24	29	7	9	6	10	7	9	12	12	9	4	3	7	6	6	8	7	4	1	1
	7	17		FLAMINGO ROAD	7	11		6	8	17				6	7	4	8	5	7	9	9	7	4	3	6	3	4	6	5	4	2	1
	<			NBC TUE-MOV			17		17	34				10	13	11	16								10							
	15	32	WPTA	HART TO HART	14	16	9	14	13	29	30	29	35	8	10	10	11	14	14	17	14	11	8	8	10	10	12	11	10	6	1	2
	46			HUT/PUT/TOTALS *	43	48	50	47	47		47	53	52	30	38	32	42	40	42	45	44	40	31	28	33	30	32	32	31	21	4	4
	1	2			3	4	5	6	7	8	10	11	12	14	15	16	17	18	19	20	21	22	23	24	25	26	27	28	29	30	31	32

TUESDAY 6.45PM-11.00PM

FEBRUARY 1981

For explanation of symbols, see page 3.
For RSE explanations, see page 2.

Courtesy of The A.C. Nielsen Co.

tion, headquartered in New York, maintains its operations center at Beltsville, Maryland. It uses diaries for local market data gathering and an electronic monitoring device for overnight ratings of network prime-time programs in the three largest markets. In addition, Arbitron offers a variety of other reports and custom services, including overnight telephone coincidental surveys. However, this company is best known for its regular ratings "sweeps," conducted simultaneously four times a year in more than 200 US television markets.

To conduct its local market studies, Arbitron has divided the entire country into geographic sampling units, which usually consist of one county each. Diaries are placed in each sampling unit on a quota basis determined by population and the expected rate of return of diaries. Following an interval-selection process, Arbitron's sample households are computer selected from master tapes obtained from a major direct mail advertising company. These computer tapes, which are updated frequently, contain listings of all telephone directories used in the United States.

Separate samples are generated for each week of the four-week rating periods, with each cooperating family keeping its diary for a seven-day period. Special interviewing techniques are used in some markets to aid in obtaining data from households whose members may have language and/or writing problems and who otherwise might not be fully represented in the sample. The average weekly program rating and share data are computed from the combined multiweekly samples.

Upon their return to Arbitron, diaries are screened for accuracy and edited for data processing. Diaries may be rejected if they are postmarked before the last day of the survey week, if fewer than seven days are included, or if they arrive after the cut-off date. Information is key-punched onto computer cards, then transferred to computer tape for data processing.

Each of the television markets researched by Arbitron is surveyed at least three and as many as eight times per year. The reports closely resemble those of Nielsen, including rating and share data for the SMSA and the larger Area of Dominant Influence (ADI). Audience totals and demographic data are provided for the Total Survey Area (TSA), which includes viewership beyond as well as within the ADI's. Each Arbitron television report includes viewing data for each program broadcast in the market, as well as day-part summaries.

Arbitron Radio conducts audience surveys up to four times annually in some 160 markets. These reports, which were expanded from four-week to 12-week periods in 1981, provide listening data for metro areas as well as for Areas of Dominant Influence. The television ADI basis was adopted in 1975 to provide advertising clients with radio data comparable with that of television. Figure 5.13 illustrates Arbitron's format for presenting average-quarter-hour and cume radio audience information.

OTHER AUDIENCE MEASUREMENT SERVICES

We have already mentioned the Trendex, TvQ, and Videodex services, which measure viewing behavior and program preferences for television. In radio, audience measurement sustained a serious blow in the late 1970s when

Figure 5.13 Sample Data From Arbitron Radio

Average Quarter-Hour and Cume Listening Estimates

NASHVILLE-DAVIDSON
OCT/NOV 1980

MONDAY-FRIDAY
6.00AM-10.00AM

STATION CALL LETTERS	ADULTS 18 +						ADULTS 18-34						ADULTS 18-49					
	TOTAL AREA		METRO SURVEY AREA				TOTAL AREA		METRO SURVEY AREA				TOTAL AREA		METRO SURVEY AREA			
	AVG. PERS (00)	CUME PERS (00)	AVG. PERS (00)	CUME PERS (00)	AVG. PERS RTG.	AVG. PERS SHR.	AVG. PERS (00)	CUME PERS (00)	AVG. PERS (00)	CUME PERS (00)	AVG. PERS RTG.	AVG. PERS SHR.	AVG. PERS (00)	CUME PERS (00)	AVG. PERS (00)	CUME PERS (00)	AVG. PERS RTG.	AVG. PERS SHR.
WAAA	27	157	27	157	.5	2.2							10	40	10	40	.3	1.2
WBBB	12	51	12	51	.2	1.0	7	27	7	27	.3	1.4	7	27	7	27	.2	.8
WBBB-FM	2	16	2	16		.2												
TOTAL	14	60	14	60	.2	1.2	7	27	7	27	.3	1.4	7	27	7	27	.2	.8
WCCC	17	95	17	95	.3	1.4	7	51	7	51	.3	1.4	9	63	9	63	.2	1.1
WDDD	51	275	51	275	.9	4.1	7	82	7	82	.3	1.4	18	162	18	162	.5	2.2
WEEE	35	168	34	149	.6	2.7	6	71	5	52	.2	1.0	17	104	16	85	.4	1.9
WFFF	83	489	70	392	1.2	5.6	71	428	66	354	2.6	13.0	81	469	68	372	1.7	8.2
WGGG	5	48	4	38	.1	.3	1	22	1	22		.2	4	30	4	30	.1	.5
WHHH	50	394	31	289	.5	2.5	47	356	28	251	1.1	5.5	48	380	29	275	.7	3.5
WIII	78	745	59	566	1.0	4.7	39	401	25	262	1.0	4.9	59	568	41	400	1.1	5.0
WJJJ	39	350	36	302	.6	2.9	34	302	31	254	1.2	6.1	38	340	35	292	.9	4.2
WKKK (FM)	51	282	51	282	.9	4.1	32	200	32	200	1.3	6.3	43	266	43	266	1.1	5.2
TOTAL	90	570	87	523	1.5	7.0	66	447	63	400	2.5	12.4	81	551	78	504	2.0	9.4
WLLL	14	43	14	43	.2	1.1	4	17	4	17	.2	.8	5	21	5	21	.1	.6
WMMM	57	359	57	344	1.0	4.6	17	97	17	97	.7	3.3	40	215	40	212	1.0	4.8
WNNN	238	1099	148	696	2.5	11.8	66	285	34	170	1.3	6.7	144	665	85	408	2.2	10.3
WOOO	242	1587	167	983	2.8	13.3	52	393	36	252	1.4	7.1	122	861	89	565	2.3	10.7
WPPP	116	665	76	484	1.3	6.1	82	436	48	290	1.9	9.4	111	573	72	413	1.8	8.7
WQQQ	90	462	89	431	1.5	7.1	54	268	53	237	2.1	10.4	84	383	83	352	2.1	10.0
WRRR	15	87	15	87	.3	1.2	5	43	5	43	.2	1.0	6	56	6	56	.2	.7
WSSS	176	1022	62	407	1.0	5.0	139	803	51	348	2.0	10.0	173	1005	61	398	1.6	7.4
WTTT	168	867	142	759	2.4	11.3	45	188	35	169	1.4	6.9	85	403	69	338	1.8	8.3

STATION CALL LETTERS	ADULTS 25-49						ADULTS 25-54						ADULTS 35-64					
	TOTAL AREA		METRO SURVEY AREA				TOTAL AREA		METRO SURVEY AREA				TOTAL AREA		METRO SURVEY AREA			
	AVG. PERS (00)	CUME PERS (00)	AVG. PERS (00)	CUME PERS (00)	AVG. PERS RTG.	AVG. PERS SHR.	AVG. PERS (00)	CUME PERS (00)	AVG. PERS (00)	CUME PERS (00)	AVG. PERS RTG.	AVG. PERS SHR.	AVG. PERS (00)	CUME PERS (00)	AVG. PERS (00)	CUME PERS (00)	AVG. PERS RTG.	AVG. PERS SHR.
WAAA	10	40	10	40	.4	1.6	15	59	15	59	.5	2.1	26	134	26	134	1.0	4.3
WBBB	7	19	7	19	.3	1.1	7	19	7	19	.2	1.0	4	15	4	15	.2	.7
WBBB-FM														7		7		
TOTAL	7	19	7	19	.3	1.1	7	19	7	19	.2	1.0	4	15	4	15	.2	.7
WCCC	6	31	6	31	.2	1.0	8	38	8	38	.3	1.1	7	36	7	36	.3	1.2
WDDD	15	116	15	116	.5	2.5	21	131	21	131	.7	3.0	41	173	41	173	1.6	6.8
WEEE	12	41	12	41	.4	2.0	20	70	20	70	.6	2.8	21	70	21	70	.8	3.5
WFFF	39	196	30	157	1.1	4.9	39	196	30	157	.9	4.2	10	41	2	18	.1	.3
WGGG	3	17	3	17	.1	.5	3	17	3	17	.1	.4	4	26	3	16	.1	.5
WHHH	12	136	10	108	.4	1.6	13	142	11	114	.3	1.6	2	30	2	30	.1	.3
WIII	38	351	29	265	1.0	4.7	46	385	36	288	1.1	5.1	35	276	30	236	1.2	5.0
WJJJ	28	200	27	184	1.0	4.4	29	210	28	194	.9	4.0	5	48	5	48	.2	.8
WKKK (FM)	23	132	23	132	.8	3.8	31	148	31	148	1.0	4.4	19	82	19	82	.8	3.2
TOTAL	51	305	50	289	1.8	8.2	60	324	59	308	1.8	8.4	24	123	24	123	1.0	4.0
WLLL	5	13	5	13	.2	.8	5	13	5	13	.2	.7	10	26	10	26	.4	1.7
WMMM	39	200	39	197	1.4	6.4	44	242	44	227	1.4	6.2	34	217	34	202	1.3	5.6
WNNN	142	647	83	390	3.0	13.6	170	779	91	435	2.8	12.9	122	612	74	368	2.9	12.3
WOOO	113	776	81	503	2.9	13.3	150	988	95	585	3.0	13.4	158	1003	100	576	4.0	16.6
WPPP	82	395	53	294	1.9	8.7	83	407	54	306	1.7	7.6	33	194	28	171	1.1	4.7
WQQQ	50	183	50	183	1.8	8.2	52	217	52	217	1.6	7.4	35	173	35	173	1.4	5.8
WRRR	6	56	6	56	.2	1.0	7	69	7	69	.2	1.0	6	36	6	36	.2	1.0
WSSS	75	466	31	173	1.1	5.1	76	470	32	177	1.0	4.5	37	214	11	54	.4	1.8
WTTT	77	375	61	310	2.2	10.0	96	485	80	420	2.5	11.3	104	542	90	463	3.6	15.0

Adults

Courtesy of The Arbitron Co.

The Pulse, Inc., folded. This service, which began measuring radio audiences in 1941, based its reports on extensive, but costly and increasingly difficult, personal interviews.

Several smaller organizations have attempted to expand to provide a second radio meaurement service which is needed to corroborate the work of Arbitron. The newer companies include the Burke organization of Cincinnati and the Birch Report of Miami. Thus far, however, neither has become a full-fledged competitor.

Media Statistics, Inc., Silver Springs, Maryland, markets its research under the name of Mediastat. This company, founded by the former owner of Arbitron, works on contract and primarily handles ascertainment surveys and small-market radio studies.

Numerous other broadcast research firms are available for contract projects. Both *Broadcasting Yearbook* and *Television Factbook* publish listings annually. In addition, many universities operate research bureaus which conduct quality audience research on a contract basis.

AUDIENCE RELATIONS

It is perhaps redundant, but nevertheless important, to remind ourselves that broadcast stations must attract and serve a viable audience to succeed. The degree of success depends largely upon the quality of the station's signal and its programming. Promotional activities and strategic scheduling also assist in audience building. Chapters 7 and 8 focus on the tactics involved in schedule and format development. However, one additional ingredient also can help a station win public acceptance—the interpersonal element that takes place whenever a member of the public makes contact with the station.

Every employee of a radio or television station should be encouraged to treat the public courteously and helpfully whenever an opportunity arises. Audience mail should be answered promptly. Telephone calls should be handled politely. And public contacts by station personnel should reflect a constructive attitude toward the station and its attempts to serve the public. Any discourtesy in person, through the mail, or on the telephone, of course, can harm a station's image. In contrast, a sincere desire to assist listeners or viewers can have a positive effect.

SUMMARY

In this chapter, we have noted that both radio and television reach vast audiences. In fact, listening and viewing are practically universal activities among the US population. However, only rarely is this behavior *en masse*. Instead, individuals tune to programs and stations that appeal to their interests. Thus, audiences become clustered into subsets along demographic and special interest lines. The only important exception is prime-time television, which is watched by a broad mixture of the population and which is dominated by the television networks. Even so, more women than men view prime-time television, and the self-selection process leads to further audience clustering along demographic and special interest lines.

We have compared the public's usage of radio and television, noting their complementary nature. Radio leads in the daytime, while television dominates at night. Television exhibits seasonal patterns to a pronounced degree, attaining tremendously high viewership during the winter season, with a sharp decline in the spring and summer. In contrast, radio's usage is fairly even throughout the year. On another point, radio's audience is much more fragmented than television's. However, program choices for viewers are increasing rapidly, which could eventually result in similar splintering among television viewers. It is ominous for broadcast TV that cable television's subscriber base now exceeds 30 percent in the United States. Again, with respect to radio, perhaps the most noticeable audience shift already experienced has been the recent emergence of FM over the older AM service. Programmers as well as the owners and managers of broadcast properties should be attuned to all such trends in audience behavior.

In addition to considering the available audience as they make programming decisions, program managers should understand *how* individuals choose programs. In our discussion, we explored the three main ways (carry-over, dial twisting, and deliberate choice), suggesting that programmers develop strategies to maximize their chances for winning viewers and listeners. Specific strategies are discussed in detail in chapters 7 and 8.

Programmers also must acquire the ability to interpret and use audience measurement studies. In this chapter, the research procedures of the major audience measurement organizations have been detailed. We also have explained, with examples, how to understand and use the data they provide.

This chapter also noted the importance of following general trends in the population, as well as societal changes within one's market. Finally, on a personal level, programmers are advised to treat all listeners, on and off the air, with utmost courtesy. It is these individuals who determine the future success of any broadcast organization.

In our next chapter, "Program Appeals and Structure," we turn our attention to individual programs. We will attempt in chapter 6 to discover what makes a successful program through a study of program "appeals." The chapter also will examine the structural organization necessary for successful programs.

ENDNOTES

1. *Radio Facts* (New York: Radio Advertising Bureau, Inc., 1981), p. 4.
2. *Nielsen Report on Television 1981* (Northbrook, Ill.: A.C. Nielsen Co., 1981), p. 3.
3. *Radio Facts, op. cit.* p. 4.
4. *Ibid.*, p. 3.
5. *Ibid.*, p. 6.
6. *Nielsen Report, op. cit.*, p. 3.
7. *Ibid.*, p. 1.
8. *Radio Facts, op. cit.*, p. 8.
9. James E. Duncan, Jr., *American Radio Spring 1981* (Kalamazoo, Mich.: James H. Duncan, Jr., September 1981), p. 4.
10. *Ibid.*, p. A-19.
11. *Nielsen Report, op. cit.*, p. 2.
12. Duncan, *op. cit.*, p. A-16.

STUDY QUESTIONS

1. Keep a diary of your personal radio and TV usage for a week. Then compare your listening and viewing patterns and your total media usage with the averages given in this chapter. How closely do your listening and viewing patterns correspond to the national averages? Explain any differences.
2. Reflect on your seasonal usage of radio and television. How does your seasonal usage of the broadcast media compare with the patterns discussed in the chapter? Explain any differences.
3. Can you identify any radio stations or formats that you use mainly as background for other activities? To which types of radio stations do you give the greatest amount of attention? Explain differences between formats and attention levels in terms of programming and your personal activities.
4. Given the present population and demographic trends, what changes in radio and TV programming would you expect during the next 10 years?
5. Which of the three basic approaches do you (or your family) follow in selecting television programs to watch?
6. Compute program ratings from the following data:
   (a) HUT = 40; Share = 30%.
   (b) HUT = 60; Share = 20%.
   Explain the significance of your findings in this computation.
7. Which of the following data-gathering systems do *you* think is best: (a) meter devices, (b) diaries, (c) personal interviews, or (d) telephone interviews? Explain your answer.
8. Why are cume audiences important to advertisers? Why does a high-reach station usually have a low average listening span, and why does a high-cume station have a short average listening span?

SUGGESTED READINGS

Banks, Mark James. *A History of Broadcast Audience Research in the United States 1920–1980 With An Emphasis on the Rating Services.* PhD dissertation, The University of Tennessee, Knoxville, 1981.

Beyond the Ratings. New York: The Arbitron Co. 1978–present. Published monthly.

Coping with the Complexity of Cable in the 80's. Northbrook, Ill.: A.C. Nielsen Co., 1979.

Duncan, James. *American Radio.* Kalamazoo, Mich.: Gilmore Advertising. Published twice yearly.

Everything You've Always Wanted to Know About TV Ratings. Northbrook, Ill.: A.C. Nielsen Co., 1978.

Inside the Arbitron Television Report. New York: The Arbitron Co., 1977.

Lichty, Lawrence W. *Broadcast Program and Audience Analysis.* Madison, Wisc.: American Printing and Publishing, 1973.

The Nielsen Ratings in Perspective. Northbrook, Ill.: A.C. Nielsen Co., 1980.

Nielsen Report on Television 1982. Northbrook, Ill.: A.C. Nielsen Co.: 1982. Published annually.

Quick Reference Guide to Arbitron Radio Market Report. New York: The Arbitron Co., 1977.

Radio Facts. New York: Radio Advertising Bureau, 1982. Published annually.

Research Guidelines for Programming Decision Makers. New York: The Arbitron Co., 1977.

6

PROGRAM PLANNING: APPEALS AND STRUCTURE

Effective programming for television and radio begins with its conceptualization, is developed through careful writing, culminates in quality production and performance, and though it may be critiqued and researched during this process, is ultimately evaluated by the audience for which it is intended.

As we have discussed in chapter 5, the ultimate purpose of any program is to attract the intended target audience, in sufficient numbers, for the station or network, and to communicate specific information and/or values to the audience. It logically follows that, for any program to succeed in achieving its purposes, it must not only attract, but also satisfy and hold its intended audience.

This chapter deals with two fundamental considerations essential to successful program development. These factors are program *appeals* and *structure*. The former relates to qualities or elements contained within a program which satisfy the audience. The latter pertains to the program's organization, design, and construction.

PROGRAM APPEALS

Over several decades of radio and television programming, creative producers have become aware that some programs and concepts succeed beautifully in gaining an audience, while others work only moderately well or even fail miserably. While other factors, such as timing, have a bearing upon a program's success, experience has shown that successful programs emphasize certain elements which we call *appeals*. These are the identifiable programming ingredients that make listeners and viewers want to tune in. Thus, appeals may be thought of as "satisfactions" derived from listening to or watching a given program. They also may be thought of as motivating factors that induce listening or viewing behavior. For our purposes, let's refer to these "make-the-viewer-want-to-watch" ingredients as *audience appeals,* or simply as *appeals*.

Program producers generally recognize seven identifiable appeals, each of which has its subdivisions and each of which may be heightened in intensity through various methods of emphasis. The seven appeals are *conflict* or *competition, comedy, romance and sex appeal, human interest, emotional stimulation, information,* and *power* or *importance*. Each will be discussed at some length in this chapter.

Recognizing that a program's attractiveness can be heightened through selective use of appeals, producers generally choose to emphasize two or more of these elements in any given program. In addition, they usually weave another two or three appeals into each program as secondary attracting devices. Very few programs provide all seven appeals; it simply isn't necessary. However, a program that manifests as many as three appeals quite strongly, given favorable scheduling, will probably attract and hold its audience quite well.

While the idea of using specific devices may smack of formula writing, it should be remembered that style and creativity are also essential to an artistically good program. The writer's handling of setting, plot line, character development and interplay all remain extremely important in any dramatic program. Nondramatic programs also require careful planning and preparation, including the selection of suitable appeals.

CONFLICT OR COMPETITION

The first appeal we shall consider, conflict, is undoubtedly the most basic of the seven. It is essential to any dramatic program and may be important to other types as well. Whether the drama is a serious play or a light situation comedy, there simply must be a problem, heavy or light, to be resolved. Furthermore, the conflict appeal becomes much stronger and more effective as an audience-attracting and holding device if there is uncertainty as to the outcome.

Numerous types of conflict occur in dramatic programs. Six will be listed here; however, they are not limited to dramatic-type shows, as we shall see. These types include (1) struggles involving danger to life or physical safety; (2) conflict based on threats to reputation or success; (3) love conflicts; (4) problem-solving conflicts; (5) conflicts of ideas; and (6) conflicts within one's self. Now let's examine each of these types.

Physical Danger Conflicts

Conflicts which pose threats to life and safety abound in popular crime and detective shows, Western dramas, and adventure programs. In such dramas, the hero frequently encounters danger or may be threatened in some manner. This type of conflict, of course, lends itself to magnification through violence, either implied or depicted, through suspense, or both.

This appeal is often found in classical drama, such as Shakespeare's *MacBeth* and *Hamlet*. It is also found in movies shown on television and in serial dramas, both the daytime and nighttime variety. Remember the suspense created in the prime-time series "Dallas" at the end of the 1979–1980 season when the villainous J.R. Ewing was shot? Millions of faithful viewers thought the character was actually dead, at least until the producers and the actor, Larry Hagman, agreed to renew their contract for the following season. So much suspense was created by this life-threatening action that someone actually stole a "Dallas" script from Lorimar Productions' studios.

In adventure programs, the threat of physical violence may be derived from nature as well as from other humans. It may also be directed toward favorite animals as well as human heroes, such as the "Lassie" series in which the beautiful and courageous collie faced many dangers but always survived. Even children's cartoon programs are replete with life-threatening situations. Those threatened may be animated people or animals. These programs, however, are generally assumed to be fantasies because of their animated form.

Newscasts represent another important type of program in which life-threatening situations generate interest. Examples include stories about war, accidents, crime, rescue attempts, and devastation by forces such as floods, hurricanes, fire, and earthquakes. These tragedies, highlighted in television news programs, serve as a powerful appeal to viewers who become witnesses to their reality. A special case in conflict reporting was television's coverage of the Viet Nam war, through which the American public became intensely informed visually about the reality of war.

Threats to Reputation or Success

At a somewhat lower level of intensity are those threats against a person or a character's reputation or goals in life. Nonthriller and nonviolent dramas often present this type of conflict. These threats also add interest to soap operas and situation comedies. In the latter case, however, the conflict usually is resolved quickly after an innocent misunderstanding has been corrected.

Again, news programs may focus on competition between individuals or organizations which are striving for mutually exclusive goals. This type of conflict particularly applies to politicians seeking the same office. The national political conventions, for example, become interesting to watch and attract viewers generally in proportion to the degree of competition for the presidential nomination. Similarly, election night coverage focuses on voting

Figure 6.1 One of the most popular TV dramas of the early 1980s was "Dallas," a weekly serialized production about a rich and corrupt Texas family. Conflict and suspense were two of its major appeals.

tabulations, the outcome of which determines which candidates have succeeded in their attempts to win public favor and important offices.

A conflict which involves a threat to reputation or success also may be the initiating device that leads to a more serious life-threatening situation, as may be seen on many crime and detective programs. Murder for its own sake is rare indeed. However, murder in real life or on television often is motivated by a threat to reveal a sordid or questionable past or from a conflict over money or other matters related to personal success.

Conflicts in Love

Again, like conflicts over reputation or success, love problems may be simple and easily resolved, or they may escalate into life-threatening situations.

Problems related to love abound on television. This appeal, of course, is used extensively on daytime soap operas and prime-time serials. In some cases, love triangle problems retain viewers' interest for months before finally being resolved. Similarly, disagreements between spouses, lovers' quarrels, and boy-girl problems frequently form the basis for plots in situation comedies. Here, however, the problems usually are minor and are easily resolved as the episode closes.

Two episodic TV dramas of recent years illustrate the use of love problems as a primary appeal. ABC's "Love, American Style" presented three or four love-related stories each week. These playlets focused on love "from all sides, young and old, rich and poor, unmarried, just married, long married, and multi-married."[1] The second show, "Love Boat," which retains its prime-time spot at this writing, similarly presents three interwoven stories each week about people who fall in love on a cruise ship. Each episode, though complicated with problems to be resolved, ends with a happy, or at least a tolerable, conclusion.

Certain game shows also have used conflict-in-love as a ploy for laughter. Both "The Newlywed Game" and "Three's a Crowd," which were essentially prime-time access syndication shows in the late 1970s, usually provoked disagreements between husbands and wives.

In contrast, serious crime dramas often rely upon love triangles as the cause for murder and other serious crimes.

Problem-Solving Conflicts

Problem solving is basically a means for involving the listener or viewer in a program or a station's activities. In the case of dramatic programs, a viewer may become an active participant if he/she does not know the solution until the episode ends. In other words, the viewer seeks to puzzle out the mystery and perhaps reaches a conclusion at the same time the detective, for example, seeks to solve the plot. This approach is sharply in contrast to the type of program in which the viewers know, but the detective does not know, the identity of the culprit or the reasons for the crime.

Problem solving may be manifested as an appeal in many other ways, as well as in mystery shows. For example, radio traffic reports assist motorists in solving the problems associated with driving to and from work. Consumer affairs reports may assist homemakers in their grocery and household purchases. And certainly a large percentage of the commercial messages broadcast by radio and television stations take the form of problem-solution advertising.

Quiz programs also engage both the home audience and their contestants in problem solving as each seeks to determine correct answers. The perennial musical quiz program, "Name That Tune," offers such a challenge, as do many other programs of the genre.

Frequently radio stations engage in audience promotion activities which solicit listeners to call in answers to questions given over the air. Solving the problem, achieving the correct answer in this case, plus getting through on the telephone may result in winning a prize.

The problem-solving conflict or challenge obviously manifests itself in many different ways, both in dramatic and nondramatic form.

Conflict of Ideas

In real life, conflicts over different ideas abound. These conflicts may relate to political affairs, governmental policy, the conduct of business, attitudes toward minority races and religions, lifestyles, personal decisions, family concerns, and many other issues on which there is room for disagreement. Conflicts like these may be quite serious or very inconsequential. They appear frequently as important appeals in newscasts, serial dramas, situation comedies, Westerns, crime shows, and many other types of programs.

The concept, for example, became the basis for Norman Lear's "All in the Family" series of the 1970s, in which the producer sought to discredit bigoted ideas through a comic format. The differences of opinion and attitude on this popular show were pimarily between Archie Bunker, a conservative bigot, and his liberal daughter and son-in-law.

Inner Conflict

Situations in which a hero, or another character, must make a difficult decision may lead to powerful inner conflicts. The more difficult or poignant the decision becomes, the stronger becomes the appeal. If the viewer also becomes involved emotionally with the character who faces such a difficult decision, the "role-playing" nature of the conflict is greatly heightened.

The movie "Psycho" and the TV series "The Psychiatrist" are examples of psychological dramas containing the element of inner conflict. Characters in soap operas also frequently deal with inner conflicts, particularly in regard to their tangled love affairs. Role playing by viewers often results as viewers ask themselves, "What would I do?" and "What will she/he do?"

One further illustration will suffice. During one episode of the "Mary Tyler Moore Show," the heroine faced a difficult decision as to whether or not she should reveal the source of information for a particular news story. While this inner conflict was used to convey a real problem of contemporary journalism to the public, Mary Richards battled the conflict and ultimately decided to spend a night in jail rather than reveal her secret.

In addition to the six types of conflict or competition discussed here, we must mention one other conflict appeal which ordinarily is not manifest in dramatic programs. This is the element of conflict in sports events. In effect, there are actually two types of conflict—those involving physical conflict without danger to life and those which do not involve physical contact. The former include such "body contact" sports as football, boxing, and wrestling. Noncontact sports which are broadcast frequently include baseball, bowling, tennis, and golf.

THE UNIVERSAL APPEAL: COMEDY

Comedy is essentially a delightful form of entertainment intended to provide pleasure through laughter. It is ordinarily light and uncomplicated, and intended for pleasant diversion. However, some comedy is written to show the absurdities of human actions. Thus, in addition to providing pleasure, comedy also may become a pleasant vehicle for the criticism of people, their behavior patterns, and society in general.

Comedy may range from slapstick, which often involves physical contact and exaggerated actions, to sophisticated satire, which requires the audience to participate mentally for full understanding of the intended humor. It is generally achieved through some form of incongruity with respect to lines, characters, actions, and situations. The incongruity, or "surprise" element, provokes laughter because it is out of context with what had been expected by the listener. Frequently, comedy is also coupled with conflict. However, con-

Figure 6.2 Tom Brookshier and Lindsey Nelson broadcast a Cotton Bowl Game on New Year's Day. The appeals of conflict, information, and suspense all are present in live sports coverage.

flicts in this context tend to relate to the light and amusing side of life and usually have a happy ending.

In addition, some comedy is topical in that it depends upon current, and sometimes local, situations for its appeal. This explains why some attempts at humor succeed in one region or country, but not in another. It also explains why some comic routines cease to be funny as circumstances change. Other humor, in contrast, is universal and may be repeated at intervals to different audiences with the same favorable results.

For example, the comic situations of the "George Burns and Gracie Allen Show" and of "I Love Lucy" remain timeless. There will always be scatter-brained wives and irritated husbands, and vice versa, and this universally understood combination is certain to provoke laughter whenever it is employed. Similarly, as long as people understand baseball, the old Abbott and Costello routine "Who's on First?" will never cease to be funny. In contrast, gags that poke fun at current movie and TV stars or whoever happens to be the current president may be intensely funny at the time they are first uttered, but quickly lose their humor.

Because people like to laugh, comedy is a highly effective program appeal. For many programs, it is the dominant appeal. For others, it is used for reinforcement as comic relief or as a segment in a comedy-variety show. The strength of the comedy appeal can easily be ascertained by examining lists of the most popular television shows in the 1970s. In one year (1974), nine of the top ten programs were comedy series.

Most comedy efforts on television fall into the situation and the "gag" categories. However, at times, the two extreme forms of slapstick and satire are present. These four forms of comedy will be discussed next.

Slapstick Comedy

Slapstick comedy tends to be "hyper" and zany by nature. It depends primarily upon the use of overdrawn characters who are usually less than intelligent and are placed in ridiculous situations. Whatever dialogue is spoken tends to insult another participant in the routine, who becomes the "butt of the joke." Instead of clever lines, there are usually highly exaggerated and ludicrous actions, including apparently harmless physical violence.

In the silent movies, Charles Chaplin was the master of slapstick comedy. On television, his counterpart was undoubtedly Red Skelton, who gave his viewers such overdrawn personages as Clem Kadiddlehopper, Sheriff Deadeye, Willie Lump-Lump, San Fernando Red, Bolivar Shagnasty, and Freddie the Freeloader. These uproarious pantomime acts, which were done solo by Skelton, were favorites of the American public for more than two decades on network television.

Other examples of slapstick are found in the routines of such comic teams as Bud Abbott and Lou Costello, the Keystone Kops, the Little Rascals, and even Ernie and Bert on "Sesame Street." Slapstick is fundamental to the humor in the country variety show, "Hee Haw," as it was in its prototype, "Laugh-In."

While shows like these depend heavily upon slapstick, others incorporate this form of humor sparingly along with a mixture of more realistic comedy. Certainly the "I Love Lucy" series included slapstick, but its appeal was based on much more than that. Two recent situation comedies, "Alice" and "The Jeffersons," occasionally contain this ingredient. The pillow fight scene in the opening montage of "The Jeffersons" is an example.

Situation Comedy

The situation comedy ("sitcom"), one of television's most enduring forms, may be categorized into two basic types: (1) farce and (2) realistic presentations. In both types, the creators of these brief, humorous dramas strive for uniqueness in terms of characters, plots, and settings.

In the farce situation comedy, both the characters and the situations tend to be exaggerated and implausible. In some cases, both may actually be ridiculous. However, once the viewer accepts the situation for what it is, comic values may be developed through the plot, the actions, and the dialogue.

In contrast, the realistic situation comedy presents believable characters placed into situations that could happen to almost anyone. As discussed in chapter 2, the realistic situation comedy has undergone a notable transformation from the "wholesome family story," which prevailed before 1971, to one which deals with contemporary, and sometimes provocative, problems. Nevertheless, both approaches fit into the realistic situation comedy genre. Now for some examples.

A list of prominent *farce* situation comedies would certainly include "The Beverly Hillbillies," "The Munsters," "Mork and Mindy," "Green Acres," and "Gilligan's Island." All are based on implausable situations.

Realistic situation comedies of the pre-1970 era include such classics as "Make Room for Daddy," "The Andy Griffith Show," "Father Knows Best," and "My Three Sons." Modern realistic sitcoms, however, often present a social message and/or deal with provocative topics. Prominent examples include "All in the Family" "M*A*S*H," "One Day at a Time," "Different Strokes," and "Barney Miller."

Figure 6.3 The "Beverly Hillbillies" was an instantaneous hit and a successful network series from 1962 until 1971. This slapstick situation comedy continues to be shown on syndicated television.

Another group of situation comedies appears to bridge the older and the newer approaches. Among these sitcoms which are contemporary, but not highly provocative, are "The Mary Tyler Moore Show," "Sanford and Son," "WKRP in Cincinnati," and "Laverne and Shirley."

The classic sitcom, "I Love Lucy," practically defies categorization. Elements of realism, farce, and slapstick are all present in this series which continues to enjoy success in syndication *thirty years after it began!*

Gag Comedy

Gag comedy is based on clever lines and anecdotes rather than physical action or dramatic dialogue. This form of comedy tends to gain popularity in part because it usually deals with topical material with which the audience is familiar. Because of its contemporary content, however, the material becomes dated quickly and rarely is useful on a rerun basis.

Two types of gag comedy prevail in present-day broadcasting. These types are (1) gag comedy using characters and (2) straight gag comedy.

Examples of gag characters in 1980s television include Benny Hill and Monty Python. And the character roles played by Bob Hope in his variety shows belong in the "gag character" category because they have spoken lines. However, Red Skelton's characters, discussed previously, do not belong under the gag category because they were portrayed only in pantomime. Turning back to the network radio era, Edgar Bergen's ventriloquist characters, such as Charlie McCarthy and Mortimer Snerd, fit the category nicely. Another radio example is the famous "Minnie Pearl" character on WSM's "Grand Ole Opry."

Although there are few gag characters in the present era, straight gag comedy is abundant among the many stand-up comedians on television. In this comic form, the comedian appears in normal attire, often wearing a business suit, presenting clever, laugh-provoking lines with no plot or situation.

Johnny Carson's monologue, which begins each "Tonight" show, is perhaps the best example of present-day straight gag comedy. Bob Hope also uses the topical monologue technique to launch his network specials. Other successful monologists over the years have included Jack Benny, George Burns, and Red Skelton.

Sophisticated Comedy

Sophisticated comedy is a variation of the "comedy of manners," the purpose of which originally was to satirize the weaknesses of the upper classes. Its purpose today is simply to satirize or poke fun at anything or anyone who might be taken too seriously. Satire often requires alert mental participation by its audience as the significance may be hidden within the comic framework.

Few programs aimed at the mass audience can succeed on the basis of sophisticated wit alone because so many listeners do not choose to participate or are unable to participate adequately to enjoy the high-level humor. Low-level satire is possible, but education for sophisticated humor is mandatory.

Figure 6.4 Comedy monologues are one of Bob Hope's specialties. This veteran comedian has entertained 20th century Americans through radio, movies, television, and on stage.

Some contemporary television programs contain humorous elements of a sophisticated nature along with mass-appeal comedy. Thus, two levels of understanding and enjoyment exist within the same program vehicle. A good example is "M*A*S*H," in which occasional gems of sophisticated wit are present.

Other Humor

In addition to the principal forms of humor and the examples given above, there are numerous minor ways in which comedy is employed in broadcast programming. These include comic relief characters in dramatic shows, such as Vera in the "Alice" series and Chester in "Gunsmoke"; audience participation programs in which contestants are encouraged to be exuberant and make funny remarks; quizmasters who use their positions to entertain with comedy material; and radio DJ's who sometimes tell jokes and engage in comic dialogue on their programs.

LOVE, ROMANCE, AND SEX APPEAL

This group of related appeals represents an important aspect of program development because of the universality of the three components. Love, romance, and sex often are interrelated, yet each appeal may be emphasized separately. Any one, or any combination of the three, may be employed either as a primary or as a supporting appeal. In this discussion, we will explore love and romance jointly, then treat sex appeal as a separate item.

Love and Romance

Love is essentially an emotional state or condition in which one person has a strong affection for another. Romance, in turn, represents the ecstasy period of a love relationship when positive feelings are at their peak. Often the perception of romance is enhanced by such accompanying devices as an exotic location, a moonlight night, and the playing of mellow love songs.

As discussed previously, stories related to problems in love and romance often serve as the basis for plots in dramatic programs. These problems, in serious dramas and in crime stories, may lead to criminal or violent actions which become the basis for a conflict plot. In light dramas, such as situation comedies, similar problems may lead to comedic effects. In either case, however, love is a secondary or supporting appeal.

On the other hand, when love and romance are primary appeals, some plot complications are still required to maintain interest in the story. Thus, conflicts may be present, but they are often insignificant and are usually resolved rather easily. Similarly, some comedy lines may be incorporated for added appeal.

The number of television programs which have emphasized the "love-romance" theme is practically endless. A few titles illustrate the extent of the practice: "Love, American Style," "Love & Marriage," "Love Boat," "Love on a Roof Top," " Love Story," "Love That Bob," "Love That Jill," "Loves Me, Loves Me Not," and "Romance."

Of these titles, "Love Boat" is perhaps the best illustration because it is most recent. On this weekly drama series, the setting is a romantic cruise ship which takes its passengers to destinations up and down the Pacific Coast. There are also moonlight nights and music, and the "promise" of the venture is thoroughly romantic. The love theme predominates as three romantic plots alternate through the hour. These love relationships may involve members of the regular crew, or they may be strictly among the guests. Inevitably, however, at the end of the program, the viewer is left with a good, satisfied feeling because, just like the Hollywood movies, the right couples usually get together on the path to matrimony.

Love and romance also have played significant roles in daytime serial dramas, as well as in such nighttime series programs as "The Dick Van Dyke Show" and "Rhoda." In the latter, Rhoda Morgenstern, a spin-off character from "The Mary Tyler Moore Show," fell in love and, after a romantic period, was married on an hour-long episode that attracted top audience ratings. The happy marriage ended, however, when Rhoda and Joe Gerard became separated and were divorced two seasons later.

In "The Mary Tyler Moore Show" itself, Mary Richards occasionally had romantic episodes, but never any serious love affairs. However, there was always a hint of possible romance between Mary and her boss, Lou Grant, played by Edward Asner.

In addition to programs that emphasize the love-romance theme, many other shows—including conflict, comedy, and nostalgic series—use love as a supporting appeal. This is often done through the portrayal of happily married couples who rarely, if ever, have problems with their relationship.

In "The Waltons," for example, a strong and warm love existed between John and Olivia Walton, as well as love between this couple and their children. It was obviously the strength of the marriage and the family relationship that supported the Waltons through the Depression of the 1930s.

In many situation comedies, there is no doubt that love exists between married partners. Such was the case with Edith and Archie Bunker in "All in the Family," who, despite numerous problems, always showed evidence of their love for each other. One of the most poignant moments in recent television programming, in fact, was Carroll O'Connor's portrayal of Archie Bunker in the (1980) episode that depicted Edith's death. Love between married partners also is evident between Louise and George Jefferson in "The Jeffersons" and Emily and Bob Hartley in "The Bob Newhart Show," and the same was true of George Burns and Gracie Allen in their radio and early TV shows.

Speaking of radio, the dominant element for most stations is music. And probably 90 percent or more of all popular songs relate to love. While musical styles come and go, the theme of love between a young girl and her beau is practically universal and timeless.

Contemporary popular songs which deal with love tend to appeal to the current youth of dating age. Even young teenage couples pick "their song" to identify their own romance. In turn, as each generation grows older, it remembers and enjoys hearing the dating songs of its youth. This concept leads to a popular strategy in radio programming in which stations appeal to target audiences by emphasizing the love songs of their demographic age group's courting years.

Other Love Appeals

While we primarily associate the love appeal with romantic love between members of the opposite sex, love is also manifest between parents and children, brothers and sisters, and between humans and their animal pets. These forms of affection frequently are presented in TV programs, even though they usually are supporting rather than primary appeals in their respective shows.

The love between parents and their children in "The Waltons" already has been discussed. A few other examples, all taken from one-parent families, include Sheriff Andy Taylor and his son Opie in "The Andy Griffith Show," Alice Hyatt and her young son in "Alice," Fred and Lamont Sanford in "Sanford and Son," and Ann Romano and her two teenage daughters in "One Day at a Time."

Love by children for their pets is nearly universal in society, and this theme has been used successfully as a program appeal on TV and in the movies. The classic case is "Lassie," the long-running series about a brave, loyal, and highly intelligent collie and her owners. A similar appeal was developed for the pet dolphin, "Flipper," and for a pet black bear in "Gentle Ben."

Incidentally, a sure-fire method for attracting viewers to any television program or commercial is to include cute children, especially babies, and attractive pets. The almost universal love for both is the basic appeal involved.

Sex Appeal

A person's sex appeal essentially is the attraction that person exudes for members of the opposite sex through his/her physical attributes, warmth of personality, or both. It is frequently used in TV programming as a device to gain the attention of specific target audience groups. Usage of sex appeal ranges from unabashed exploitation of physical attributes to the casting in television roles of warm and charming individuals whose appeal lies primarily in their personalities. Thus, sex appeal may be used in both blatant and subtle ways by the media.

One of television's earliest usage of sex appeal was in a 1952 program known as "Dagmar's Canteen." The canteen for sevicemen was quite real, as was the extraordinary figure of the actress who played the Dagmar character. During this era, a great deal of television viewing took place in bars in Northern cities, and it was believed that Dagmar's presence would help sell home television receivers.

During the 1950s and 1960s, blatant sex appeal was minimal on television. However, during the 1970s, with the lowering of taboos and rising protests against the portrayal of violence, sex appeal (and sexual material) rebounded vigorously. This emphasis ultimately resulted in protest action by various pressure groups which opposed the extent of sexual material and innuendo on television.

One of the prime examples of modern-day sex appeal on television is "Charlie's Angels," a detective show which exploited the physical attractiveness of three young actresses who frequently appeared in bikinis or other scanty attire. Other examples of blatant sex appeal include the voluptuous Jennifer Marlowe, played by Loni Anderson, on "WKRP in Cincinnati," and Major Margaret ("Hot Lips") Houlihan, played by Loretta Swit on "M*A*S*H." Much more subtle, however, was the warm and wholesome sex appeal of Mary Tyler Moore on "The Dick Van Dyke Show" and her own series. Similarly, former Miss America Lee Meriwether portrayed the appealing daughter-in-law of "Barnaby Jones" on that dramatic series.

The use of physically attractive persons on television includes males as well as females. Physical attraction often is a major asset for male newscasters, program hosts, and heroes in dramatic programs. A few examples of the latter include James Garner on "The Rockford Files," Telly Savalas as "Kojak," Alan Alda as "Hawkeye" on "M*A*S*H," Robert Young as Dr. Marcus Welby, and Edward Asner as "Lou Grant."

Finally, sex appeal is not confined to the visual medium of television. Radio's great capability to stimulate the imagination contributes to the sex appeal of announcers, male and female, and other performers who project warmth of personality through the speaking voice. The rapport established by announcers with their listeners plays an important role in perpetuating radio as a companion medium.

HUMAN INTEREST

The way people act and react, whether as real individuals or as characters in dramatic shows, can fascinate the general audience. Thus, interest in human behavior, or *human interest,* may be added to the list of appeals which programmers can use to attract viewers or listeners.

Human interest, of course, arises from the natural curiosity that we have about the behavior of others, including their problems, their reactions, and the things that interest them. It includes fascination with famous people, such as movie stars, television celebrities, renowned athletes, and politicians, as well as ordinary, undistinguished persons.

Human interest usually is a moderately strong appeal, used to enhance the drawing power of a program whose primary emphasis rests on a conflict, comedy, or love theme. In some cases, however, human interest can be the dominant program appeal.

Three television shows illustrate the use of human interest as a dominant appeal. These programs are "Candid Camera," "Real People," and "Games People Play." Allen Funt's "Candid Camera," the successor to "Candid Microphone," uses the basic ploy of photographing unsuspecting people with hidden cameras to see how they react to bizarre, contrived situations. "Candid Camera" was carried by all three TV networks at some time between 1948 and 1967. It is still going strong on pay-cable TV in an adult version not permitted on commercial television. "Real People," launched by NBC in 1979, follows a similar approach. In "Games People Play," both ordinary individuals and quasiprofessional performers display their abilities in various forms of contests and stunts. The success of these three programs lies in the reaction of ordinary people to stimuating and usually humorous circumstances.

As a secondary appeal, interest in "ordinary folks" takes a number of forms, including audience participation shows in which the contestants are typical citizens, dramatic programs in which human interest is heightened through everyday characters and situations, emphasis on problems of ordinary people, and the display of common, humanizing traits by professional entertainers.

Several of the TV game shows illustrate the human interest concept quite well. Two examples are "The Gong Show" and "Family Feud." In "The Gong Show," performers of questionable talent attempted to sing, dance, or do whatever act they chose until the panel of judges voted to ring the "gong." "Family Feud" is a somewhat more dignified production, in which two families compete against each other in answering a series of questions. The real appeal of both shows, however, lies in the spontaneous reaction of the participants.

Human interest as exemplified in dramatic TV programs may be illustrated by such wholesome family dramas as "The Waltons" and "Little House on the Prairie." Both shows reveal the qualities of character and strength which were so essential to survival during the difficult time periods they portray. Certain situation comedies, such as "The Andy Griffith Show" and "The Real McCoys," also generated interest because their unpretentious characters were so typical of ordinary people who live in grass roots America.

In some cases, however, human interest has been heightened by putting ordinary people into unusual circumstances or by placing sophisticated people into ordinary settings. These two "twists" are illustrated respectively by "The Beverly Hillbillies" and by "Green Acres." Another successful twist of the ordinary family situation comedy took place in "The Brady Bunch," in which the children of two families were brought together by the marriage of the father of one group to the mother of the second clan. Thus developed a highly unusual situation for the development of ordinary family problems.

Programs which focus on the problems of ordinary people also may generate human interest as viewers seek to find out how the subjects deal with those difficulties. For many years, radio and television soap operas followed this concept. In recent years, however, these programs have tended to follow the lives of more sophisticated persons. Nevertheless, the daytime serial drama succeeds, in part, because of the audience's interest in their reactions to problems.

Other examples include the "Donahue" TV-talk show, the television series "Divorce Court," and the radio feature hosted by columnist Ann Landers. Landers' radio series basically follows the pattern of her newspaper column in that she replies with advice to listeners who seek her counsel.

A number of professional entertainers have adopted common, but out of character, personality traits to develop human interest in their programs. One of the most memorable was Jack Benny's alleged stinginess. Thus, the superlative comedian was perceived by his audience as very human indeed.

Another radio-television performer whose style of communication was simple, direct, and "ordinary," but also highly effective, was Arthur Godfrey. Perhaps Godfrey's greatest contribution to broadcasting was that of delivering his commercial messages as if he were speaking with his average listener on a one-to-one basis. His technique ultimately became standard radio practice, replacing the early announcing style that was quite formal and stuffy.

Finally, human interest manifests itself in programs about and with well-known personages. While the public may enjoy the professional performances of actors and actresses, singers, athletes, and politicians, they also become curious about their lives. The gossip columns provide this type of information in the print media. Walter Winchell and Louella Parsons broadcast similar material on radio during the 1940s. Today, the preferred vehicle is the talk show in which celebrity guests are interviewed by the program's host. The "Tonight" show is a prime example. A number of syndicated talk shows, including "The Mike Douglas Show," "The Merv Griffin Show," and "The John Davidson Show," are broadcast throughout the country.

EMOTIONAL STIMULATION

Although closely related to human interest, emotional stimulation as a program appeal goes far beyond mere interest in the behavior of persons or characters in television and radio programs. This heightened form of interest often results in viewer identification with a certain character or characters and the development of empathy with the individual characters. Thus, the viewer may emotionally live the role of the character and feel the emotions that are appropriate to the character.

Sympathy is probably the most prevalent emotion stimulated by broadcast programs. However, depending upon the plot, the emotionally stimulated viewer may suffer fear as the character encounters a frightful situation, or the viewer may develop a dislike or even hatred for another character who mistreats the favored one. For example, those actors and actresses who play villainous roles on television, especially on daytime serial dramas, occasionally have been rebuked or even physically attacked when seen in public by emotionally stimulated viewers.

Emotional stimulation also may be generated through the emphasis of content themes which have special appeal among the audience. For example, religious, patriotic, and nostalgic themes appeal emotionally to many persons. The wave of nostalgia programming during the 1970s, the decade of the national bicentennial, stands out as an example. Included among the dramas depicting life in earlier decades were such popular television shows as "Happy Days," "Laverne and Shirley," "The Waltons," and "Little House on the Prairie."

INFORMATION

Information programming includes all types of broadcasts which communicate knowledge or facts to the public. The predominant type, of course, is news itself. Other information-based programming includes interview programs, talk shows, documentaries, special events broadcasts, and sports play-by-play accounts. Information also may be woven into entertainment programs even though the facts given may be somewhat trivial. For example, radio disc jockeys frequently provide bits of information about the recording artists whose music is played.

Increasingly, news programs are being taken more seriously by station licensees and by the publics they serve. Newscasts often include a number of types of content, such as reports of governmental affairs, warfare, economic developments, tragedies, and human interest stories. In addition, most television newscasts also contain information on sports, weather, and commodity and stock markets, plus occasional commentaries and consumer affairs items. While no single person may be interested in every item presented, a strongly appealing newscast can be developed through the inclusion of varied types of information needed by the diverse segments of the public.

Newscasts also play a major role in radio programming, but program patterns differ noticeably from that of television. For most stations, the concept of a brief newscast every hour prevails. However, several large markets now support all-news radio stations which frequently attract large cumulative audiences.[2]

Special events broadcasts historically have had great appeal because television and radio enable viewers and listeners to observe history being made. Radio broadcasting, of course, officially began with the coverage of the 1920 presidential election in Pittsburgh. Since then, practically every event of national importance has been covered live.

In addition to historic special events, radio and television become extraordinary public servants when they provide extended coverage of life-threatening floods, hurricanes, tornadoes, and other disasters. Special events broadcasting indeed represents a shining opportunity for networks and stations to serve their audiences.

Figure 6.5 Local and national news broadcasts exemplify the information appeal. Shown here is the "Newscenter 7" team at WHIO-TV, Dayton, Ohio.

Photo courtesy of Cox Communications, Inc.

Documentary programming, once low-rated, has come into its own through the "magazine" format which usually incorporates three or four major features, balanced for varied appeal, in an hour time period. The success of such network documentaries as "60 Minutes" and "20/20" depends in part on the balanced appeal resulting from varied informational content, plus hard-hitting investigative reporting and the public's desire for information.

Information is a major appeal for radio stations, extending beyond newscasts to a number of unique services which are particularly well suited to the medium. Reports of traffic conditions beamed to drivers is one example of radio's capability to meet an immediate need of its listeners. So important is the mobile audience during peak traffic hours that most stations identify these morning and afternoon periods as "drive time."

Radio listeners also have been known to form their listening habits on the basis of which stations consistently provide them with weather reports and time checks, as well as fast-breaking coverage of news stories.

IMPORTANCE

This last appeal, as its name suggests, relates to what listeners and viewers perceive as being important in programs. *Importance,* which may be either a primary or reinforcing appeal, can be found in both informational and entertainment programs.

Informational programming inherently contains the appeal of importance. Its degree, however, depends largely upon how much the subject matter affects the audience. For example, the story of a local flood in a newscast contains a stronger importance appeal than one in a far distant land. On the other hand, a relatively unimportant or distant news item also may become important because of its uniqueness and the build-up it has received from the media. Thus, newscasts typically appeal to their audiences through careful selection of stories which couple the two appeals of information and importance.

Public affairs programs, such as documentaries, interviews, and discussion broadcasts, also usually attract the audience in proportion to the importance of the subject and its degree of inherent controversy.

In addition to newscasts and discussion programs, special events broadcasts attract audiences because of the importance attached to witnessing live happenings. The audience historically has responded positively to live broadcasts of unfolding events, both planned and unplanned. Certainly the most spectacular broadcast coverage of all time was the lunar landing by Neil Armstrong in 1969, which was viewed by more than half a billion people throughout the world. However, even on a local scale, live coverage of a major event can powerfully attract an audience for the broadcasting media.

In entertainment programming, importance is manifest through the drawing power of well-known performers whose names can be promoted and whose presence all but guarantees a large audience. Television's one-time special shows typically include four or more prominent entertainers, usually carefully chosen for balance to make the program appeal to various target groups.

Also in some entertainment shows, the appeal of importance becomes manifest through lavish production. For example, many television specials are laced with impressive dance numbers and large casts of performers. Like prominent performers, these facts also can be promoted, thus lending a perception of importance to the program.

Finally, a third way in which importance frequently is achieved is through scheduling of important theatrical movies on television. When the name of the movie itself suggests its own importance, the network involved reaps the benefits of a large audience. Both networks and local stations alike often schedule their biggest and best-known entertainment attractions, including movies and one-time specials, during rating "sweeps" so as to maximize their audience data.

EFFECTIVE PROGRAM STRUCTURE

In addition to providing its audience with carefully chosen appeals, or "rewards," a program also must be put together well in order to win and hold its target audience. The ideal program, therefore, is one which strongly attracts viewers or listeners, then proceeds smoothly through its internal segments or "units," so that the central idea, theme, or mood is easy for the audience to follow. Thus, effectiveness results from logical arrangement of the structural parts of a program, as well as from inclusion of the appropriate appeals in the right proportion.

For a program to have effective structure, it must fully satisfy five basic structural requirements. These requirements include (1) an attractive opening and closing; (2) a strong beginning; (3) program unity; (4) effective pacing, variety of content, and unit change; and (5) effective building and climax.

While these five requirements especially relate to dramatic programs, they also apply to all other types of TV and radio programs, including newscasts, musical programs, and variety shows.

ATTRACTIVE OPENING AND CLOSING

The opening of a program is essentially a signature to alert the audience to the upcoming show. Thus, those who want to watch or listen are made aware that the program is about to begin.

Radio programs for many years used theme songs for identification. Most series TV shows now couple standard visual openings with theme music. In some cases, such standard openings consist of a montage of memorable scenes from past broadcasts.

In any case, an effective opening for a television show ideally should provide quickly grasped identification through theme, visualization, and the program's title. More than anything else, it should arouse interest in watching the program.

One-time shows and some anthology series occasionally use openings which incorporate dramatic highlights from within the program itself to grab the interest of the viewer quickly. In such cases, the program's title is given only after the attracting device presumably has involved the viewer in the plot.

A title, like that of a book, should reveal or suggest the nature of the program. Ideally, it should be catchy and distinctive and not likely to be confused with that of any other show. The title should provoke interest and be easy to remember. And, because of space constraints, it should be short enough to fit into a newspaper log column. One-word titles, initiated by NBC's "Today" and "Tonight," are especially preferred.

A program closing, which is given after the end of the episode, serves as the final program identification. It brings the broadcast to an orderly ending and may encourage the viewers to tune in the next program in the series. Most likely, the closing repeats the theme music, the visual device, and the title. It also provides an opportunity to recognize performers, writers, and members of the production team through on-air credits.

Standard closings often are used for an entire season. In some cases, however, closings may differ from program to program. A summary montage, for example, has been used on several series, including "The Mary Tyler Moore Show" and "Lou Grant."

Closings sometimes are produced in different lengths and also may contain "pad" time to facilitate adjustment to the lengths of episodes.

A STRONG BEGINNING

For any type of program, it is vitally important to capture the audience's attention immediately and then to hold the viewer's interest throughout the program. First, an interest-arousing opening is needed for quick involvement. Otherwise, the start becomes weak and the audience may shop around for alternative programs to watch. Thus, the faster the program proper gets underway, the more secure is the audience.

A few typical examples of strong beginnings for a television show include (1) an action scene to start a dramatic program; (2) a lively production number for a variety show; (3) a laugh-provoking monologue for a comedy-variety show; (4) a bright and lively musical selection to begin a musical program; and (5) a major news item to start a newscast.

Similarly, a radio disc jockey program following a newscast may begin with a bright popular tune to grasp the audience at the show's beginning. In contrast, the program opening should not be long enough to delay the start unnecessarily. Neither should commercials be placed too early in the program because of the risk of the audience shopping around for alternative program choices.

In brief, nothing should be done that would unnecessarily risk dissipating the strength of a program's beginning.

PROGRAM UNITY

In the 5th century BC, the Greek dramatists developed three ancient principles of dramatic construction which have influenced all forms of drama since that time. These principles, known as the three "unities," were set down by Aristotle in his *Poetics*.

First, according to the ancient playwrights, the "unity of time" requires that events presented in a play must cover a period that is no longer than 24 hours. The "unity of place" requires that the events given in a play must take place within a single locality. And the "unity of action" requires that no events or characters be introduced which are inconsistent with the central theme or mood of the play.

Many playwrights of later centuries, including Shakespeare, chose to ignore one or more of the three classic unities. However, even today, it is considered desirable that a dramatic production be tightly woven around a unifying theme and that every ingredient in that play contribute to the development of the story.

The fact that television and radio have such rigid time constraints also emphasizes the demand that every action must count toward the central purpose of the program. This same requirement also applies to nondramatic programs, such as variety and musical shows, as much as it does to drama itself.

In broadcasting, especially in television, we tend to think of programs as packaged and titled commodities which can be scheduled for specific time slots. Program managers typically place programs in such periods as the hour or the half-hour on the basis of their appeal to the intended audience, as well as their ability to maintain interest and build a carry-over audience for subsequent programs.

However, programs are much more than mere shows to be dropped into a station's or a network's schedule. Closer study reveals that any program, regardless of its type, consists of many structural units. These units are identifiable segments in which one type of subject matter is presented, or in which one recognizable idea dominates the action.

A typical half-hour television drama, such as a light situation comedy, usually contains between 10 and 14 subject-matter units, exclusive of commercials. Similarly, an hour-long drama ordinarily includes between 18 and 26 units. In contrast, however, an hour-long variety show will consist of only seven or eight acts, or units.

Subject-matter units are typically introduced into a program through one of the following devices: (1) a change of scene; (2) the introduction of a new type of material, such as a new act in a variety show; (3) the beginning of a new musical number; (4) the entry of a new character into a drama; (5) the introduction of a new idea into a talk; (6) a change to a different form of presentation, such as from dialogue to monologue, or from monologue to interview; and (7) a change in the mood of a program.

With these techniques of introduction or unit change in mind, let us go further to describe several typical program units, as follows:

1. A "discovery scene" in a crime-detective show;
2. A "kitchen scene" in a situation comedy;
3. A husband-wife conflict encounter in a soap opera;
4. A comedian's monologue (e.g., Johnny Carson of "Tonight" and Bob Hope on his specials);
5. A dialogue between two personalities (e.g., Johnny Carson and Ed McMahon on "Tonight");
6. A musical selection by a band or vocalist;
7. A choreographic number;
8. A commercial or public service announcement;
9. A narrator's transition in a documentary broadcast;
10. Each single question and answer in an interview program;
11. Each half-inning in the broadcast of a baseball game; and
12. Each story in a newscast. News stories, however, are usually grouped into larger subject-matter units in news broadcasts.

The list could go on indefinitely. The point, however, is that each unit, whether long or short, is a building block used in constructing the total program. And the implication is that each unit should contribute directly to the totality, or "unity," of the broadcast.

In a dramatic program, each unit exists for a specific purpose. Some units introduce characters. Others introduce the problem and its complications, while other units plant clues or add comic relief. All such units exist to move the plot forward toward its ultimate resolution.

Such singleness of theme, while mandatory in a drama, is also highly recommended as a device for maintaining unity in nondramatic programs. A variety show, for example, may focus on a seasonal theme, such as springtime or autumn, or a holiday event, such as Christmas or the Fourth of July. A musical program also may emphasize such themes as the seasons, music of an era, or songs by a particular composer.

The length of program units depends primarily upon the intended audience for a specific program. No audience can be expected to remain interested in any single subject for a long period of time because of limited attention spans. These tolerance spans tend to be quite short for young children, but are somewhat longer for adults.

In some cases, adults willingly tolerate dull subject matter because of circumstances. A bored ticket-paying theatre-goer, for example, will not likely subject himself or herself to the embarrassment of leaving. However, a bored TV viewer will turn the channel at the slightest whim. It's a good rule of thumb to adjust unit lengths to the target audience. Two highly successful children's programs bear out this concept. Both "Sesame Street" and "The Electric Company," produced by the Children's Television Workshop, frequently contain units as short as 30 seconds.

What about the adult audience? "Laugh-In" pioneered the use of the short unit for adult television. Other shows, including "Hee-Haw," have adopted the approach. While grown-ups will tolerate longer segments, frequent change is still desirable to retain maximum viewer interest. Units in dramatic programs intended for mature audiences may average two minutes in length and may range from 40 seconds to perhaps four minutes or more. Sample unit structures for different types of programs are shown in Figure 6.6.

While interest in a program can be sustained through frequent changes of unit, interest levels also can be boosted by varying the camera angles on the subject matter. The unit, therefore, may contain numerous camera shots, taken from different angles, to maintain variety in presentation. For example, the use of multiple shots is common within variety show acts, which tend to average six to eight minutes in length.

In addition to program structure, the unity of a program also may be enhanced through several other devices. One is the effective use of transitions and lead-ins, which serve to link together the major units with a thread of continuity.

Another device is the use of a single featured personality whose presence and transitional remarks provide a unifying focus for an entire program. A classic example is "The Ed Sullivan Show," the long-running variety broadcast that was held together almost entirely by the presence of its host. Present-day variety shows usually follow a similar pattern, although the host may also take a performing role. In newscasts, the anchorperson serves a similar function by introducing field reports and reading brief transitional items.

Finally, another technique for improving the unity of a series is week-to-week continuity. This device calls for the regular appearance of the same characters, at least the principals, with their predictable behavior patterns revealed on program after program. Week-to-week continuity also may be developed through the use of similar types of plots or ploys in entertainment programming.

EFFECTIVE PACING, VARIED CONTENT, AND UNIT CHANGE

These three aspects of presentation are grouped together because they are basic techniques for maintaining the interest of the audience in a given program.

The *pacing* of a broadcast relates to the perception of moving ahead with the plot or other material. We have just discussed unit structure in connection with program unity and have learned that, in a dramatic program, each subject matter unit has a specific purpose. We also have learned that each unit is expected to move the story forward toward its climax and resolution. A program with proper pacing gives the viewer or listener a positive sense of moving toward that resolution.

Figure 6.6 Unit Structures for Typical Programs

(1) Television Variety Show (One hour)

Unit No.	Unit Description	Length (minutes)
1	Program Opening	1-2
2	Opening Monologue	6-7
	COMMERCIAL BREAK	
3	Choreographic Number	7-8
	COMMERCIAL BREAK	
4	Comedy Skit	7-8
	COMMERCIAL AND LOCAL STATION BREAK	
5	Musical Number	7-8
	COMMERCIAL BREAK	
6	Comedy Act	7-8
	COMMERCIAL BREAK	
7	Musical Finale	7-8
	COMMERCIAL BREAK	
8	Host's Closing Remarks and Program Closing	2-3

(2) Television Detective Show (One hour)

Unit No.	Unit Description	Length (minutes)
1	Program Opening	1-1½
2	Orientation Scene	2-3
3	Murder Event	2-3
4	Discovery Scene	2-3
5	Discoverer Approaches Private Detective	2-4
6	Detective Surveys Death Scene	2-4
	COMMERCIAL BREAK	
7	Detective and Associate Discuss Case	2-3
8	Detective Examines Fragmentary Evidence	2-3
9	Detective Confers with Police	2-3
10	Detective Meets with Associate "A" of Victim	2-4
11	Associate "B" (the Murderer) Arrives at the Scene, Talks with Detective	2-3
12	Detective Leaves for Office	1
13	A and B Discuss the Murder, the Suspicions of the Detective, Reveal their Complicity	2-4
	COMMERCIAL AND LOCAL STATION BREAK	
14	Detective Returns to Murder Scene, Discovers New Evidence, Becomes Suspicious of B	2-4
15	Detective Calls on Associate B, Asks Probing Questions, Leaves for Office	2-4
16	Detective Gets Lab Report Positively Implicating B	1
17	Detective and Associate Discuss the Solution	1-2
	COMMERCIAL BREAK	
18	A and B Confer, Plan to Kill Detective	2-3
19	Detective Receives Call from A, Arranges Meeting for Voluntary Testimony	1
20	A and B Hidden at Rendezvous Point	½
21	Detective Arrives in Car, Gets Out, Walks	½
22	A Emerges, Starts Talking with Detective	½
23	B Emerges, Establishing Life Threatening Situation for Detective	½
24	Brief Dialogue, Followed by Emergence of Detective's Associate	½
25	Fight Ensues, Detective and His Associate Win	1½
	COMMERCIAL BREAK	
26	Postlude Discussion Scene	1-1½
27	Program Closing	1

Along the way, however, the perceived rate of movement must vary. If it doesn't, the program forever would be on a static plane, either high or low, with no dramatic peaks to stand above the more tranquil scenes. Thus, as in a dynamic musical composition, some units should be action oriented, while others are included to offset the fast pace and provide a balance from tenser moments.

Action segments generally are given longer air time in dramatic programs than are more slowly paced scenes. In fact, any slow-moving element should be given only a brief time to maintain the audience's interest. However, they are necessary to provide balance.

The sense of movement ordinarily can be heightened through rapid cutting between camera shots as well as by fast action on the screen. Pace also can be slowed down through the use of camera movement, such as zooms in and out and panning across the subject, rather than by cutting from one camera to another.

Pace in a variety show may be achieved by alternating tense or exciting acts with tranquil ones. For example, a tense acrobatic act or a hilarious comedy routine might well be followed by a relaxing medley of songs. Similarly, a musical program can achieve both pace and balance by playing tunes through sequences of fast and slow numbers, including transitional selections to bridge the gap.

Any program without internal *variety* tends to bore its audience. Just as pace is important to keep a program moving, variety in content and presentation is needed to keep a program interesting.

In a musical broadcast, variety may be achieved through use of selections of various types and tempos which adhere to the basic program theme. Varied settings, characters, and types of action add dimension to dramatic programs. And, of course, variety shows are built around an assortment of different entertainment acts.

Other ways that variety may be introduced into a broadcast include the use of various types of characters or performers and varied methods of presentation. As suggested above, casts of characters for a dramatic program may be balanced to include both straight and comic relief characters, as well as a balance between male and female and juvenile and mature characters.

In musical programs, variety may be achieved by alternating between types of performers. In a radio disc jockey program, such an example might consist of a sequence beginning with a vocal group, followed by a male vocalist, an instrumental number, and then a female vocalist.

Methods of presentation also may be varied. For example, a talk show may alternate between monologue, dialogue, and interview. Or a variety show might rotate between comedy, music, and dance acts.

Unit-to-unit change is another device that is widely used to maintain the interest of the audience. As suggested previously, each unit must conform and contribute to the overall unity of the program. However, a subject-matter unit may be quite different from the preceding unit and still maintain unity. In many dramatic programs, for example, a series of plots is alternated through a progression of units. Unit-to-unit change also is easily handled in musical and variety shows where continuity is less pronounced.

A useful analogy here is the rubber band. The challenge in programming is to stretch the difference between units as much as possible, but not so much that the continuity snaps.

EFFECTIVE BUILDING AND CLIMAX

The final requirement of good program structure is that viewer or listener interest must be maintained throughout the program and then satisfied in the final resolution.

The climax, which is the culmination and the most gripping single unit in a program, usually comes just before the final resolution of the problem or conflict. In a dramatic program, the final resolution, or "denouement," is usually the last unit. Thus, it is a strategic decision usually to place the climax near the end of the program to maintain interest as long as possible. Similarly, the highlight of a variety show usually is saved until the final act to hold the audience through anticipation. Thus, the elements of suspense and anticipation are very useful in maintaining the audience's interest.

Secondary climaxes also may be used as a device to bridge viewer interest across crucial breaks in a long program or in a series. For example, a dramatic high point often is placed just before the end of an act in a TV play to build interest in that which follows. Thus, a half-hour dramatic comedy show may have a secondary climax at the end of its first act, while a four-act hour-long drama may have three secondary climaxes, followed by the culmination and final resolution very near the end of the last act.

The use of secondary climaxes, or high and suspenseful points, is also quite common among serial dramas. Each daily episode usually ends with such a highlight to keep viewers curious enough to tune in the next day. Such secondary climaxes tend to be stronger and more provocative on Fridays than other days because of the greater lapse of time before the next broadcast.

SUMMARY

As stated at the beginning, a program is successful only if it attracts and sustains the interest of its intended audience. In this chapter, we have learned that program appeals and structural unity are fundamental considerations in program building. Furthermore, we have identified seven basic appeals available to program originators, as well as the seven essential facets of structural unity. Adroit selection and implementation of three or four of those audience appeals and careful adherence to the principles of structural unity form a strong basis for successful program development.

We have gained insights in this chapter into some vital internal aspects of individual programs. Our next chapter takes us into television schedule building, in which individual programs are looked upon as building blocks in the totality of a station or network's programming effort.

ENDNOTES

1. Tim Brooks and Earle Marsh, *The Complete Directory to Prime Time Network TV Shows 1946–Present* (New York: Ballentine Books, 1979), p. 360.
2. All-news television programming became a reality in 1982 with Turner Broadcasting's Cable News Network (CNN), a 24-hour information service. CNN-2 was launched by Turner in 1982. Another cable news service, a joint venture of ABC-TV and Westinghouse Broadcasting, also was scheduled for a 1982 debut.

STUDY QUESTIONS

1. Select a current television program and analyze it in terms of its structure and appeals. What are the program's strongest appeals? How effective are they for the program's intended audience? What additional supporting appeals are used? How effective are they? How well is the program designed in terms of structural unity?
2. Compare and contrast the program appeals and structure between specific programs of two types, as follows:
   (a) a situation comedy and a serious dramatic program;
   (b) a variety show and a serious drama;
   (c) a newscast and a talk show;
   (d) a children's program and a late-night talk/variety show.
3. Select a radio station format and analyze it in terms of its programming appeals and structure. What are the strengths and weaknesses of the format and its execution?
4. Develop a prospectus for a new series of dramatic television programs. You may choose any program genre. Include details regarding the program's setting, characters, and theme. Also include an outline of a sample plot, as well as a listing of other plot possibilities. Keep in mind that the program should have a basic formula so new episodes can be developed easily while maintaining the program's basic premise.

SUGGESTED READINGS

Adler, Richard P. *All in the Family: A Critical Appraisal.* New York: Praeger, 1979.

Alvorado, Manuel, and Edward Buscombi. *Hazell: The Making of a TV Series.* London: The British Film Institute, 1978.

Bluem, A.W., and R. Manvell, eds.. *Television: The Creative Experience.* New York: Hastings House, 1967.

Cantor, Muriel G. *The Hollywood Producer: His Work and His Audience.* New York: Basic Books, 1972.

Gerrold, David. *The World of Star Trek.* New York: Ballentine Books, 1973.

Shanks, Bob. *The Cool Fire: How to Make It in Television.* New York: W.W. Norton, 1976.

Wolper, David L., and Quincy Troupe. *The Inside Story of TV's "Roots."* New York: Warner Books, 1978.

7

COMMERCIAL TELEVISION PROGRAMMING

Competitive programming is the cornerstone of commercial television in the United States. As noted previously, the twin goals to which every commercial licensee must subscribe are to earn profits and to serve the public interest (both because a broadcast license is a trusteeship to the public airwaves and because it's good business). Profits rise when programs win popular favor, but they also fall and sometimes even disappear when programs fail to win an adequately large audience. Television programming, which is very expensive, is at the very heart of a successful commercial TV operation.

This chapter seeks to explain the fundamentals of television programming through an examination of programming goals, objectives, and strategies, sources of programs, and the basics of TV schedule building.

TV PROGRAMMING GOALS AND OBJECTIVES

To implement the goals of making a profit and serving the public interest, a number of fundamental objectives as well as tactical strategies come into focus. These basic objectives for commercial television are as follows:

1. *To build a competitive schedule that will attract the largest possible audience,* particularly of the desired demographic component, at each point on the schedule. The target audience of a network or local TV station will differ at various times within its weekly schedule, of

course, depending upon what audience is available to watch and what type of viewers the station needs to reach for advertising or public service purposes. In the case of specialized-appeal television stations, the target audience usually is narrowly defined, but it still may vary somewhat throughout the week.

2. *To provide a balanced schedule of programs,* including commercial positions, suitable for the requirements of the sales department. Most TV stations are expected to serve a variety of different audiences at some time each week as part of their service obligation. The same expectation holds true for station sales departments. Although there must be sufficient programming directed to the most sought-after demographic groups, the typical sales department also needs to serve a broad list of clients, for which a sufficiently varied schedule is desirable.
3. *To satisfy the public interest obligations*—news, public affairs, and other nonentertainment programming—for which the licensee has made commitments to the Federal Communications Commission. This programming, of course, may attract substantial audiences and contribute to the station's profitability as well as fulfill the promises made when the license was obtained.
4. *To develop a favorable station image among the viewing public.* A station's image, which often influences viewing behavior, is simply a composite of the personality and reputation of the station as perceived through all facets of its programming. Although intangible, station image is of utmost imortance and requires careful nurturing by management.

THE TV MEDIA AND THEIR INTENDED AUDIENCES

To the public, television is a receiving set and a variety of programming sources that can be tuned in. These sources may be divided into broadcast, cable, and prerecorded media. Excluding sources of video records, six types of telecommunications organizations provide TV programming to the public. These include five types of broadcast media—television networks, network TV affiliates, general independent stations, specialty independent outlets, and subscription TV stations—as well as cable television systems. Although cable television is not broadcasting in a strict sense, it is a delivery system that resembles broadcast TV as well as a rapidly growing competitor and companion to over-the-air television. Before we explore programming sources and techniques, let's look at these media types.

First, there are the *national networks,* whose coverage extends broadly throughout the country, allowing them to serve the vast and diverse national population. Because their advertising revenues are pegged to national program ratings, network programming efforts are directed toward two principal goals: (1) reaching as large an audience as possible at any given time, particularly among those viewers who exhibit the demographic characteristics sought by consumer advertisers; and (2) reaching all of the desirable, specialized audience groups at some time during the broadcast week. Each network tries to develop a diversified program schedule with sufficient appeal to permit effective competition for viewership and advertisers.

The primary focus of US television programming rests upon the commercial networks. ABC, CBS, and NBC each provides approximately 90 hours of programming per week to some 200 individual stations, including both network-*owned* and network-*affiliated* outlets. These networks both originate programs and secure TV productions from outside sources.

Second, *network-affiliated stations,* which include the vast majority of the country's TV outlets, depend upon their network affiliation for most of their programming needs. Both affiliates and network-owned stations typically fill nearly 70 percent of their schedules with network programs. These stations usually follow the network pattern by placing primary emphasis on mass appeal programming, with secondary emphasis on specialized programs that appeal to large audiences.

Third, *general independent stations* attempt to compete with the network affiliates for the broad mass audiences in their markets. However, independent stations must program practically all of their air time with nonnetwork material. They rely heavily on syndicated programming, "occasional networks," and local live production. Since network programming usually represents "first-choice" viewing by the public, general independent stations usually follow programming strategies which, as we shall see, respond to their major competitors. A few stations of this type (for example, WTBS, Atlanta, and WGN-TV, Chicago) have emerged as "super stations," rivaling even the networks in national coverage through satellite transmission of their signals to cable systems.

Fourth, there are *specialty independent stations,* usually UHF operations, which seek narrowly defined audiences *throughout* their schedules. These stations usually exist *in addition to* one or more general independent stations in their markets. Target audiences often include Spanish-speaking Americans, other foreign-language groups (examples include Japanese, Chinese, Korean, German, and Greek), Blacks, followers of certain religions, and persons interested in news/business/financial information. Only when these unique audiences are sufficiently large, however, can such specialty stations be commercially viable.

Fifth, *subscription TV stations* are independent outlets which provide over-the-air pay television service, coupled with either general or specialty independent programming. Subscription (STV) stations, which began to proliferate during the late 1970s, usually provide free (unscrambled) programming during some daytime hours in addition to their scrambled programs, which are receivable only by paying customers. The pay-TV material carried by STV stations usually consists of recent movies, sports, and entertainment specials.

Figure 7.1 charts the spectrum of broadcast TV stations in three large cities, indicating each station's network affiliation or principal programming specialty.

Sixth, *cable television systems* serve as distribution vehicles for both broadcast programming and cable-oriented material. In addition, the more advanced CATV systems offer a variety of consumer services through two-way communications capability. Cable systems offer their services to the general public

Figure 7.1 On-Air Programming in Three Major Markets

Network or Programming Specialty	Boston		Chicago		San Francisco	
	Call	Channel	Call	Channel	Call	Channel
ABC	WCVB	5	WLS	7	KGO	7
CBS	WNEV	7	WBBM	2	KPIX	5
NBC	WBZ	4	WMAQ	5	KRON	4
Spanish Int'l Network	—	—	WCIU	26	KDTV	14
PBS	WGBH	2	WTTW	11	KQED	9
PBS	WGBX	44	WCME	20	KQEC	32
Independent (General)	WSBK	38	WGN	9	KTVU	2
Independent (General)	WLVI	56	WFLD	32	KBHK	44
Independent (General)	—	—	—	—	KTZO	20
Independent (Pay TV)	WQTV	68	WSNS	44	KTSF	26
Independent (Religious)	WXNE	25	WCFC	38	KVOF	38

on a subscription basis, providing their customers with wired reception of over-the-air stations and nonbroadcast programming.

The normal complement of broadcast sources on a cable system consists of all local TV stations, including network affiliates, independents, and public stations, as well as some out-of-market independent stations. Cable origination programming usually includes service/information channels (weather, stock market reports, community announcements), local production channels (movies and community-related programming), cable networks (sports, news, religion, children's programs, etc.), and pay-cable program services. Numerous pay-TV services are available to cable systems through satellite delivery. Most emphasize movies and stage shows; the material ranges from general to X-rated.

Although cable subscribers represent a broad population segment, specific programming frequently is directed toward narrowly based target audiences.

WHERE DO BROADCASTERS GET PROGRAMS?

The demand for television programming is immense. The three major networks, their hundreds of affiliates, the independent stations, and cable telecasters all have vast schedules to fill. It is trite, but accurate, to state that television has a voracious appetite for material, challenging and taxing the capacity of the creative community involved in program production. In this section, we will look at sources of programs from the perspective of the TV networks and local television stations.

PROGRAMMING SOURCES FOR NETWORKS

Two program sources are available to the television networks: (1) the network itself and (2) independent production firms. The most important types of programming originated by the networks are news and public affairs broadcasts. Each network budgets more than $100,000,000 annually for informational programming, including nightly newscasts, news breaks throughout the day, discussion programs, coverage of special events, and documentary broadcasts. The networks also produce sports coverage, children's programs, and some entertainment shows, including daytime serial dramas.

During television's formative years, the networks produced most of their entertainment programming. Today, however, they obtain almost all of their prime-time shows and much of their daytime material from outside sources. Many independent producers vie with each other for network exhibition of their product, which in turn can create a lucrative market later through syndication. Familiar names such as Tandem Productions, Quinn-Martin, Universal Television, Columbia Pictures TV, Hanna-Barbera, 20th Century Fox Studios, Paramount Television, and MTM Productions dominate the schedules. Selecting entertainment shows from such producers reduces much of the speculative risk from network operations, while also stimulating creative production for the network market.

Each year the independents, mostly based in Hollywood, churn out about 100 pilot shows for consideration by the network program departments. All pilots are carefully scrutinized by network executives and advertising agencies before they're purchased and scheduled. Even earlier, pilot shows are usually pretested before live audiences in theatre settings; sometimes they're broadcast as special programs so the public's reaction can be studied.

Specfic network schedules normally are announced each spring for the fall season which starts in September. Changes can be made as late as August, however, and in-season changes are made frequently in response to audience ratings.

Network program budgets relate closely to the potential audience that may be attracted at various times of the day or week. A rule-of-thumb at the beginning of the 1980s was that prime-time network TV shows incurred production costs averaging $10,000 per minute of air time. Thus, typical half-hour prime-time episodes cost about $250,000 to produce, allowing for commercial time. Some programs, of course, are much more expensive. Programs with unusual special effects, important talent, and big-name guest stars fall into this category, along with "blockbuster" movies. One of the most expensive TV series programs of all time was "Buck Rogers in the 25th Century," a space travel show that required elaborate sets and special effects. This show cost more than $750,000 for each 30-minute production. Networks have paid such staggering prices as $10,000,000 for rights to "The Godfather," $5,000,000 for "Gone With the Wind," and $4,000,000 for "Dr. Zhivago." In contrast, Saturday morning cartoons cost about $150,000, soap operas average $60,000, and many games shows only cost about $12,000 per show.[1]

PROGRAMMING SOURCES FOR LOCAL TV STATIONS

Local TV stations obtain programming from national networks, syndicated program distributors, special networks, and, of course, their own local efforts.

Network Programming

The relationship between networks and their local stations, as discussed previously, is a contractual one, subject to FCC rules on chain broadcasting. Each local outlet receives compensation at an agreed-upon rate for carrying network commercial broadcasts. The most important fact, however, is that program managers of affiliated stations can rely heavily upon their networks for the bulk of their programming needs.

Under the FCC's rules, each individual station licensee is totally responsible for its programming, retaining the right to turn down a network program for any reason whatsoever. Practically speaking, however, affiliates clear almost all of the programs their networks offer. To do otherwise would increase program costs and risk loss of affiliation. In some cases, however, a station will refuse a program because (1) it is considered objectionable for the area served; (2) another broadcast, such as a special local sports event, may be given higher priority; (3) it has low ratings locally; or (4) the station can make more money by carrying another program. Whenever a network affiliate declines such a program, however, an independent station in the market likely will pick it up.

Weekly network schedules are generally divided into six program blocks: (1) evening prime time, (2) evening news, (3) daytime, (4) early morning, (5) late night, and (6) weekend daytime. The programs scheduled during each period fundamentally reflect the interests of the available audiences.

Evening Prime Time As noted earlier, television's largest audience assembles before millions of TV sets every night. Each network begins its prime-time schedule at 8:00 (EST) and generally fills the next three hours with programs suitable for family viewing, including comedies, dramas, variety shows, news magazines, and occasional sports and specials. Under the FCC's prime-time access rule, TV stations in the top 50 markets may carry no more than three hours of network or off-network programs between 7:00 and 11:00 PM except Sunday, when the rule permits four hours.[2]

Evening News Each of the three national networks currently produces a half-hour early evening newscast. Local affiliates have a choice of two feeds from the network. Most carry this newscast just after their own half-hour or hour local newscast. However, some affiliates broadcast a half-hour local newscast before and after the network news in a "wrap-around" approach.

The idea of an hour-long newscast has been advanced periodically by the national networks. This expansion has not materialized to date, primarily because affiliates have been reluctant to give up the time.[3] However, each network has added brief news reports during prime-time hours and additional newscasts during nonevening periods. Additional network newscasts are projected for the early morning, late night, and even the 2:00 to 5:00 AM period.

In addition to the national networks, a special news network for independent stations has been established by WPIX-TV, New York. The Independent News Network (INN), which operates on a barter basis, provides two daily half-hour newcasts—one during late evening and the other during midday—for more than 80 independent television stations.

Daytime Daytime network programs, between 10:00 AM and 4:00 PM (EST), consist largely of serial dramas, game shows, and reruns of former prime-time shows. One of the most significant developments in daytime television during the past decade has been the expansion of serial dramas from 30 minutes to a full hour. (Remember when NBC Radio had 20 daily 15-minute serial programs each weekday afternoon?) Homemakers constitute the principal target audience; however, an increasingly important concern is the growing number of working women who are no longer available to watch television during these hours.

Early Morning Early morning network programming, which consists mainly of news and informational material, serves much the same purpose as early morning radio. NBC pioneered this time block with its "Today" show. Now all three networks offer news and information programming between 7:00 and 9:00 AM. ABC's "Good Morning, America" has been NBC's strongest rival during recent years. CBS broadcasts a two-hour news program known as "Morning." At this writing, the long-standing children's series, "Captain Kangaroo," is scheduled on weekend mornings. Viewership during the early morning period consists largely of adults and young children.

Late Night The late night network block, again pioneered by NBC with its "Tonight" show, attracts an audience composed predominantly of young adults and late-shift factory workers. ABC currently provides a nightly news recap, "Nightline," plus reruns of dramatic shows, while CBS programs reruns and movies. Postmidnight programming also was initiated by NBC with its "Tomorrow" talk and entertainment series.

Weekend Daytime Finally, the networks use weekend daytime periods to reach specialized audiences that are difficult to attract during the week. Cartoon shows and other children's fare dominate Saturday mornings, while the early afternoons are directed toward older children and teenagers. Each network conducts a press conference on Sundays with reporters questioning prominent national and international figures. Sunday morning news programs have been a recent addition to network schedules. Probably the most important weekend audience subset is the hard-to-reach adult male, who may be attracted to network news and sports programs and play-by-play broadcasts.

Syndicated Programming

Local TV stations rely heavily upon syndicated programs to fill their non-network time, and independent stations are far more dependent on this source than affiliates. Syndicated programs, which are sold on an exclusive basis to one station in any given broadcast market, fall into four categories:

(1) first run or original productions made for the syndication market, (2) reruns of "off-network" shows, (3) feature movie films, and (4) shared production programs.

The chief advantage of using syndicated material is that, by spreading the cost among many users, stations may obtain quality program products at a relatively low production cost. Until very recently, physical delivery of film prints or video tape copies of syndicated shows was necessary. However, syndicators are now experimenting with satellite delivery to individual stations. It is quite likely that satellite delivery for local video taping will become the normal mode of distribution when the majority of television stations are equipped with earth receiving dishes.

First Run Syndication First run syndicated programs have become increasingly available since the mid-1970s, largely because demand expanded with the growth of independent stations. However, network affiliates also bid for syndicated product for much of their nonnetwork time. Prominent first run syndicated shows at the time of publication include "Donahue," "The Merv Griffin Show," and "Hour Show."

New syndicated shows frequently are offered to stations on a barter basis. In such cases, production costs are underwritten by one or more sponsors, who provide the program to stations at no cost in exchange for free broadcast of their commercials within the show. Three widely used barter programs during the early 1980s were "Hee Haw," "The Lawrence Welk Show," and Mutual of Omaha's "Wild Kingdom."

Off-Network Syndication Upon completion of successful runs on network TV, most prime-time series, other than variety shows, go into syndication.[4] Some programs are in such demand that local stations obtain syndication rights one or two years before the shows end their network runs and become available for local use. Obviously, reruns of well-established shows can be used effectively to meet programming needs and to serve as advertising vehicles on local stations.

An off-network program needs to have at least 100 episodes "in the can" to have any real value in syndication because reruns bought by stations generally are "stripped"—scheduled across-the-board at the same hour Monday through Friday—even though they were made as one-per-week episodes. Thus five weeks of original network programming are used in one week. Since the typical weekly network series consists of 24 new episodes per year, a show has to run for almost five years before it becomes a strong candidate for syndication. Most independent producers aspire to produce durable programs which can eventually go into syndication because the financial rewards—after residual payments to actors, directors, and writers—substantially exceed the proceeds from network exhibition.

A few of the dozens of successfully syndicated off-network programs include "Gilligan's Island," "I Love Lucy," "The Mary Tyler Moore Show," "Gunsmoke," "Barnaby Jones," "M*A*S*H," "Sanford and Son," "Happy Days," "Star Trek," and "The Andy Griffith Show." Literally dozens of others could be added to the list. Figure 7.2 lists major shows handled by three of the largest syndicators in 1982.

Figure 7.2 Typical Syndicated Programming Product From Three Major Distributors

Program Type	Viacom, Inc.		Warner Brothers TV		Worldvision Enterprises	
	Program	No. Episodes	Program	No. Episodes	Program	No. Episodes
Off-Network Shows	All in the Family	207	Alice		Barnaby Jones	177
	Beverly Hillbillies	216	Chico and The Man	88	Ben Casey	153
	Bob Newhart Show	142	F Troop	65	Combat	152
	Dick Van Dyke Show	158	Harry O		Dark Shadows	
	Family Affair	138	Kung Fu	62	Doris Day Show	128
	Gomer Pyle	150	Maverick	124	Little House on the Prairie	168
	Grizzly Adams	35	Tarzan	57	Love Boat	150
	Gunsmoke	226	The FBI	234	Man from Atlantis	20
	Hawaii Five-O	200	The Waltons		Mod Squad	124
	Hogan's Heroes	168	Welcome Back, Kotter	95	The Invaders	43
	I Love Lucy	179	Wonder Woman	61	The Fugitive	120
	My Three Sons	160				
	Perry Mason	245				
	The Rookies	90				
	The Twilight Zone	134				
	Wild, Wild West	104				
First-Run (Original) Shows	Family Feud (half-hour)				Don Lane Show (one hour)	
	Hittin' Home (one hour)				Newlywed Game (half-hour)	
	The TV Star (half-hour)					
	To Tell the Truth (half-hour)					
Specials & Mini-series	A Cosmic Christmas (half-hour)		Roots (12 hours)		Holocaust (10 hours)	
	Circus (half-hour)		Roots: The Next Generation (14 hours)		Against the Wind (13 hours)	
	Devil & Dan'l Mouse (half-hour)		Pearl (6 hours)			
	Easter Fever (half-hour)					
	Intergalactic Thanksgiving (half-hour)					
	Spy (one hour)					
Feature Film Packages	Various packages		Various packages		Various packages	
Cartoon Features	Terrytoons (1,200 cartoons)		Bugs Bunny & Friends (100 cartoons)		Banana Splits & Friends (125 half-hours)	
			Porky Pig & Friends (156 cartoons)		Casper, Friendly Ghost (244 cartoons)	
					Fun World of Hanna-Barbera (84 half-hours)	
					Top Cat (30 half-hours)	

Rental fees charged for each episode of a syndicated program, whether off-network or first run, vary according to market size, competition, desirability of the specific show, the intended time slot, and the number of previous showings in the market (some shows have been aired more than 50 times in major markets). Not to be excluded, of course, are the reputation of the syndicator and the negotiating skill of the buyer and seller.

Some top-rated off-network programs (for example, "Three's Company," "Laverne & Shirley," and "Happy Days Again") have commanded prices in excess of $50,000 per episode and currently (1982) cost large market stations as much as $65,000 to $70,000.[5] By comparison, some small market TV stations obtain half-hour programs for less than $100. Obviously, from a station's standpoint, prices that are negotiated must make economic sense with respect to audience and advertising potential.

Feature Films Feature films, movies originally produced for theatrical showing, also are available to local television stations from syndicators. A variety of types of movie packages, ranging from vintage to recent films, may be acquired. Again, costs vary considerably, usually corresponding closely to recency and success at the box office, as well as market size and competition.

Shared Production Syndication Another form of program syndication is "shared production," in which a given TV station produced part of a program while obtaining other segments from the syndicator. An early program of this type was "Romper Room," a children's show produced locally in markets across the country. A more recent example of shared production syndication is "PM Magazine," a prime-time access magazine show syndicated by Group W. "PM Magazine" features local cohosts in each market, plus a mixture of local items and material shared by other participating stations. Each station is required to follow rigid production standards set forth and maintained by the syndicator.

Finally, another form of shared programming involves exchanges between stations, usually those licensed to the same group owner. Program exchanges of both entertainment and news material usually are facilitated through satellite interconnection of commonly owned television stations. Among the major groups which utilize satellite technology for internal news feeds and program exchanges are Storer, Metromedia, Cox, and the Group W (Westinghouse) stations.

A later section will explore methods for evaluating syndicated programs for local station use.

Special Networks

As mentioned earlier, several organizations put together "ad hoc" TV networks to carry special programs. Most typical are the sports networks, such as TV Sports, Inc., Hughes TV Network, and Mis-Lou Productions, which specialize in secondary football bowls and basketball tournaments that are not broadcast by the major networks. "Operation Prime Time" is the most prominent occasional network for entertainment programming. TV stations frequently obtain such special network programming on a barter basis.

Local Live Production

The major production effort by most local TV stations usually consists of two nightly newscasts, one during the early evening and another after the prime-time network feed. Noontime newscasts and daytime variety shows also have increased during recent years. Other forms of local programming have been scant throughout most of television's history; however, with increased competition, local origination is vital for building station image and profitability.

The amount and quality of local production varies widely among commercial TV stations throughout the country. Some have built reputations as strong "production stations" by turning out significant amounts of quality programming. A few examples include WBTV, Charlotte; WBNS-TV, Columbus, and WEWS-TV, Cleveland, Ohio; and KTVU-TV, San Francisco. Some stations, including WCVB-TV, Boston, WGN-TV, Chicago, and WNEW-TV, New York, produce for the syndication market.

CRITERIA FOR EVALUATING PROGRAMS

Whether it be a network or a local situation, program decision makers must firmly grasp their circumstances before attempting to evaluate specific programs. In this section, we will discuss some basic principles regarding the broadcast situation upon which judgments can be based, and then we will examine some specifics of program evaluation.

KNOW THE AUDIENCE

First, the programmer must understand the characteristics of the potential audience—whether it's the entire national population in the case of a major network or the local/regional public for a single TV station. Since successful programming efforts must be compatible with the desires of the potential audience, the program manager should learn the prevalent interests, tastes, and habits of the population. The program manager must know *when they are available to watch*. For example, at what hour do most workers arrive home? When is dinner customary in the community? He/she must also know the important *audience subsets and their interests*. Some communities, for example, are literally "sports crazy" in their devotion to a local professional or collegiate team (e.g., Knoxville, East Lansing, Pittsburgh, and Columbus, Ohio). Others have unusually strong interest in motion pictures (Los Angeles), country music (Nashville), or news (Washington and New York).

The program director also must learn what types of programs usually win viewers best and what types are rejected by viewers in the market. What types of people watch which kinds of programs? And what popularity trends are evident? To understand such peculiarities, the programmer must study carefully the ratings history of the various stations in the market.

KNOW YOUR COMPETITION

Second, the program director needs to know what the other stations are doing and to assess why they are following that course in their programming.

Thus, the alert programmer finds out what the competitors are presenting at each point in the schedule, what audience they seek, what strategies they use, what image they are attempting to project, and how successful they are in each of these endeavors. Furthermore, role-playing *their* jobs, as well as one's own, also enables a program manager to anticipate moves by the opposition.

By gaining a thorough insight into the strengths and weaknesses of the programming efforts of rival stations, which must be done largely by observation and inference, the program director can better determine the most effective ways to compete for viewers.

KNOW WHAT PROGRAMMING IS AVAILABLE

An astute programmer, whether for a network or a local outlet, keeps up with all options, including both new and present programs. With sources of programming for television on the increase, this aspect of the program manager's job has become more time consuming.

Not to be overlooked, first, are the programs currently on the schedule. How well are they faring in the competitive struggle? Then, what alternative programs are available? Network program executives constantly search for promising new shows, both pilots from outside producers and concepts for production by the network itself. At the same time, they are keenly aware that the best program is the on-going, tried-and-true success! (For how many years have the Bob Hope specials run?)

Similarly, local TV program managers must keep up with current network schedules, available syndicated shows, ideas for local origination, and of course, the track records of current programs. In practice, the program director likely will spend more time evaluating syndicated programs than any other type. Sometimes, however, group owners provide strong assistance in this regard to their local stations through the expertise of their programming and research staffs. In any case, the local program director can make intelligent decisions only after analyzing available programming in terms of the goals and needs of specific time periods. Is the slot a crucial lead-off period? A transition slot? A "throw-away" time? The answer will affect any scheduling decision.

The program director needs to know which syndicated programs are now available (exclusive in the market) and which ones are coming up. Track records may be examined to discover, for example, how well an off-network show rated *locally* while on the network. If the program has been used elsewhere, how has it fared in similar markets, at various time periods, and against various types of competitive programming? To what audience does it appeal, and is it right for the time slot? If it's a rerun, how many showings have there been in that market, and is it still viable? Finally, what contribution would the program make to the overall programming strategy of the station?

Although the intuition of an experienced programmer can be invaluable, quantitative data should be examined closely when buying syndicated programs. Both Arbitron and Nielsen regularly publish data on currently syndicated shows, including lead-ins and various competitive programming for all markets in which each show is broadcast. Another valuable resource is the *TVQ Syndicated National Report,* published by Marketing Evaluations, Inc., which scores programs on the basis of their familiarity among the viewing public. Figure 7.3 reproduces typical items from Arbitron's "Syndicated Program Analysis," and Figure 7.4 shows a sample page from the *TVQ Report*.

In addition to analyzing syndicated material, local program managers, like their network counterparts, should not neglect possible local productions using their stations' writers, producers, and staff or free-lance talent. No monopoly exists on resourcefulness and ideas; therefore, the astute program

Figure 7.3 Sample Data From Arbitron Television's Syndicated Program Analysis

HAPPY DAYS AGAIN HAPPY DAYS AGAIN

146 **MARKETS TELECASTING**
146 **STATIONS TELECASTING**
4 **PREVIOUS SPA'S**
NOV 79 **FIRST SPA**

PROGRAM TYPE: SITUATION COMEDY
PROGRAM DURATION: 30 **MINUTES**
TVHH IN ADI MKTS: 690,790
ADI MKTS % U.S. 89.42

DISTRIBUTOR: PARAMOUNT TV SALES, INC.
ADI TVHH RATING 10.4
ADI TVHH SHARE: 22.1

DAYPARTS IN WHICH TELECASTS BEGAN	AVG ADI ESTIMATES BY STATIONS PER MARKET: 4+ STA. NO. MKTS / TVHH R SH	3 STA. NO. MKTS / TVHH R SH	2 STA. NO. MKTS / TVHH R SH	1 STA. NO. MKTS / TVHH R SH	ALL STA. NO. MKTS / TVHH R SH	NO. OF STNS BY DAY-PART	AGGREGATE TSA PROGRAM TOTALS FOR HOME STATIONS IN THOUSANDS (000): TOTAL TVHH	WOMEN 18+	WOMEN 18-49	MEN 18+	MEN 18-49	TEENS 12-17	CHILD 2-11
M-F MORNING	1 3 11				1 3 11	1	4	2					
M-F AFTERNOON	4 7 24	4 5 19	1 8 23		9 6 23	9	279	145	116	73	51	111	99
M-F TOTAL DAYTIME	5 7 24	4 5 19	1 8 23		10 6 23	10	283	147	118	73	51	111	100
M-F EARLY FRINGE	48 10 20	40 13 30	14 12 29	3 23 57	105 10 21	105	7010	3730	2919	2856	2283	2803	4133
MN-SA PRIME ACCESS	4 19 32	19 16 28	5 19 31		28 17 30	28	1075	738	524	642	467	372	538
SU-SA PRIME		1 19 32			1 19 32	1	62	61		49			
M-F LATE NIGHT	1 3 32				1 3 32	1	30	21	14	18	13	2	1
SAT MORNING													
SU-SA SGN/ON-SGN/OFF	58 10 20	65 13 29	20 13 29	3 23 57	146 10 22	TOTAL PRGM 146	8506	4727	3626	3660	2853	3312	4812

MARKET NAME SGN-ON/SGN-OFF SH DAY/TIME/TELECASTS TSA (000) COMPETING PROGRAMS	CALL LETTER	ADI TV HH: HH RTG RT IDX (000)	HH SH SH IDX	WOMEN 18+ R SH (000)	WOMEN 18-49 R SH (000)	MEN 18+ R SH (000)	MEN 18-49 R SH (000)	TEENS 12-17 RTG (000)	CHILD 2-11 RTG (000)	LEAD-IN HALF-HOUR PROGRAM NAME	ADI TV HH R SH (000)	WOMEN 18+ R SH (000)	WOMEN 18-49 R SH (000)	MEN 18+ R SH (000)	MEN 18-49 R SH (000)	TEENS 12-17 RTG (000)	CHILD 2-11 RTG (000)	LEADOUT ADI TV HH R SH (000)
ABILENE-SWTWATER			18S/S															
M-F 06:30P 20T/C	KTXS	10 97	15 68	7 14	12 26	7 16	11 27	6	10	MASH-S	6 9	4 8	6 17	4 9	6 17	4	2	14 20
TSA (000)		13		10	8	8	7	2	5	TSA (000)	7	5	4	4	4	2	1	
TC TAC DOUGH	KRBC+	28	40	25 45	10 23	16 34	8 19	9	6	NEWSWATCH	28 43	24 49	10 28	18 40	7 21	3	1	24 35
HLYWD SQUARE	KTAB*	9	13	6 11	5 12	7 15	4 11	10	5	6P NWSTAB 32	13 20	10 21	10 28	10 22	9 26	8	2	12 16
ALBANY, GA			55S/S															
M-F 05:30P 17T/C	WALB	22 210	59 267	15 65	18 67	10 63	11 71	29	21	A GRIFFITH	23 61	15 65	17 65	10 62	10 66	32	21	47 72
TSA (000)		35		25	18	14	10	17	20	TSA (000)	34	24	17	14	10	15	17	
ALBNY-SCHDY-TROY			33S/S															
M-F 04:30P 20T/C	WRGB	10 96	32 145	3 21	5 35	3 24	4 32	15	22	TOM-JERRY	9 31	2 16	3 25	2 16	2 16	9	23	12 33
TSA (000)		50		19	14	15	11	20	40	TSA (000)	45	13	9	8	4	12	41	
MERV GRIFFIN>	WTEN+	9	29	8 50	5 36	5 37	3 22	1	1	MERV GRIFFI>	9 29	8 52	5 39	4 39	2 26	2	1	8 23
KUNG FU	WAST	4	13	2 13	2 12	3 24	3 30	3	1	KUNG FU	4 13	2 13	2 13	3 26	3 34	3	1	8 23
ALBUQUERQUE			36S/S															
M-F 06:30P 18T/C	KOAT	20 188	34 154	14 31	16 39	13 32	15 38	24	24	ACTN NEWS 6	22 37	19 39	17 41	17 39	14 38	6	6	22 37
TSA (000)		67		48	36	44	32	26	40	TSA (000)	79	68	41	60	33	8	10	
PM MAGAZINE	KOB	15	24	11 25	11 28	12 29	12 30	5	6	EYWITNESS NW	16 27	12 24	11 28	13 29	12 32	4	5	17 28
TC TAC DOUGH	KGGM	14	24	14 31	8 19	8 20	5 12	4	5	JOKERS WILD	14 23	13 27	8 20	8 18	5 12	5	7	13 21
ALBUQUERQUE			36S/S															
AVG 06:30P 22T/C	KOAT	19 180	33 149	14 31	15 38	13 32	14 37	22	23	ACTN NEWS 6	21 37	18 40	17 42	16 40	13 38	6	6	23 39
TSA (000)		63		47	35	41	29	24	38	TSA (000)	76	66	39	57	31	8	10	
PM MAGAZINE >	KOB	15	26	11 26	12 30	11 28	11 30	5	8	EYWITNESS NW	15 26	11 24	11 27	12 28	11 30	4	4	16 27
TC TAC DOUGH>	KGGM	14	24	13 29	7 18	8 21	5 14	4	5	JOKERS WILD>	14 23	12 26	8 20	8 19	5 15	5	6	12 21
AMARILLO			38S/S															
M-F 05:00P 20T/C	KVII+	16 149	39 176	9 35	11 43	8 40	9 48	21	18	GOMER PYLE >	10 33	5 25	7 36	3 26	3 35	16	23	27 48
TSA (000)		27		17	12	13	10	10	13	TSA (000)	19	10	8	5	3	9	17	
CROSS-WITS	KAMR	7	16	6 24	3 11	3 13	2 8			MERV GRIFFIN	8 25	8 37	3 17	3 33	2 20	1		12 20
BARNEY MILER	KFDA	6	15	5 17	5 17	4 20	4 20	2		ONE DAY-D	5 17	3 17	4 18	2 20	2 21	5	4	5 8
ARDMORE-ADA			38S/S															
M-F 06:30P 20T/C	KXII	26 246	40 181	18 38	24 52	14 35	14 44	20	36	NW/WEA/SPT 6	30 44	25 48	25 52	19 43	12 41	4	6	25 39
TSA (000)		24		19	11	12	5	4	10	TSA (000)	30	25	12	19	8	1	2	
BARNEY MILER	KTEN	10	15	7 15	8 17	9 23	8 23	2	3	MASH-S	13 19	8 16	11 23	11 25	9 31	11	9	16 24
ATLANTA			30S/S															
M-F 05:00P 19T/C	WSB	11 104	30 136	6 27	7 38	4 24	4 30	15	9	BIONIC WOMA>	6 18	4 21	4 26	2 17	2 17	7	5	12 32
TSA (000)		109		67	54	36	27	44	42	TSA (000)	59	39	28	18	12	20	24	
JOHN DAVIDSN	WAGA	9	26	8 35	5 23	4 26	2 16	3	2	JOHN DAVIDSN	9 28	7 42	4 28	3 32	2 21	4	2	10 25
JIM ROCKFORD	WXIA	7	18	4 18	3 16	5 35	4 33	3	2	STAR TREK	5 14	2 12	3 17	3 27	3 35	3	2	7 17
AUGUSTA			35S/S															
M-F 05:00P 20T/C	WRDW	13 123	35 158	6 33	8 40	5 35	5 38	14	14	GILLIGANS IS	9 27	4 27	6 34	3 36	4 39	10	12	18 41
TSA (000)		24		13	11	9	6	9	14	TSA (000)	17	9	8	6	4	6	12	
TOM-JERRY >	WJBF	13	36	5 29	7 33	4 25	4 28	11	21	TOM-JERRY >	14 42	6 40	7 40	3 33	3 35	10	24	15 34
JOHN DAVIDSN	WATU*	6	15	4 24	3 16	3 21	2 15	1	1	SUPERMAN	5 15	3 16	3 14	1 14	1 8	6	6	5 12
AUSTIN, TX			29S/S															
M-F 06:30P 20T/C	KVUE*	18 168	31 140	12 26	16 46	10 29	12 45	22	26	ACTION NWS E	18 32	14 32	17 52	12 33	13 49	11	10	18 31
TSA (000)		42		31	26	27	23	14	27	TSA (000)	42	36	27	30	24	7	10	
PM MAGAZINE	KTBC	17	29	14 31	9 26	10 28	6 23	8	5	NEWS 6-M-F	22 38	17 39	8 25	13 37	7 26	6	2	16 28
TC TAC DOUGH	KTVV*	10	18	10 22	4 11	6 16	3 10	5	2	NWSCTR 36 6	7 11	5 11	2 7	4 11	2 7	2		12 22
BAKERSFIELD			22S/S															
M-F 04:00P> 17T/C	KBAK*	3 30	13 59	2 16	2 23	1 10	1 18	4	3	VARIOUS	4 17	3 30	4 40	5		4	2	3 9
TSA (000)		5		2	2	1	1	2	3	TSA (000)	5	4	3			2	1	
JOHN DAVIDSN	KPWR*	2	10	2 17	1 11	3		1		JOHN DAVIDSN	2 8	1 9	1 7	7		1		3 9
TONI TENNILE	KERO*	2	10	2 13	1 10	5	4	2		TONI TENNIL>	3 14	2 18	1 7	7	5	2		4 15

PAGE 428

Courtesy of The Arbitron Co.

Figure 7.4 Sample Data From TVQ's Syndicated National Report

PROGRAMS AIRED: 01/09/81 - 03/08/81 HART TO HART PAGE 41
ABC TUESDAY 10:00 PM-11:00 PM MYSTERY DRAMA

	FAMILIARITY			POSITIVE TVQ			SCALE POINTS						NEGATIVE Q		
		NORMS			NORMS									NORMS	
	FAM	PGM TYPE	ALL PGMS	TVQ	PGM TYPE	ALL PGMS	FAVOR-ITE	VERY GOOD	GOOD	FAIR	POOR	NOT SEEN	NEG Q	PGM TYPE	ALL PGMS
TOTAL SAMPLE	66	54	60	24	25	21	16	15	19	12	5	34	25	28	34
TOTAL INDIVIDUALS															
6 - 11	41	37	49	45	48	41	19	6	9	3	5	59	19	23	23
12 - 17	78	62	70	30	31	26	23	14	24	12	4	22	20	20	30
18 - 34	78	60	66	17	21	18	13	23	22	16	4	22	25	31	36
35 - 49	75	62	63	26	22	17	19	15	19	14	7	25	28	30	38
50 AND OVER	51	45	51	26	22	20	13	9	16	9	4	49	24	27	34
18 - 49	77	61	65	20	21	18	15	21	21	15	5	23	26	31	37
18 AND OVER	68	55	60	21	21	19	15	17	19	13	5	32	26	30	36
TOTAL MALES															
6 AND OVER	64	55	59	20	24	21	13	18	17	11	6	36	26	29	36
18 - 34	76	61	65	13	20	17	10	31	16	15	5	24	25	31	38
35 - 49	75	63	61	19	20	15	14	16	22	16	6	25	30	31	40
50 AND OVER	45	44	49	22	20	18	10	7	16	6	6	55	27	31	36
18 - 49	76	62	64	15	20	17	12	26	18	15	5	24	27	31	38
18 AND OVER	65	56	59	17	20	17	11	20	17	12	5	35	27	31	38
TOTAL FEMALES															
6 AND OVER	69	53	61	28	25	22	19	13	21	13	4	31	24	27	33
18 - 34	80	59	66	20	21	20	16	16	28	17	4	20	26	31	34
35 - 49	76	62	66	32	25	19	24	15	16	12	8	24	27	30	37
50 AND OVER	57	46	52	28	23	22	16	11	17	11	2	43	22	25	33
18 - 49	79	60	66	24	22	19	19	16	24	15	5	21	26	30	35
18 AND OVER	70	55	61	25	23	20	18	14	21	14	4	30	25	29	34
INCOME															
UNDER $15,000	63	53	59	31	28	26	19	14	17	10	3	37	20	25	31
$15,000 - $19,999	64	53	60	19	23	19	12	13	19	12	7	36	29	28	36
$20,000 - $24,999	68	57	65	15	20	18	10	19	20	14	4	32	27	27	35
$25,000 AND OVER	72	54	60	24	23	20	17	16	20	13	6	28	26	32	36
EDUCATION (ADULT)															
HIGH SCHOOL OR LESS	68	55	60	19	22	20	13	18	21	11	5	32	24	27	33
SOME COLLEGE/DEGREE	69	55	60	24	21	17	16	15	18	15	4	32	28	32	39
OCCUPATION (ADULT)															
WHITE COLLAR	63	57	61	21	18	15	15	18	18	14	3	32	26	32	39
BLUE COLLAR	74	56	61	18	25	20	13	24	21	10	6	26	21	24	34
RACE															
WHITE	66	54	60	21	22	20	14	16	19	12	5	34	25	29	35
BLACK	66	54	58	52	41	33	34	8	15	8	1	34	14	21	27
COUNTY SIZE															
A	69	54	59	26	26	23	18	15	19	13	4	31	24	28	33
B	73	58	63	23	24	20	17	18	21	12	5	27	23	27	33
C AND D	59	52	59	22	23	21	13	13	17	11	5	41	26	29	36
REGION															
EAST	60	53	57	16	21	19	10	15	18	12	6	40	30	29	35
NORTH CENTRAL	71	54	61	27	24	22	19	17	21	11	2	29	18	27	32
SOUTH	66	55	61	24	26	23	16	15	17	13	5	34	27	29	34
FAR WEST	69	53	60	28	27	22	19	13	20	11	6	31	25	27	36

Courtesy of Marketing Evaluations, Inc.

director attempts to assemble a compatible and talented staff that can produce local programs of acceptable quality. After all, it is a station's local programming that most influences its image among the viewers.

KNOW YOUR BUDGET

Programming decisions are far from purely artistic judgments. Broadcasting is a business, and each program usually is expected to generate its share of profits. Exceptions are time periods of low audience potential, in which inexpensive programs usually are used, and "leader" programming, which may be subsidized to attract viewers at the crucial beginning of an important time block. The economics of programming will be considered in greater detail later in this chapter.

FUNDAMENTAL CONCEPTS IN TV SCHEDULE BUILDING

Having looked at the television medium, sources of programming, and criteria for evaluating programs, we turn now to a group of basic concepts for building a successful television schedule. The concepts which follow are widely adhered to in the TV industry.

1. *Select programs which appeal to the largest demographic segment of the available audience.* The same axiom also can be expressed this way: *Place programs at the most opportune time for reaching a maximum number of target viewers.* Either way, fulfilling the goal of achieving maximum audience response results from offering the audience what it wants when it is available to watch it.

A few examples from contemporary television illustrate the concept.

(a) Family programs traditionally are scheduled during prime time, when the audience potential includes adult men and women, teenagers, and children.
(b) "Adult" programs are broadcast late at night when young children presumably are not watching.
(c) Cartoon shows are presented on Saturday mornings when young children are not in school.
(d) And sports programs are scheduled mainly on weekends when most males are off from work.

These examples reveal the important relationship between programs and audiences: each part of the day has its audience characteristics for which distinct types of programs work best; each program, in turn, has its most advantageous time based on audience appeal.

2. *Program to an unserved or underserved audience.* Many times two or more networks or stations compete for the same type of viewers simultaneously through "power" programming. If so, possibly another significant audience is being ignored. By identifying important demographic audiences

or interest groups that are not being served, a station may move in with different programming and cultivate a viable audience. This principle of providing an alternative program to overlooked audiences underlies the strategy of "counter" programming.

3. *Lead with strength and establish positive audience flow by scheduling similar programs in sequence.* Each part of the day in a TV schedule may be regarded as a unit or block through which viewers may be carried over from one show to another. It is therefore very important that the initial program in any sequence be strong enough to attract a large share of the viewers and that subsequent shows be compatible in appeal to continue the audience-building process and to minimize the flow of viewers to other stations. Thus, "block" programming rests on the concept of establishing, building, and retaining viewers through several hours of similar programming.

The networks provide us with excellent examples of this practice. Invariably, each network leads off its nightly prime-time block with a strong program, although the three respective programs may be quite different. Subsequent shows follow in the same genre, whether it be situation comedy, nostalgic drama, a detective show, an extravagant special, or whatever. In practice, each program attracts some new viewers and loses some from the previous show; but if the sequencing strategy works well, a positive audience flow results.

In addition, it is also wise to schedule a strong lead-in program immediately before any crucial show to generate prior audience and, hopefully, to enhance the viewership for the primary program through positive audience carry-over. For example, most programmers place strong shows before their local newscasts to maximize the audience and profit potential of news programs.

4. *Place transitional programs between blocks of disparate programming or between any two shows of different types to minimize audience outflow.* Sharp contrasts between two adjacent programs simply invite the audience to search for other programming, thus disrupting established viewing patterns. Transitional programs, having some characteristics and appeals of both the preceding and following programs, bridge these gaps and facilitate smooth changes in programming and audience flow.

One of the most difficult periods to schedule is late afternoon, from 4:00 to 6:00, because this period bridges the daytime "housewife" viewing hours and the evening family audience period. The potential audience changes drastically through this time as teenagers and children come home from school and workers return from their jobs. Homemakers are still available, although their chores related to preparing the evening meal may keep them away from the TV set. Working men and women return home, but different occupational groups arrive at various times. Factory workers may leave their plants at 3:00 or 4:00 PM, depending upon their company's schedule, while sales and office workers rarely leave for home until 5:00, 5:30, or even 6:00 PM. The local situation needs careful analysis when making program decisions for this volatile time period.

5. *Programs destined to do poorly should be given obscure rather than prominent times.* This is the "least harm" concept, which dictates that weak programs that must be tolerated should be scheduled at times when they will

do minimum harm to the station's ratings or audience flow. For example, just as the networks lead with strong programs, they also tend to place their weakest shows late in their blocks to minimize tune-out by viewers.

Other ways in which this concept is implemented include (1) saving low share programming for nonrating periods rather than using it during audience measurement sweeps; (2) running weak programs opposite the competition's major hits, reasoning that whatever you schedule there will be clobbered (what do you run opposite the Super Bowl?); and (3) placing low rated programs during low audience periods—promoting them to their target audiences, of course, but avoiding harm to audience levels during crucial periods.

6. *Cater to the person most likely to control the TV set.* The idea here is to attract the key viewer as early as possible, preferably with a lead-in program *before* an important block begins. Most often the key to a family's viewing is the wife, since women *almost always* outnumber men in television's audience. Adult males, however, usually initiate viewing for sports and news programs; and children exert a strong influence on late afternoon viewing patterns. The latter is quite important in terms of audience carry-over into the early evening news block.

TV PROGRAMMING STRATEGIES AT WORK

In the competitive American broadcasting system, television networks and stations use a variety of strategies to attract and hold viewers. These competitive tactics, which may be divided into primary and secondary approaches, are largely derived from the concepts just discussed.

PRIMARY COMPETITIVE STRATEGIES

The five most important competitive programming strategies are *block, across-the-board, blockbuster, power,* and *counter programming.* Each of these primary tactics will be discussed below.

Block Programming

The most common strategy for achieving favorable audience carry-over from one program to the next involves scheduling a series of shows with similar audience appeal consecutively through a block of time. Often called "vertical" programming, a typical block usually extends through two or more hours of the schedule. As explained earlier, this approach usually works well because viewers, once attracted to a strong lead-off show, will stay tuned for subsequent programs which satisfy the same need.

An example of block programming from the 1982–83 CBS-TV schedule includes four half-hour situation comedies scheduled in sequence on Sunday nights. From 8:00 to 10:00 PM (EST), the network carried "Archie Bunker's Place," "Gloria," "The Jeffersons," and "One Day at a Time."

Across-the-Board

Whereas block programming takes advantage of the tendency of viewers to remain tuned as long as similar programming is offered, *across-the-board* scheduling takes advantage of the tendency of individuals to form regular daily viewing habits. Also known as "strip" or "horizontal" programming, this approach involves scheduling a given program at the same time every day, usually Monday through Friday. Most daytime programs, evening newscasts, and prime-time access shows adhere to this form of scheduling.

In contrast, the practice of placing a different show in a time period each day of the week also is followed to a degree. This "checkerboard" approach, the opposite of strip programming, is most observable in the prime-time access period on some stations and on the networks during prime time itself. In the latter, however, the principal strategies of *block, power,* and *counter programming* undergird the schedule.

How to compete against an opposing station's high rated shows is indeed a challenge faced by every TV station or network at some time. Essentially, three basic strategies are available: the blockbuster approach and power and counter programming, which are diametrically opposed to each other.

The Blockbuster

The *blockbuster* is a strong, single program lasting 90 to 120 minutes, which is scheduled directly opposite a competitor's block of shorter programs. In some cases, a blockbuster begins before the start of the opposition's block to gain a head start and to discourage switching to the opponent's block. In either case, the intent is to weaken the effectiveness of the competitor's programming by capturing viewers early and holding their interest through a long period of time.

A blockbuster may be a regular weekly series, a movie slot in which the show varies from week to week, or a special one-time broadcast.

Power Programming

Power programming occurs when one competitor pits a strong show against one already entrenched on another station or network. Usually the aggressor appeals to the same type audience in an attempt to draw viewers from the competition. Thus, viewers are forced to choose between two (or more) desirable programs. While power programming has worked in some instances, stations do risk wasting a strong program by engaging in such a struggle. A frequent result is withdrawal of one of the competitive shows after audience ratings reveal the winner of the confrontation.

One of the most memorable examples of power programming at the network level occurred during a national ratings sweep in the late 1970s. In this particular case, on one Sunday evening, NBC scheduled "Gone With the Wind," CBS had the movie "One Flew Over the Cuckoo's Nest," and ABC carried an Elvis Presley special. With three blockbuster shows power-programmed against each other, however, none of the networks gained an advantage in the ratings.

Counter Programming

In *counter programming,* it's conceded that an entrenched show will continue to do well. Instead of enagaging in a wasteful power struggle, a competing station offers viewers a sharply different kind of show. Counter programming not only saves strong shows from destructive competition, but it also tends to enlarge total viewership by attracting additional viewers through an alternative choice.

At the network level, there have been many examples of counter programming, such as placing "60 Minutes" opposite the "Wonderful World of Disney," and scheduling adventure shows against situation comedies ("Emergency" vs. "All in the Family," for example). Independent stations also make great use of counter programming (as well as across-the-board scheduling). Typical examples involve scheduling entertainment fare at the time network stations carry newscasts and, in contrast, programming 10:00 PM late newscasts while affiliated stations are still running network prime-time shows.

SECONDARY STRATEGIES

As television has become fiercely competitive for audiences, a number of secondary competitive techniques have been devised by ingenious programmers. Perhaps the oldest of this group is the television "*spectacular.*" Other secondary techniques include the *hammock,* the *mini-series, serialization of regular shows, long form, stunting, front loading,* and *alternative programming.*

TV Specials

Although the majority of television's shows are regular weekly program series, the networks schedule numerous one-time spectacular broadcasts each year. These specials usually outdraw even the most popular regular programs when they're well conceived and attractively promoted. Keys to successful specials include elaborate budgets, prominent talent, careful production, and a lot of creative imagination. Whereas the production costs for an average hour of prime-time network programming may approach $600,000, an elaborate special may be budgeted at twice as much.

Hammock

In *hammock* programming, the slot between two successful shows is used to provide exposure to a new program or a program that needs a boost. The weaker program should benefit from the advantageous middle position, thus gaining the audience carry-over from the preceding show and the anticipatory audience tuning in for the following program.

Mini-Series

A *mini-series* is a short series of full-length programs devoted to a subject of great importance or wide interest. Successful mini-series usually have been based upon historical fact and/or historical novels. A mini-series usually runs two or three hours per episode and extends over several consecutive evenings. The programming usually attains high impact resulting from a variety of appeals, including emotional stimulation and suspense. "Roots," "Holocaust," and "Shogun" have been among the most successful mini-series thus far on network television.

Serialization of Regular Shows

During recent years network programmers occasionally have transformed regular episode programs into two- or three-part series to build week-to-week suspense. Thus, by spreading a single plot across two or more weeks, the program may achieve higher overall ratings than it would with separate plots. This form of *serialization* usually is undertaken during rating sweeps, but only with highly popular programs. Three shows which have been given this treatment are "All in the Family," "The Jeffersons," and "M*A*S*H."

Long Form Programs

Another competitive tactic sometimes employed is that of extending the length of a popular program to boost overall network ratings during a sweep period. Typically, half-hour shows are expanded to a full hour, but sometimes hour-long programs are extended to two hours. As with serialization, the *long form* approach is used only for top-rated shows. Typically, the time added to these programs comes from the regular time of weaker ones, such as "hammocked" shows.

Stunting

The term *stunting* usually connotes bizarre or highly unusual tactics used to draw audiences to a network or station. In one sense, serialization and long form programming are among the unusual approaches. However, stunting may go much further into the sensational.

One of television's most successful stunts of all time undoubtedly was the suspense build-up of "Dallas" over the summer of 1981. The J.R. Ewing character, you will recall, was shot by an unknown assailant during the final episode of the spring season. Only when new productions were released in the fall did viewers learn the identity of the assailant, her motive, and the fact that J.R. survived. The most prominent one-liner of the summer became "Who shot J.R.?" Interestingly, actor Larry Hagman, who played the J.R. role, was demanding a substantial salary increase at the time the shooting scene was produced. It was generally thought that the character would be written out of the series if the actor and the producer failed to agree on terms.

Another form of stunting is that of *front loading,* in which early programs in a series are loaded with unusually strong personalities or appeals. Another variation involves scheduling very strong movies early in the season (or during any rating sweep) in order to maximize the all-important first ratings. The practice also tends to develop viewing habits which remain in effect when later and less costly programs are shown.

Alternative Programming

Providing viewers with an *alternative* choice in programming resembles counter programming. However, as used in public television and on specialty independent stations, the term implies offering viewers specialized appeal programs rather than mass appeal shows. This form of programming, which complements the dominant form, broadens the offerings of television with cultural and other special interest fare.

TYPICAL STRATEGIES OF NETWORKS AND STATIONS

All of the strategies discussed so far are available to the television networks, their affiliates, independent stations, and public TV outlets. However, the networks set the competition because of their pervasiveness in the industry. Affiliates inherit the strategy of their networks, but may engage in competitive tactics of their own choosing during nonnetwork periods. Independent stations, which traditionally have operated at a great disadvantage, have much more flexibility in scheduling their hours than do network affiliates. Finally, public stations, by choice, tend to complement commercial television by providing alternative programming fare.

Typically the networks, one by one, release their program schedules each May for the coming fall season. Those schedules usually are revised somewhat before September as the networks employ various competitive strategies to launch the season in the most advantageous way. Other adjustments, of course, are made during the season as the ratings come in and reveal public acceptance of each network program.

Affiliated stations, as we have seen, rely heavily upon network material and therefore use much less syndicated programming than the independents do. However, during certain periods, the affiliates are essentially "independents." The most important of these times is from 4:00 to 8:00 PM (EST), when the networks are not in service. The affiliates and independent stations alike employ competitive tactics—block, blockbusters, power, and counter programming—against each other during these periods.

Because they lack network commitments, independent TV stations have great programming flexibility. For example, they can schedule extensive sports coverage, including daily major league baseball games as well as basketball, football, and hockey. Affiliates usually experience difficulty clearing time for such on-going team sports because the networks frown upon extensive preemption of regular programs. Pay TV and specialized programming are two other options available to many independent stations.

With their programming freedom, independent stations also can effectively employ competitive strategies. This is especially the case with counter programming, although basic block and strip scheduling also are used. The 4:00 to 8:00 PM period is particularly productive for most independents because they compete equally with affiliates during this nonnetwork period. Another frequently used tactic is the early-starting blockbuster programmed against network prime-time schedules.

Independent stations have grown immensely in audience favor during recent years, largely because of the growing quantity and improved quality of program material, imaginative scheduling, and the public's desire for wider viewing choices. Figure 7.5 shows a typical day's schedule for a competitive TV market during the 1981–82 season.

Figure 7.5 This Typical Newspaper Log Shows the Diversity of TV Programming Available in Large US Cities

1/28	4 NBC WRC	5 WTTG	7 ABC WJLA	9 CBS WDVM	20 WDCA	26 PBS WETA	2 NBC WMAR	11 CBS WBAL	13 ABC WJZ
6:00	Health Field	Panorama	Bauman Bible	J. Swaggart	Jim Bakker		Tom & Jerry		Int'l Zone
6:30	Tony Brown		News	Kangaroo			Romper Room	Learn To Do	Stretch
7:00	Today	New Zoo Revue	Good Morning, America	Morning With Charles Kuralt	Bugs Bunny		Today	Morning With Charles Kuralt	Good Morning, America
7:30		Great Space Coaster			Woody Woodpecker				
8:00		Porky Pig			Mighty Mouse	Lilias Yoga			
8:30		Bugs & Popeye			Cartoons	MacNeil-Lehrer			
9:00	Leave It to the Women	I Love Lucy	Richard Simmons	Phil Donahue	W.O.W.!	Sesame Street	Phil Donahue	Richard Simmons	People Are Talking
9:30	Password Plus	My Three Sons	Good Morn. Washington		Romper Room			Carol Burnett	
10:00	Regis Philbin	Leave It to Beaver	Family Feud	Morning Break	700 Club	Sesame Street	Regis Philbin	One Day at a Time	Hour Magazine
10:30	Blockbusters	Rhoda	Edge of Night				Blockbusters	Alice	
11:00	Wheel of Fortune	Medical Center	Love Boat	The Price Is Right		A Tribute to FDR	Wheel of Fortune	The Price Is Right	Love Boat
11:30	Battlestars				News		Bullseye		
12:00	Charlie Rose	Panorama	News	News	Gilligan's Island	Focus on Society	News	News	News
12:30	The Doctors		Ryan's Hope	Young and the Restless	Hogan's Heroes	Dick Cavett	The Doctors	Young and the Restless	Ryan's Hope
1:00	Days of Our Lives	Movie: "Showdown"	All My Children		Get Smart	Kennedy Center Tonight	Days of Our Lives		All My Children
1:30				As the World Turns	The Munsters			As the World Turns	
2:00	Another World		One Life To Live		Newsprobe	Write On!	Another World		One Life To Live
2:30				Search for Tomorrow	Kids Break			Search for Tomorrow	
3:00	Texas	Tom & Jerry	General Hospital	Guiding Light	Krofft Superstars	History of a Sunbeam	Texas	Guiding Light	General Hospital
3:30		Superman			Huck & Yogi	Villa Alegre			
4:00	Charlie's Angels	Incredible Hulk	Movie: "Serpico" Part 2	John Davidson	Scooby Doo	Sesame Street	Good Times	Happy Days Again	Edge of Night
4:30					Bugs Bunny		Laverne & Shirley	Carter Country	John Davidson
5:00	People's Court	I Love Lucy			Woody Woodpecker	Mister Rogers	All in the Family	M*A*S*H	
5:30	News	Andy Griffith	News	News	What's Happening!!	3-2-1 Contact	News	News	The Muppets
6:00	News	Carol Burnett	News	News	The Muppets	Villa Alegre	News	News	News
6:30		Happy Days Again			Laverne & Shirley	Business Report	NBC News	CBS News	
7:00	NBC News	Welcome Back, Kotter	ABC News	CBS News	Barney Miller	Over Easy	Tic Tac Dough	Family Feud	ABC News
7:30	Family Feud	M*A*S*H	Entertainment Tonight	P.M. Magazine	Laverne & Shirley	MacNeil-Lehrer	Joker's Wild	People's Court	Evening Magazine
8:00	Fame	Movie: "Save the Tiger"	Mork and Mindy	Magnum	Movie: "The Paradine Case"	Sneak Previews	Fame	Magnum	Mork and Mindy
8:30			Best of the West			The Lawmakers			Best of the West
9:00	Diff'rent Strokes		Barney Miller	Knots Landing		The White Tribe of Africa	Diff'rent Strokes	Knots Landing	Barney Miller
9:30	Gimme a Break		News Special				Gimme a Break		Taxi
10:00	Hill Street Blues	News	20/20	Nurse		Nova: "Roger Tory Peterson"	Hill Street Blues	Nurse	20/20
10:30					Twilight Zone				
11:00	News	M*A*S*H	News	News	Benny Hill	Dick Cavett	News	News	News
11:30	Tonight	Odd Couple	ABC News Nightline	After Hours	Saturday Night	Captioned ABC News	Tonight	Barney Miller	ABC News Nightline
12:00		Perry Mason	Vega$					Quincy	Hawaii Five-0
12:30	Tomorrow				Jim Bakker		Rockford Files		
1:00	Coast-to-Coast	Starsky & Hutch	I Spy	Hawaii Five-0				The Saint	Vega$
1:30					News				

Courtesy of *The Washington Post.*

STATION IMAGE

The term *station image* refers to the personality projected through a station's choice of programs, on-air talent, and the manner in which it produces its programs. Station image is what the public thinks of a particular station—a perception that strongly influences viewing patterns. Affiliated stations, as suggested earlier, reflect to a great extent the personalitites of their networks. Thus, a TV station often is known primarily as "the ABC, CBS, or NBC station" in its market. Since affiliates also devote much of their local time to syndicated shows, they have fewer opportunities than independent stations (or radio stations) to exhibit individual characteristics. Even though independent stations also use syndicated material quite heavily, their scheduling flexibility permits image building based on such themes as "the sports station," "the movie station," or "the station with the all-time great [rerun] shows."

Apart from network and syndicated programming, alert and creative managements can develop distinctive station images during local program segments and even during station-break intervals. In addition, the quality of station production, especially the *absence* of attention-getting technical foul-ups, and the involvement of a station in its community also contribute to viewer perceptions of a station.

Since news is the most prominent form of local programming, a TV station's newscasts are usually the principal vehicle for developing a positive station image. Newscasts serve as vehicles for displaying a station's talent, for revealing its involvement in the community, and for showcasing its journalistic and production capabilities. Much attention has been given recently to upgrading local TV news because of the belief that vital, aggressive news reporting produces a favorable image, which enhances a station's entire schedule. News consultants often are engaged to analyze the strengths and weaknesses of newscasts and to recommend ways to improve public acceptance.

Another device for image enhancement is the use of special station graphics. For example, WMC-TV, Memphis, incorporates a sketch of a Mississippi riverboat, complete with audio foghorn, into its station breaks as a means of tying the station to the region in serves. Other stations, typified by KRON-TV, San Fransisco, and KWGN-TV, Denver, display prominent features of the landscape in their station ID's. The call letters of Seattle's KING-TV spell the name of the county in which the station is located. In other instances, station buildings have become community landmarks through on-air publicity. One of the first was WSB-TV, Atlanta, whose antebellum home is known as "White Columns." Knoxville's WATE-TV similarly promotes its historic Victorian-style mansion as "Greystone." Several station ID graphics, reproduced in Figure 7.6, illustrate various techniques for enhancing a station's image.

Viewer impressions of stations may range across a wide gamut: from trustworthy to unreliable, from warm and sincere to cold and indifferent, from enthusiastic to boring, and from ethical to unprofessional. Nuances of station images held by the public can be discovered only through in-depth qualitative research. As collective perceptions of a station's personality, these images must be of great concern to station managements.

Figure 7.6 Station Identification Graphics

Courtesy of KRON-TV, San Francisco; KING-TV, Seattle; WMC-TV, Memphis; KWGN-TV, Denver; and the Telemation Corporation.

PROGRAMMING ECONOMICS

Programming is both a major item of expense and the key to profits in a television station or network operation. Because advertising revenues correlate closely with the popularity of programming, economic factors are important considerations in decisions affecting program schedules.

Program managers ordinarily operate under a budget system in which they have an allocation of funds with which to buy or produce programs. These budgets usually are divided into day-part categories and may even be subdivided for individual time slots, based upon advertising revenue projections for the specific periods. Thus, each program (or day-part) may be thought of as a profit center that can be analyzed in terms of both production or acquisition cost and revenue produced. Station managers, including the program director and sales manager, usually project the cost and revenue for each program under consideration. Previously mentioned factors, such as time of day, available audience, competition, and past ratings of the program, also belong in the discussion.

Syndicated programs usually are acquired on a multiple run syndication basis, in which a portion of the total cost of each episode is allocated to each performance. Instead of straight line amortization, however, program costs ordinarily are amortized on an accelerated basis. Thus, the first and second runs are assigned a higher proportion of the package cost than the less productive (saleable) third, fourth, or fifth runs. For example, in a two-run situation, a station may amortize the cost of the episode on a 50/50 or a 60/40 basis. If three runs are involved, the costs might be assigned at 55 percent for the first run, 30 percent for the second, and 15 percent for the third. If there are even more runs, the amortization pattern might be 40 percent for the first run, 25 percent for the second, 15 percent third, 10 percent fourth, 5 percent fifth, and 5 percent sixth. Many variations of accelerated program cost amortization are possible under the present regulations of the Internal Revenue Service. Because of multiple-run program purchases, the program director needs to plot strategy over a period of time.

Let's establish a hypothetical situation to illustrate how economics influences the selection of programs. For this purpose, we shall assume that a popular syndicated show is acquired for scheduling during the 7:30–8:00 PM prime-time access period. We shall also assume that the pro-rata assigned cost of the program for the initial showing is $1,000, while the station operating costs for the period are $500. (For cost analysis purposes, station expenses may be assigned among various time periods on a uniform basis, or they may be assigned on a scaled basis to reflect differing revenue potentials of various time slots.) Thus, if this particular program is acquired, the total applicable cost for the time period becomes $1,500.

Next, we must project the revenue to be generated by the station through use of the particular show. Stations usually assume about an 80 percent sellout of any syndicated program. Making this assumption, an average of 6.5 30-second spot commercials would be sold from the three minutes of spot positions within the program and the one-minute station break at its close. However, the prices that can be obtained for each commercial depend upon the size of the audience reached. Our assumption will be a $3.00 cost-per-thousand basis, the approximate basis for rate computation in 1982. Let's also assume that, based upon ratings of the same program in other markets, we estimate audience size to range between 75,000 and 125,000 households. Based upon these "givens," now we can projects a number of scenarios, including the following low (A), medium (B), and high (C) projections.

	A	B	C
Projected Households	75,000	100,000	125,000
Price per 30-sec. spot	$225	$300	$375
Projected income from 6.5 spots	$1462.50	$1950.00	$2437.50
Less program and operating costs	$1500.00	$1500.00	$1500.00
Projected profit/loss	($37.50)	$450.00	$937.50

Thus, should the program achieve the median projected audience, it would return a profit of $450 per episode, or 30 percent more than the cost of programming and overhead. If the maximum audience projection is attained, the profit rises to $937.50, or 62.5 percent; but if only the minimum projection is reached, a $37.50 deficit occurs, which is a 2.5 percent loss on the program period. Thus, in this hypothetical case, the profit potential appears quite favorable, with only a slight risk of loss. In contrast, however, it would be unwise to purchase a similar program at $1,500 per episode, since, using the same projections, that would result in a $537.50 loss with the minimum audience projection and a $50 loss with the median projection. Only the most optimistic projection yields a profit ($437.50) with this change.

Program budgets, of course, vary with the day-parts to coincide with the size of the potential audience. Both networks and local stations, for example, generally allocate much lower budgets per hour for daytime programming than for the evening or nighttime hours. A daytime serial drama, consisting of five hourly episodes each week, usually is budgeted by the television networks at approximately $400,000 per week (1981), versus about $600,000 per hour of prime-time programming.

Just as local stations must consider the breakeven factor in making their programming decisions, the networks also consider theirs as they develop and modify their schedules. The following brief discussion explains why the ratings for individual network shows are crucial to a program's retention on the schedule.

First, we must remember that the television networks, like local stations, incur operating costs in addition to the direct funds expended for programming. Thus, in addition to approximately $600,000 spent per hour for typical prime-time programming (1982), the networks must include payments to affiliates, interconnection fees, and administrative and promotional costs in their computations to arrive at their breakeven points.

It is generally assumed by knowledgeable people in the industry that a prime-time network program breaks even financially with an average rating of about 15 during the fall-winter season. Lower ratings result in a loss, while higher ratings produce a profit. The lower the ratings are *below* 15, the greater is the loss; while the higher the ratings are *above* 15, the greater the profits. Because of the significance of 15 as a breakeven rating during the fall-winter television season, programs that only attain or fall below that mark frequently are dropped or are rescheduled into a different time period. Figure 7.7 suggests the success levels of prime-time network programs, based on the standards of the early 1980s.

Figure 7.7 Success Levels of Prime-time Network Shows

	Share-of Audience (HUT = 60%)	Prime-Time Rating
A "hit"	33–50% and above	20–34+
Acceptable/good	29–33%	17–20
Questionable/poor	23–29%	14–17
A "miss"	0–23%	0–14

SUMMARY

In this chapter, we have attempted to depict the many facets of schedule building for commercial TV stations and networks. We also have explored the goals and objectives of programmers in each of the major television media forms.

Our examination of schedule development also has focused on sources of programs and criteria for their evaluation, as well as competitive scheduling strategies. We have seen, too, that programming for television involves the balancing of audience, artistic, public service, and economic considerations. Because telecommunications technology promises to become increasingly complex and the medium more competitive, programming undoubtedly will continue to be one of the foremost challenges in commercial television.

Our next chapter takes us into the world of commercial radio broadcasting. Again, our focus will be on how to program successfully to achieve the medium's goals and objectives.

ENDNOTES

1. Anthony Cook, "The Peculiar Economics of Television," *TV Guide*, June 14, 1980, p. 4.
2. The additional hour of network programming on Sundays may be carried by top 50 market stations provided it is primarily intended for children or that it is of a public affairs character. The prime-time access rule also allows stations to carry network newscasts during the 7:00 to 7:30 period on weekdays.
3. It is the authors' opinion that hour-long newscasts will be adopted by one or more of the networks during the 1980s.
4. One reason variety shows generally do not go into syndication is the excessive residual cost of musicians and musical talent. Some variety shows are available, but the prices always run high.
5. Although these quotations are for individual episodes, a station normally obtains rights for multiple airings of each episode, usually over a period of several years.

STUDY QUESTIONS

1. Compare the schedules of the commercial TV stations that serve your market in terms of their (a) schedule balance, (b) competitive strategies, (c) creative local programming, and (d) public service programming. Which stations lead the market? Can you explain why?
2. Compare the programming strategies employed by a local independent station, if any, with those of the network affiliated stations. At what times does the independent appear to be most competitive? What strategies does it use most effectively?
3. Is there a subscription TV station or a specialty independent present in your market? If so, describe its programming and explain how it differs from that of the general independent stations.
4. Devise an ideal schedule for an independent television station in your market. Include both original local programs and syndicated shows. Assume for this assignment that any syndicated programming is available to you. Explain both your choices of programs and the strategies you use in developing the schedule.
5. Analyze the station image of each television station in your market. Which station, in your opinion, has the most favorable image? Explain your answer.

SUGGESTED READINGS

Balakrishnan, Trichur R. *A Game Theory Approach to Programming Prime Time Network Television.* PhD dissertation, University of Illinois, 1974.

Clift, Charles, III, and Archie Greer. *Broadcast Programming: The Current Perspective.* Washington: University Press of America. 1974–present. Updated annually.

Eastman, Susan Tyler, Sydney W. Head, and Lewis Klein. *Broadcast Programming.* Belmont, Calif.: Wadsworth Publishing, 1981.

McAlpine, Dennis B. *The Television Programming Industry.* New York: Tucker Anthony and R.L. Day, 1975.

Moore, Barbara A. *Syndication of First-Run Television Programming: Its Development and Current Status.* PhD dissertation, Ohio University, 1979.

Morgenstern, Steve, ed. *Inside the TV Business.* New York: Sterling Publishers, 1979.

Tuchman, Gaye, ed. *The TV Establishment: Programming for Power and Profit.* Englewood Cliffs, N.J.: Prentice-Hall, 1974.

Virts, Paul H. *Television Entertainment Gatekeeping: A Study of Local Television Program Directors' Decision-Making.* PhD dissertation, University of Iowa, 1979.

Wolf, Frank. *Television Programming for News and Public Affairs.* New York: Praeger Publishers, 1972.

8

PROGRAMMING THE COMMERCIAL RADIO STATION

Radio, like television, is a competitive enterprise in which programming plays a vital role. Since audience acceptance and profitability usually go hand-in-hand, a chief goal is to achieve a high level of listenership among the target audience through competitive programming.

There are vastly more radio than television stations; the New York and Los Angeles markets each have nearly 100 operating stations. The result is a high degree of program specialization and audience fragmentation.

Since radio stations are so numerous, the basic strategy is to devise formats and station images that differentiate each outlet from all others for the purpose of attracting a steady, loyal listenership. No longer is it feasible for radio programmers to shoot for the public at large or even large demographic age groups. Instead, each station must struggle to find its own niche, and that often means programming to surprisingly narrow audiences. As a result, research and programming consultants have become increasingly important adjuncts in the pursuit of viable audiences.

The purpose of this chapter is to explore the basics of radio programming through examination of station goals, target audiences, program ingredients, and sources of material. Special attention will be given to types of formats, format development, and contemporary competitive strategies.

RADIO PROGRAMMING GOALS AND OBJECTIVES

Radio's fundamental goals are essentially the same as those for television—to earn profits and serve the public interest. But these objectives are accomplished through strategies which differ in detail from those of television. First, let's summarize the basic objectives in radio programming.

1. *To build a competitive format—or schedule—that will win the largest possible audience and/or a substantial and loyal audience among a desirable demographic or special interest subset of the general population.* Again, the economic well-being of a radio station depends upon its audience in terms of size and characteristics. Few radio stations today can attract a broad heterogeneous mixture of listeners. Therefore, with the exception of a few large city "general service stations" and small "home town" outlets, most stations forego as futile any attempt to provide "something for everybody" in favor of developing a loyal listenership among a specific audience subgroup.

2. *To satisfy public interest obligations.* All programming, including entertainment, must be in the public interest. However, radio stations, like TV outlets, also provide substantial service to the public through news, public affairs, community announcements, and other nonentertainment programs. This programming, when well implemented, can attract listeners and produce profits, as well as fulfill the public interest expectations of the Federal Communications Commission.

3. *To develop a favorable station image among the listeners of the intended target audience.* Station image, the public's perception of a station's personality, is vitally important in radio because of the large number of services available to most listeners. It is closely entwined with program format and also encompasses such items as on-air talent, quality of production, services provided the public, and the attitude exhibited toward the listeners. In summary, a station achieves a positive image when its programming becomes *valuable* to its intended audience. A high level of rapport with its audience is perhaps the most valuable resource a radio station can possess.

THE RADIO MEDIA AND THEIR INTENDED AUDIENCES

Although radio broadcasting is composed of both networks and local stations, it is mainly a local medium. Programming is individually tailored by each station, while the networks mainly serve as sources of information. National and international news, special events, sports, and feature material are their principal services to affiliated stations. We must note, however, that some radio syndicators have begun to distribute music-format programming via live network interconnection of stations through the use of communication satellites.

The *national radio networks* maintain broad coverage throughout the United States, though the caliber of their affiliates varies from place to place. Since 1980, there has been an explosion of radio networking. Instead of a few networks seeking mass audiences, we now have about 20 radio networks, which are programmed, like most stations, to reach segmented audiences. The *regional radio networks* are patterned after the national chains, with emphasis on regional or state news coverage.

Radio stations themselves tend to be localized in their programming to serve the people of their communities—whether they are small towns such as Copperhill, Tennessee (population 600) or New York (population 12,000,000). The stations are divided into AM and FM outlets and often are categorized in terms of their program formats. During the late 1970s, as we discussed in chapter 5, FM radio forged ahead of AM in total listenership in most large markets in the United States.

Despite the prevalence of audience fragmentation, many radio stations thrive economically and practically all survive by defining and serving specific target audiences. Powerful stations with large geographic coverage (such as 50,000 watt AM and 100,000 watt, class C, FM facilities) are positioned best to appeal to broader audience segments, whereas lower power stations must focus more sharply on smaller audience subsets.

In regard to audience size, very few large city radio stations achieve shares-of-listening higher than 12 percent because of the number of competing stations. Even so, total listenership of some radio stations is very substantial. During spring 1981, for example, 14 stations—located in New York, Chicago, Detroit, Pittsburgh, and Los Angeles—each attracted between 100,000 and 200,000 listeners during an average quarter hour. Only two of those stations, however, exceeded 12 percent shares in their respective markets, according to Arbitron data published in *American Radio* by James Duncan, Jr.[1]

BASIC PROGRAMMING MODES: BLOCK AND FORMAT

Two basic modes of programming prevail in modern radio broadcasting: *block* and *format*. In block-programmed stations, the schedule is divided into segments of time, or "blocks," each of which is devoted to a different type of material. The alternative is the format approach, in which a consistent and continuous pattern of programming is followed throughout the broadcast day.

BLOCK PROGRAMMING: SOMETHING FOR EVERYBODY

The block programming approach permits a station to serve several types of listeners, as well as different categories of advertisers, through varied programming. However, block operation poses a serious problem because the breaks between program blocks interrrupt the audience flow. With each break, an audience likely is lost to other stations; in turn, a new audience must be established. For this practical reason, block programming has been abandoned by large numbers of stations in favor of format operation, which poses no such problems.

Block programming, once very common, is most often practiced today by small town radio stations where competition is minimal and a need exists for several types of programming. It is also found among a few large market stations which still attempt to serve broad audiences. These stations usually divide their schedules into news blocks, talk shows, sports broadcasts, and musical programs. The block-programming schedule of WGN Radio,

Figure 8.1 This weekly program chart depicts a large market, block-programmed radio station.

PROGRAM SCHEDULE
effective OCTOBER 12, 1981

WGN Radio 720 Chicago

LEGEND
SFR: Special Feature Rate
CA: Community Affairs
S: Sponsored
AAA, AA, A, B, C: Rate Card Time Classification
***:** Program segment and spot rates available in farm supplement to rate card.

WGN BUSINESS REPORTS
Monday thru Friday: 10:30 & 11:30am
12:30, 2:30, 4:30 & 6:05pm

NEWS
5 minutes on the hour & 5:30pm & 6:30pm
2 minutes on the half-hour
5:30am, 6:30am, 7:30am & 8:30am

WEEKDAYS

5:05 **MORNING SHOW** with Max Armstrong B*
5:30 **THE WALLY PHILLIPS SHOW** 6:00
7:00-7:10 NEWS
8:00-8:10 NEWS
Trafficopter Reports 6:55-9:10am AAA
10:00 **THE ROY LEONARD SHOW** A
12:00 **THE NOON SHOW** with Orion Samuelson & Max Armstrong A*
1:00 ROY LEONARD SHOW 1-2PM 1:00 A
2:00 THE BOB COLLINS SHOW 3:00 A / AAA
On The Hour NEWS
Trafficopter Reports 4:15 & 5:50 SFR AAA
6:00 THE BILL BERG SHOW 7:30
6:00-6:10 NEWS
6:10 BUSINESS FINAL AAA 8:00
6:20-6:35 SPORTS TODAY AAA
Trafficopter Reports 6:15 & 6:35 SFR 8:30 A
9:00 **THE JOAN McGRATH SHOW** Mondays C / **EXTENSION 720 with Milt Rosenberg** 10:00 C
10:55 **SPORTS SPECIAL**
11:00 11:05pm - 5:00am **GREAT MUSIC FROM CHICAGO** with Jay Andres
ALL-NIGHT NEWS (on the hour) S

SATURDAY

MORNING SHOW B*
GREAT OUTDOORS with Bill Cullerton A
7:00-7:10 NEWS
8:00-8:10 NEWS
THE ROY LEONARD SHOW AA
THE NOON SHOW with Orion Samuelson & Max Armstrong A*
BIG TEN FOOTBALL GAME OF THE WEEK
Non-Football Days: Afternoon in Chicago S
SCOREBOARD with Floyd Brown 4:30
AFTERNOON IN CHICAGO A 5:00
TEN PIN TATTLER S 5:55
WHEN MUSIC WAS MUSIC with Mike Rapchak 7:00 A / C
THE NORMAN ROSS SHOW S
BACK TO GOD S
WORDS OF HOPE S
UNSHACKLED S
11:05pm - 5:00am **GREAT MUSIC FROM CHICAGO** with Jay Andres
ALL-NIGHT NEWS (on the hour) S

SUNDAY

SUNDAY MORNING IN CHICAGO with Virginia Gale 6:30
THE WORLD TOMORROW S 7:00
LUTHERAN HOUR S 7:30
MUSIC UNLIMITED A 10:00
THE JIM LOUGHMAN SHOW A 1:00
2:00
DR. DAN KILEY A 4:00
THE SPORTSWRITERS 5:00 S 6:00
THE FLOYD BROWN SHOW 7:00 A / C
OLD-TIME RADIO 8:30-9:00pm C 9:30
THE NORMAN ROSS SHOW S 10:30
HISPANIC HAPPENINGS CA 10:55
SPORTS SPECIAL S 11:00
11:05pm - 5:00am **GREAT MUSIC FROM CHICAGO** with Jay Andres
ALL-NIGHT NEWS (on the hour) S

Courtesy of WGN Radio, WGN Continental Broadcasting Company, Chicago.

Chicago, is shown in Figure 8.1. Some foreign language stations also divide their schedule into blocks to serve different ethnic groups.

FORMAT PROGRAMMING: THE SPECIALIZED APPROACH

The aim of format radio is to offer a distinctive program service that is consistent throughout the station's operation. The programmer hopes listeners will be attracted to his/her particular station because of its sound and services. A later section of this chapter will explore the details of major format types. However, in this introduction, let's note that radio formats may be classified into three broad categories: (1) *music-based formats,* (2) *information formats,* and (3) *specialty formats.*

Format stations do not attempt to provide a balanced schedule as do most block-programmed stations. However, balanced programming results within a given community through the variety of different formats usually available. Since radio encountered difficulty being all things to all people, it became transformed into what it is today—a highly specialized medium characterized by a plethora of stations competing for a slice of the audience pie.

Format stations also limit themselves considerably in regard to advertising clientele. While they must forego inappropriate types of advertisers (for the demographics of their listenership), format stations provide advertisers with an excellent opportunity for selective target audience campaigns. We will examine several prominent types of formats in detail later in the chapter.

ELEMENTS AND SOURCES OF RADIO PROGRAMMING

Regardless of the mode of operation—block or format—radio stations must build their programming from a group of easily identified elements. These programming ingredients include music, news, other forms of information, personalities, commercials, and promotions. Differences between stations result from the choice of elements and the emphasis and treatment given each one.

This section will explore the basic elements available for radio programming, including sources from which they may be obtained.

MUSIC: TO ENTERTAIN RADIO'S LISTENERS

Music occupies more air time than any other single element in modern radio broadcasting. This item is so important that most stations are identified by the public and the broadcasting industry by their predominant type of music. And, because there are so many radio competitors, most stations emphasize a particular category of music to establish sharp identities. Thus, among others, stations are known as "adult contemporary," "soft rock," "easy listening," "top 40," and "country music" operations, depending on management's choice.

The number of music formats has proliferated greatly during the past decade. In general, however, the higher power stations adopt formats with the broadest appeal, leaving less desirable formats for weaker outlets. When more than one station in a given market decides to air the same type of music format, the direct competitors usually attempt to outperform each other through various competitive techniques, including music mixture and rotation plans, promotions, personalities, and audience research to help identify and anticipate music trends.

Many changes have taken place in music programming since the earliest period of format radio. One of the most noticeable is the blending of types of music across lines that once firmly separated popular, country, and rock sounds. In a great many cases, a given popular record, performed by a "cross-over" artist, will be broadcast by stations of all three format types.

For most prominent radio stations, free copies of current records are supplied by the manufacturers to gain valuable air play. Smaller stations usually can obtain copies of current singles and albums at a nominal cost direct from the various record companies or their distributors.

Another source of programming is syndicated program services. Hundreds of radio stations now subscribe to such packaged programming, which is available on audio tape and via live satellite feeds. A multitude of packaged formats are available, designed for specific target audiences. Many of these syndicated services are produced by consultants who customize their material to some extent for their client stations. These packaged formats, which range in cost up to $10,000 per month, are usually designed for stations that have automated or semiautomated on-air production operation. Figure 8.2 lists several of the leading format syndicators and their program services.

In addition to formats, there are a number of popular syndicated radio shows. Casey Kasem's "American Top-40" and "Country Countdown," in syndication from Watermark Productions, are among the most popular and profitable shows on radio. Others include Drake-Chenault's "Weekly Top-30" and "Musicland U.S.A." for Roger Carroll Enterprises.

Because of music's importance in radio, most competitive stations employ a music director to solicit, screen, and select music for broadcast, or a consultant to advise all phases of music programming.

Figure 8.2 Major Radio Syndicators and Their Products

Syndicator	Music Formats	Syndicated Shows
Bonneville Broadcast Consultants (Tenafly, N.J.)	Beautiful Music	
Century 21 Productions (Dallas, Texas)	12 automated formats (mostly religious and country music)	
Drake-Chenault, Inc. (Los Angeles)	"Great American Country"	"History of Rock and Roll" "The Weekly Top-30"
FM 100 (Chicago)	Beautiful Music Adult Contemporary Country Music	
Satellite Music Network	Country Coast-to-Coast StarStation	
Schulke Productions (South Plainfield, N.J.)	Beautiful Music MOR	
T-M Companies (Dallas)	Stereo Rock Soft Rock Country Music Alpha One (R&B) Adult MOR	Specials
Watermark Productions (North Hollywood, Calif.)		"American Top-40" "Country Countdown"

NEWS: TO SATISFY A CONSTANT NEED TO KNOW

Although the total amount of air time allocated to news is far less than that provided for music, news is a highly important program ingredient for most radio stations. A research study conducted for the Associated Press suggests that news closely rivals music in attracting listeners.[2] This may be explained by the fact that station *involvement* in news (as opposed to a "rip-and-read" operation), special events, and other public affairs broadcasting connotes an image of authority and participation in the life of the station's community. When the public strongly identifies a station with news, its overall credibility is almost certainly enhanced.

Most radio stations broadcast at least one newscast, usually about five minutes in length, every hour of their operation. These newscasts typically are carried at a fixed point on the clock—such as the "top of the hour" or on the half-hour—so listeners can become accustomed to the fixed time and tune in whenever they desire an updated report. Some music-type stations, however, emphasize news more heavily during the morning hours and afternoon "drive time," but carry fewer newscasts at night. Some stations, as noted before, provide all-news formats or include extended news blocks in their schedules. News programming also includes special events coverage, as well as interview programs, commentaries, and editorials.

A radio station's news effort usually consists of coverage of local and area developments as well as reports of state, national, and international events. Most stations obtain the latter from one or more wire services and/or a radio network. Figure 8.3 shows the weekly schedule of "The Source," NBC Radio's youth-oriented radio network. Coverage of local news requires an adequate, capable, and resourceful staff of broadcast journalists. For maximum effectiveness, a local news department also requires a strong news director for leadership and a long-range financial commitment by station management. However, the rewards of the investment usually are translated into an enhanced station image and greater profits.

OTHER INFORMATION PROGRAMMING: TO SERVE SPECIAL NEEDS

A wide range of material may be included under the umbrella of *other informational programming*. This category includes sports, weather, market reports, traffic surveillance, community bulletin boards, and consumer affairs material. In addition, the category includes talk and interview programs related to such fields as agriculture, education, health, hobbies, nutrition, and religion. Some of the above, such as weather, traffic, and market reports, hold such immediate usefulness that many listeners habitually tune to the stations which satisfy these important and timely information needs.

Some of the major forms of nonnews information programming will be discussed in the following paragraphs.

Sports Programming

The two principal types of sports programs are sportscasts, summaries of sports stories and scores which resemble newscasts in form, and play-by-play

Figure 8.3 A Weekly Radio Network Schedule: The Source (NBC)

SCHEDULE
ALL SCHEDULED TIMES (NYT)

EFFECTIVE: MONDAY, JANUARY 12, 1981

TITLE/(VOICE)	RUNNING TIME	Mon	Tue	Wed	Thu	Fri	Sat	Sun
Bulk Prefeed (Various)		1:20:00AM (10 minutes)	1:20:00AM (10 minutes)	1:20:00AM (10 minutes)	1:20:00AM (10 minutes)	1:20:00AM (16 minutes)	X	X
THE ROCK REPORT (Bill Fantini)	(1:30)	6:10:00AM 9:10:00AM	6:10:00AM 9:10:00AM	6:10:00AM 9:10:00AM	6:10:00AM 9:10:00AM	6:10:00AM 9:10:00AM	6:10:00AM 9:10:00AM	X X
TODAY IN ROCK HISTORY (Dan Formento)	(1:00)	6:40:00AM 12:10:00PM	6:40:00AM 12:10:00PM	6:40:00AM 12:10:00PM	6:40:00AM 12:10:00PM	6:40:00AM 12:10:00PM	6:40:00AM 12:10:00PM	6:20:00AM 12:10:00PM
COPING WITH... (John McGhan) (Writer—John Parikhal)	(1:30)	6:41:00AM 12:11:00PM	6:41:00AM 12:11:00PM	6:41:00AM 12:11:00PM	6:41:00AM 12:11:00PM	6:41:00AM 12:11:00PM	X X	X X
MAKIN' IT (Bob Madigan)	(1:30)	7:10:00AM 5:10:00PM	7:10:00 AM 5:10:00 PM	7:10:00AM 5:10:00PM	7:10:00 AM 5:10:00 PM	7:10:00AM 5:10:00PM	X X	X X
UNEXPLAINED PHENOMENA (Lee Speigel)	(1:30)	8:10:00AM 8:10:00PM	8:10:00AM 8:10:00PM	8:10:00AM 8:10:00PM	8:10:00AM 8:10:00PM	8:10:00AM 8:10:00PM	X X	X X
SCREEN SCENES (Laura Davis)	(1:00)	7:11:30 AM 5:11:30 PM	7:11:30 AM 5:11:30 PM	7:11:30 AM 5:11:30 PM	X	X	X	X
ONE MINUTE WITH... (John McGahn/Dan Formento)	(1:00)	X	X	X	7:11:30 AM 5:11:30 PM	7:11:30 AM 5:11:30 PM	X	X
AUDIO FILE (C.D. Jaco)	(1:30)	4:10:00PM 7:10:00PM	4:10:00PM 7:10:00PM	4:10:00PM 7:10:00PM	4:10:00PM 7:10:00PM	4:10:00PM 7:10:00PM	X X	X X
ROCK COMEDY (Various)	(9:30)	10:20:00PM	X	X	X	X	X	X
THE SOURCE REPORT (Jim Cameron)	(29:30)	X	X	X	10:20:00PM	X	X	X
SOURCECASTS	(2:00)	Are fed Monday through Sunday at :15 after the hour, 24 hours per day with an additional feed at :45 Monday through Friday 6:45AM-11:45AM NYT.						

Courtesy of NBC Radio (National Broadcasting Company, Inc.).

accounts of athletic competition. A third form which has gained some prominence is the sports talk broadcast.

Some radio networks provide daily sportscasts and play-by-play broadcasts for their affiliated stations, and the wire services also feed several sports wrap-ups each day. These national reports may be supplemented with local sports information, usually gathered by the station's sports director, interviews, call-in shows, and local sports play-by-play. As a result, sports can be developed into a major component of a radio station's programming and an important contributor to its overall image.

It's important, of course, to determine how significant sports is to one's community, as well as which sports activities command the greatest number of enthusiasts. Although most fans prefer televised sports, many events are not telecast and many persons without access to a TV set want a radio account since they cannot see a televised game. Still others prefer to watch on television, but listen to the game's description on radio because it is usually more detailed than the TV commentary. For these reasons, sports continues to be an impressive audience attraction on radio.

What's the Weather?

Perhaps nothing affects the public more vitally than the weather. And because radio can flash environmental information quickly and repeatedly, most individuals rely heavily on radio for knowledge of current and future weather conditions. This dependence, of course, varies in intensity from periods of tranquil weather to those of disruptive and disturbing conditions. Also, we must remember that some geographical areas are more subject than others to severe weather problems.

On the basis of radio reports, workers decide how to dress and whether or not to carry an umbrella. Farmers make plans for planting, cultivating, and harvesting crops. And school officials ponder the need for closings during wintertime snow and ice storms, based largely upon radio's fast weather reporting. In turn, school systems depend upon both radio and television to inform students when closings are necessary. Other weather-related cancellations and closings, such as factories, churches, highways, and transportation systems, are broadcast to serve vital needs of listeners.

Each station must determine the scope of its listeners' concerns about weather, as well as the most appropriate times for these reports. If a station serves listeners throughout most of a state or in several states, more than one regional forecast likely is needed. Similarly, a station that serves tourists, long-haul truck drivers, and other motorists needs to pay attention to weather outside the station's immediate listening area. Long-range forecasts are particularly important to farmers, ranchers, and commercial fishermen, too. Thus, in regard to weather coverage, a station's management needs to analyze its service area and all those who may benefit from weather information.

Morning weather reports are probably the most important since listeners need to know how to plan for the day ahead. Second in importance are evening reports, which offer forecasts for the following day. Temperature reports and forecasts also are given throughout the broadcast day, usually at regular intervals, on most stations.

Finally, when potentially devastating weather conditions arise, radio's presence often makes the difference between life and death. Discontinuance of regular programming for life-saving warnings and related information may be warranted during times of flooding, hurricanes, tornadoes, and other disasters. Numerous stations have distinguished records for their contributions during such disturbances. A few examples include WHAS, Louisville, and WLW, Cincinnati, during various Ohio River floods; WIBW, Topeka, Kansas, and KCMO, Kansas City, during periods of tornadoes; and WWL, New Orleans, in times of hurricane activity along the Gulf coast.

The principal source of weather information is the National Weather Service, a division of the National Oceanic and Atmospheric Administration (NOAA). This governmental service feeds a special weather wire to which stations may subscribe at nominal cost. In many areas, NOAA also operates special radio transmitters that provide continuous weather reports for the public and for retransmission by broadcast stations. In addition, numerous private meteorological services prepare customized weather forecasts for client stations. These private services usually operate on a syndicated basis, providing updated local weather forecasts for their client stations, usually by telephone from a distant city.

Having a staff meteorologist on a fulltime basis is another possibility; however, this is a very expensive approach which only a few stations deem worth the expense. In addition, a number of radio stations have installed radar screen-slaves from nearby TV stations so their announcers can see the radar screen and comment knowledgeably about current weather conditions.

Market Reports

Market reports represent another form of timely information that radio can deliver quickly to those who need current trading data in their business and investment activities. Agricultural and financial markets are the two main categories. Specific items of interest vary among the sections of the country, depending upon their agricultural and mining products and commercial interests.

Agricultural market reports typically include daily trading figures and futures quotations for livestock, grain, and other farm commodities. Important markets include the Chicago Board of Trade, the New York Cotton Exchange, the Kansas City Board of Trade, the Minneapolis Grain Exchange, and the Winnipeg Commodity Exchange. Local and regional markets also are important to farm listeners. For example, tobacco market prices generate great interest during the auction season in Florida, the Carolinas, Virginia, Kentucky, and Tennessee. Daily quotations from most national and regional markets are provided by the Associated Press and United Press International wire services.

Financial market reports usually focus on stock trading on the New York and American Stock Exchanges in New York. Typical reports include trading indexes, particularly the Dow Jones average, trading volume, high volume stocks, and stocks of local or regional interest. Trading in metals, such as gold, silver, and copper, and in petroleum also is important to commercial interests in some cities.

Just as with farm market reports, timeliness is vital to listeners who tune in for financial information. Thus, stations that seek a high income audience usually broadcast periodic market updates throughout the trading day, as well as end-of-day summaries. Financial reports are provided on some hourly network newscasts, by the AP and UPI wires, and in greater detail by the Dow Jones & Co. (*Wall Street Journal*) wire service. Brokerage firms also may be solicited for voice reports on stocks of local interest.

Traffic Reports: A Unique Radio Service

Radio stations have a unique capability for communicating traffic information to listeners in moving vehicles. In most large cities, several stations provide traffic-flow information, including periodic reports of congested areas and alternate routes, during morning and afternoon "drive times" when traffic is heaviest. In the author's home city, long noted for its "Malfunction Junction," half a dozen radio outlets provide regular reports to assist travelers through congestion and a mammoth road-building program.

The best vantage point for obtaining traffic information, of course, is from the air. Typical reports are given from helicopters and airplanes which navigate high above the traffic to various points around a city (see Figure 8.4). In some cases, local police departments assign traffic officers to airborne duty to give reports and suggestions to motorists in hopes of improving traffic flow. Although maintenance of aircraft is very expensive, accurate and reliable traffic reports usually produce a competitive edge for the originating station. Also local public transit authorities sometimes provide ground-based reports to supplement aerial coverage and as a back-up during inclement weather when aerial reports are impossible.

Bulletin Boards: Providing Community Information

Another type of information programming offered by many stations is the "bulletin board," in which announcements of up-coming community activities are broadcast. These brief programs serve as vehicles for stations to assist cultural, civic, religious, and educational organizations in promoting their activities. Such broadcasts provide an especially important service when weather conditions force the cancellation of scheduled events.

A special type of bulletin board which offers a unique service to listeners is the "lost pet" announcement. Many stations have remarkable records for locating missing animals, both pets and livestock, a rewarding service that builds immense goodwill for the station among listeners who have been assisted.

PERSONALITIES

Every radio station, as noted throughout this book, has a personality of its own. We usually call it "station image." This image reflects every element of the station's programming, but especially the presentation style of the on-air talent staff. For this reason, announcers, newscasters, talk-show hosts, and other air personnel must be selected carefully and supervised continuously to maintain the station image desired by management.

Figure 8.4 A Helicopter Traffic Report Begins Here

Courtesy of WSB Radio, Cox Communications, Inc., Atlanta, Ga.

Strong air personalities, especially those of long tenure with a station, often develop a high degree of rapport with listeners. These announcers may attract a loyal following for the station, adding to its popularity and contributing to the effectiveness of the commercial and public service announcements it broadcasts. Many stations, therefore, encourage their announcers to project their personalities, within bounds, on the air. Many contemporary music stations, for example, heavily promote their DJs as one means of differentiating their programs from competitors which play much the same music. Other types of stations, including most easy-listening and soft-contemporary outlets, however, usually deemphasize individual personalities in favor of highlighting the music.

The choice and use of personalities is simply another option for the program manager in molding the sound of a radio station. Whether personality is emphasized or minimized, professionalism should prevail at all times in the on-air sound presented by a station's talent staff.

COMMERCIALS AND OTHER ANNOUNCEMENTS

Although we do not usually think of announcements as basic programming material, commercials and public service announcements (PSA's) add a dimension to a station's image because of their prominence. While commercials are essential for a station's economic success and PSA's demonstrate public service, a number of policy questions arise. They do so because commercials and PSA's can both enhance and harm a station's image. Some of these policy questions follow.

1. *How many commercials should be permitted per hour?* Radio broadcasters know that "too many" commercials at the expense of music or other programming materials will drive listeners away. Historically, the NAB Radio Code has recommended, and the FCC has sanctioned, a maximum load of 18 minutes of announcements per hour.[3] However, few radio stations in competitive markets dare carry 18 minutes of commercials today because of the proliferation of alternative stations from which listeners may choose. Actually, FM stations led the trend toward lower hourly commercial loads. Most typical at present are commercial loads of 10 to 14 minutes per hour, a modest number which seems to be tolerated by most listeners.

2. *Should commercials be clustered in groups or dispersed one at a time throughout a station's hourly format?* Studies indicate that most listeners react more negatively to a large number of program interruptions than to the number of commercials themselves. Therefore, a recent trend has been to cluster commercial announcements in groups of three or four messages, with only four to six clusters per hour, to minimize interruption and facilitate continuous programming. This trend is followed noticeably by easy listening, adult contemporary, and other "soft" format stations. Top 40, rock, and country stations often spread the spot load more evenly throughout their programming.

3. *What commercials should be accepted by a station?* Just as advertisers choose stations to carry their messages because those particular stations reach needed target audiences, stations also should be discriminating about the commercials they *accept*—to protect the valuable station image.

The NAB Radio Code, the broadcasting industry's principal guide to program standards, advises that great care should be taken to prevent the presentation of "false, misleading or deceptive advertising."[4] It also recommends that all stations refrain from carrying certain types of questionable advertising, such as hard liquor, fortune telling, and tip sheets, because "radio broadcasting is designed for the home and the entire family."[5] NAB also advises special care in advertising medical and personal hygiene products. Some stations don't follow the Code, of course, but others even go beyond the NAB's recommendations and refuse other categories which, in their judgment, are contrary to the best interests of listeners or are incompatible with their formats. Examples include beer and wine, X-rated movies, and patent medicines.

Another consideration with respect to advertising acceptance is production technique and quality. Certainly all commercials carried should be compatible with the sound being nurtured by the management. An easy listening station, therefore, may reject a loud, boisterous commercial because it doesn't fit well with the programming, while a rock music station could broadcast the same announcement without fear of alienating listeners.

It should be noted that many stations, especially economically marginal operations, do not reject many commercials since they cannot afford the financial loss. Such stations typically refuse only the ones that might get them in trouble with the FCC.

4. *Do commercials sound interesting?* Local radio stations usually must create and produce announcements for many local advertising clients and for some public service organizations. Because listeners become bored easily, it's important that a station's best creative effort go into the writing and production of locally originated material. Interesting, sincere sounding, well-produced announcements maintain an audience's attention while also working effectively for the client. On the other hand, dull, poorly produced material insults listeners and promotes their tuning out. A wise rule in this respect is to encourage a staff's creativity and put nothing on the air unless it has a genuine creative spark.

With the fragile nature of listenership in today's supercompetitive radio environment, program managers cannot pay too much attention to the announcement material broadcast on their stations.

PROMOTION AND AUDIENCE PARTICIPATION

Finally, promotions and audience participation activities are important ingredients in the programming mixture for many stations. These activities are intended to build a station's audience through prizes, suspense, participation, and recognition.

On-air promotions frequently take the form of contests in which listeners are invited to participate. What began as relatively simple and inexpensive promotions, however, have escalated until prizes sometimes reach enormous proportions. For example, the *Wall Steet Journal* reported that one Miami station manager "is betting two $8,400 Mazda RX7 sports cars, a couple of 16-foot catamaran sailboats, a $2,500 hot tub and several vacation trips that he can gain ground on a lot of tough competitors in South Florida's rich Gold Coast market."[6] In all, the station's promotion, which lasted seven weeks during the fall (1978) rating period, was said to have cost about $250,000, including prizes, TV spots, bus signs, and bumper stickers.

Other Miami stations during the same period offered to pay a year's rent or mortgage up to $4,800, a year's electricity bills up to $1,200, and other cash prizes up to $10,000. However, during the fall of 1980, Cincinnati's WKRQ-FM, in a "million dollar contest," established a record in prize money by awarding $25,000 annually for life to a 16-year-old listener.

Theoretically, in a large metropolitan area, an increase of only one point in the ratings can significantly offset the cost of an expensive promotion contest. However, the benefits from such costly promotion events are not always realized. With each major station in a market attempting to win increased listenership through "hypoing" techniques, many experts believe big prize promotions nullify each other, leaving stations at the *status quo*. Therefore, many stations engage in prize promotions only as a protective measure, and some outlets have turned away from giving large prizes to a few lucky people in favor of awarding hundreds or even thousands of modest prizes to many different listeners. Examples of the latter typically include tickets to plays, movies, and concerts; free record albums; and other small items of merchandise.

The big prize approach to audience promotion, of course, builds suspense and excitement for a station during its rating period, even though only a small percentage of the listenership participates actively. However, because only a few people win prizes, many may be disappointed. The "small prize for everybody" approach, in contrast, generates a lower level of excitement, but many more individuals receive a bonus for listening to the station. In the final analysis, station management must determine which philosophy to adopt, if it awards prizes at all, on the basis of cost versus potential economic benefit.

Other forms of audience participation also are available to radio programmers. These include access programs which allow listeners to express their opinions on the air and "recognition features," which give public recognition to listeners for their accomplishments, anniversaries, and other meaningful occasions. For example, WSB, Atlanta, broadcasts numerous recognition features on a regular basis. This station extends greetings to newcomers in the city, congratulates individuals for civic accomplishments, and extends best wishes to listeners celebrating birthdays, wedding anniversaries, and other special events. Other features, also based on the premise that everyone likes to be recognized, include salutes to churches, schools, teachers, ministers, and students throughout the listening area. Such features as these call for creativity and some research, but their cost is minimal.

SUMMARY OF RADIO PROGRAMMING ELEMENTS

In this section, we have discussed the basic elements used in modern radio programming. Stations differ from each other, even within a format category, mainly through the selection and emphasis given these elements, the manner in which they are mixed, and the style added through production and presentation techniques. The programmer's goal is to choose the right elements and put them together in a pleasing and interesting format that entertains and informs the audience and, in the process, wins an acceptable share of the audience.

Next, we will examine the major formats of the 1980s, including their choice of program ingredients.

MAJOR RADIO FORMATS

Numerous formats have evolved over the past three decades, each designed to appeal to a particular age group and/or socioeconomic stratum. With time, some of the basic formats have divided and subdivided, resulting in many distinctive approaches to radio programming today. Shifting demographics, changing lifestyles, new technology, and the expansion of FM all have contributed to the proliferation. However, the broad classifications remain: music, information, and specialty formats.

MUSIC-BASED FORMATS

Music is the cornerstone of programming for most radio stations, along with news and service features. Popular music formats are generally divided into three major categories: the contemporary group, middle-of-the-road (MOR), and beautiful music. Other categories include country and classical. These divisions, with their respective major formats, are shown below.

Contemporary Group
1. Top 40
2. Adult Contemporary
3. Album-Oriented Rock (AOR)
4. Disco
5. Jazz

Middle-of-the-Road
1. Traditional MOR
2. Soft Contemporary
3. Nostalgic ("Golden Oldies," "Big Band," etc.)

Beautiful Music
1. Easy Listening

Country Formats
1. Traditional Country & Western
2. Modern Country

Classical

Of these formats, seven usually attract significant shares in competitive markets: (1) Top 40, (2) Adult Contemporary, (3) Album-Oriented Rock, (4) Middle-of-the-Road, (5) Easy Listening, (6) Soft Contemporary, and (7) Modern Country.

A typical music-and-news station follows an hourly "clock," with specific items—such as news, types of music selections, commercial sets, and features—programmed at fixed times each hour of the day. Some stations follow the basic pattern, but make minor modifications in the tempo of the music to accommodate demographic changes in the available audience during various listening periods. This practice is commonly called *day-parting*.

Figure 8.5 illustrates a "clock" for a popular music radio station. Note the absence of commercial breaks, or "stop sets," from 10 to 20 minutes past the hour and from 20 to 10 minutes before the hour. This break-free period permits a music sweep across the critical quarter-hour breaks, calculated to hold listeners through two consecutive quarter-hour periods. When successful, the station receives listening credit in sample diaries for both quarter hours because five minutes of listening occurred in each. In contrast, ten minutes of listening by an individual in a single quarter hour produces only one credit for the station under Arbitron's five-minute listening criterion. Similarly, five minutes of listening divided between two 15-minute periods gains no credit for a station. Thus, the "quarter-hour sweep" strategy is intended to gain the maximum possible audience credit for a station.

Once a music category has been selected for a station, the programmer must determine the sequencing and rotation pattern for the selections that meet the playlist criteria. Because no programmer wants to risk losing listeners, research often is undertaken to find out what songs appeal to the demographic group to which the programming is directed.

Another important term needs to be introduced here—*modal*. A modal (from the statistical term "mode") music approach attempts to maintain a core of musical types and artists which all of the station's audience likes. The basis for determining "modal records" is *psychographic* research: the analysis of listener types based on their psychological reactions to songs. The

Figure 8.5 Format clocks are used by many radio stations to depict graphically their repetitive hourly programming patterns. This clock provides for music sweeps across quarter-hour marks and the clustering of commercials.

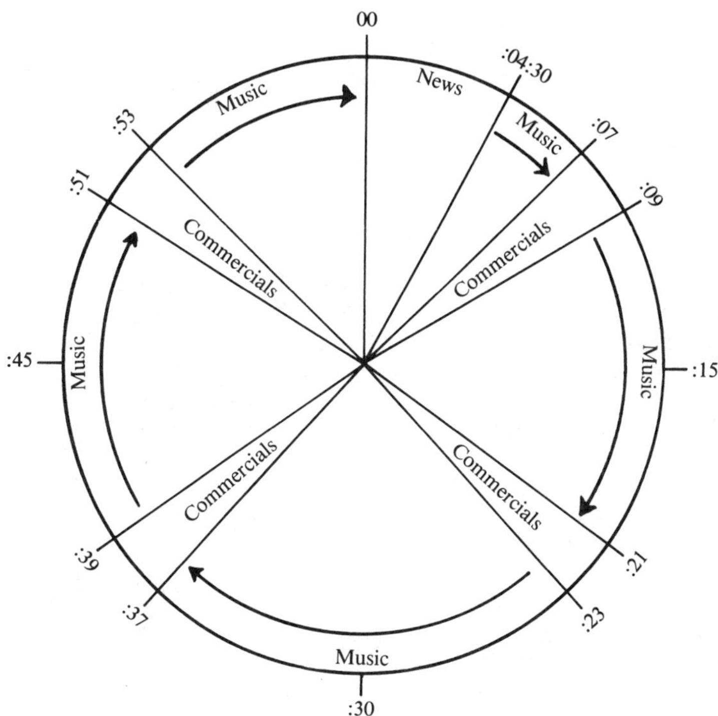

key concept is to determine which core of artists and records are liked by all (or nearly all) of a station's listeners and then to play *only* those artists and records. Thus, maximizing listenership among the desired demographic group is the goal. However, a disadvantage is that the playlist becomes quite narrow and the same "energy level," or loudness and intensity, may prevail from selection to selection.

Although the modal procedure is usually associated with Album-Oriented Rock (AOR) formats, the concept of narrow (modal) vs. broad (varied) music playlists is an important strategic consideration with all music-based formats.

Approaches to *music rotation* differ markedly among various formats. Listeners to popular music stations want to hear their favorite selections played often. Therefore, Top 40 programmers establish rotation plans that call for airplay roughly in proportion to a song's popularity. Thus, a top hit may be played at intervals of every 75 minutes or so, while a low-ranking selection on the current chart is broadcast once every six hours. In contrast, most noncontemporary formats usually do not *allow* repetition of a given selection during the same daypart within a week, or even a longer period of time. The emphasis, instead, is placed upon variety, pace, and the flow of music. Specific rotation techniques will be discussed more fully under each of the music-based formats.

The Contemporary Group: Today's Music

The contemporary music stations represent the majority of all formats on the air today. Among this group are such generic names as "Mass Appeal Top 40," "Adult Contemporary," "Album-Oriented Rock," "Disco," "Urban Contemporary," and "Jazz." Although some essential differences exist among these formats, they all appeal to some segment of the 12 to 34 age group.

Mass Appeal Top 40 Early Top 40 radio stations were known for continuous repetition of the 40 most popular current records. Few, if any, other selections were broadcast. The records simply were ranked and played in order, with the rotation cycle repeated after the 40th selection was played. This form of Top 40 no longer exists, having given way to a weighted form of rotation.

Contemporary Mass Appeal Top 40 stations emphasize current hit selections, but rotate the songs in proportion to their rank on the music chart. In addition, the music mix usually includes an occasional "oldie," a hit from perhaps as far back as 15 years, selected new records that may become hits, and perhaps songs by a featured artist of the day.

The top 40 records are usually divided into three groups, for example: Group "A," hits 1–5; Group "B," tunes ranked 6–20; and Group "C," 21–40. The "A" group is given the heaviest rotation, with each of the top five hits being played once every 75 minutes. This rotation insures that an average listener, whose listening span is perhaps 45 minutes, will hear three or four of the top hits during that period. "B" and "C" records are played less frequently. Ordinarily, little latitude is given the disc jockeys, who are expected to play every selection from a category before they can repeat any selection.

The overall rotation pattern for a Mass Appeal Top 40 station, then, looks something like the "hot clock" shown in Figure 8.6.

Strong personalities, heavy promotion, and a heavy news commitment are other characteristics of Mass Appeal Top 40 stations. Although these stations seek to attract the 12 to 34 demographic range, they particularly appeal to teenage listeners. Mass Appeal Top 40 is best exemplified by such 50,000 watt "rockers" of the 1960s and '70s as WABC, New York, and WLS, Chicago.

Adult Contemporary (AC) Adult Contemporary, which emerged as a leading format around 1980, developed largely because of the declining teenage population and the aging of the youth audiences that grew up listening to Top 40 radio. Adult Contemporary attempts to maintain these former Top 40 listeners into their young adult years through a hefty mixture of older songs, current hits, music trivia contests, lifestyle-oriented news, and a Top 40 type of execution. AC works well on powerful AM stations that have seen their Top 40 audience migrate to FM rock outlets. It is not uncommon for an Adult Contemporary station to proclaim itself "the station that you grew up

Figure 8.6 A "Hot Clock" for a Mass Appeal Top 40 Station. This format clock depicts the typical rotation scheme for a mass appeal top 40 station.

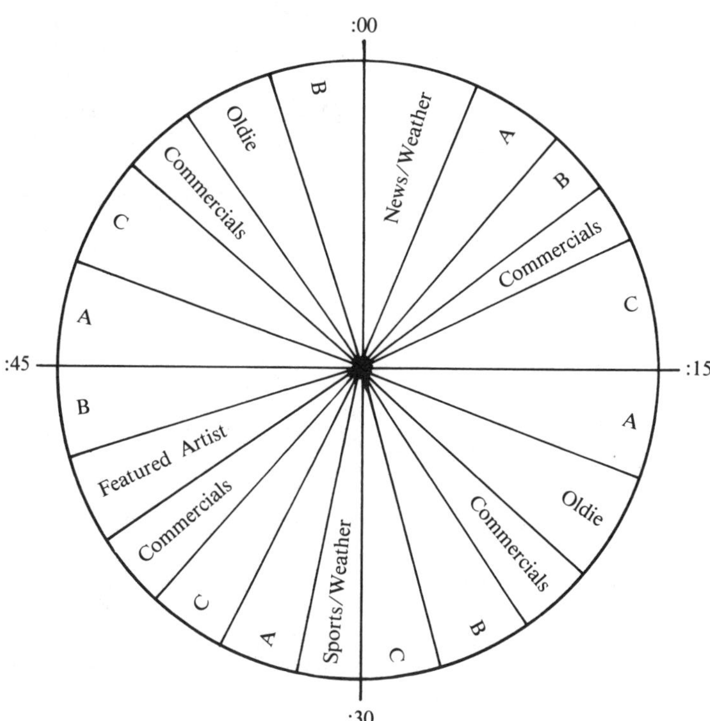

with" in the hope of keeping an audience that discovered and enjoyed radio before the era of FM dominance.

The music rotation of an AC station is more complicated than that of Top 40 stations. Because age demographic groups can be attracted by playing the music of their youthful "courting years," careful attention is given to the year each "oldie" was popular, as well as the type of music to which it belonged (e.g., Soul, Beach, Protest). Current records are ranked and weighted as are the oldies. Current records are usually divided into three groups:

"A"	"B"	"C"
Chart Positions	Chart Positions	Chart Positions
1–15	16–35	36–40

The "A" records are the "hottest" ones, but notice that more selections are included in this category with the Adult Contemporary format than with the Top 40. The "B" records are either moving up or down the popularity chart. The "C" records mainly are the new records which could become next month's "A's" or "B's." The oldies are usually divided into categories by groups of years. Assuming a 1984 operation, the oldie priorities might look something like this:

1960–1965	1966–1971	1972–1977	1978–1981
PRIORITY 5	PRIORITY 4	PRIORITY 3	PRIORITY 2

In addition, a group called *Recurrents* may be assigned to PRIORITY 1. In contemporary music programming, the recurrents are hits just off the current list, but not yet oldies—typically hit music from six months to two years old.

The typical Adult Contemporary rotation looks something like this:

:00	A	A
	PRIORITY 1	PRIORITY 4
	B	A
	A	C
	PRIORITY 2	PRIORITY 5
	A	A
	B	B–fill to top of hour (backtimed)
	PRIORITY 3	

Note that much more older music is played by AC than by Top 40, and that usually only one "C" record is played per hour. The priority oldie categories also may be different on rotation clocks of different day-parts.

Adult Contemporary stations, like Top 40 outlets, usually provide hourly newscasts and feature strong air personalities. Some AC stations emphasize other information programming as well, which places them in the General Service Station category, a broad-appeal type of station to be discussed later.

Album-Oriented Rock (AOR) Album-Oriented Rock, one of the most successful FM formats, has capitalized on the evolution of "rock and roll" into progressive music and the emergence of FM dominance in radio. AOR is a "lifestyle" format concept aimed at the narrow target demographic group of 18- to 34-year-old males. Album rock selections, rather than hit singles, are featured.

AOR music rotations differ noticeably from those of other contemporary formats. Since FM stations customarily have minimal news and public affairs commitments, there is no compelling need for talk on the hour (other than the required station ID). Therefore, a "flow" pattern of music rotation is employed instead of repeating an hourly "hot clock." AOR also employs the "sweep and cluster" approach: long segments of music with commercial and other talk material scheduled in occasional clusters.

AOR stations usually emphasize psychographic research to determine which artists and album cuts are preferred by their listeners. These stations, which tend to follow the "modal" approach to music selection, are usually assisted by program consultants.

Other Contemporary Formats Three other types of contemporary music formats persist in popularity, though at a lower level than the three mentioned above. Found only in selected markets, these types are Disco (for "discotheque"); its successor, Urban Contemporary; and Jazz.

For a period of several years during the late 1970s, a disco FM station led all of New York City's radio outlets in audience numbers. Since the disco format appeals heavily to members of certain ethnic groups, this format is seldom successful in noncosmopolitan centers. In fact, at this writing, all-disco has virtually disappeared in favor of the urban contemporary approach, which includes some disco music. On the other hand, jazz programming is found in many cities, large and small, because that form of music appeals to broader segments of the population.

Middle-of-the-Road: Broad-Based Adult Music

This group of formats, called *Middle-of-the-Road* (MOR) because they came to occupy a central position between contemporary rock and easy listening formats, is one of the oldest and most durable types of music programming within format radio. It includes Traditional MOR, Nostalgic, and Soft Contemporary approaches. The target audience is adults of both sexes, age 35 and older.

Traditional Middle-of-the-Road (MOR) Popular standard music is the staple of Traditional MOR stations, which emphasize melody more than beat in their music selections. MOR playlists consist of standards (e.g., Frank Sinatra, Perry Como, Tony Bennett, Ella Fitzgerald, and Peggy Lee), mixed with contemporary adult music (e.g., Sergio Mendez, Helen Reddy, Olivia Newton-John, Roger Whittaker, and Ray Conniff) that is compatible with the traditional melodic sound. Since the target audience is older than with contemporary formats, the music reaches farther back in time.

The traditional method of programming MOR music involves three rotations executed simultaneously: Artist Category (Male, Female, Group, and Instrumental), New or Old, and Standard or Contemporary. Individual selections for the rotation often are left to the air personality, who is usually highly experienced. The format repeats itself each hour, usually after news presented on the hour. A typical MOR music sequence would be:

Male		Female		Group		Instrumental
Current	→	Old	→	Current	→	Old
Standard		Contemporary		Standard		Contemporary

A conservative MOR station likely would play two standards and two old selections for every contemporary and current tune. A contemporary MOR outlet, however, would reverse the ratio. This procedure also serves to stagger the rotation so as to avoid the same combinations repeating themselves before the entire pool of possibilities has been exhausted.

There are fewer Traditional MOR stations now than in the 1960s and early 1970s, largely reflecting a shift to Adult Contemporary formats. However, a few large city stations (e.g., WNEW, New York) continue to program with MOR, usually supplementing the music with heavy news and information programming.

Other MOR Formats Several minor formats exist under the Middle-of-the-Road umbrella of standard popular music. Big Band and Golden Oldies are two types which emerged during the nostalgic era of the 1970s. The former emphasizes dance band music with occasional vocal soloists and groups, while the reverse ratio is generally followed by Golden Oldies stations.

A third type of MOR format, so classified because of its mellow sound, is Soft Contemporary. This approach features a blend of current melodic music to the exclusion of anything with a heavy beat. In this format, contemporary music may be reorchestrated to achieve the desired mellowness. Rotation plans are employed in all three of these MOR types.

Beautiful Music: A Format for Quiet Listening

Emphasis on lush instrumental and vocal arrangements characterizes Beautiful Music Stations, which are among the most successful on the air today. Almost every major city has a Beautiful Music, or Easy Listening, station among the top three or four outlets. There is some criticism that these stations serve only as background music sources rather than as high attention-level "foreground" stations. Nevertheless, Beautiful Music stations are highly popular, appealing especially to the 35+ demographic segment.

Beautiful Music, which is an FM stereo phenomenon, is usually automated to some degree—either completely or in a "live assist" manner. Furthermore, most of these stations employ one of the highly successful packaged formats, such as Schulke or Bonneville, which is carefully sequenced with original and reorchestrated music. This type of format, in fact, was the first to be packaged for automated station operation. Now, however, practically all formats can be obtained from syndicated producers.

Two primary differences are found among Beautiful Music stations with respect to music rotation: *matched flow* and *random access*. In a matched flow rotation, selections are sequenced or "tempo paired," with a series of selections on a single tape. Only two tape decks are required. In contrast, when random access is used, each individual selection is separated on the reel (by tones or other methods), and four reel-to-reel tape decks are needed for playback. The music flow in random access rotation comes from some combination of the four reels.

MATCHED FLOW	RANDOM ACCESS
Reel Deck 1 music segment—	Reel Deck 1 →Reel Deck 2→
Reel Deck 2 music segment	Reel Deck 3 →Reel Deck 4

The advantage of matched flow is also its major drawback. The music can be paired more carefully by the programmer; but since several selections are segued on a single tape roll, the same selections appear in the same order each time the tape is played. However, by simply changing the sequence of random access, any number of combinations of pairings can be accomplished in that system (i.e., 1-2-3-4, 1-3-2-4, 1-4-3-2, 1-2-3-2-4-3-1, etc.).

Country Music: More than Rural Appeal

Country music has been an important part of radio broadcasting since the industry's earliest years. The success of live country jamborees, such as WSM's perennial "Grand Ole Opry," inevitably led to full-scale country music programming when format radio arrived. At first, these were called "Country and Western" because of their combination of hillbilly, folk, bluegrass, and cowboy music. Today, of course, country music is contemporary and broad-based in its appeal. Country stations are popular in practically all areas of the United States, attracting a wide adult demographic audience, especially if a station complements the music with full service informational broadcasting.

The two basic subdivisions of country music programming are the traditional Country and Western and the Modern Country formats. The former represents a broader mix of types of country music, not unlike Traditional MOR in its musical variety, while the latter concentrates more on contemporary music of the country field.

Rotation plans of Country and Western outlets usually follow the MOR pattern, while Modern Country stations essentially follow the Adult Contemporary or weighted Top 40 approach. There is really little difference between programming country radio, from a format standpoint, and programming any other type of music format that includes both current and old selections. A well-trained programmer with knowledge of country music's history is needed, but only the records, personalities, and promotions would change.

Classical Music Formats: For Discriminating Listeners

When one thinks of classical music stations, public radio often comes to mind. However, in some large cities, classical formats are programmed successfully by commercial stations. These stations are "lifestyle" oriented, appealing mainly to discriminating listeners, usually among older demographic groups of upper income and educational levels.

Serious music programming consists of commercial recordings, as well as live and taped concerts. Programmers may emphasize either the older classics or modern compositions, or a mixture of both, in various programs. Frequent repetition of individual selections, however, is generally avoided so as to broaden the range of selections presented. This is necessary, in part, because serious music works are typically long by broadcast standards. However, because of the need to accommodate commercial material, programmers tend to choose shorter selections for daytime hours and schedule longer concert pieces in the evenings. In both cases, however, commercials are clustered to avoid frequent program interrruptions.

News of cultural events and the arts, as well as regular newscasts, usually are emphasized as important contributors to the "class" image of these stations.

INFORMATION-BASED FORMATS

A significant number of large market radio stations have successfully adopted all-information programming. All-News, All-Talk, and News-Talk are the three principal formats. Variations exist, however, in General Service Radio and sports and agricultural subformats. These programming approaches generally appeal to adults over the age of 35.

All-News

Because of its huge staffing requirements, All-News is by far the most expensive format in modern radio. Despite its high cost, this format is competitive with most music formats in large population centers. The potential audience, however, must be quite large in order to maintain significant shares, since high audience turnover is a characteristic of the format. Two important sources of audio news material, other than a station's local effort, are CNN Radio, operated by the Cable News Network, and Associated Press Radio. Other radio networks are also utilized.

The All-News format calls for a definite rotation plan, not completely unlike that of popular music stations. Based on the concept that typical listeners tune in for short spans, stations currently programming All-News are based on 18-minute to half-hour repetitive cycles. During each cycle, the format takes the listener through a sequence of types of news. A typical cycle consists of national/international, regional/state, local, sports, financial, and weather blocks, plus perhaps a commentary or feature. This cycle, of course, is subject to change whenever breaking news stories occur. Thus, each cycle provides busy listeners with a capsule of the major stories in several categories, whereupon typical listeners tune out and presumably new ones tune in. At the same time, an effort is usually made to keep hard-core news listeners for a longer period through constant updating and rewriting, a variety of secondary stories, and new features and commentaries. A representative All-News station is described in Figure 8.7.

Despite its high cost, All-News radio stations have achieved a more stable audience base than many of their music-oriented AM counterparts which must compete head-on with FM for the music-listening audience.

All-Talk

All-Talk radio began a few decades ago with late night call-in broadcasts on clear-channel radio stations. These talk programs attracted insomniacs and other nighttime listeners who called in to the stations. Gradually this form of radio programming emerged during the daytime hours on a few big city stations, including KMOX, St. Louis, a CBS-owned facility. Today, this format is found in many large markets and, like All-News, is almost always on AM stations.

Strictly speaking, talk radio may include any type of talk, including news, play-by-play sports, serious and light interviews, and telephone conversations between the host (and sometimes his/her guests) and listeners. The most common approach, however, relies mainly on two-way conversations which permit listeners to have their say on the air.

The key to success with two-way talk radio is the program host, or "talkmaster," who determines the course of the broadcast. His/her job is to keep the program interesting and, whenever possible, even exciting through the selection and interviewing of guests and by stimulating and pacing the phone calls. Thus, the host represents the audience. In this role, the host encourages callers who have interesting things to say and politely dismisses those who do not. It is also wise to have callers prescreened by a production assistant before they are turned over to the host of the program. A successful talk show host, of course, must be well informed on many subjects to conduct a talk show intelligently. Topics discussed usually are far-ranging, including current events, consumer affairs, personal problems, sports, or practically any subject of broad general interest.

Figure 8.7 The broadcast hour of All-News WINS Radio, New York, is structured around three 20-minute news cycles. Within each cycle, listeners hear a flow of the latest news plus updates on fast-breaking stories. Complementing the news is a variety of regularly scheduled features, such as those shown here.

REGULARLY SCHEDULED FEATURES 1010 WINS RADIO

CONSUMER

BUSINESS REPORTS *Monday-Friday*
5:27 am, 5:57 am, 6:27 am, 6:57 am, 7:57 am, 8:57 am, 9:27 am, 9:57 am

STOCK MARKET REPORTS *Monday-Friday*
At :27 and :57 past the hour throughout the trading day.

BUSINESS ANALYSIS *with Larry Wachtel*
Monday-Friday 7:27 am, 8:27 am, 12:27 pm, 4:57 pm, 6:27 pm

MEDICAL REPORTS *with William Hines*
Monday-Friday & Sunday
Monday-Friday: 5:25 am, 9:06 am, 11:06 am
Sunday: 8:33 am, 9:33 am, 10:33 am, 11:33 am, 1:33 pm

PERSONAL FINANCE REPORTS *with Gerry Rosen*
Monday-Friday & Sunday
Monday-Friday: 5:57 am, 10:33 am, 1:33 pm
Sunday: 8:06 am, 9:06 am, 10:06 am, 12:06 pm, 1:06 pm

INFLATION FIGHTER REPORTS *with Eileen Douglas*
Monday-Sunday
Monday-Friday: 6:33 am, 10:06 am, 1:06 pm, 3:06 pm
Saturday: 6:54 am, 8:54 am, 10:54 am, 12:54 pm
Sunday: 7:06 am, 11:06 am, 2:54 pm, 6:06 pm

ENTERTAINMENT REVIEWS
with Leida Snow/Theater and Bob Salmaggi/Movies
Monday-Friday 5:33 am, 9:11 am, 2:33 pm

FOOD AND WINE REPORTS *with Don Brewer*
Thursday-Saturday
Thursday (Food) and Friday (Wine): 11:12 am, 2:06 pm, 7:06 pm
Saturday: 1:33 pm (Food), 2:33 pm (Wine), 4:33 pm (Food), 5:33 pm (Wine)

INFORMATION

ACCU-WEATHER REPORTS *Monday-Sunday*
Continuous updates throughout the day.

SHADOW TRAFFIC REPORTS
Monday-Friday 6:00-9:00 am, 4:00-7:00 pm
Every 20 minutes.

WINS NEWS CONFERENCE
Sunday, 10:00 pm

MIDDLE EAST DIARY *with Jay Bushinsky*
Monday-Wednesday 11:12 am, 2:06 pm, 7:06 pm

SPORTS

SPORTS REPORTS *Monday-Sunday*
Quarter of and quarter after every hour.

FISHING REPORTS
Friday and Saturday, in season.
Friday: 5:06 am, 10:12 am, 12:06 pm, 4:06 pm, 7:11 pm, 11:06 pm
Saturday: 5:06 am, 6:12 am, 8:06 am, 4:06 pm, 7:11 pm, 11:06 pm

SKIING REPORTS *Wednesday-Saturday, in season.*
Wednesday: 6:33 pm, 9:06 pm, 11:06 pm
Thursday and Friday: 6:12 am, 8:06 am, 6:33 pm, 9:06 pm, 11:06 pm
Saturday: 6:12 am, 8:06 am

OPINION

GROUP W COMMENTARIES
with Vernon Jordan, Jacqueline Wexler, Franklin Williams
Monday-Sunday
Monday-Friday: 9:33 am, 12:33 pm, 3:33 pm, 10:33 pm
Saturday: 9:33 am, 12:33 pm, 3:33 pm
Sunday: 9:33 am, 12:33 pm

RELIGIOUS COMMENTARIES:
Sister Camille D'Arienzo
Sunday: 8:57 am, 3:57 pm, 10:57 pm
Reverend Roy Lloyd
Saturday: 11:54 am, 3:57 pm, 7:57 pm, 11:57 pm
Sunday: 6:57 am, 1:57 pm, 8:57 pm
Rabbi Marc Tannenbaum
Sunday: 7:57 am, 7:57 pm, 12:57 pm

WINS EDITORIALS AND FEEDBACK
3:37 am, 4:37 am, 5:37 am, 8:37 am, 4:37 pm, 8:37 pm, 11:37 pm

1010 WINS . . . You give us 22 minutes. We'll give you the world.

GROUP W WESTINGHOUSE BROADCASTING COMPANY

RAR RADIO ADVERTISING REPRESENTATIVES, INC.

Although the call-in program is the main item in the All-Talk format, these stations usually carry hourly newscasts, sports reports, play-by-play accounts, and feature material as well.

News-Talk

A hybrid format combining the strengths of both All-News and All-Talk has emerged as News-Talk radio. This type of radio station usually broadcasts lengthy news blocks during the morning and afternoon drive-time period and heavy play-by-play sports at night and on weekends, with the remaining time used for listener call-in broadcasts. The call-in shows usually achieve higher listenership than all-news during the midday hours in most markets, and they are less costly to produce. For those reasons, some formerly All-News stations have gravitated toward the News-Talk format in recent years.

A typical day's programming on a News-Talk station might resemble the following schedule:

6–10 AM	Morning News Block
10–12 N	Call-in Talk Show
12– 1 PM	Noon News Block
1– 4 PM	Call-in Talk Show
4– 7 PM	Afternoon News Block
7– 8 PM	Call-in Sports Talk Show
8–10 PM	Sports Play-by-Play
10–12 M	Late Night Call-in Show

General Service Radio

Although most radio stations have adopted distinctive formats, many also superimpose upon their basic format—whether it's a music or an information type—a strong information service. These stations are commonly called *general service stations.* They are characterized by a strong and credible news department, usually complemented by a major network, with talk shows, sports, play-by-play, helicopter traffic, market reports, extensive weather coverage, and other information services.

General service programming, which appeals primarily to persons above age 35, also may add a strong second demographic audience in addition to that attracted by the station's basic format. The public's dependence upon general service radio for useful and sometimes vital information often propels these stations into dominant positions in their markets.

Large market general service stations almost always are 50,000 watt clear channel AM outlets which have broad market penetration. Examples are WCCO, Minneapolis; WGN, Chicago; WJR, Detroit; WSB, Atlanta; KDKA, Pittsburgh; KFAB, Omaha; WTIC, Hartford; and KSL, Salt Lake City.

Information Subformats

Two other types of information programming—sports and agricultural—occupy large amounts of time on some stations. Rarely, if ever, do these types of information constitute a station's total format. However, their extensive programming and importance in many geographical areas qualify both as "subformats."

For some radio stations, sports is a permeating factor. For example, one or two radio outlets in major league cities devote much time to play-by-play accounts of professional baseball, football, and other games. Pregame shows and postgame scoreboards add to the sports package. Talk shows and interview programs focus on the local teams. Even disc jockeys may get into the act with comments, game time weather forecasts, and pre- and postgame traffic reports. Similarly, collegiate athletics may form a nucleus for extensive sports programming in university cities.

Agricultural information similarly receives a great amount of attention on regional stations in the Central and Southern states. Farm programming is usually scheduled for early morning and noontime blocks, but it sometimes extends into other time periods.

Typical agricultural programming includes farm market and extended weather reports, interviews with county agents and other agricultural leaders, information about new and improved products and farming techniques, and news of farmers' organizations. In addition, farmer-directed advertising adds to the agricultural flavor of such stations.

One example of an agriculturally-oriented station is KRVN, a 50,000 watt AM station in Lexington, Nebraska. This station, licensed to the Nebraska Rural Radio Association (a farmers' cooperative venture), broadcasts nearly 30 hours of farm information each week. A few of the other stations which emphasize agricultural programming include WHO, Des Moines, Iowa; KCMO, Kansas City, Missouri; WPTF, Raleigh, North Carolina; and WDAY, Fargo, North Dakota.

SPECIALTY FORMATS

Several forms of specialty programming are found in American radio broadcasting. The most common are ethnic and religious formats.

Black Formats

The most widespread form of specialty broadcasting is that of Black-oriented radio. These stations may be found in all large cities that have substantial Black populations and in smaller communities throughout the South. Actually, the formats used are mere variations of those discussed above. The principal difference is that the information and services are particularly appropriate for Black listeners. Their music programming retains a "soul" and "rhythm and blues" flavor; but with the cross-over phenomenon in popular music, it increasingly resembles the contemporary approach. Air personalities, of course, are almost always Black.

In addition to Black programming, an increasing number of radio stations are coming under Black ownership. Both the FCC and the National Association of Broadcasters have encouraged this development. As noted in chapter 1, two networks provide national newscasts for Black-oriented stations in the United States.

Other Ethnic Programming

Spanish-language stations constitute a second important type of ethnic specialty programming. These stations generally are located in the Sunbelt states, particularly Florida, Texas, Arizona, and California, as well as such major cities as New York and Chicago. Music, news, and information for Spanish-Americans in Spanish is the usual procedure. In Miami and some other cities, Spanish-language radio stations consistently rank among the leaders in audience shares.

In addition to fulltime stations broadcasting Spanish, block programming in other languages may be heard in various cosmopolitan centers. Ethnic stations in New York City, for example, broadcast in Polish, Italian, Russian, and a number of other languages. Polish, Italian, and Greek broadcasts are prominent in Chicago. And in San Francisco and Los Angeles, Chinese, Korean, Japanese, and other oriental groups receive radio service from ethnic specialty stations. Finally, a few stations program in native dialects to American Indians in such states as New Mexico, Oklahoma, and the Dakotas, while Eskimo broadcasts are common in Alaska.

Religious Formats

Another rapidly emerging programming specialty is all-religious broadcasting. All-religious stations, which have been established in most large cities, may be either institutional or commercial in nature. Institutional religious stations are licensed to churches, church-related colleges, and nonprofit religious organizations. Commercial religious stations are privately owned, operated for profit, and secure revenues from the sale of time to evangelists, churches, religious organizations, and commercial advertisers.

Typical programming offered by religious stations includes preaching or sermons, inspirational talk programs, and traditional church or gospel music. Both block and format programming are used.

CHOOSING A FORMAT

Selecting a format for a radio station and deciding how to execute it are fundamental decisions that require thoughtful attention by program management. A final format determination must be based on analysis of the community served, the competitive environment, including specific competitor stations, and the station to be programmed. In adddition, programmers need to understand the basic characteristics of each format considered, particularly the demographic segments to which it most appeals, national format popularity trends, and format execution procedures.

The following sections include some of the most important questions that need to be answered before deciding on the adoption of a format.

CONSIDER THE COMMUNITY

Every community has unique characteristics which relate to economic pursuits, social characteristics, individual interests, and collective habits. A thorough understanding of these and other special characteristics of the community/service area is a necessary starting point in making basic programming decisions.

The following are appropriate questions regarding the community.

1. What are the major economic pursuits of the community (commerce, manufacturing, financial, retailing, agriculture, government, service, etc.)?
2. What are the demographic characteristics of the community (age, sex, and ethnic composition)?
3. What demographic and geographic trends are found (e.g., a declining teenage demographic, a growing 25–49 segment, rapid suburbanization)?
4. What are the social characteristics (income and educational levels)?
5. What are the major cultural interests (sports, the arts, religion, entertainment, etc.)?
6. What are the prevailing musical tastes of the population (contemporary, country, classical, standard, etc.)?
7. What are the major information needs (local, state, national, international news; traffic reports; weather; markets; sports; etc.)?
8. What are the peculiar habits of the community (e.g., prevailing AM and PM commuting hours, prevailing dinner hour, major recreational pursuits)?

CONSIDER THE COMPETITION

The next step in the analytical process is to study the competitive environment and, in particular, the programming of all competitor stations that serve the market.

These are some of the questions that may guide this part of the analysis.

1. How competitive is the radio market? (The answer would include the number of stations and the intensity of competition between them.)
2. What formats are presented in the market? (This answer also will reveal any significant formats that are not present.)
3. How many competitors are there within each format? (There may be room for more than one station within a given format. Each station, of course, would seek to develop a strong identity to differentiate it from the others.)
4. How well are the present formats executed? (This answer could reveal strengths or weaknesses in the area of program execution.)
5. How successful is each station and what other advantages or disadvantages does each station have? (A station may be successful in spite of weak execution if it has little direct competition. It also may be successful at present, but vulnerable to a challenger with greater geographic coverage, better hours of operation, better production facilities, or better technical sound.)
6. Are any significant demographic groups, musical tastes, or cultural interest groups not being served adequately? (If so, does the audience represented have enough potential to justify a fulltime format? If not, how much programming might be justified?)

7. What are the track records of various stations and formats in the market? (A format not presently programmed may have been attempted previously with unsatisfactory results. If so, why was it not successful? Also, a dominant station may have been challenged in the past, but without satisfactory results. Why not?)

CONSIDER YOUR STATION

The characteristics of the station to be programmed are vitally important in making a format decision. The programmer must know what he/she has to work with and how those facilities compare with those of potential competitors.

Here are a few pertinent questions.

1. Is the station AM or FM? (The high fidelity characteristic of frequency modulation transmissions enables FM stations to compete well with music formats. On the other hand, information-type formats, which do not require high fidelity, do comparatively well on AM radio.)
2. Is the station new—seeking its first format—or is it an existing operation considering a change? (In either case, the station will either find a programming void and fill it, or challenge an existing station's format.)
3. If the station already exists, what is its format and ratings history? (How successful has it been with each previous format? How successful is it now, and what recent listenership trends has it experienced?)
4. Would a change of format likely improve the station's overall audience share or the demographic composition of its audience? (The decision should take into account the new competition faced, the loyalty and rapport that may be lost with the existing audience, and the technical facilities with which the station competes.)
5. How extensive is the station's coverage in comparison with potential competitors? (Wide coverage is a definite advantage for stations with broad-appeal formats. Coverage superiority over a format competitor, coupled with equal or superior format execution, usually assures success. However, coverage inferiority, coupled with superior format execution, rarely succeeds. Stations with limited geographical coverage face a definite disadvantage in competition with stations that have greater signal reach; however, they still may be viable provided they identify and serve compact populations with common interests. These unique audiences may include ethnic groups, suburban communities, and other identifiable populations.)

FINAL CONSIDERATIONS

When adopting a format, a number of additional items related to execution must be determined. They include the following.

1. Will the music playlist be broad or narrow? (A high power, wide coverage station generally succeeds better in achieving broad audience reach and, therefore, can program a broad range of music effectively. Lower power stations competing against high power outlets often are most successful when they follow a narrow playlist appealing to hard-core adherents of a type of music.)
2. Shall the station adopt a power strategy by directly challenging another station, or a strategy of complementing the available programming through a format unique to the market? (The real question here is whether to become aggressively competitive for a large potential audience or to seek a noncompetitive niche for a unique type of service in the market.)
3 Should a switch in format be sudden or gradual? (If sudden, most previous listeners may become alienated and turn elsewhere, while it also requires time to build the new audience. This can affect advertising sales adversely. If gradual, some previous listeners may be retained, but the promotional edge may be lessened.)
4. How shall the station's new format be promoted? (Promotion via other media—newspaper, TV, outdoor billboards, etc.—as well as on-air contests is a fact of life in competitive radio broadcasting.)
5. Should the station be automated or programmed on a live announce basis? (Much debate and discussion could develop on this point as the pro's and con's of automation are debated. Remember that most formats now are available from program packagers for automated and semiautomated stations. Excellent quality packaged formats, coupled with quality automation equipment, produces a pleasing professional sound. Some spontaneity, however, may be sacrificed.)

SUMMARY

In chapter 8, we began with the notion that radio is a vital communications medium. It's also unique. Radio stations serve the public in ways that are different from television because radio is audio only, highly mobile, and fragmented into numerous formats that reach different demographic segments of the public. Radio is also highly localized in its service. To be competitive, viable financially, and a servant of the public are among commercial radio's principal goals.

A radio station's programming may be divided into various time blocks, each with different programming, or it may be formatted for a uniform sound whenever the station is on the air. The latter approach is more common. Music, news, other types of information, personalities, announcements, and promotions are among the most important available programming elements.

We also classified radio formats into three broad categories—*music-based, all-information,* and *specialty*—and then identified specific formats that belong in each category. Finally, chapter 8 concluded with a set of criteria for choosing a radio station format.

In the next chapter, we turn to a different form of radio and television programming as we examine public broadcasting.

ENDNOTES

1. James Duncan, Jr., *American Radio Spring 1981.* (Kalamazoo, Mich.: James H. Duncan, Jr., September 1981).
2. *Attitudes and Opinions Toward Radio News in the United States.* (Marion, Iowa: Frank N. Magid Associates, Inc., April 1978).
3. Under the FCC's 1981 deregulation orders, radio stations no longer must inform the FCC of the extent of their commercial material.
4. National Association of Broadcasters, *The Radio Code,* 22d ed. (Washington, D.C.: National Association of Broadcasters, 1980), p. 14.
5. *Ibid.*
6. Jim Montgomery, "Like a Paid Day Off? Like to Raid the Bank? Turn Your Radio On," *Wall Street Journal* (November 13, 1978), p.1.

STUDY QUESTIONS

1. Make a list of the radio stations in your city (or a nearby large city), indicating whether each is block or format programmed. Designate type of format, whenever appropriate.
2. Classify the formats shown in question 1 by category: (1) music; (2) information; and (3) specialty.
3. How many different formats are used in the market? What type of format is used by the greatest number of stations? How do these stations differentiate their programming from that of the other intraformat competitors?
4. Are any important formats missing from the market? If so, would that (or those) formats be viable? Why?
5. Analyze in detail the format of a radio station in your area. Your instructor may wish to make specific assignments for this exercise.
6. Analyze in detail the news and weather programming of a radio station in your area. Again, your instructor may make specific assignments.
7. Analyze the radio promotions conducted by stations in your city. Be sure to indicate the most lavish prize given by a station during the most recent audience measurement period.
8. Design a radio station format in detail, using a clock diagram, showing placement of news, music, commercials, weather, and any other elements to be used during a typical hour.

SUGGESTED READINGS

Barnes, Rey L. *Program Decision-Making in Small Market AM Radio Stations.* PhD dissertation, University of Iowa, 1970.

Denisoff, R. Serge. *Solid Gold: The Popular Record Industry.* Edison, N.J.: Transaction Press, 1974.

Eastman, Susan Tyler, Sydney W. Head, and Lewis Klein. *Broadcast Programming.* Belmont, Calif.: Wadsworth Publishing, 1981.

Hall, Claude, and Barbara Hall. *The Business of Radio Programming*. New York: Billboard Publications, 1977.

Johnson, Joseph S., and Kenneth K. Jones. *Modern Radio Station Practices,* 2d ed. Belmont, Calif.: Wadsworth Publishing, 1978.

Miles, Daniel J., Betty T. Miles, and Martin J. Miles. *The Miles Chart Display of Popular Music: Volume II, 1971–1975*. New York: Arno Press, 1977.

Routt, Edd, James B. McGrath, and Frederick A. Weiss. *The Radio Format Conundrum*. New York: Hastings House, 1978.

Taylor, Sherril W., ed. *Radio Programming in Action*. New York: Hastings House, 1967.

9

PROGRAMMING THE PUBLIC BROADCAST STATION

Kent Sidel

Public broadcasting in the United States consists of some 1,100 noncommercial radio and 300 noncommercial TV stations, their national member-controlled programming organizations, and various regional associations.

Just as competitive programming characterizes commercial radio and television, "alternative" programming is the specialty of noncommercial broadcasting. At first, alternative programming, whether for philosophical, pedagogical, or social reasons, tended to originate from educational institutions with which the earliest noncommercial stations were affiliated. Thus, noncommercial programming came to be called generically *educational broadcasting*. Later, following the passage of the Public Broadcasting Act of 1967, the term *public broadcasting* was adopted.

Noncommercial broadcasting in the United States actually dates back to the earliest days of radio. However, it has not been as powerful a social, political, or economic institution as its commercial counterpart. Indeed, even today, public broadcasting experiences difficulty amassing enough financial support to do more than merely survive each short-term crisis. Nevertheless, public broadcasting has attained a certain status of acceptance; despite its chronic financial difficulties, it provides an important service to the American public.

Although the name *public broadcasting* has replaced *educational broadcasting,* we must note that each of these terms also connotes specific types of programming widely provided by noncommercial radio and TV stations. *Public broadcasting* refers to cultural and public affairs programs which are disseminated over these stations. In contrast, *educational broadcasting* is primarily instructional in content and purpose. Both, of course, are *alternative programming* in that they provide a clear-cut option to much of the programming produced by commercial networks and stations.

The purpose of this chapter is to develop an understanding of the structure of noncommercial broadcasting, its goals and objectives, and the various approaches to programming followed by its diverse body of licensees. We shall begin with a brief overview of public broadcasting's historical background.

PUBLIC BROADCASTING TO 1967

The most important single milestone in public broadcasting was the passage of the Public Broadcasting Act of 1967 and, following that enactment, the establishment of the Corporation for Public Broadcasting (CPB) to encourage and fund public television and radio. However, the roots of public broadcasting are much deeper.

Several educational radio stations have been in existence longer than most commercial broadcast outlets. Station 9XM, Madison, Wisconsin, went on the air with an experimental AM operation in 1919. Later renamed WHA, this station was a product of the University of Wisconsin physics laboratory. In 1922, educational groups had 74 of the 500 station licenses. By 1925, this number had grown to 171. However, a combination of circumstances, including undesirable frequency assignments, acquisitions by commercial interests, and lack of funds, rapidly depleted the number. By 1934, the year the Federal Communications Commission was established, there were very few AM licenses remaining in noncommercial hands.

Today, only about 25 public radio stations operate in the AM band. The same outlets that were fortunate enough to survive the rapid development of commercial broadcasting 50 years ago are still the dominant non-FM public radio stations. A few examples include WILL, Urbana, Illinois; WBAA, West Lafayette, Indiana; WOI, Ames, Iowa; WNYC, New York City; WKAR, East Lansing, Michigan; WOSU, Columbus, Ohio; KWSU, Pullman, Washington; and WHA, Madison, Wisconsin.

Although Congress failed to designate additional AM frequencies for educational use in the Communications Act of 1934, the FCC in 1938 did reserve channels in the 41–42 megahertz portion of the spectrum for future educational FM broadcasting. However, noncommercial broadcasters had to wait another decade for further developments. In 1948, the FCC followed the precedent of earlier government policies which encouraged development of unused land through homesteading. The Commission's action authorized low power (10 watt) noncommercial stations on reserved FM channels (88–92 MHz), providing the most substantial boost to educational broadcasting since the early days of radio.

Reasonable initial investment coupled with reduced maintenance requirements provided the impetus for a two-stage process leading to the successful development of the FM band. First, more stations meant more available programming for listeners. This led to an increased desire to receive the material and, in turn, created a consumer climate conducive to the development and manufacture of low cost receivers. Many of today's leading public radio stations grew from those early 10 watt FM operations.

Noncommercial television followed many of the same trends as radio, but TV seemed to fare slightly better. Commercial television began regular broadcasting in 1941. Eleven years later, following World War II and a lengthy freeze on new station development, the FCC assigned 242 television channels for educational use.

The first noncommercial TV station, KUHT in Houston, went on the air in 1953. Thereafter, growth was slow but steady—10 stations by 1954, 17 by 1955, 44 by 1959. Noncommercial television, or educational television (ETV), then received its boost in growth, much as FM had experienced through low power authorizations, with the passage of the Educational Television Facilities Act in 1962. This Act provided up to $1,000,000 in matching grants to each state for equipment purchases. By 1963, 75 ETV stations were operating, and this number jumped to 101 by 1965 and to 126 by 1967.

Although ETV received most of its operating income from state and local governments before 1967 (as did noncommercial radio), the Ford Foundation's contributions were a major factor in keeping the system solvent. Through the establishment in 1952 of the Educational Radio and Television Center—renamed National Educational Television (NET) in 1959—the Foundation financed programs to be shared by ETV stations. These shared programs reached 10 hours weekly in 1963. The creation of the Ford-funded Public Broadcasting Laboratory (PBL) in 1966 provided a series of cultural and public affairs programs that were distributed simultaneously to all ETV stations. Foundations contributed almost 15 percent of ETV's total income of $58,000,000 in 1966. Ford, of course, provided the majority of this support.

Educational broadcasting prior to 1967 revealed a mixed picture of success. AM radio's growth had all but stagnated since the mid-1930s. FM was growing, but many of the stations were low power, low budget, and low profile operations. Television existed, but it maintained a tenuous existence because of inadequate operating funds. Programming was largely educational, with some nationally produced cultural and public affairs material distributed by NET.

THE PUBLIC BROADCASTING ACT OF 1967

No national public policy for noncommercial broadcasting existed before 1967. With the growth of noncommercial TV following the Educational Television Facilities Act of 1962, a need emerged for a comprehensive mechanism to allocate funds and supervise future growth. This problem was examined by a high level Carnegie Commission on Educational Television at the urging of the National Association of Educational Broadcasters. President Lyndon Johnson endorsed the Carnegie Commission's recommendations, and the passage of the Public Broadcasting Act of 1967 soon followed.

The most important feature of the Public Broadcasting Act was the creation of the Corporation for Public Broadcasting to disburse annual Congressional appropriations to noncommercial radio and TV stations. The formal establishment of the Corporation in 1968 marked the beginning of more than a decade of dramatic and sometimes politically controversial growth of public broadcasting. Public broadcasting as we know it today took shape during this period.

WHO'S INVOLVED IN PUBLIC BROADCASTING

Noncommercial radio and television stations exist under a number of types of ownership across the country. Licensees include colleges and universities, state boards of education, state television authorities, municipalities, local boards of education, public libraries, and nonprofit community organizations. Figure 9.1 gives examples of each type.

The three prominent national organizations in public broadcasting are the Corporation for Public Broadcasting, already introduced, the Public Broadcasting Service (PBS), and National Public Radio (NPR). As we discussed earlier, the Corporation for Public Broadcasting distributes federal grants for public broadcast facilities and programs. Since CPB was prohibited by Congress from interconnecting the stations to which it allocates funds, PBS was established as a membership organization of public TV stations to establish and maintain the program distribution service for its member stations. National Public Radio is noncommercial radio's counterpart for PBS.

Regional membership associations also have been established to facilitate the exchange of programs between stations within geographic regions. A few examples include the Eastern Educational Network (EEN), Southern Educational Communications Association (SECA), Central Educational Network (CEN), and the Pacific Mountain Network (PMN). Finally, the Agency for Instructional Television (AIT) produces and distributes educational and instructional programs. All of these groups except the Corporation itself are sources of programming for individual public broadcast stations.

THE CPB AND PUBLIC BROADCASTING FUNDING

The Corporation for Public Broadcasting began to provide grants for both programs and broadcast facilities soon after its formation. The first CPB grant, made in 1968, went to "Black Journal," a TV magazine program about Black Americans. A year later, a group of foundations and the federal government funded an effort to teach basic cognitive skills to preschool children. Within a year, the program "Sesame Street" became the most heavily watched broadcast on public television. Its success was attributed largely to the integration of modern television production techniques with innovative writing and sound educational principles. The Children's Television Workshop (CTW) was the program's originator.

The first CPB grants to individual stations were made in 1969, when each noncommercial TV licensee was awarded $10,000. Then, in 1971, the Corpor-

Figure 9.1 Typical Licensees of Public Stations (number of stations in parentheses)

Colleges and Universities	Boards of Education	State Television Authorities	Community Organizations	Municipalities, Libraries, and Other
University of Southern Colorado (KTSC-TV)	Tennessee State Board of Education (4)	State Educational Radio & TV Facility Board of Iowa (8)	Community TV of Southern California (KCET-TV)	City of New York (WNYC-TV)
University of Houston (KUHT-TV)	Spokane (WA) School District (KSPS-TV)	Nebraska ETV Commission (8)	Memphis Community TV Foundation (WKNO-TV)	Louisville (KY) Free Public Library (WFPK-FM)
Michigan State University (WKAR-TV)	Fresno (CA) County Dept. of Education (KMTF-TV)	Maryland Public Broadcasting Commission (4)	Greater Washington (DC) Telecommunications Assn. (WETA)	Public Library of Nashville/ Davidson County (TN) (WPLN-FM)
University of North Carolina (8)	Kentucky State Board of Education (16)	Alabama ETV Commission (9)	Metropolitan Indianapolis TV Assn. (WFYI-TV)	Kentucky Technical Institute (WLRS-FM)
University System of Georgia (WGTV)	Georgia State Board of Education (8)	Louisiana ETV Authority (5)	Blue Ridge ETV Assn. (VA) (3)	
Ohio University (WOUB/WOUB-TV)	Atlanta (GA) Board of Education (WETV)	South Carolina ETV Commission (10)	WGBH Educational Foundation (Boston) (WGBH/WGBX/WGBY)	
University of New Hampshire (5)	Dade County (FLA) School Board (WLRN/WTHS)	Arkansas ETV Commission (5)	Chicago Public Television (WTTW)	

ation and PBS agreed on a detailed process for disbursing funds to member stations. This agreement designated three major stations—WNET-TV, New York; WETA-TV, Washington; and KCET-TV, Los Angeles—as the principal production centers for the Public Broadcasting Service. The remaining program funds were to be awarded to other PBS stations on an open competition basis.

While more funding for public stations comes from the licensees, there are several other outside sources of production funds. For example, the National Endowment for the Arts (NEA) has provided financial assistance for cultural and historical programs. Included among the major series backed by NEA are "Earplay," "Dance in America," "Live from Lincoln Center," and "Live from the Metropolitan Opera."

The US Department of Education is another government agency that assists in producing programs for public broadcasting. The Department is especially interested in program proposals which serve the interests of teenagers and parents. For example, its "Footsteps" TV series supported the parenting activities of people with children under seven. Another program underwritten by the Department of Education is NPR's popular series "Options in Education."

Another pattern of funding, corporate underwriting, emerged during the early 1970s and has continued to the present. In 1970, the Xerox Corporation gave PBS two British program series, "Forsyte Saga" and "Civilisation." A year later, a gift from Mobil Oil made possible "Masterpiece Theatre," another highly regarded British dramatic series. Subsequently, many other US corporations assisted PBS by underwriting various programs.

American productions shown on PBS during the 1970s included "Washington in Review," "Thirty Minutes With," and "The Great American Dream Machine." Noteworthy material from National Public Radio, which was incorporated in 1970, included live coverage of the 1971 Senate Foreign Relations Committee Hearings on Viet Nam and the daily news magazine program "All Things Considered."

In addition to jurisdictional and funding disputes between CPB and PBS during the formative years, the early 1970s also saw intervention into public broadcasting from the White House. President Nixon expressed a growing concern that the public television system was evolving into a fourth national network at the expense of the system's legislative mandate to localism. The dispute was settled in 1973 with a joint CPB-PBS partnershp agreement in which PBS remained in charge of the interconnection service which feeds programs to member stations, but also was given a diminished role in determining which programs were to be funded by the Corporation.

PUBLIC BROADCASTING'S PHILOSOPHY AND STRATEGIES

The basic thrust of public broadcasting centers on providing an alternative to commercial programming fare. Discussions with public broadcasters consistently reveal an overriding sense that their programs must be different, that their audiences *expect* this. It isn't that all programs must be "high-brow," but that any program selected incorporates a perspective *unavailable elsewhere.*

Commercial television, for example, seldom commits itself to the quality and quantity of dramatic presentations found on public stations. There are the commercial blockbusters such as "Roots" and "Holocaust," but not the consistently dependable works such as those of "Masterpiece Theatre." Similarly, the time devoted to the discussion of technical or scientific issues on commercial television is insignificant when compared to the public TV commitment to such series as "Nova," the "National Geographic Specials," "Ascent of Man," and "Cosmos."

On radio, public stations each week air a broad spectrum of material untouched in any detail on commercial radio. In its attempt to offer the alternative, public radio outlets typically fill the voids in both music and information programming that are left by commercial radio. Music areas such as classical, jazz, ethnic, and some traditional forms are staples in public radio.

The public affairs capstones of "All Things Considered" and "Morning Edition," both produced by NPR, provide more information-oriented programming in one day than many commercial stations broadcast in several weeks. However, these two series are supplemented by a wide range of programs which cover the spectrum of contemporary ideas. The "Options" series, "National Town Meeting," and "Communique" are examples. Modern radio drama also has been kept alive by the efforts of National Public Radio and its members. "Masterpiece Radio Theatre" presents classic dramas in current form, while "Earplay" provides one of the few forums to showcase the talents of both modern writers and technical audio experimenters.

Although little is done on public radio in the instructional field, public TV provides superlative supplemental assistance to the primary school classroom teacher. Series such as "Zoom," "Mr. Rogers' Neighborhood," "Sesame Street," and "Electric Company" have been staples for millions of American children. Other, more specific educational programs include "Wordsmith," "3-2-1 Contact," "Vegetable Soup," "Ripples," "Villa Alegre," and "Math Factory."

PUBLIC TV STRATEGIES: A DIFFERENT PROGRAMMING APPROACH

The programming strategies of America's public television stations are complicated by their several objectives: to educate, to inform, and to provide alternative, cultural programming. Public TV's morning and afternoon dayparts usually consist of educational type material for enrichment of in-school teaching. Placement of individual programs or classes is dictated partially by instructional needs and class schedules.

When it comes to evening hours, the goal is to maximize audience numbers within the alternative programming concept. What is perceived to be the most popular program of the evening is usually placed in prime-time center—around 8:00 PM. Occasionally such favorable placement is dictated by underwriting considerations, as we shall see in the upcoming case studies. Other prime-time program placement is based on counter programming the commercial networks. For instance, the program director of a public TV station might schedule a dramatic series or a science-oriented program opposite three situation comedies. The Boston Pops might compete with network adventure shows or a movie. In contrast, news-oriented broadcasts such as the "MacNeil/Lehrer Report" may be placed to *complement* rather than compete with the commercial network or local news programs. Programming in sequence for effective audience flow is a consideration in public television just as in commercial TV broadcasting. After all, the goal of public broadcasting is to serve audiences.

One of the most unusual characteristics of public television programming is the high frequency of program repetitions. This pattern occurs primarily to achieve higher cumulative viewing levels and, in many cases, simply because there is a dearth of acceptable programming to fill the schedule. Repetition also helps many public stations to obtain maximum effectiveness from their limited program budgets.

PUBLIC RADIO PROGRAMMING: ALTERNATIVE AUDIO

Filling the voids left by commercial stations is the usual objective of public radio stations. How this is done also differs considerably from the continuous format approach so common in commercial radio. Most public radio programmers rely instead on the decades-old strategy of modified block programming. Public stations usually carry a much higher proportion of nonmusic material than do most commercial stations, and this talk material naturally fits well into the block programming approach because it can be booked in half-hour or hour segments. The modified block approach also accommodates both the uncertain time parameters of symphonies and variable length discussion programs.

A traditional day-part breakdown for public radio typically includes a classical music morning broadcast with local and/or national news inserts from sign-on until noon, possibly an hour of informational programming or public affairs, and then a return to classical music until late afternoon and the start of NPR's "All Things Considered." Early evening likely includes additional public affairs material, an evening concert, and possibly a late evening specialty program such as jazz or big-band music until sign-off.

There is a growing trend toward 24-hour operation by public radio stations, as well as increased usage of NPR's "Morning Edition" news show. It's interesting that while practically all NPR stations air "All Things Considered" in its entirety (90 minutes), there is some reluctance to carry all of "Morning Edition." Program directors may simply believe they surrender enough of their station's time to the network, or they may feel that music rather than talk is preferred for early morning.

The development of NPR's satellite distribution system has posed new questions for public radio programmers, while also enhancing the technical quality and programming choices available. Rather than the usual telephone quality single line from a network, NPR stations equipped with satellite receiving dishes have the capability to select from 20 channels of high quality audio. This raises questions of waste and network dominance. A station certainly would be hard-pressed to use all the material sent by National Public Radio on 20 different channels. As a result, many programs will have reduced audiences, not because of content deficiencies but because they were never aired. Such programs are victims of overabundance.

The companion question regarding the satellite delivery system is one of relinquishing control over large portions of one's program schedule to outside producers. For small stations with limited resources, the availability of large amounts of high quality programming results in a very good air sound. Still, such a dependence upon the network raises concerns about local public service. Is such a station merely a translator of its network? Large NPR stations, as we shall see in the up-coming case studies, are in a position to maintain programming autonomy—utilizing NPR material as an adjunct to their locally produced broadcasts. These same concerns also apply to public television stations, most of which receive multiple channels of PBS television programming.

In our next section, we will examine the Public Broadcasting Service, its programming activities, and the ways in which local public TV stations select from its offerings. This discussion will be followed by a group of selected station case studies. Later in the chapter, we will present a similar discussion of National Public Radio as a programming source, together with radio programming case studies.

PROGRAMMING THE PUBLIC TV STATION

Just as with commercial television, public TV stations obtain their programs from a national interconnection (network) service, national nonnetwork syndication sources, and regional networks, and through their own production efforts. The most important source by far, however, is the Public Broadcasting Service.

PBS: THE NONCOMMERCIAL "NETWORK"

The Public Broadcasting Service was created as a private nonprofit organization to establish and operate a national program distribution service for its member television stations. Through its National Program Service, PBS offers both series and special programming from a variety of sources. Interestingly, however, PBS produces no programs on its own. Individual public TV stations account for the largest share of the programming, with the balance provided by American and foreign independent producers. Even though PBS is not a network in the usual sense, the organization provides its members with a broad range of support services in such areas as research, promotion, program development, and fund raising.

PBS programming is fed to its stations through the multichannel Public Television Satellite Interconnection System. Four transponders (A, B, C, and D) are utilized to provide maximum programming flexibility for individual stations. Transponder A provides the basic program feed for the Eastern Time Zone, while B and C repeat the programming for later time zones. Transponder D is used mainly to feed special programs, most of which are taped by local stations for later broadcast. A PBS station may pick up any two of the four transponder channels simultaneously. Figure 9.2 shows a typical PBS operations log with transmission schedules for the four channels.

Figure 9.2 A Typical PBS Satellite Transmission Schedule Utilizing Four Transponders

OPERATIONS LOG FOR FRIDAY NOVEMBER 13 , 1981 PREPARED 13-Oct-81 PAGE 103

SCHEDULE A		SCHEDULE B		SCHEDULE C		SCHEDULE D	
TIME	PROGRAM	TIME	PROGRAM	TIME	PROGRAM	TIME	PROGRAM
1900:01/A	THE MACNEIL/LEHRER REPORT #7098 HFD /D/ 28:46*	1900:01/B	MISTEROGERS' NEIGHBORHOOD #1045 MOT /D/ 29:07	1900:01/C	SESAME STREET #1570 (CLOSED CAPTIONS) VOCA: 56:40/:60 MOT /D/ 58:49	1900:01/D	OVER EASY #5035 (CLOSED CAPTIONS) MOT /D/ 28:46*
1928:47/A	BLACK 1:14					1928:47/D	BLACK 1:14
		1929:08/B	BLACK :53				
1930:01/A	THE MACNEIL/LEHRER REPORT #7098 MOT /D/ 28:46*	1930:01/B	THE ELECTRIC COMPANY #025A MOT /D/ 28:43			1930:01/D	THE DICK CAVETT SHOW #5020 (C/B&W) MOT /D/ 28:46*
		1958:44/B	PROMO BREAK #082 1:17				
1958:47/A	BLACK 1:14					1958:47/D	BLACK 1:14
				1958:50/C	PROMO BREAK #081 1:11		
2000:01/A	WASHINGTON WEEK IN REVIEW #2121 MOT /D/ 28:46*	2000:01/B	STUDIO SEE #216 "COWBOY" VOCA: 27:27/:44 MOT /D/ 28:46	2000:01/C	MISTEROGERS' NEIGHBORHOOD #1045 MOT /D/ 29:07	2000:01/D	PMN FEED SPORTS AMERICA #203 DEN 58:46*
2028:47/A	PROMO BREAK #084 1:14	2028:47/B	PROMO BREAK #083 1:14				
				2029:08/C	BLACK :53		

OPERATIONS LOG FOR FRIDAY NOVEMBER 13 , 1981 PREPARED 13-Oct-81 PAGE 103

Courtesy of Public Broadcasting Service and WSJK-TV, Sneedville (Knoxville), TN.

Structurally the Public Broadcasting Service is organized into three program services in an effort to provide a wide range of diversified programming to its viewers. PTV-1 is reponsible for the presentation of prime-time general audience programs. Program types include dramatic productions; public affairs; stage, concert hall, and festival performances; and science programs. PTV-2 provides special interest programs to specific audiences, particularly women and minority groups. PTV-3 concentrates on educational and instructional material for children and adults, both in and out of school.

Who Finances PBS?

Funding for the PBS National Program Service comes from a variety of sources in addition to the Corporation for Public Broadcasting. These sources and their percentages in 1980–1981 were as follows: corporate underwriting (24 percent); member stations (22 percent); federal agencies, such as the Department of Education, the National Endowments, and the National Science Foundation (20 percent); the CPB itself (14 percent); foundations (7 percent); and various other sources (13 percent). At the beginning of the 1980s, the yearly schedule of original programs for PBS costs about $100,000,000 versus about $40,000,000 per week for the prime-time schedules of the three commercial networks.

In one recent year 54 member stations produced programs for distribution on PBS. These programs filled about 80 percent of the schedule, while independent producers provided the remaining 20 percent of first-run material. Furthermore, 11 percent of the schedule originated abroad because of the significant savings in production costs—an average foreign price of $8,500 per hour, compared with more than $300,000 in the United States.

Although program production is not a PBS function, the organization works closely with stations and outside producers to match its scheduling needs with station proposals. One of the principal mechanisms used to facilitate this interaction is the Station Program Cooperative (SPC), through which stations select their national programs.

The Station Program Cooperative: A TV Clearing House

The Station Program Cooperative, formed in 1974, serves two principal purposes. First, it allows individual PBS stations to select specific programs. Second, the SPC creates a pool of funds from member stations which provides a portion of the financial support for high quality national programming.

The SPC actually is one of the most democratic organizations in broadcasting, annually allocating about one-quarter of the total public broadcast programming fund for program production. These funds exceeded $30,000,000 during the early 1980s. Through the Station Program Cooperative, PBS members make their choices for the up-coming season on a program-by-program basis. Although the actual process appears cumbersome, in reality it is relatively simple.

SPC 8: A Case-Study

The national programs that appear on public television screens result from a process that could best be described as "electronic social Darwinism." These programs are the survivors of the annual Station Program Cooperative Program Fair, which is held early each year. Our case study deals with the eighth Fair, held in 1981.

Prior to each Program Fair, PBS and its member stations define the year's programming needs. Producers then submit program proposals. The Fair begins with the issuance of a 100-plus page catalog of program proposals, which includes a compendium of the well-known and the obscure program choices for the coming year. The SPC-8 catalog began with 155 programs, about one-third of which came from independent producers. The programs fall into four principal categories: culture, educational and children's programs, public affairs, and sports. However, many different subjects are represented, including music, history, health, food, books, dance, folklore, business, and psychology.

Each program proposal submitted to the Program Fair includes three pages of pertinent information, including the number of programs in the series, their length, their cost, a description, and a statement on minorities and women involved in the production. The producers have only one page in which to sell their concept to the program buyers. A typical proposal is shown in Figure 9.3.

Pilot programs are screened at the annual PBS Programming Conference. Afterwards, each station's representative selects programs which he/she is interested in buying for the up-coming season. The selections then are computer tabulated and program expenses are calculated, based on the number of stations willing to share the total cost. Pricing for an individual station also takes into account the station's potential audience and its yearly operating budget. For example, a station in Los Angeles (a market of 4,200,000 TV households) will pay more for a program than one in Austin or Baton Rouge (markets of about 200,000 TV homes each). Those programs which receive the least votes are then excluded from the next round of selection.

The SPC system is planned so that the more stations that vote for a specific program, the lower the cost of that program becomes for each station. Program directors are aware of how many other stations are selecting each program and the cost to them at any point in the selection process. This procedure unfortunately can produce a snow-balling effect in which unknown programs receive few votes and are rapidly eliminated from consideration. The result is a schedule in which perennial favorite programs continually surface. To minimize this effect, stations are encouraged to participate in a "universal buy" which packages the better known programs along with a few new titles and offers them at a reduced price.

Since the costs for each series are shared by all stations that purchase it, each program has a different group of supporting stations. As shown in Figure 9.4, station WSJK-TV, Knoxville, Tennessee, bought 26 different programs in the SPC-8 Program Fair for a total cost of $139,597. The station's program director, Hop Edwards, stated that the two key factors in his selec-

Figure 9.3 A Typical PBS (SPC) Program Proposal: The MacNeil/Lehrer Report

Proposal Code: 72
(Assigned b

SPC PROGRAM PROPOSAL
EXHIBIT A

1. TITLE OF PROGRAM/SERIES: THE MacNEIL/LEHRER REPORT

2. CONTENT: A nightly, in-depth news report on a current major news event.

SUBJECT: Public Affairs

TREATMENT: Discussion SPECIAL INTEREST: General

SERIES: [X] SINGLE PROGRAM: [ ] ACQUISITION: [ ]
If acquisition, indicate following:
Original producer:
Previous distribution other than PBS:

3. SUBMITTING STATION/AGENCY: WNET/WETA CONTACT: Robert Kotlowitz/ Gerry Slater

ADDRESS: 356 W.58th St. N.Y.C. 10019/ 955 L'Enfant Plaza, S.W. Wash. D.C. TELEPHONE: (212)560-2070 (202)998-2600

PRODUCER: Al Vecchione DIRECTOR:

4. NUMBER OF PROGRAMS: 261 PROGRAM LENGTH: 30 min.

5. DATE AUDIO: Yes: [ ] Specify content: No: [ ]

6. COLOR: [X] B&W: [ ] TAPE: [ ] LIVE: [X] Origination: N.Y.C./ Wash. D.C.

7. PRODUCTION SCHEDULE TARGET DATES:
Start: July 1, 1981 Completion: June 30, 1982
Available for scheduling by: July 1, 1981

8. PILOT AVAILABLE: Yes: [X] No: [ ] SAMPLER AVAILABLE: Yes: [ ] No: [ ]

9. PRODUCTION FUNDING:

A. Total Production Funding $ 6,775,745

B. Other Funding (Source:) $ 2,000,745

C. Purchase Price (without surcharges) $ 4,775,000

10. RIGHTS (complete fully; see Program Use Policies):

A. RIGHTS LICENSED TO PBS

BROADCAST:
Standard (4 releases in 3 years): [X] Other:
School 7-day off-air re-record: Yes: [X] No: [ ] Other:

CABLE (non-pay, non-sponsored):
Unserved areas only: [X] Other: Unavailable: [ ]

COMMERCIAL BROADCAST (sustaining):
Unserved areas only: [X] Other: Unavailable: [ ]

RADIO (sustaining):
Cleared: [ ] Subject to step-ups: [X] Unavailable: [ ]

SIMULCAST:
Public radio: Cleared: [ ] Subject to step-ups: [X] Unavailable: [ ]
Commercial radio (sustaining): Yes: [X] No: [ ]

B. RIGHTS AVAILABLE TO PRODUCER

	Cleared	Subject to step-ups	Unavailable
Audio-Visual:	[ ]	[X]	[ ]
Foreign Broadcast:	[ ]	[X]	[ ]
Foreign Nonbroadcast:	[ ]	[X]	[ ]
Home Rights:	[ ]	[ ]	[X]
Pay-Cable:	[ ]	[ ]	[X]
STV:	[ ]	[ ]	[X]

C. EXCLUSIVITY: Producer must describe plans, if any, for pay-cable, STV and/or theatrical release in program description.

11. ANCILLARY/SUPPORT MATERIAL BUDGETED (describe):
None: [X]

Courtesy of Public Broadcasting Service and WSJK-TV, Sneedville (Knoxville), TN.

tion were cost and projected audience acceptance. Because WSJK-TV was prohibited from on-air fund-raising efforts at the time, it shouldered the majority of this expenditure from its state-supported budget. A typical station, however, will not have to defray the total purchase price. Some programs may be funded partially by corporate underwriting, foundation grants, or the stations that propose them.

Figure 9.4 A Typical Public TV Station's SPC Program Purchases

WSJK SPC 8 JANUARY MARKET PURCHASES

802	AUSTIN CITY LIMITS	2483.	13/60
812	#DENMARK VESEYS REBELN	86.	1/90
813	THE DICK CAVETT SHOW	5718.	100/30
814	THE ELECTRIC COMPANY	1583.	130/30
815	EVENING AT POPS	6440.	8/60
819	FIRING LINE	2856.	39/60
823	GREAT PERFORMANCES	3134.	18/ —
827	MACNEIL LEHRER REPORT	21959.	261/30
828	MARK RUSSELL SPECIALS	720.	6/30
829	MATINEE AT THE BIJOU	752.	16/90
830	MEDIA PROBES	1475.	8/30
833	MR ROGERS NEIGHBORHOOD	4034.	260/30 – 3/60
835	NON FICTION TELEVISION	1770.	12/60
836	NOVA	18395.	20/60
840	OVER EASY	10927.	65/30
842	PLAYHOUSE	21975.	22/ —
847	SESAME STREET	11616.	130/60
849	SNEAK PREVIEWS	3283.	40/30
850	SOCCER MADE IN GERMANY	1932.	52/60
853	SOUNDSTAGE	3428.	10/60
854	THE SPECIALS FUND	5311.	20/60
858	#UP & COMING	501.	10/30
859	VICTORY GARDEN	4088.	39/30
860	WALL STREET WEEK	2204.	52/30
863	#WITH OSSIE & RUBY!	722.	13/30
865	WORLD SPECIALS	2202.	6/60

WSJK TOTAL SPC 8 PURCHASES 139597.*

* AS A RESULT OF YOUR PARTICIPATION IN THE SPC 8 UNIVERSAL BUY, YOUR TOTAL OBLIGATION FOR THE ABOVE PROGRAMS HAS BEEN REDUCED TO 124718.

IN ACCORDANCE WITH THE FOLLOWING SCHEDULE, WSJK COST IS AS FOLLOWS:

PAYMENT POSTMARKED BY	AMOUNT
JULY 30, 1981	$ 100481.
AUGUST 31	$ 101344.
SEPTEMBER 30	$ 102206.
OCTOBER 31	$ 103069.
NOVEMBER 30	$ 103932.
DECEMBER 31	$ 107050.
JANUARY 31, 1982	$ 109128.
FEBRUARY 28	$ 111207.
MARCH 31	$ 114325.
APRIL 30	$ 124718.

Courtesy of WSJK-TV, Sneedville (Knoxville), Tennessee.

Since SPC material accounts for only about 40 percent of a typical station's schedule, the remaining programming comes from a variety of sources. A program, for example, might originate with a regional network and not be offered nationally through the Station Program Cooperative. In this case, it may be bought directly from the station's regional network office. In some cases, regional network programs are offered through the program cooperative. However, a station may be able to secure a better price through an adjunct to the SPC, the Station Acquisition Market (SAM). This service is operated by PBS to allow a group of stations to buy an existing program on reasonably short notice any time during the year.

Programs also come from the PBS Public Television Library or the Flexible Program Service, which loans a wide variety of material under specific restrictions on its use. Material also can be secured from commercial syndication services and from a station's own local production. The amount and type of local program origination vary widely among noncommercial stations. Some public TV stations, for example, do not attempt to compete with commercial stations in local news; others, usually those located in communities without local commercial TV service, provide extensive news coverage. Two examples of the latter are WSIU-TV, Carbondale, Illinois, and WOUB-TV, Athens, Ohio. Finally, a special service, the Stations Independent Programs Service (SIP), offers, to those noncommercial stations involved in fund raising, programs which contain five- or ten-minute "windows" for local solicitation.

PUBLIC TV PROGRAMMING: THREE LOCAL STATIONS

With these various program sources and mechanisms in mind, we can begin to formulate an actual program schedule that meets the needs of a particular community. Three public TV stations were chosen for our case studies, representing large, medium, and small market operations in three different geographic regions. These stations, respectively, are WTTW-TV, Chicago; KPTS-TV, Wichita, Kansas; and KIXE-TV, Redding, California. All three stations supplied a copy of their program schedules for Wednesday, January 30, 1980, that week's program guide, and a statement of their mission. In addition, a list of PBS programs was obtained for the same date. The comparative schedules for WTTW, KPTS, and KIXE are shown in Figure 9.5.

Large Market: WTTW-TV, Chicago

WTTW-TV, licensed to the Chicago Educational Television Association, holds the distinction of being the most heavily watched public TV station in the country. It first went on the air in 1955. WTTW's literature declares it "is used to teach and illuminate and inspire—through the development of a public broadcasting facility whose management and programming are responsive to the public's varied interests and needs in public affairs, education and the arts."[1] Policy [not program] guidance is supplied by 51 trustees from the community. Each serves a three-year term. Program decisions are the responsibility of the General Manager.

Figure 9.5 Comparative Public TV Schedules

January 30, 1980

Local Time	WTTW (TV) Chicago	KPTS-TV Wichita-Hutchison	KIXE-TV Redding, Calif.
7:30 AM	Sesame Street		
8:00		Sesame Street	Mister Rogers
8:30	Mister Rogers		3-2-1 Contact
9:00	Sesame Street	Wordsmith/Ripples	Sesame Street
9:30		Freestyle	
10:00	3-2-1 Contact	Electric Company	Electric Company
10:30	Electric Company	Universe & I	Upstairs, Downstairs
11:00	Bread & Butterflies	Vegetable Soup	
11:30	Insight	Mister Rogers	Nova
12:00 N		Sesame Street	
12:30 PM	Over Easy		Instructional Programs
1:00	Dick Cavett Show	Explorers/Bread & B.	
1:30	Movie	Math Factory	
2:00		Metric System	
2:30		Villa Alegre	Two-Thirty
3:00	Villa Alegre	Sesame Street	Best of Cavett
3:30	Mister Rogers		Mister Rogers
4:00	Sesame Street	Mister Rogers	Sesame Street
4:30		Electric Company	
5:00	3-2-1 Contact	3-2-1 Contact	3-2-1 Contact
5:30	As We See It	Over Easy	Electric Company
6:00	Over Easy	Dick Cavett Show	Growing Years
6:30	MacNeil/Lehrer Report	MacNeil/Lehrer Report	Over Easy
7:00	Chicago Feedback	Story of Popular Music	MacNeil/Lehrer Report
7:30			Dick Cavett Show
8:00	Great Performances	Great Performances	Great Performances
9:00	Cousteau Odyssey	Every Four Years	Every Four Years
10:00	Dick Cavett Show	Untamed World	F.Y.I.: Coal Power
10:30	Every Four Years	Captioned ABC News	
11:00		Sign Off	MacNeil/Lehrer Report
11:30	Movie		Captioned ABC News
12:00 M			
1:00 AM	Captioned ABC News		

Like many community-based stations, WTTW's principal support is from viewer subscriptions. With more than 140,000 subscribers, the community provides 68 percent of the station's $10,400,000 annual budget. About 22 percent is derived from program and production contracts, 7 percent from the Corporation for Public Broadcasting, and 3 percent from other sources. A significant part of WTTW's budget goes for locally created programs, which ideally will be selected or purchased for regional or national distribution.

Program Discussion WTTW's schedule runs to almost 18 hours each day. WTTW follows the usual pattern for public TV stations, beginning the day with material targeted toward the preschool and young school audience. WTTW also schedules several series more than once during the broadcast day, a common practice among noncommercial television stations. While "Sesame Street" and "3-2-1 Contact" both were run three times, none of the programs were reruns. Instead, each was a different show of the same series. This also was the case with "Over Easy" and "Mister Rogers," both of which were scheduled twice.

Placement of these series corresponds to the times children are usually available for viewing—preschoolers or half-day students in the morning and older children during the after-school hours. "Over Easy" traditionally has been aimed at the more mature audience with its lunchtime and early evening slots. Spanish-language programming is covered in the children's show "Villa Alegre." The remainder of the day's schedule is filled out with material from the Station Program Cooperative, syndicators, and local programs.

An interesting point should be noted regarding WTTW's evening schedule. "Great Performances" is aired at 8:00 PM directly from the network feed. As we shall see, the other public stations to be examined also aired "Great Performances" at the same time. This results from the fact that four nights a week (Sunday through Wednesday) PBS offers stations a two-hour block of programs referred to as "common carriage." About 90 percent of the PBS stations participate in common carriage, thus assuring nationwide coverage for PBS and a high degree of saturation for its program underwriters.

Medium Market: KPTS-TV, Wichita, Kansas

KPTS-TV, Wichita, which is licensed to the Kansas Public Telecommunications Service, Inc., began operations in 1970. Its public mission is defined as follows: "to serve the ascertained needs and identified interests of the people in our service area through public telecommunications program services."[2]

At the beginning of fiscal year 1982, more than 18,000 individual subscribers annually provided about 38 percent of KPTS's $1,362,000 budget. Other sources include the Corporation for Public Broadcasting (20 percent), corporate underwriting (27 percent), and the remainder (15 percent) comes primarily from auctions, donations, and a state grant. Policy guidance comes from a board of 28 trustees.

Program Discussion KPTS broadcasts 70 hours each week, a schedule that includes no instructional TV offerings. During the week of January 30, 1980, many of the programs were the same as those aired by WTTW, including "Sesame Street," "Electric Company," "3-2-1 Contact," "Bread and Butterflies," "Mister Rogers' Neighborhood," "Villa Alegre," and "Over Easy."

The evening schedules of both KPTS and WTTW began with the PBS feed of "The MacNeil/Lehrer Report" at 6:30. Afterwards, the two stations ran three of the same programs, although two were at different times. Both took the direct network feed of "Great Performances," and both ran "Every Four Years—A Look at the Presidency" and "Captioned ABC Evening News." KPTS's "Untamed World" deals with various aspects of the wilds, and its "Story of Popular Music" traces the development of American song.

Small Market: KIXE-TV, Redding, California

KIXE-TV, licensed to the Northern California Educational Television Association, began operation at Redding in 1964. KIXE's stated mission is "to provide the viewing area with excellence in alternative programming. The station will provide local, regional and national programming that will inform, educate, entertain and involve viewers with the issues and interests collected through the ascertainment process."[3] Thirteen percent of the station's $421,600 budget (1980) comes from viewers through an annual auction.

Program Discussion KIXE's morning and afternoon schedule clearly resembles portions of those from WTTW and KPTS. Many of the morning children's programs are the same, although the times differ slightly. As with KPTS, "Mister Rogers' Neighborhood," "3-2-1 Contact," "Sesame Street," and "Electric Company" also are carried in the afternoon. While the first two are different programs of the same series, the "Sesame Street" and "Electric Company" shows are the same for both broadcasts.

The instructional programming block from 12:30 to 2:30 PM bears less resemblance to the programming of the other two public stations discussed here. Major morning differences include the insertion of "Upstairs, Downstairs" at 10:30 and the previous evening's "Nova" at 11:30. "The Best of Cavett" at 3:00 is a weekly program, as is the public affairs program "Two-Thirty" at 2:30. A bit of "checkerboard" programming is practiced here, since the 2:30 slot is occupied on other days of the week by such shows as "Bill Moyers' Journal," "Masterpiece Theatre," "World," and "Pavarotti at Juilliard."

The evening programs at KIXE-TV include six that also are carried by WTTW-TV and KPTS-TV. Again, this demonstrates the adherence to common carriage which PBS advocates for the evening hours.

A Comparison: The Network Feed and Our Cases

An examination of the PBS feed for January 30, 1980, reveals some interesting programming strategies regarding the use of live versus tape-delayed material. First, the two smaller stations, KPTS-TV and KIXE-TV, taped few programs for rebroadcast. Instead, they carried most programming straight from the network feed. "Sesame Street" is a good example. Both KPTS-TV and KIXE-TV aired the popular children's show right off the network, while WTTW-TV elected to carry delayed broadcasts of the series. Apparently WTTW-TV had taped a backlog of "Sesame Street" shows for use in succeeding weeks.

Except for "Wordsmith," a 15-minute program aired from 9:00 to 9:15, KPTS-TV broadcast the entire morning PBS feed from 7:45 to 11:00 on the date being studied; and the Redding, California, station obtained practically all of its afternoon and evening programs direct from the PBS feed. Similarly, KPTS-TV in Wichita carried the network feed from "Villa Alegre" at 2:30 through "The MacNeil/Lehrer Report" at 7:00 in addition to its evening PBS schedule. In sharp contrast, WTTW-TV, Chicago, only aired five programs directly from the network: "A.M. Weather," "3-2-1 Contact," "The MacNeil/Lehrer Report," "Great Performances," and "The Dick Cavett Show." WTTW's other material was either live production from its own studio, film, or taped PBS material from previous network feeds.

On the basis of this examination, the extent to which a public television station relies directly on the PBS hook-up seems to be determined by the size of the operation. The smaller stations surely find it more convenient and less expensive to rely directly on the network rather than taping material for later rebroadcast. However, the larger stations appear to exercise more control over their program schedules.

Although public television stations have considerable influence over the types of programs produced and distributed nationally (through the Station

Program Cooperative), PBS seems to be evolving slowly into a more traditional network with its control (by default) over major portions of station programming. This trend is especially noticeable among the smaller public television stations.

EDUCATIONAL AND INSTRUCTIONAL TV PROGRAMMING

According to the second Carnegie Commission report on public broadcasting, the typical public TV station devotes about 40 percent of its schedule to instructional material. These programs consist of both network-delivered and locally produced telecasts. The latter tend to be emphasized most by stations licensed to universities and local or state school boards.

Instructional programming, of course, gave educational television its original impetus. Great enthusiasm prevailed for televised delivery of lectures and classroom teaching for both public schools and higher education when the nation's first educational television station was launched in 1955. Furthermore, considerable financial support was provided for instructional programming, especially by the Ford Foundation, until the establishment of the Corporation for Public Broadcasting.

Although there were exceptions such as NBC's "Sunrise Semester," most early instructional programs consisted of a televised lecture or round-table discussion. However sound these programs were academically, their instructional value was open to question. Not until "Sesame Street" appeared in 1968 did public broadcasting begin to take advantage of the available production techniques to make a program interesting as well as educational. In 1971, the "Electric Company" introduced for in-school use the same approach perfected for preschoolers in "Sesame Street." Thus, the Children's Television Workshop, the originator of both of these programs, proved that well-planned and produced educational programs can attract and hold their intended audiences.

SOURCES OF INSTRUCTIONAL PROGRAMS

In addition to the Children's Television Workshop, another prominent educational organization supplying high quality educational series is the Agency for Instructional Television (AIT). AIT is a consortium of state and Canadian educational interests, with its headquarters located at Bloomington, Indiana. AIT's titles include "Ripples," "Inside/Out," and "All About You." "Think About" is a successful in-school series of sixty 15-minute programs designed to aid fifth and sixth graders in developing language arts, mathematics, and study skills.

Still another successful approach has involved the use of prime-time public TV series for educational purposes. "Ascent of Man" and "Adams Chronicles," for example, have been used by numerous school systems as the basis of credit courses in science and history. Other broadly educational programs shown during prime time include "Nova," "National Geographic Specials," and "Theatre in America."

Other sources of quality educational telecasts include numerous state public radio and TV networks, such as those in Nebraska, South Carolina, Kentucky, Mississippi, and Maryland. For instance, in adult education, the Kentucky Authority for Educational Television has emphasized programs to help adults prepare for the high school equivalency examination. Regional public networks, such as the Southern Educational Communications Association (SECA) and the Central Educational Network (CEN), also have been quite active in producing both educational and general interest telecasts. For example, CEN's "Farm Digest," a consumer-oriented agribusiness program, focuses on the effects of farm issues on the economy.

CONTINUING EDUCATION AND COLLEGE CREDIT BROADCASTS

Another important facet of educational broadcasting is that which awards college credit to students taught through televised instruction. To date, several American versions of the British Open University have emerged. Perhaps the most notable of these is the National University Consortum (NUC), a group of ten public TV stations and seven colleges which offer degrees in the humanities, technology and management, and the behavioral and social sciences.

NUC students register with one of the participating colleges and receive televised instruction distributed by satellite to one of the participating TV stations or cable systems. A student with no previous college experience would need about six years to earn a bachelor's degree. The National University Consortium has been spearheaded by the Maryland Center for Public Broadcasting and the University of Maryland.

Instructional programming for credit also is planned by several other organizations. The University of Mid-America, a consortium of 11 state universities with headquarters in Lincoln, Nebraska, intends to offer both undergraduate and graduate instruction via television. The Appalachian Community Service Network, an offshoot of the Appalachian Regional Commission, also plans to distribute up to 64 hours of instruction weekly by satellite to cable systems across the country. Other professionally oriented continuing education courses are provided by the American Educational Television Network, a profit-making corporation in Irvine, California.

SPECIAL TECHNOLOGIES AND EDUCATIONAL BROADCASTING

In addition to over-the-air instruction, certain other nonbroadcast technologies are used in educational television. The Instructional Television Fixed Services (ITFS) is perhaps the best example. ITFS is a limited range microwave service used by many school systems to distribute locally produced educational material. A large-scale university model using such a system is underway at the University of Maryland. Patterned after a similar service at Stanford University, the Maryland ITFS project allows courses in engineering, science, and business administration to be transmitted live from the College Park campus to government and industrial installations within a 30-mile radius of the campus.

The Maryland system consists of two classrooms in which students and a professor conduct a normal class. Cameras and microphones transmit the proceedings to participating telecourse students at their various locations. Those students receive the material through special receivers and antennae. Instant feedback is accomplished through a telephone talk-back system to the Maryland campus. The obvious advantages of such a system are that it allows students to remain at their places of employment, avoiding travel time and expense, while taking part in classes as if they were on campus.

PROGRAMMING THE PUBLIC RADIO STATION

Much like public television, noncommercial radio stations are licensed to several types of organizations. However, two distinct types of stations are most evident. Most prominent are the *public stations,* which usually broadcast with maximum power and serve the general public at least 18 hours daily. In contrast, there are hundreds of low power FM stations that are used mainly as laboratories for broadcast training. The former usually are members of National Public Radio and receive some financial support from CPB, while the latter do not.

Corporation for Public Broadcasting funding has been an important factor in the advances made by public radio during recent years. CPB funding, however, is restricted to NPR stations that meet certain basic criteria. To qualify, a station must have all of the following:

1. A fulltime staff of at least five professional members employed 12 months a year;
2. A minimum annual budget of $90,000;
3. An effective radiated power (FM) of at least 3,000 watts with an antenna height of at least 300 feet, or a minimum of 250 watts for an AM station;
4. Two adequately equipped production studios and at least one control room; and
5. A minimum broadcast schedule of 18 hours per day, 365 days per year.

There are currently about 220 qualified NPR stations out of a total universe of 1,100 noncommercial radio stations.

NATIONAL PUBLIC RADIO

Public radio stations typically rely upon the National Public Radio network for much of their programming, just as public TV outlets depend upon PBS. Unlike PBS, however, National Public Radio actively produces programs for distribution to its member stations. NPR's production facilities are centralized in Washington, primarily because much of its programming focuses on news and public affairs material. NPR also serves as a clearinghouse for member-produced material.

NPR's Financing and Control

Federal funds for program production flow from Congress through the Corporation for Public Broadcasting to NPR. Station fees also are important in the network's financing. For a $9,000 annual fee (1980), member stations had their pick of any or all programs which came over four satellite audio channels. These programs are collectively called the National Program Service (NPS). Control of National Public Radio is retained by member stations through their representation on the NPR board.

NPR's Programming Service

The most notable program produced by National Public Radio is the daily news show "All Things Considered" (ATC). Begun in 1971, ATC has long been considered the nation's oustanding radio news show. It was joined in 1980 by "Morning Edition," a comparable early program. Other standard NPR programs include "Options in Education," "Folk Festival U.S.A.," "Recital Hall," and "Communique." NPR also feeds coverage of important Congressional debates to its stations.

A look at the NPR network feed schedule, shown in Figure 9.6, for January 30, 1980, shows a typical pattern in scheduling news and feature programming. This schedule is for the *telephone line feed* from NPR in Washington. However, the NPR *satellite interconnection system* provides each satellite-fed station with up to 20 channels of high quality information. With increased federal awareness of the potential of public radio and the development of NPR's high quality satellite distribution system, local programmers have come under increasing pressure to accept more national and regional material, thereby reducing the time available for local programs.

The telephone feed begins at 6:00 AM (E.S.T.) with "Morning Edition." This national news and discussion program is transmitted live for two hours and then is repeated on tape from 8:00 to 10:00 AM and from 10:00 AM to 12:00 Noon (E.S.T.) for later time zones. Such repetitions also are provided for the 90-minute "All Things Considered" broadcast in the late afternoon. Most stations which air these two programs take them live off the network line instead of taping for later rebroadcast. However, many stations choose to tape other NPR programs throughout the day for later and more convenient scheduling. Of the three stations in our case studies, none directly broadcasts the NPR feed except for "All Things Considered" and "Morning Edition."

The program director of a public station must be able to size up the offerings of the commercial stations in the market and program his/her station to best serve the perceived needs of its audience. This type of analysis often results in the taping of network material for later use, a common practice among public radio stations because of the flexibility it provides in building alternative programming strategies.

OTHER PUBLIC RADIO PROGRAM SOURCES

Many public radio outlets supplement the NPR and their local programming efforts with material from additional sources. Perhaps the most impor-

Figure 9.6 A Typical NPR Transmission Schedule

```
1305  1359-  3+4   NPS STEREO PROMOS I                     N  NFB      -
                    81-078-00098
1315  1344-  1     F/S:S.A.M.S.                            N  #410-DE  -
                    81-231-00049
1330  1529   5     PRC/JAZZ SESSION                        E  0909.14  -
                    81-147-00221
1345  1359   7     REVISA                                  E  #724-JN  -
                    81-317-00023
1345  1359-  1     ROBERT CROMIE MODULES                   N  #2129JL  -
                    81-361-00010
1400  1459   7+8   BALLADS, BARDS & BAGPIPES               E  #911-AP  -
                    81-123-00049
1415  1444   3+4   MUSIC IN THE BLACK CHURCH (PRE)         N  1012.02  -
                    81-000-00332
1500  1529   7+8   DIGITAL TRANSMISSION TEST               N  NFB      -
                    81-000-00426
1500  1559   3+4   EXPLORING OPERA                         E  0804.15  -
                    81-240-00024
1500  1559   6     ORANGEBURG TODAY                        E  1118.12  -
                    81-407-00003
1505  1604-  1     BBC:"WLD RPT/INTL MONEY/DATELINE"       N  STAND    -
                    81-038-00049
1530  1559   7     COMMON GROUND                           E  0925.01  -
                    81-156-00023
1600  1614   7     OHIO NEWS REPORTS                       E  903-JL   -
                    81-150-00244
1600  1629   6     ATLANTIC DATELINE                       E  #517-JN  -
                    81-143-00049
1600  1659   3+4   THE ORGAN LOFT                          E  #1129AU  -
                    81-164-00049
1630  1659   7+8   MICROLOGUS (RPT)                        E  #1414JA  -
                    81-253-00044
1630  1724-  5+6   CHRISTMAS MODULES/RL #1 (PRE)           N  1012.02  -
                    81-000-00328
1700  1829   1     ALL THINGS CONSIDERED I                 N  STAND    -
                    81-004-00244
1725  1814-  5+6   CHRISTMAS MODULES/RL #2 (PRE)           N  1012.02  -
                    81-000-00328
1815  1909-  7+8   CHRISTMAS IN THE COLONIES/RL 1--PRE     N  1012.02  -
                    80-000-00235
1830  1859   1     OPTIONS IN EDUCATION II                 N  STAND    -
                    81-011-00048
1830  1959   6     AS IT HAPPENS                           E  0914.09  -
                    81-327-00027
1900  1929   3+4   S WEB/ALICE THRU LOOKING GLASS, PT2     N  STAND    -
                    81-024-00103
1910  1959-  7+8   CHRISTMAS IN THE COLONIES/RL 2--PRE     N  1012.02  -
                    80-000-00235
1930  1959   3+4   NPR PH/LORD OF THE RINGS (RPT)          N  #1015JL  -
                    81-344-00019
2000  2129   1     ALL THINGS CONSIDERED II                N  STAND    -
                    81-005-00244
2000  2159-  3+4   INTERNATIONAL CONCERT HALL #8149        N  STAND    -
                    81-018-00049
```

Courtesy of National Public Radio and WUOT-FM, The University of Tennessee, Knoxville.

tant such source is the Public Radio Cooperative, a nonprofit membership organization of public radio stations encompassing 129 stations in 42 states from Alaska to Maine. Formed in 1980 as a station-controlled mechanism to organize the satellite program marketplace, the Cooperative provides a means for the acquisition and satellite distribution of high quality radio programming at the lowest cost per station. The Cooperative, a program subsidiary of the Eastern Public Radio Network, is governed by a Board of Directors, consisting of the managers of the EPRN stations.

Any CPB-qualified station may join the Public Radio Cooperative. Members are entitled to numerous benefits, specials, and low program fees not available to nonmembers. Occasionally, programs are available to nonmembers, but at a higher fee. The Cooperative distributes programs from a variety of sources, including independent producers, public radio stations, and some commercial sources. The PRC's services to producers include scheduling satellite time and providing marketing services. Because of volume, the Cooperative is able to pass along savings on satellite costs to producers, as well as to member stations.

Programs available to member stations of the Public Radio Cooperative are quite varied, as shown in Figure 9.7. Typical offerings include live musical performances, public affairs features and documentaries, drama, poetry, and "classical" jazz.

Various other producers also utilize some of the unused time on the public radio satellite since NPR uses only about 35 percent of its capacity. In addition to the PRC, these producers include Minnesota Public Radio ("Prairie Home Companion," the Minnesota Orchestra, and the St. Paul Chamber Orchestra), the California Public Radio Consortium, and the commercial syndicator Parkway Productions ("First Hearing," "Radio Smithsonian," and "Early Music"). Concerts of various symphony orchestras also are available via satellite.

Other national program material is obtained by public radio stations from special networks such as the Texaco-Metropolitan Opera Network,[4] tape networks, and tape-exchange agreements between stations. Public radio stations also make extensive use of commercial records, particularly classical jazz, but sometimes other types of music as well. Finally, local live production is undertaken at a great many public radio outlets.

Although public radio has historically devoted far less time to instruction than television, an occasional educational program may be found. An excellent example is "The Spiders," a series originated in 1972 by WGBH, Boston. This series features stories, interviews, poetry, and folk songs.

PUBLIC RADIO CASE STUDIES: THREE LOCAL STATIONS

This section contains three radio case studies: a public station from a large market, one from a medium-size city, and a third from a small rural community. Each station to a degree represents its size market; however, individual station characteristics, of necessity, reflect the communities served. A comparative day's schedule for the three stations is shown in Figure 9.8.

Figure 9.7 This is a typical listing of programs available to member stations of the Public Radio Cooperative. The programs are distributed via the Public Radio Satellite.

PUBLIC RADIO COOPERATIVE
SPRING QUARTER 1982 SATELLITE TRANSMISSION SCHEDULE

DAY/TIME	PROGRAM TITLE	START DATE/ END DATE	CHANNEL/MODE	#/PROGRAM LENGTH	RIGHTS
MONDAYS					
12:45 - 13:14	MUSIC MAKERS	4/05 - 6/28	3&4/stereo	13/29:00	One broadcast w/in one year
13:15 - 14:14	FOLK SAMPLER	4/05 - 6/28	3&4/stereo	13/59:00	Unlimited/one year
14:15 - 15:14	WOODY'S CHILDREN	4/05 - 6/28	3&4/stereo	13/59:00	One broadcast w/in one year
TUESDAYS*					
13:30 - 15:29	JAZZ SESSION	4/06 - 6/29	5/mono	13/2 hrs.	Unlimited/one year
*WEDNESDAYS**					
12:30 - 13:29	GREAT ARTISTS	4/07 - 6/30	3&4/stereo	13/59:00	One broadcast w/in one year
THURSDAYS					
12:00 - 12:59	A NOTE TO YOU	4/01 - 6/24	5&6/stereo	12/59:00	Unlimited/one year
13:00 - 13:59	CINEMA SOUNDTRACK	4/01 - 6/24	5&6/stereo	13/59:00	Unlimited/one year
14:00 - 14:29	ESKIMO STORIES	4/01 - 6/03	3&4/stereo	10/29:00	Unlimited thru 12/31/82
15:30 - 16:29	ELLINGTONIA	4/01 - 6/24	3&4/stereo	13/59:00	Two uses/one year
16:30 - 18:44	LIBRARY OF CONGRESS CHAMBER MUSIC SERIES	12/03 - 2/25	3&4/stereo	80:00 - 13/120:00	See Winter Packet listing
18:00 - 18:29	THE MIND'S EYE	4/01 - 6/24	5/mono	13/25:00 - 27:00	Air between 4/01 & 8/31/82
18:30 - 18:59	KINDRED SPIRITS	4/01 - 6/24	5/mono	13/29:00	Unlimited/notify producer of carriage

Courtesy of WUOT-FM, Knoxvile, and the Public Radio Cooperative.

Large Market: WGBH-FM, Boston

WGBH, Boston, licensed to the WGBH Educational Foundation, began broadcasting in 1951. The WGBH foundation was formed in 1946 as a loose federation of 17 Boston area universities and cultural institutions seeking to develop educational radio programs. WGBH currently receives more than 75 percent of its operating costs (more than $600,000 annually) from individual listeners. Policy guidance comes from a board of 25 persons who represent the sponsoring institutions and the community.

WGBH-FM operates with 100,000 watts (ERP), the maximum power presently allowed under the FM rules. Significantly, WGBH carries the highest rating of any public radio station in the top 20 markets.

Program Discussion WGBH's 24-hour daily program schedule consists mainly of recorded music, mostly classical, and news/public affairs programming. Each weekday begins with NPR's news magazine "Morning Edition"

Figure 9.8 Comparative Public Radio Schedules

Local Time	WGBH-FM Boston	WUOT-FM Knoxville	KEYA-FM Belcourt, N.D.
6:00 AM	Morning Edition	Early Morning Program	Country Morning
7:00	Morning Pro Musica	(NPR News) Early Morning	
8:00		(NPR News) Early Morning	
9:00		(News) Morning Concert	
10:00		Morning Concert	Request Show
11:00			
11:30		Music & Talk Series	
12:00 N	(News) Music America	Noontime	
1:00 PM	Music America	Afternoon Concert	Music's Alive!
2:00			
3:00			
4:00		Jazz Interlude	All Things Considered
4:30	Public Affairs		
5:00	All Things Considered	All Things Considered	
5:30			Radio Dramas
6:00			High School Radio
6:30	GBH Journal	Music & Talk Series	
7:00	Talk Programs		
8:00	Varied Concerts	Varied Concerts	Considerin'
9:00			Night Owl's Nest
10:00	Public Affairs Series	Jazz Workshop	
11:00	Artists in the Night		
12:00 M		New Morning	
1:00 AM			Sign Off

from 6:00 to 7:00 AM. However, "Morning Edition" is only aired for one of its two hours because listeners prefer a long-running local origination program. "Morning Pro Musica," programmed from 7:00 until 12:00 Noon, consists of news and interviews, recorded and live classical music, and weather. The program always begins with bird songs and the music that best suits the early morning hours, such as medieval, baroque, and the early classics. Longer works and contemporary music follow. ("Morning Pro Musica" is available to PRC member stations on Saturday and Sunday mornings via satellite transmission.)

Following a ten-minute noontime newscast, "Music America" begins on WGBH, with a format of indigenous selections until 4:30. The next half-hour contains a strip of public affairs programs, just ahead of NPR's "All Things Considered." Local talk programs, including news and oral literature, continue until 8:00 PM, when a two-hour concert begins. At 10:00, there is an hour for public affairs broadcasts. "Artists in the Night" commences at 11:00, featuring jazz until 6:00 AM and the beginning of the following day's schedule.

Significantly, WGBH's programming reflects a Boston orientation even though NPR and recorded programming dominate the schedule. It's also interesting to note the blocking of talk and music programming and the use of transitional nighttime public affairs programs between the classical and jazz music blocks.

Medium Market: WUOT-FM, Knoxville, Tennessee

WUOT-FM, licensed to and funded primarily by The University of Tennessee, began broadcasting in 1949. It serves metropolitan Knoxville, including Oak Ridge and surrounding parts of East Tennessee, with a 100,000 watt signal. WUOT's programming also is rebroadcast in the Chattanooga area by a sister station, WUTC-FM. Policy guidance originates with the University's vice-president for continuing education.

Operating in a 20-station market, WUOT's goal is to provide a clear and obvious alternative service to the area's commercial outlets. Program manager Norris Dryer adds, "It makes no sense whatever to spend taxpayers' money to duplicate what is already available commercially."[5] During recent years, WUOT has ranked as high as fifth place in its market in cume audience.

Program Discussion WUOT's programming closely resembles that of WGBH. Its 24-hour broadcast day consists largely of classical and jazz music, news, and public affairs programs. The day begins at 7:00 AM with the "Early Morning Program" of classical music, news, and weather briefs hosted by a station announcer. WUOT carries the hourly five-minute newscast from NPR; however, station management made a conscious decision not to broadcast the full "Morning Edition" because of listener preference for the local program over network news and feature material. A "Morning Concert" from 9:10 to 11:30 features a preselected classical repertoire. The remaining half-hour before noon is devoted to varied music and talk series.

"Noontime," an hour-long broadcast, consists of classical music, brief interviews, and feature news cohosted by a male-female announcing team. Classical music continues at 1:00 PM with WUOT's long-established "Afternoon Concert," using selections programmed by the music director of the station. Then a "Jazz Interlude" is broadcast from 4:00 to 5:00. WUOT's most-listened-to broadcast, NPR's "All Things Considered," is carried from 5:00 until 6:30, followed by a 90-minute talk-and-music block prior to the evening's classical music. These nightly concerts utilize tapes from such organizations as the Boston, St. Louis, and Chicago Symphonies, and the New York Philharmonic Orchestra.[6] Jazz music is carried from 10:00 until midnight. Then WUOT returns to classical music, including both recorded selections and syndicated programming, until 7:00 AM in a program called "New Morning." The syndicated shows provide breaks during the long night for the announcer on duty. Typical early morning syndicated programs include "BBC Concert Hall," "Dutch Concert Hall," and " America in Concert." Such programs may be obtained from a variety of sources, including Parkway Productions, Radio Nederland, the Association of German Broadcasters, Radio Canada, and Radio Moscow.[7]

WUOT and WGBH are quite similar in that their programming centers on three elements: classical music, jazz, and talk. Both rely on classical music as their programming mainstay, and they use speech programs as transitions into other day-parts. "All Things Considered" is the kingpin of the dinnertime talk segment, which precedes the evening concert block. Although one might expect jazz in the late hours, WUOT alters the pattern by inserting classical material during its postmidnight schedule.

Both WUOT and WGBH publish a monthly program guide which includes listings of individual music selections. Material from a WUOT guide is shown in Figure 9.9.

Small Market: KEYA-FM, Belcourt, North Dakota

Our third radio case study is definitely not typical of most public radio stations. KEYA-FM, Belcourt, N.D., operates with 19,000 watts (ERP) and serves a 45-mile radius, which includes parts of southern Manitoba. This station orients its programming primarily to the residents of the Turtle Mountain Chippewa Indian Reservation in North Dakota. Begun in 1975, KEYA is one of the few radio signals that can be received in the area. Funding comes from the CPB, local underwriting, and two school districts on the reservation. One of the school districts is the station's licensee.

KEYA's programming varies widely from the classical and jazz music so frequently found on public radio stations. Instead, the station presents a great amount of country, contemporary, and Canadian fiddle music. In addition, KEYA's public affairs programs tend to be oriented to the needs and interests of the Chippewa Indians.

Program Discussion KEYA's programming approach is much more like commercial radio than either WGBH or WUOT. In the absence of adequate commercial service, however, KEYA's approach *is* alternative programming. Since KEYA serves as the principal media outlet in its area, it tends to program in shorter segments rather than the longer block programming found at most public outlets.

KEYA's "Early Morning Show," which begins at 6:00 AM, features fiddle and country music along with essential information to start the new day. Newscasts include both national material from NPR and state and regional stories from a wire service. The "Early Morning Show" and "Country Morning" carry brief excerpts from NPR's "Morning Edition" prior to 8:00. The morning programming is interlaced with such public service features as bulletin boards, "Mother Earth News," "Feeling Good," consumer reports, vocational education, fish and game reports, and agricultural items, as well as public service announcements.

The "Request Show" from 10:00 AM to 1:00 PM allows listeners to phone in requests in honor of special events such as birthdays, anniversaries, and other personal events. "Music's Alive" from 1:00 to 4:00 features contemporary soft rock and country selections. Newscasts are presented hourly, including local reports and national news from NPR.

"All Things Considered" is carried live from 4:00 to 5:30 PM (C.S.T.). Afterwards, KEYA's programming consists of the "Radio Drama," which varies from early radio productions to more recent material from NPR. Then the early evening hours are programmed with a "High School Radio Show" that includes music requests and dedications, as well as news of school activites. The programming becomes more serious with "Considerin'," an hour-long broadcast from 8:00 to 9:00 PM. This program covers a wide range of material, from discussion by Indian people on the Chippewa scene, NPR's "Options," and local presentations, to Canadian Broadcasting Corporation

Figure 9.9

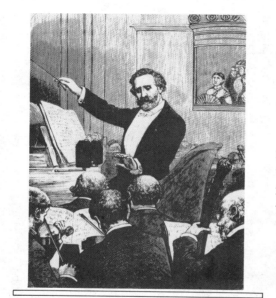

WUOT·FM
PUBLIC RADIO/STEREO 92

January, 1982

WUOT-FM/Knoxville & WUTC-FM/Chattanooga

Affiliates of National Public Radio

Every effort is made to broadcast the program exactly as listed, but changes occasionally may be necessary.

Friday, January 1

5:00a **Eileen Farrell's American Popular Singers**
6:00a NPR News
6:05a **Early Morning Program**
7:00a NPR News
7:05a Early Morning Program
8:00a NPR News
8:05a Arts Calendar
8:10a Early Morning Program
9:00a **BBC Radio Newsreel**
9:15a **MORNING CONCERT —** HANDEL: Royal Fireworks Music
9:40a MENDELSSOHN: Octet, Eb, Op. 20
10:15a YARDUMIAN: Symphony No. 1
10:42a BRUCKNER: Five Unaccompanied Motets
11:00a VAUGHAN WILLIAMS: Greensleeves and English Folksong Suite
11:15a HAYDN: Piano Sonata No. 19, e
11:30a **NPR Playhouse — Music in a New World**
12:00p **Noontime**
1:00p **AFTERNOON CONCERT** HUGO WOLF: 46 Moerike Lieder
3:35p BACH: Toccata & Fugue, d, BWV 565
3:45p LASZLO ROOTH: Variations on a Sephardic-Jewish Romance, "Paxaro de Hermosura"
3:50p **Commentary**
4:00p **Jazz Interlude**
5:00p **ALL THINGS CONSIDERED**
5:25p Arts Calendar
5:30p **ATC** cont'd
6:30p **New Dimensions** — Ginsberg Remembers, with Allen Ginsberg (New Dimensions in January is underwritten by J. David Buckwalter of Knoxville)
7:30p **Music of the Southern Mountains**
8:00p **Talking About Music**
8:30p **BOSTON SYMPHONY ORCHESTRA** — Leonard Bernstein, conductor/Doriot Anthony Dwyer, flute. BERNSTEIN: Overture to Candide; Suite from "On the Waterfront"; Halil; Symphonic Dances from "West Side Story"; Divertimento for Orchestra **Music for the Day's End**
10:30p **Jazz Workshop — Jazz Alive!** Saxophonist Dewey Redman, pianist Ronnie Mathews and singer Joe Lee Wilson

American soprano EILEEN FARRELL, singer DAVID ALLYN, and pianist/arranger LOONIS McGLOHON look over the score for a popular '50s tune during the premiere program of EILEEN FARRELL'S AMERICAN POPULAR SINGERS. The 13-part series, which explores the world of popular song with some of its most famous interpreters, airs Friday mornings at 5.

Saturday, January 2

12:00a **New Morning** — All-request. Phone (615) 974-5375
7:00a **Early Morning Program**
9:00a **Man and Molecules**
9:15a **MORNING CONCERT** MOZART: Oboe Quartet, F, K., 370
9:32a MENDELSSOHN: Violin Concerto, e, Op. 64
10:01a STRAVINSKY: The Firebird
10:46a RACHMANINOFF: Symphonic Dance, Op. 45, No. 1

6

Courtesy of Department of Radio Services, Division of Statewide Continuing Education, The University of Tennessee.

specials. KEYA's broadcast day concludes with the four-hour "Night Owl's Nest," a mixture of contemporary and country music from 9:00 PM to 1:00 AM.

Most public radio stations serve areas in which commercial outlets provide news, information, and popular music. In turn, they concentrate on alternative areas such as classical music in longer blocks. However, KEYA is virtually alone and must fill the needs of all of its community. That means it must provide a more traditional service instead of the prototype form of public radio which WGBH and WUOT exemplify. Even so, KEYA does carry some material not likely to be heard on commercial radio outlets.

OTHER NONCOMMERCIAL RADIO PROGRAMMING

Although primary attention has been given to public radio, three other forms of noncommercial broadcasting deserve special mention because of their impact as alternative program sources.

First, about 50 listener-supported licensees belong to the National Federation of Community Broadcasters. These stations, which coproduce and exchange material, emphasize public affairs and cultural material. The best known member of the Federation is the Pacifica group, which operates radio stations in New York, Washington, Los Angeles, Berkeley, and Houston.

Second, religious broadcasting is a growing force in the electronic media. The success of the Christian Broadcasting Network and religious station groups, such as "Your Family Radio," have added momentum to a growing awareness on the part of church leaders that broadcasting is a very effective method for reaching their special audiences. Both institutional church denominations and independent groups are involved. The National Association of Religious Broadcasters serves as the national coordinator for most of these broadcasters.

A third group includes the noncommercial radio licensees who operate low power student-training stations. Most of these stations are licensed to communications departments in colleges and universities. Unlike the CPB qualified stations, these low wattage campus outlets provide programming of particular local (student) interest. Their main clearing house for program exchange is the Intercollegiate Broadcasting System (IBS).

In addition to these three forms, some FM radio stations aid in the dissemination of audio instructional material through a subsidiary communications authorization (SCA) which allows them to transmit a separate program on the same frequency with their regular programming. This service most often involves readings for the blind, but it also has been used to distribute specifically targeted postprofessional instruction to physicians and lawyers.

PUBLIC BROADCASTING AND THE FUTURE

Although public broadcasting is at least as old as commercial radio, it has been plagued with financial problems throughout the years of its existence.

Foundations and the federal government have been the mainstay in bringing public radio and television to their present level as important and established broadcasting services. However, both of these sources are subject to economic conditions, and the latter has been notoriously subject to political whim.

Through a series of new initiatives, PBS hopes to lessen its dependence on the federal treasury. One proposal would see PBS making a greater effort to solicit corporate underwriting to establish a pay television network for high quality cultural programming. Such a Public Subscription Network would use the existing PBS satellite delivery system. As proposed, it would carry professional improvement and skills programming for adults, secondary schools, colleges, and corporations during the day. Then, at night, it would concentrate on a 90-minute to three-hour cultural block for which the home subscriber would pay a monthly fee.

A second proposal calls for public television stations and PBS to carry a limited amount of advertising to help defray operating costs. Those who advocate this approach usually suggest that the amount of advertising be limited and that the messages be restricted to the institutional type. Corporate underwriters already may show their company trade signs, emblems, and logotypes on the programs which they fund.

Other possible nonbroadcast sources of revenue include the marketing of video cassettes and video discs through a centrally operated video cassette club. Ancillary services would include a public TV video cassette catalog, a record label, video cassette recorder and disc player, an arts and cultural magazine, and a travel service which would organize cultural tours.

SUMMARY

In this chapter, we have explored the historical development, current practices, and future prospects of noncommercial radio and television. Noncommercial broadcasting first developed as *educational radio,* then *educational television,* largely because the first stations were owned by academic institutions which used them for instructional purposes. Noncommercial broadcasting evolved into *public broadcasting* after federal funding was made available in the 1960s. Until that time, these stations were unevenly distributed across the country and were almost always underfunded. Nurturing by the Ford Foundation and other philanthropies enabled them to survive.

The real impetus for public broadcasting in the United States came with the passage of the Public Broadcasting Act of 1967. This Act stimulated the development and upgrading of public radio and TV stations, resulting in their present coverage of all important populated centers in the country. Its principal mechanism is the Corporation for Public Broadcasting, which allocates federal funds for broadcast facilities and programming. Two associations of local member stations, the Public Broadcasting Service and National Public Radio, are responsible for distributing programs to their station members through satellite and telephone distribution networks. To a great extent, however, the member stations determine which programs will be fed through the interconnection system.

The basic programming concept of public radio and television is *alternative service,* providing viewers and listeners with quality programs of various types that are unavailable from commercial media. Six case studies—three television and three radio stations—revealed how alternative programming is practiced in public broadcasting. Particularly noteworthy is National Public Radio's daily news magazine, "All Things Considered," and the highly successful instructional television programming of the Children's Television Workshop, including "Sesame Street" and the "Electric Company."

Despite the prominence of public affairs, cultural, and enrichment programs, instructional or "teaching" uses of noncommercial television still exist. In fact, adult education and college credit courses via television are expanding through such organizations as the National University Consortium and the University of Mid-America.

Finally, we have seen that public broadcasting, as presently structured, is subject to financial uncertainty. At this writing, a number of proposals, including pay television and commercial advertising, are under consideration as possible avenues for greater financial stability. In any case, it is highly probable that public broadcasting will continue to perform its valuable role as an alternative programming service for many years to come.

In our next chapter, we will explore the broad field of programming criticism, with particular attention given to those aspects most applicable to the program director's job.

ENDNOTES

1. WTTW Program Guide, January 1980.
2. Personal correspondence between Jim Lewis, KPTS-TV Director of Programming, and the author. October 28, 1981.
3. Personal correspondence between Hal Bouton, KIXE-TV General Manager, and the author. October 19, 1981.
4. Saturday afternoon performances of the Metropolitan Opera have been broadcast on network radio since the 1930s under sponsorship by Texaco, Inc. Although a few commercial stations continue to broadcast the operas, this long-standing program is carried now by dozens of public radio stations. Texaco continues to underwrite the production costs.
5. Personal interview with Norris Dryer, WUOT-FM Program Director, January 15, 1982.
6. Recorded performances are available from several other prominent orchestras and opera companies in the United States. These groups include the Los Angeles Philharmonic Orchestra, the Cleveland Symphony, the Philadelphia Orchestra, the Milwaukee Symphony Orchestra, the Kansas City Lyric Opera Company, the San Francisco Opera Company, and the Houston Grand Opera Company.
7. A few other sources of taped noncommercial programming include the Italian Radio TV System, the Library of Congress (Music Division), the University of Chicago's Office of Radio and Television, the Swiss Broadcasting Corporation, the Broadcasting Foundation of America, Georgetown University, the Swedish Broadcasting Corporation, Radio Smithsonian, and the United Nations Radio Service.

STUDY QUESTIONS

1. List the educational or public radio and television stations that can be received in your area. What type of ownership holds the license for each station? From what sources does each station obtain its operating funds?

2. Examine and analyze the current program schedule of a public radio station in your area. How does this station fit into the overall mosaic of radio service in the market? What programming strategies does the station emphasize? Give examples. How does this station serve the peculiar needs of its community?
3. Examine and analyze the current program schedule of a public TV station in your area. How does this station fit into the total television service available in the market? What programming strategies does it utilize? Give examples. How does this television station serve the peculiar needs of its community?
4. Discuss the instructional programming available from local public stations. Which are more prominent—enrichment programs, in-school telecasts, or adult education broadcasts? Do you believe the predominant form of instructional programming is the most suitable type for your area? Why?
5. Develop a prospectus for a new program series for public radio or television. Include in your proposal (a) the program's purpose; (b) its format; (c) its setting; (d) its principal characters or personalities; and (e) its major appeals. Why do you think this program should be produced?

SUGGESTED READINGS

Blakely, Robert J. *The People's Instrument: A Philosophy of Programming for Public Television*. Washington: Public Affairs Press, 1971.

Burke, Richard C., ed. *Instructional Television: Bold New Venture*. Bloomington: Indiana University Press, 1971.

Carnegie Commission on Educational Television. *Public Television: A Program for Action*. New York: Harper & Row, 1967.

Cater, Douglass. "The Politics of Public TV," *Columbia Journalism Review* (July/August 1972), pp. 8-15.

Cater, Douglass, and Michael J. Nyhan. *The Future of Public Broadcasting*. New York: Praeger Publishers; Palo Alto, Calif.: Aspen Institute for Humanistic Studies (copublishers), 1976.

Costello, L.F., and G.N. Gordon. *Teach with Television: A Guide to Instructional TV*. New York: Hastings House, 1965.

Gibson, G.H. *Public Broadcasting: The Role of the Federal Government, 1912–1976*. New York: Praeger Publishers, 1977.

Katzman, Natan. *Program Decisions in Public Television*. Washington, D.C.: Corporation for Public Broadcasting and National Association of Educational Broadcasters, 1976.

Kirkish, J.B. *A Descriptive History of America's First National Public Radio Network: National Public Radio, 1970 to 1974*. PhD dissertation, The University of Michigan, 1980.

Koenig, A.E., and R.B. Hill, eds. *The Farther Vision*. Madison: University of Wisconsin Press, 1970.

Robertson Associates, Inc. *Local Station Utilization of PBS Programming: A Study for the TV Manager's Council of NAEB*. Washington, D.C.: National Association of Educational Broadcasters, 1977.

Springola, R.F. *Non-Commercial Radio Stations in the United States and Territories: Programming and Organization, 1971*. PhD dissertation, Indiana University, 1972.

10

PROGRAM CRITICISM

Darrel Holt

Courtesy of *The Knoxville Journal.*

This cartoon gives you a look at what this chapter is about—the criticism of broadcast programming, especially television. Radio has received its share, of course, but since television took over as the dominant electronic medium, it has assumed the deluge of complaints that once were reserved for radio. What's more, by April 1981, the Federal Communications Commission

(FCC) deregulated commercial radio in several significant ways—clear evidence that fears concerning radio have subsided, if not died, over the years.

Although the complaints about broadcasting cover an awesome range, the purpose of this chapter is not to attack these media. Rather, our purpose is to examine carefully some of the most common charges and observations so that, as a serious student of programming, you will acquire the understanding upon which to construct your own value system concerning "good" and "bad" content and practices.

To achieve this purpose, we believe it important to place each of the charges and its rebuttal in a pragmatic (and sometimes philosophical) perspective. Doing that will permit you to understand the *why,* as well as the nature and scope, of the debate, and thus come away with a better foundation for decision making than would be true with some other approach to a chapter on criticism.

Unfortunately, the following analysis cannot include a scholarly proof or denial of any charge because there is no incontrovertible proof among the literally thousands of scholarly studies and thoughtful essays. What's more, many of the research results and opinions have changed, and will change, with newly emerging evidence. And so we hope only to provide a general overview and synthesis of what a good many intelligent observers believe about broadcast programming.

CRITICISM: MEANING

What *is* criticism? Most of us think of criticism as a kind of negative comment or censure—sometimes labeled *destructive criticism.* Conversely, there is constructive criticism, in which we link an upbeat comment or observation with a suggestion for improvement.

Another kind of criticism involves an educated judgment or evaluation of the merit or quality of something according to a body of criteria. In this sense, criticism copes with the form and substance of the thing evaluated (criticized) and concludes that it is good or bad or whatever because it does or does not conform to the various criteria.

Literature, dance, music, fine art, film, and even architecture lend themselves to formal criticism. They have been around long enough for commonly accepted criteria to have emerged through systematic study. Television has not. For that reason, added to the facts that TV is such a "cafeteria" of dissimilar program offerings and that each program occupies such a fleeting moment in time, genuine criticism is in short supply. Often, columnists who write under the label "TV Critic" are little more than "I like" or "I don't like" program reviewers. That's an entirely different kind of judgment.

Thus, we can easily understand why there is so much confusion and disagreement about broadcasting generally, and television specifically. In the absence of commonly accepted, formal, objective criteria, much of the criticism emerges from individualized, informal, subjective values. The problem calls to mind the account of six blind men trying to describe an elephant. Each man "saw" the beast differently because each was feeling a different portion of the elephant's anatomy.

CRITICISM: RADIO

First, let's review the evolution of radio from its so-called "Golden Age" of the 1930s and early 1940s up to the 1980s. Clearly, radio programming today is much different from those days of fifty-plus years ago. Back then, radio programming was also a "cafeteria" and received many of the same slings and arrows that shower upon television today. But those complaints were not quite so voluminous, nor usually so ferocious, as those of the television age.

One reason is that, despite the popularity of radio, it never exerted the same degree of "reality" upon us. Let's recall that early radio equipment was bulky and cumbersome, not the miniaturized and easily portable units we enjoy today. Today, we can "be there" and "live" the event when electronic news-gathering equipment lets us see/hear it immediately as it occurs. In short, the capabilities of TV tend to make its fare more "real" and "lifelike" because TV is easier to believe.

A second reason is that America in the early days of radio was—or appeared to be—a different kind of society. Granted, the nation was born in violence. Granted, too, the 1930s and 1940s suffered from a considerable amount of violent crime. But there didn't seem to be the incidence of mindless atrocities that crash so frequently into the headlines and newscasts today.

In the 1980s, we have many more media, all equipped with the tools to take us anywhere an event occurs. These media continue to tell/show us things which suggest that certain aspects of our society are not so desirable as we would like them to be. Human nature prompts us to place the blame somewhere.

As television nudged radio aside to become the something-for-every-taste medium, radio gave up that role in favor of a here's-my-specialty kind of programming. If you like a diet of rock 'n' roll, tune in Station A. If you thrive on country-western, Station B will be your choice. As radio programming changed, so did many of the complaints about it.

OBSCENITY AND INDECENCY

In their efforts to hold or increase audiences in a post-TV era, some radio stations resorted to programming practices which brought charges of obscenity and/or indecency. Considering all the stations there are, such charges have been relatively few. There might have been more, except that what constitutes actionable obscenity or indecency was and is difficult to apply to specific program content. What is indecent or obscene to one may become another's classic favorite.

And so, even though federal criminal law prohibits the broadcasting of obscene, indecent, or profane material, for several reasons the FCC has moved cautiously in its efforts to squelch such material. One is that courts have declared broadcasting to be protected by the First Amendment. Another is that Section 326 of the Federal Communications Act specifically forbids the FCC to censor broadcast material.

We're not entirely at sea regarding obscenity, because the *Miller* decision[1] gave us some words and concepts to examine. In *Miller,* the Supreme Court ruled that material was obscene if, taken as a whole, it violated contemporary community standards and appealed to prurient interests; depicted or described, in a patently offensive manner, sexual conduct specifically defined by state law; and if the material lacked serious literary, artistic, political, or scientific value.

Despite the difficulty in getting any large group of people to agree that a program meets those three tests (let alone to agree as to what the tests mean), the FCC was successful in stopping what could have become an "obscene trend" in early 1970s radio.

Subsequently referred to as "topless radio," these programs invited telephone call-ins. Those who called in—mostly women—typically discussed various aspects of their sex lives, sometimes in lurid detail. And thus many of the discussions were—if not obscene to everyone—noticeably gamey! By early 1973 there were quite a number of such programs, and at least one of them was put into syndication to more than 20 stations.

There is no question that these sex-oriented programs were popular with a sizable part of the population. A Connecticut station, which created its own sizzler, noted a "30% jump in midday audience" soon after it commenced the program. Later, it noticed a "30% drop when the station pulled it off the air."[2]

Interestingly, previous commissions and some courts have advanced the principle that it's the consumer's right to hear, not the programmer's right to be heard, that is of utmost importance. What's more, the FCC has noted that all major segments of the population enjoy the right to have their tastes satisfied to some extent. Clearly, though, this kind of fare was not what the FCC had in mind. And so, a few FCC-levied fines and some Congressional pressure ultimately eliminated "topless radio."

Obscenity's partner is indecency. In the early 1960s there occurred a case which overlapped the boundary between obscenity and indecency. Commonly known as the "Charlie Walker Case," it received a great deal of national visibility. On the one hand, it was one of the early instances in which, under a then-new FCC policy, the hearing would be held in the city to which the station was licensed. On the other hand, it was an early opportunity for the FCC (and later the court) to test an obscenity or indecency definition. Interestingly, neither chose to do so.

In any event, Charlie Walker was an air personality for WDKD in Kingstree, South Carolina. His program enjoyed a substantial following— of admirers *and* detractors—because the content was anything but bland. In addition to his outspoken opinions on almost any topic or person, he injected his own brand of humor into his patter. The content of that humor ultimately prompted a complaint to the FCC.

After considerable time and litigation, Charlie Walker was found guilty of using obscene and indecent language on the air. He was sentenced to five years' probation. WDKD lost its license because the station had tolerated Walker's use of broadcast material that was "coarse, vulgar, suggestive, and susceptible of indecent double meaning."[3] This statement, of course, did not constitute any kind of definition of indecency—only that, whatever indecency is, Walker's comments contained it.

The FCC surmounted the definition problem, finally, in the *Pacifica Foundation* case. Pacifica's New York station, WBAI-FM, played a long cut from a George Carlin album in which Carlin discussed the seven "Filthy Words" that should never be said on the air. Although most of us have heard those words now and then in individual contexts, to hear them all at one time in this fashion was likely to singe a number of eardrums.

After a substantial battle which ended up in the Supreme Court, the FCC was able to clarify its standards of indecency. Broadcast content is likely to be indecent if it uses language that is "patently offensive" according to "contemporary community standards for the broadcast medium," and if it uses that language to describe "sexual or excretory activities and organs," especially if the material is broadcast "at times of the day when there is a reasonable risk that children may be in the audience."[4]

Later, the FCC further clarified its intention, stating that such material might be acceptable as part of a news or public affairs program. It might even be acceptable otherwise if the material has a redeeming social value and is broadcast when children are not likely to be in the audience. In either case, there must be adequate warning to the audience of the nature of this forthcoming material.

The idea of adequate warning, as two observers put it,

> ...introduced a new and novel dilemma for broadcasters: the listener's right *not* to hear. Given the "uniquely pervasive presence" of broadcast media...the public's need to be untrammeled by objectionable programming also warrants Constitutional protection. More succinctly, certain kinds of broadcast expressions may constitute a form of intrusion and thus violate the listener's right of privacy.[5]

Nonetheless, the FCC did not punish WBAI-FM. Instead, the complaint was filed away, possibly to be reconsidered should further complaints be received about the station. The *Pacifica* case should serve, as it apparently did, to alert other broadcasters to be extremely cautious in their attempt to appeal to the audience with this kind of material.

MUSIC AND NEWS

As we have seen, a majority of today's radio stations fall into the music-and-news category. The programming is mostly music, with a five-minute newscast on or near the hour and, perhaps, additional news on or near the half-hour. Traditional patterns will become increasingly flexible, however, as more satellite-distributed radio services become available.

The most common complaints over the years regarding radio music are: (1) drug-oriented lyrics, (2) sex-oriented lyrics, and (3) payola. The first offends some listeners because the lyrics seem to tout the notion that there are positive values—psychological, at least—in taking drugs. The second, some believe, ranges from simple bawdiness to outright promotion of free love. The third is part of unethical and illegal practices; in this case, it causes certain songs to be played because someone was "bought off" to play them. Payola need not concern us right now.

Drug-oriented lyrics pose a problem at two levels. At one level is the charge that youthful, persuasive listeners are lured into the use of drugs in order to find those "values." This view sees such music as a threat to society. Certainly, the use of drugs is widespread. Equally demonstrable is the fact that there has been a serious increase in violent crimes in recent years. The two often go together, because many of those crimes are thought to be committed in order to support a drug addiction.

At the second level is the problem which may continue even today to confront station authorities. Usually of an older generation, many of these managers don't always understand the jargon in which these lyrics are couched. Unless counseled by someone who is "literate" in the counterculture language, a good many managers don't know which songs to take off the air if they are so inclined.

Let's assume that some listeners *are* affected by the lyrics. Let's further assume that most managers now understand the language. On what basis will the managers decide to eliminate these songs from the playlist? If a given song is popular, one can argue, a station of the appropriate format ought to play it. A popular song, by definition, is one that a good many listeners want to hear. And most of those will simply enjoy it, then go about their business; that is, most of them won't rush right out for a "fix."

At the same time, appealing to a suitably large audience is important to the economic health of a station. Certainly, management has an obligation to the stockholders. It is counterproductive, therefore, to eliminate a "bad" song unless one's competitors enjoy consciences of equal dimensions. Otherwise, they get the audience which flees from the "good" station.

The same kind of dilemma exists when we consider songs that are sexually oriented. The problem, critics fear, is not that there are *some* of these songs, but that there are *so many* of them and they receive such repeated airplay. The result, goes this line of thinking, is that we hear so many of these songs so often, and performed by well-known, popular people, that we come to perceive this kind of behavior as normal and acceptable.

These are troublesome questions, certainly, but few believe that the solution lies in granting authority to the FCC or some other superpower to say that *this* song is acceptable but *that* song must stay off the air. An opposing view, moreover, holds that these songs don't cause us to be the way we are. Instead, we who are already that way write and perform the songs, and they simply mirror society as it has become through a number of causes.

Whatever the opinion, the conscientious and socially minded broadcaster faces an awesome responsibility when considering whether a given song is acceptable in terms of what he/she thinks it says. Numerous studies strongly suggest that what an individual perceives and understands from *any* communication depends in large part on what he/she brings to that communication—mood, prejudices, intelligence level and the like. More about that later.

Fewer complaints seem to exist specifically concerning radio news, even though some radio stations put very little effort into news gathering and reporting. At best, some of them provide only a rip 'n' read token. And when a disc jockey must dash to the AP or UPI printer during a record, rip off a few items, then assemble them during the next song, the purpose and value of journalism take a back seat.

Fortunately, most radio executives realize that a genuinely effective and meaningful news operation requires special priority and attention because so little time is allotted to the typical newscast. Allowing for open, close, and commercial(s), the so-called five-minute newscast will actually offer three-plus minutes of surface-only information.

Others question how much in-depth news is required of each medium when so many media are available. And it may be that some people simply prefer a "bulletin board" of radio headlines.

Sometimes, too, news policy or practice emerges more from a concern for sponsors or audience size than it does from professional news judgment. Consider the problems posed when the son of the station's largest advertiser is arrested for some unbelievable behavior. If the station has already established a let-the-chips-fall-where-they-may reputation for news integrity, that's one thing. Otherwise, there will be one nervous news director.

In the same ballpark lies the potential for unethical practices by talk show personalities. On March 30, 1981, for example, an attempt was made on President Ronald Reagan's life. A little later, a talk show on a Las Vegas TV station featured a Los Angeles psychic who predicted the attempt. Her segment, said to have been taped nearly two months earlier, contained details that were spookily close to what happened. Unfortunately, it came to light that the tape had, in fact, been cut the day *following* the assassination attempt. In the meantime, though, her predictions received wide distribution because they were also televised in good faith over NBC and Cable News Network.

This is the kind of problem that respects no medium. Moreover, it betrays a faithful and trusting audience.

COMMERCIALS AND CONTESTS

Most of the complaints which orbit around advertising apply equally to radio and TV. The values and problems of advertising, as such, merit treatment beyond the reach of this chapter. However, there are a few considerations we need to explore regarding radio commercials. Many of them stem from radio's essentially local nature.

One common complaint is simply that there are too many. Often, a commercial—or perhaps more than one—will follow each record. When these are followed by a public service announcement, then a promotional spot for an up-coming feature, then a station break, some listeners feel as if they are deluged with commercial "clutter." Stations which overschedule haphazardly are likely to lose audence.

On the positive side, many people don't object to commercials. In fact, some of us rely on well-written, informative commercials to tell us where today's best buys are located. Stations which carefully create and schedule these informational messages are likely to gain listeners—a point the program manager will keep clearly in mind.

The writing of local commercials, too, can cause problems. Often, they are handled by sales personnel or copywriters who may not be fully up-to-date on the various laws and regulations which govern questionable or downright illegal merchandising practices. Some of these practices are noted in chapter 3, and you may wish to review them.

There are also many possible pitfalls lurking in audience participation contests. The FCC is very clear in its lists of do's and don't's. They add up to the admonition that each contest should be exactly what it appears to be—an unrigged opportunity for participants to win all the prizes described in the contest promotional material. There should be no hidden gimmicks or conditions.

Moreover, contestants must not be encouraged to do things which may place them in danger. In the mid-1970s, for example, a California radio station was sued for "a wrongful death" which allegedly resulted from participation in the station's contest. The contest asked people "to locate a disc jockey who was driving about in a metropolitan area giving away money prizes." Some "youthful motorists, who were listening to said station...forced the victim's automobile off the roadway."

> As the California Supreme Court noted, the action of the radio station constituted an "attempt...to generate a competitive pursuit on public streets, accelerated by repeated importuning by radio to be the very first to arrive at a particular destination," and an integral part of competition which the Court found to be inherently, gravely dangerous.[6]

We have touched on only a few of the rights, responsibilities, and hazards that "come with the territory" when broadcasters try to communicate with the general public. More and more, public complaints turn into public actions—actions which can turn out to be disadvantageous to the stations affected. It is a matter of conscience and ethics to do what is right. It is a matter of pragmatics to do what is safe; that is, to give very careful consideration to both the intent and the possible consequences of any communication.

CRITICISM: TELEVISION

To open up a discussion of television criticism is to be like the Dutch boy who pulled his finger out of the dike. As early as February 21, 1977, asserted a *Newsweek* article, more than 2,300 studies had been conducted on the effects of television. Almost all the studies suggest that a steady diet of television programs does in fact do something *to* or *for* viewers, children and adults alike. Specific conclusions, however, differ considerably.

For example, political observer Anne Rawley Saldich recognizes TV as a great democratizer.[7] The late Paddy Chayefsky (author of *Network* and other probing works for TV and film) described television as "democracy at its ugliest."[8] Additional hyperbole comes from a professor of sociology, who is quoted as saying, "Next to the H-bomb, television is the most dangerous thing in the world today."[9] Conversely, even Robert Lewis Shayon—one of the most perceptive and long-lived critics of TV—acknowledges that the medium has fulfilled certain important needs for certain people.

Perhaps all the negative concerns can be summarized by recalling the Zamora case.[10] In 1978, Ronny Zamora was charged with four crimes, including first degree murder. His defense before the Florida court was "involuntary subliminal television intoxication." More simply, his considerable TV viewing had altered him mentally without his knowing it. The plea didn't work, but the fact that it was offered with a straight face suggests how the defense attorney perceived public attitudes toward television's influence.

The truth certainly lies between the extremes of "good" and "bad." That's why the modern program director must define his/her own values. The medium must appeal to sufficient numbers of people, but it must also discharge its responsibility to those people. To accomplish both goals is a formidable task because, as some critics charge, what appeals to us may in the long run be harmful.

But broadcast stations *are* licensed to serve the public interest, convenience, and necessity. Though we may debate the meaning of that phrase, it certainly does *not* mean a constant schedule of programs which contribute to flaky attitudes, counterproductive behavior, or false perceptions of reality.

Does television do that? Nobody knows for certain, but a great many intelligent researchers and observers fear that it does. In fact, even a simple list of all the negative charges placed against TV would consume the rest of this chapter. But space allows us to provide only a modest overview of the most pervasive concerns. And so, we will consider these under the following category labels.

1. Television and Lifestyle. What does the very existence of TV do to our lives?
2. Entertainment Programming. Is that *all* the "fun" shows do to or for us?
3. News and Information. Are Americans the *best* informed or only the *most* informed?
4. Advertising. Does it mostly explain or exploit?
5. What About Children? Is TV instructive or destructive?

As we will notice, these categories are not mutually exclusive; some of the concerns overlap. For example, certain fears apply to people of all ages, not just children. Some charges are leveled at all program types, and advertising as well. The overlap can't be helped, given a monstrous number of concerns, unless we create a monstrous number of categories.

TELEVISION AND LIFESTYLE

The major problem with the typical family's owning a TV set is that they turn it on. Not just now and then, or with a ho-hum attitude, but more than seven hours each day (in the winter), and with something akin to addiction. Not many individuals watch that much, of course, but by definition a heavy viewer watches three or more hours each day.

This concerns some observers, who point out that you can't do much living of your own life if you plop down in front of a phosphorescent screen to watch others live their lives. To do so, they fear, will result in the general deterioration of family life and socialization, and create individual passivity and withdrawal.

Passivity

Years ago, one savant made a prophecy which said, in effect, when man first steps out onto another planet, he will see a great deal of lichen and moss. These will be the vestigial remains of a civilization that watched too much television. Talk show host Dick Cavett is among the many who fear that TV leads to excessive passivity. In a *U.S. News & World Report* interview, Cavett expressed fears that television may have created a "nation of spectators." He worries that too many evenings in front of the set "cannot help but numb the brain."[11]

The key idea here is passivity. Does TV turn us into inactive watchers instead of doers? One study discovered that people who watch 20 or more hours weekly do tend to be less active than light viewers, except in media use generally. That is, heavy viewers tend to go to movies, read magazines and newspapers, and listen to radio, along with their staring at the tube. Another study found that heavy viewers tend to be homebodies and, for a variety of reasons, unemployed. Interestingly, most of these heavy viewers are under 30 years of age. But, as the researchers suspected, these heavy viewers have not attained the education or income levels of average and light viewers. The heavy viewers are also less likely to be socially active in church or job-related groups. The researchers concluded that many of the heavy viewers simply choose TV over other activities.[12]

In rebuttal, others point to the significant increases in various activities and hobbies: tennis, racquetball, the numerous arts and crafts, to name a few. Ah yes, comes the rejoinder, but those increases may well reflect the activities of light-to-average viewers, because heavy viewers don't have enough time for more worthwhile things.

One of those important "things," of course, is reading. Consider this: as early as the 1970s, according to the New York Times News Service, publishers began to resort to "simplified language in their [text]books to adjust to a new element in higher education—the college student who cannot read at traditional college levels."[13] As recently as March, 1981, according to a United Press International story, the US Army complained that too many of its high school graduates "can't read or write beyond fifth- or sixth-grade levels." What's more, many of these graduates "lack the skills for the most routine jobs" and, they add, "the problem is getting worse."[14]

The point is that we can learn how to *talk* by listening to parents and, later, conversing with family and friends. But we learn to use *language* effectively by reading. Effective and precise use of language is important because we think our thoughts in words and sentences. If we're inept in our use of language, we're likely to be inept in our ability to think and communicate. And that state of affairs, lament the critics, is unnerving enough if we are talking only about our children. It's worse to realize that many TV-reared children are now approaching their thirties and must cope as adults with an increasingly complex and technological world.

Among those who point to the other side of the ledger is Dr. Frank Stanton, former CBS executive. He reminds us that almost everything about the print media has increased during the years of TV's existence. While this country's population was growing by 43 percent, for example, the number of book titles published annually nearly quadrupled. The sales of paperback books increased tenfold, while the circulation of daily newspapers also increased. Moreover, public library circulation virtually doubled during the same period.[15]

Others like to point to the tremendous sale of books following TV specials made from those books. *Roots, Shogun,* and *Washington: Behind Closed Doors* are examples of several successful specials which led to startingly great book sales.

Family Life

Equally controversial, even though examples are much more widespread and observable, is the question of TV's effect on the typical family's lifestyle. That TV has indeed altered family living is hardly arguable. Whether the consequences are good or bad is a topic which continues to excite people of both persuasions.

Traditionally, we have thought of the family unit as the foundation not only of society, but of individual growth and socialization as well. Since television arrived, charge the critics, much of that has changed. Granted, in its earliest days, TV often encouraged sociability to the extent that those without sets continued to visit friends who bought sets. Conversely, some TV-less families discovered that Dad was spending more and more time at a nearby bar, cheering his favorite ball club.

It wasn't long, though, until a great many families had TV sets. Winston Kirby, professionally involved with TV over the years, recalls that by the time Bishop Sheen challenged Milton Berle for top ratings, "television receivers had proliferated and viewing was no longer a social event. Television now kept people home, isolated and increasingly alone."[16] Visits between families occurred less frequently.

Within each TV family, too, numerous changes were taking place. The sequence and timing of many of the old activities were rearranged to accommodate TV schedules.

In some families, dinnertime becomes a race with the clock: hurry up, the show's about to begin. In others, the TV set is moved in front of the dinner table so that they can view and chew simultaneously. Either way, the ability and desire for family socialization deteriorates as each family member enters his/her own little electronic cocoon.

Another problem began to emerge. "A 1979 Roper poll (financed by the television industry) conducted a survey of 3,001 married couples which showed that the leading cause of matrimonial disputes was disagreement about which television show to watch."[17] Additional sets help that problem, but separate the family geographically as well as psychologically.

Even the most ardent defenders of TV agree that contemporary family life is not what it once was. But, they point out, television at worst is only one of numerous factors which may correlate with those changes.

In fact, one respected researcher discovered TV to be a "wonderful invention having immense positive social significance that draws men, women, and children back into the home and thus strengthens family life." This is explained by the idea that "contemporary man is the victim of alienating forces" and that "only certain forms of collective communication, above all television, seem to be capable of restoring the lost sense of unity."[18]

Value Structures

And unity is important to society. For a group of people to create and perpetuate a society, the majority of them must share essentially the same value structure. If they are able to implement and maintain those values, then the society is "good" and so is the quality of life there. If a substantial group of people acquire different values which tend to replace or destroy the earlier "good" values, then society is weakened and the quality of life declines for those who hold the older values.

As more and more of our citizens—especially the younger ones—begin to exhibit new and different value structures, other citizens begin to worry and wonder *why*. Most often, they suspect that the *why* ties in with television viewing. Here's the reasoning.

Each of us can learn only so much from first-hand experience. All the rest of what we "know" we acquire second-hand. Our parents, peer groups, teachers, churches, and the media become the most prominent of our secondary sources. Although each of these may be the only source of learning in this or that area, they generally complement or conflict with each other over a broad range of value areas.

If these sources are often in conflict, then which of them wins out most often, and with what kind(s) of value orientation? Worried observers point to family disintegration as a decline in parental influence. They point to decreasing Scholastic Aptitude Test (SAT) scores and simplification of textbooks as evidence of declining influence in the schools. They accept concerns voiced by several religious denominations as proof of decline in church influence. Then they turn to peer groups and the media.

Some scholars believe that peer group influence and media influence are interrelated. One theory holds that members of a group tend to speak alike, dress alike, behave alike, and so on. These commonalities, goes the theory, directly reflect the general influence of the mass media. Another theory asserts that each of us looks to an opinion leader for guidance on a given matter. Which person represents that leader will likely vary according to the nature of the matter, but this theory contends that leaders will be people most exposed to the media. Thus they become what Winston Kirby calls media "carriers," conveying their interpretations of the original messages to the opinion followers.

The programmer's reponsibility is great, because such a long communications chain offers the possibility of misperception and/or misinterpretation in each of its links. Unless carefully created, the message ultimately received may not be the message the programmer intended.

This writer remembers a story from his own school days concerning the Russian government's perception of the 1940 movie version of John Steinbeck's *The Grapes of Wrath*. The plot follows some terribly poor people as they try to escape from the Oklahoma Dust Bowl and make their way to California in a decrepit automobile. The Russians began to show it to their peasants as proof of how poor Americans are under the capitalistic system. They hastily withdrew the film, though, when they discovered that many viewers perceived it differently: no matter how poor you are in America, you can own a car. Even if this story is apocryphal, it illustrates the point.

Next, let's add the idea of subliminal communication, in which the communicator may unknowingly convey something or the receiver may unknowingly perceive something. The possibility that media content provides many subliminal perceptions may cause problems, some fear. Such perceptions can become an important part of our thinking and value patterns, thus affecting our behavior. But, because we do not consciously receive, evaluate, and then accept them, they can make negative as well as positive contributions to our behavior.

Let's summarize where we are up to this point. A society and its quality of life are good when its members share common values and implement those values. Each of us usually behaves according to our values, many of which we learn or acquire from second-hand sources. Although we *knowingly* learn some things and thus are able to accept or reject them, we also *unknowingly* learn other things, which makes their evaluation much more difficult. Some believe that we learn most from television. Therefore, what television offers us is of utmost importance to us as individuals and to society in general.

This leads to the fundamental question of whether some kinds of programs help us to learn the wrong kinds of values. At the same time, by the absence of other kinds of programs, does television inhibit our learning other, worthwhile values? Will a constant barrage of shoot-em-up action shows, for example, subtly teach us to accept violence and death as acceptable problem-solving techniques?

The best way to accommodate these questions and a few others is to take a closer look at specific program types and the charges leveled at them. Let's begin with the entertainment shows.

ENTERTAINMENT PROGRAMMING

Entertainment programs exist because they create large audiences, and American mass media entrepreneurs are excited by big numbers. Once a hardcover book reaches the 100,000 mark, for example, it's on its way to becoming a best seller. A popular paperback will sell 1,000,000 or more copies. Our largest newspaper enjoys a circulation of about 2,000,000. In the magazine field, *TV Guide* crowds the 20,000,000 mark, as does *Reader's Digest*. A blockbuster movie will draw 10,000,000 to the box office.

Regarding television, there are nearly 82,000,000 American homes with one or more sets. Often, more than one viewer is in front of the set in each home at a given time. If the typical viewer watches about four hours a day, the result is a great deal of viewing by a great number of individuals. And for that reason, a prime-time TV program that can boast only 20,000,000 viewers may be headed for cancellation. Cynics refer to the numbers competition in television as The Ratings Game.

Ratings

Even a short visit with a few bibliographical sources will produce a very long list of quotations which add up to this thought: most TV programs are created not with concern about quality and value, but with all-consuming concern for their appeal to the greatest number of people. It's not surprising to discover that newspaper and magazine TV critics share this view. Terrence O'Flaherty of the *San Francisco Chronicle* is one who puts it succinctly: "Television doesn't care about the quality of their shows, only ratings." But then, he also wonders, "Why are we [critics] advising those people how to run their business? They are multi-millionaires. Television is a huge success. The people love it and don't want to change it."[19]

It *is* surprising, though, to hear a broadcaster take the same view. Voluble Ted Turner, well-known for his Atlanta superstation, Channel 17, and his Cable News Network, is vehement: "I'm not a broadcaster....I don't even want to be classed with them. I *was* a broadcaster, and I'm ashamed of what I did. A broadcaster just puts on the shows. He doesn't care what the show is as long as it's cheap and it gets the highest rating so he can get the highest dollar."[20]

To reach for the "highest dollar" means to maximize profits—a goal that will not always serve the public interest. Even so, we cannot conclude that "profit " is a dirty word. Some of our people must always be able to earn a profit. Taxes on those profits help finance a number of benefits that we, as individuals, can't pay for ourselves—e.g., higher education.

Despite that fact, goes the complaint, most programs appeal to the lowest common denominator of intelligence. The inevitable results include a low-level and banal sameness in the programs. Moreover, there are so many of them that they leave little room for "good" programs. If there are few or no good programs, it follows that program content which enriches us culturally and teaches us good taste is stranded in limbo. Let's examine some of these charges.

Sameness? There's bound to be! One reason is that programs are intended to attract viewers and please them, not to offend and drive them away. Past attempts to be more "real" and more "relevant" have usually met with audience rejection.

Another reason is that the costs of programming are enormous. Few entrepreneurs in any field are willing to risk large sums of money unless their crystal ball predicts acceptable odds for success. Barry Cole tells us: "By 1980 the three networks together were spending $3.5 billion for their programming, about 5000 hours for each network. The cost of prime-time evening programming alone jumped forty per cent between 1978 and 1980, to a combined cost of $40 million each week." Then he adds: "CBS president Gene Jankowski told the press in early 1980 that a single one-hour pilot film cost CBS $1 million. For the fall of 1980, the networks financed approximately one hundred pilot shows of which only twenty to twenty-five were expected to become series. Historically, no more than one in every four new series is renewed by the networks for a second year."[21]

Fortunately, an extremely popular series can help recoup the losses suffered by a failure. No wonder, then, that programmers search for another "M*A*S*H" instead of another "East Side, West Side." (Despite George C. Scott and well-scripted, "relevant" stories, the latter failed.) And no wonder that competing programmers constantly look over each others' shoulders. If one of them comes up with a hit, the others try to come up with something similar.

Within any one genre of program—say, action-adventure—the sameness will be greater yet. Remember that television consumes material at a monstrous rate. If, as someone has suggested, there are only about 15 basic plots, there are only so many variations that can give even the appearance of being different.

Indeed, two professors of telecommunications offer the idea that the very fact of standardized plots and stock characters gives a feeling of familiarity with the programs. We can predict, to some extent, how things are going and how they will turn out. "This familiarity becomes a comfort to persons who use television strictly as entertainment," they conclude. What's more, "much of the audience finds change uncomfortable and stability welcome"; and so, "the very sameness of broadcasting is one of its greatest strengths."[22]

Many also lament the "debasement of culture" and the "vulgarization of taste" they perceive in all of this lowest-common-denominator sameness. These phrases usually mean that TV content encourages us to accept "art" that is at worst lowbrow and at best commonplace because there is no room in the program schedule for programs which expose us to higher forms of art.

A humanities professor carried the debate one step further, asserting that TV "has not only failed to transfer other arts into its form, but...has almost completely failed to find any expressive art form which is peculiarly its own."[23]

That criticism may be unfair, because no medium can do more than what it is capable of doing. It's a fact that TV has stimulated a new awareness of and interest in ballet, but a two-dimensional screen cannot reproduce the excitement of the three-dimensional tableau, the pit orchestra, or the contagious crowd psychology for those who are actually *there*. Similarly, a TV camera can be installed so that it takes in the entire stage during a Broadway production of, say, *Hamlet*. Any critique of the product, though, should be of the stage play, not of the TV reproduction: what we see on the tube is only an example of TV as a recording device.

Nonetheless, there are, in fact, many cultural programs on TV, and most of us applaud that fact. But we don't watch them. We seem to say, "There ought to be more good programs—not for me, but for you clods who need them."

And so, cultural taste remains a subjective thing. Agreed, say the critics, but subjectivity can only explain, not excuse, our lack of motivation and/or ability to appreciate the finer things. "Anyone is free to enjoy any art form he chooses, for personal enjoyment is one legitimate standard for aesthetic judgements; but this rationale puts grandma's delight in the Sunday School Christmas pageant into the same bag with George Bernard Shaw's delight in *Das Rheingold;* that is, they both 'liked the show.'"[24]

Furthermore, TV helps shape our taste by telling us how to respond emotionally. Canned laughter is a good example. Dr. John Phelan explains it this way: "Great literature makes assumptions about its receivers that are flattering; they are presumed curious, eager to get out of themselves, ready for growth, critical, yet open; in short, ready for the truth of life and the truth of the imagination. What does canned laughter reveal about producers' assumptions regarding their audience? What must they think we are like? Are they right?"[25]

If canned laughter reduces our ability to discriminate between the good and the bad, the writer's incentive for maximum creativity is reduced. Andrew Siegel, vice president in charge of comedy development for MTM Enterprises, asserts that "they put on the laugh machine and blow everybody away. And because they know they're gonna *sound* funny, they don't have to write as well. And that is genuinely destructive to the creative process."

Some find it convenient to combine all these charges—lack of creativity, debasement of culture, vulgarization of taste, and the rest of them—under one noun, *banality*. Especially in entertainment programming, the content is thought trivial, trite, commonplace, hackneyed, and mindless, calling for emotional reaction rather than intellectual response. Banality bothers some more than does the sex-and-violence question. "To me, violence isn't the issue, nor is sex. Both have been present in what all of us recognize as some of the finest drama our culture has produced....What *is* the issue is mindlessness: violence or sex for its own sake; vapid material; television to do chores by."[26]

The Ratings Game, in short, results in sameness, in blandness, in giving us more of what we demand. The chief reason is, as two knowledgeable observers put it: "This national medium is, at bottom, not a way to purvey news and public affairs to the viewers, not a way to entertain millions of Americans with comedy, drama, and music, not a way to educate and inform— but the most profitable method ever devised by man to deliver huge audiences to advertisers, who then deliver their commercial messages."[27]

If all of this is true, and if it is bad, then that fact says something negative about us viewers. The programmers will gladly offer us all the good programming we want. Not what we *say* we want, but what we will actually tune in to watch. We need to develop the courage to sample some programs of higher quality than we think we want. But we can't let too much more time slip away, because many of us already have proved George Bernard Shaw's oft-quoted admonition: "Get what you want, or you will soon get to like what you are given."

False Pictures of Reality

Apart from the contribution that TV programming does or does not make to our cultural growth, what relationship exists between TV's content and reality? Does it bring closer together, or does it push farther apart, "the world outside and the pictures in our heads"? In his *Public Opinion,* Walter Lippmann noted that distinction and added, "Man is a creature of evolution who can just about span a sufficient portion of reality to manage his survival."

A key point here is that each of us lives in a world that exists as a series of "pictures in our heads." Reality is that which each of us creates it to be by perceiving what's out there, then assembling those perceptions into a cognitive structure with which we can cope. And few of us will create reality in precisely the same way, partly because a variety of psychological and demographic factors will influence how we perceive a given thing at a given time. The example often cited is that in which several people witness an automobile accident, but their accounts of what happened vary widely.

Another key point, as mentioned earlier, is that none of us knows very much through direct experience. Most of what we know and consider to be reality comes to us second-hand—and most of that through the media, especially television. In what ways, and to what extent, does TV then become a "window" that lets us look out upon the real world? TV's defenders assert that it *is* such a window. Or sometimes they liken it to a mirror which reflects the society that created TV and now nurtures it. TV's detractors, conversely, contend that it is a window which looks out upon a reality of its own creation. Or, if you like the mirror analogy, TV reflects reality like those grossly distorted mirrors we used to see in circuses and fun houses.

Whichever view we accept, a problem still remains for many of us. All these second-hand stimuli reach us and we must assemble them in a meaningful way. But new technology, new knowledge, and new crises continually create *so much new* reality! Many of us lack the education, experience, or some other things necessary to perceive and assemble all these ingredients correctly. Thus, we become overwhelmed and need "to get away from it all" now and then. And so, although some of us may deliberately look to entertainment programming for help in organizing our constructs, many of us use the tube as an escape from reality.

Perhaps, comes the rejoinder, but "now and then" means three to four hours a day for the typical viewer. Anyway, even escapists will perceive stimuli which they must assemble into something meaningful; otherwise, they'll tune out. Because TV entertainment programs contain a limited number of themes and implied values which are repeated and restated over and over, they tend to reinforce themselves. And because these same themes and values are reinforced by the other mass media as well, they inevitably must become a part of us—a part of our learning. So, then, what do we learn? The charges are endless, but here are a few.

We learn to be mistrustful and fearful. A number of studies draw that conclusion. According to one of them, heavy TV viewers "tend to feel pessimistic about the future. Compared to average and light viewers they are more likely to fear going out at night, and to acquire guns, locks, and dogs for purpose of protection."[28]

Stereotypes

Another thing we learn from television's break with reality is that which comes from the creation or reinforcement of stereotypes. For purposes here, let us define *stereotype* as an overgeneralized belief, attitude, concept, or "feeling" which results from our accepting stimuli that have by-passed the analytical thinking process. This is not to say that all stereotypical communication is bad. Indeed, in some instances video and audio conventions are useful in that they can provide us with instantaneous—i.e., cliché-like—understanding of what might otherwise require a labored explanation. Or, as T.W. Adorno puts it, some "stereotypes are an indispensable element of the organization and anticipation of experience, preventing us from falling into mental disorganization."

But a good many of the stereotypes we find on television are misleading at best and potentially injurious at worst—precisely because they promote an overgeneralized picture of reality. As a result, several dissatisfied groups have complained about their images as presented on (or missing from) television. The complaints typically concern ethnic groups, sex roles, age, and more recently, occupations.

Among the first of television's ethnic stereotypes was that of our Black citizens, a habit inherited from movies and radio. The roles that Blacks played in situation comedies and an occasional drama usually portrayed them unfavorably. One of the most popular radio shows was *Amos 'n' Andy,* played by two white men. The transfer to TV, using Black talent, failed to change the image. In 1951, the National Association for the Advancement of Colored People asked that the show be taken off the air. Among the several reasons was that the series "tends to strengthen the conclusion among uninformed and prejudiced people that Negroes are inferior, lazy, dumb and dishonest."[29]

Some research shows that, although the proportion of Blacks to whites appearing on TV approximates their proportion in society, most of the Blacks we see are females under the age of 20. There are almost no elderly Black people to be seen. More: "a disproportionate number of black characters are confined to a handful of shows which strongly emphasize black family and black neighborhood situations."[30] Some fear that the kinds of people thus portrayed, as well as the environments in which they live, place them outside the Black experience.

Italians, too, have come in for their share of stereotyping. An early example of the most common stereotype arose in *The Untouchables,* a violent series dealing with organized crime in the 1920s. A great many of the criminal characters were given Italian names. That fact, added to the fact of large audiences for the program, prompted Italian-Americans to complain about the "gangster image" being perpetuated.

Other studies point to the virtual absence of TV characters who are of Hispanic origin. Even though these people represent our fastest growing minority, they seldom appear in "normal" roles. The mass media have offended a number of them enough to prompt the formation of the Mexican-American Anti-Defamation Committee. The committee's goal is to eliminate the Mexican stereotypes created by "the Anglo"—especially those which portray the typical Mexican as a bandit or as very sleepy.

The American Indian hasn't fared very well, either, according to one researcher who recalls these images: "the Noble Red Man, the Savage Warrior, and the Faithful Companion Tonto." Among those who took offense were members of the Oklahoma Legislature who passed a "strongly-worded resolution denouncing the television industry for Indian stereotypes."[31]

Asian-Americans typically share the same fate. As is true of the ethnic groups mentioned above, much of what we see on TV is the replay of old Hollywood movies. Asian males are usually gardeners or house servants, or conversely, cunning villains like Fu Manchu. Of course, there was also the superdetective, Charlie Chan, who exhibited the calm, inscrutable visage of the Orient. Asian women are stereotyped as either obedient, docile creatures or sensual dragon-lady types.

Much criticism has arisen concerning the stereotyped portrayal of females, whatever their nationalities. The majority of the complaints can be summarized: women are too often shown as sex objects or otherwise depicted as inferior to males. When not playing demeaning roles, they are assigned to the traditional sex roles of secretary, nurse, manicurist, all-knowing mother, and the like.

Interestingly, though, Ted Turner takes an unusual counterposition. Addressing a Veterans of Foreign Wars convention in Philadelphia in mid-August of 1981, according to UPI, he described television as being anti-motherhood. "They are trying to make women dissatisfied because the most difficult job in the world is being a mother," is the way UPI quoted him.

Nonetheless, many believe that women do not share proportionately in the meaningful roles—those which show women achieving and influencing as so many of them do in real life. One report summarized it this way:

> Women and girls have always been underrepresented in commercial television drama. Research dating back to the early 1950s documents that female characters

> have consistently constituted between 25 and 30 percent of all characters. While a recent spate of new shows featuring young women suggests that the proportion of women on television may be increasing, the ways in which many of them are depicted suggest that women, like minorities, are sometimes abused by television. "Girls" in highly revealing costumes are often seen in "jiggly" shows. Furthermore, there is evidence that the frequency of this type of portrayal...is increasing.[32]

If some believe that women receive too few "good" roles, the problem multiplies for elderly people of both sexes. To see and understand the aging process, with all its positives and negatives, is an important experience for those who do not yet understand or reconcile themselves to it. One perceptive observer worried:

> When I think of our children's ignorance concerning the aged, I wonder how cruel the treatment of the elderly will be in another twenty years. We think the Eskimos are barbarians because they set grandmother out on the ice when she is too old to work, and we pride ourselves on our refinement in sending her to an old ladies' home. What will our next generation do with grandmother?[33]

Various vocations and professions come under fire as well. Politicians, for example, are frequently portrayed as incompetent or dishonest. Law enforcement? Many action-adventure programs show them as honest and dedicated. Many others, though, perpetuate the image of the Southern-sheriff type, while others suggest that legally constituted authorities are well-meaning obstructionists the private eye must work around in order to get the case solved properly.

As for businessmen, *Time* concluded, "Television may do for businessmen what a Borgia banquet did for casual dining." Earlier, *The Wall Street Journal* asked, "Should that ruthless snake in the grass J.R. Ewing [of 'Dallas'] be named Businessman of the Year?" These and other comments arose from a study called "Crooks, Conmen and Clowns: Businessmen in TV Entertainment."[34]

Surveying 200 prime-time entertainment programs during the 1979–1980 season, the researchers perceived that "two out of three TV businessmen are portrayed as foolish, greedy or evil." They also found that more than half of corporate chiefs are portrayed as committing illegal acts which range from fraud to murder. Conversely, only 3 percent of the businessmen are portrayed as doing something socially useful or economically productive.

Blue collar workers, too, come in for their share of the tarnished image. If we judge by the number of times they appear, union members are less important than crooks, prostitutes, singers, police officers, waitresses, truck drivers, and TV camera operators. An Associated Press report of July 6, 1981, said surveys of TV programs show union members to be "clumsy, violent, uneducated louts who drink, smoke and obstruct commerce," when they *do* show up in a program. A practical consequence of this, say union officials, is that there is an increasing shortage of skilled blue collar craftsmen, and TV's image of them offers no enticement to bring young people into these crafts.

Although we could continue in this vein, our discussion so far provides a basis for understanding the broad range of stereotypes and their contributions to the distortion of reality. Some programs provide false images by dealing in caricatures instead of "real people," while others imply unimportance by ignoring some people altogether. An alleged consequence of these is that some young people have no positive role models to follow, while others may accept those negative images as role models.

And as regards the distortion of reality generally, a number of TV script writers have complained now and then about having to write to a formula rather than to the needs of art. David Rintels, a former officer of the Writers Guild of America, once stated that there were about 3,000 writers who created network scripts for comedies, drama, and variety programs. Of these, some 81 percent believed that those programs offered "a distorted picture of U.S. politics, economy and racial situation." He added that most of the programs we see are "deliberately designed to have no resemblance at all to reality."[35]

However true that may be, the charge ignores the purpose for which most of us watch story-telling programs: entertainment. The typical story involves conflict—a problem which the person who has it tries to solve. Plot complications delay the solution and increase the suspense. Whatever it is we get out of these stories results from our empathy for the protagonist. Doing so may let us escape our own problems for a short time, or, at least, make them seem less burdensome by comparison.

Moreover, because TV is a motion medium, it tries to explore conflicts which are visual rather than cerebral. Perhaps daytime soap opera fans will accept limited sets and characters who mostly sit around and talk, interrupting themselves now and then with alternating smiles and grimaces. Prime-time audiences, however, will not. And so, prime-time plots emphasize conflicts which require the protagonist, in grand settings, to run, fight, crash a car, fall off a horse, or undertake some equally visual behavior.

Most of our own problems are not like that, and so we are not like those characters. That's one reason we can lose ourselves in their exciting and unusual problems. Dr. Greenberg's research team study, cited above, agrees that fictional characters on TV don't correspond to real people, but contends that they don't need to. Fictional characters are chosen because they are more peculiar than they are regular; they "are identified because they stand out rather than because they are normative."

That reasoning may explain prime-time schedules; but, according to the critics, it doesn't justify them. Negative consequences are no less negative simply because of an interesting explanation. The fact remains that a steady diet of abnormal people doing abnormal things to solve abnormal conficts leads us into a counterproductive never-never land. A good many of our most important problems *are in fact* cerebral; they *must* be solved by rational analysis and not irrational or violent behavior. They cannot be solved within the alloted 30- or 60-minute time frame, and they will not be followed by a commercial which tells us all will be right with the world if only we will use Gurtzon's Goo immediately upon rising. Or, as former FCC Commissioner Nicholas Johnson admonished in *How to Talk Back to Your Television Set,* "[T]elevision's salesmen cannot have it both ways. They cannot point with pride to the power of their medium to affect the attitudes and behavior associated with product selection and consumption, and then take the position that everything else on television has no impact whatsoever upon attitudes and behavior."

Sex and Violence

Much of the fear concerning attitudes and behavior is that they will coincide more and more with the "lessons" learned from so much sex and violence on the tube. The specific charges are numerous, but they add up to the belief that this programming contributes to a general breakdown in what we like to think of as appropriate morality. Kathy Nolan, when she was president of the Screen Actors Guild, offered this summary: The network chiefs have "trashed up the airwaves almost beyond repair. It's a subhuman situation."

One of the specific charges is that many of these programs portray women in a way that's degrading and disrespectful at worst or that minimizes their importance at best. Although we considered some of this in our discussion of stereotypes, we need to cover a few more points here—briefly, because so much easily accessible literature already exists.

Too often, women are portrayed as physical or psychological "tools" of the male characters. Males are macho; females are submissive. And so, a male character can "use" a woman—either literally or figuratively in the sense that she must be supportive of his goals. Much less often will she be a dominant character whose own goals constitute the major plot ingredient in a program of dramatic quality.

The so-called jiggle shows are among those which seem to provide not a gripping story or a stage for the females' acting abilities, but rather a legal means of male voyeurism. She may be a waitress, a private investigator, or a scantily clad hillbilly, but rarely will the depth and significance of her character distract us from the jiggle.

An offshoot of that concern lies in the charge that too many programs "teach" the idea that chastity is no longer important and that promiscuity is an acceptable way of life. That bothers those who believe that television effectively transmits values, including sexual values.

The pinnacle of that mountain, apparently, lies in the daytime soap operas. Studies reported in the Summer, 1981, issue of *Journal of Communication* support that contention. For example, "Daytime Serial Drama: The Continuing Story," draws several interesting conclusions. One of them is that there is more sex depicted in soaps than in prime-time drama. In the soaps, more hanky-panky takes place between unmarried than married characters. And when married characters even talk about sex, they usually discuss the goings-on of unmarried characters. And so, those who are unworldly—especially the young—might easily conclude that married couples don't indulge in sex, whereas unmarried couples rarely take time out for anything else.

By 1981, though, several groups were making headway in their efforts to minimize bawdy programming. An advertising executive foresaw less sex but more cops and robbers. But a less sex and more violence prophecy supports Les Brown's belief. "They alternate; like sides of a coin, when one is down (suppressed), the other is up."

Clearly, which side of the coin is up will vary from season to season. But the point to be made is that TV takes the romance out of man-woman relationships. Women are simply objects for whom the male need feel no emotion or accept no responsibility. The next step—and only a modest step, some fear—is rape.

Many believe rape to be an act of violent aggression rather than a sexual act. Whichever, it suggests another concern which overlaps both sex and violence—that of aggressive imitation: monkey-see-monkey-do. Examples abound with regularity in the print media. In a 1981 UPI item, the National Coalition on Television Violence announced that 16 people died when they lost at Russian roulette, apparently imitating a scene from *Deer Hunter*, which had been shown earlier on TV. Another time, two teenagers saw a TV program which gave them the idea to rob a grocery store and shoot the owner. They even tried to wear clothes like those of their TV counterparts. Still another time, two young men ambushed a Greyhound bus—prompted by a stagecoach hold-up they saw on *Gunsmoke*.

Not only do such programs motivate people, comes the charge, but many of them show *how* to commit a variety of crimes. One program may show a detailed close-up of how to hot-wire a car; another may explain how to jimmy a door latch or deactivate a security system.

Even those who are not propelled into antisocial behavior can suffer from overexposure by adapting to a new level of tolerance. Those thoughts and deeds which used to sadden or outrage us no longer do so. After we've seen enough people violently destroyed in fiction programs, a real-life slaying on the evening news hardly raises an eyebrow.

Some explain these things as inevitable as our society evolves into a new, 20th century morality. Wrong, argue others; we are simply losing our ability to feel what we ought to feel when confronted by the grim and genuine problems of society.

Television's defenders, both within and without the industry, have an interesting point to make. Certain programs can and do trigger some people into negative behavior, but various studies strongly suggest that these people are unstable to begin with. Only the most courageous programmer can reject a show that millions want to see simply because it might trigger a few others.

Another key problem is the matter of perception: we don't know what a person will read into an event. Some attention-getting examples are offered by Stephen F. Rohde.[36] A man named Heinrich Pommerenke went to see Cecil B. De Mille's *The Ten Commandments*. A scene in which some women dance around a golden calf convinced him that women create all the world's troubles. He left the theatre and slew his first victim, then went on to become infamous as a rapist and mass slayer of women.

Still another argument contends that TV is blamed for things of which it is not guilty. For example, says a child psychologist, the children of extremely poor people sometimes drift into crime. "The fault, we are told, lies with television. Too much violence on the home screen, say the judges and teachers."[37] But "TV is not the villain in these wretched families. Often it is the only pleasure, the only window on the world of ideas, of love and compassion. Much of television is violent and stupid, yes. But there are glimpses of grace and beauty. There are stories that make a firm moral point." Then she concludes, "It is easier to blame television."

Another child psychologist agrees, reminding us that "*millions* of our children *under thirteen* spend hours at home with no adult present."[38] Teachers continually tell him of the painful stories they hear from students about broken homes, drug and alcohol abuse, and the like. He contends that, for the already hurt and bewildered children he knows, "the television screen, with its banalities and flights of preposterous or mean-spirited fancy, ends up being one of the more reassuring elements...something there, and relatively reliable, lively, giving."

The unfortunate fact is that, despite all our knowledge, we know very little about the human mind—at any age—or how it works. The researchers continue their studies, but they often argue among themselves as to whether this or that methodology provides data of greater validity, or whether we sometimes try to make mountainous inferences from molehills of data.

In the end, however, those who fear so much sex and violence on TV seem to be in the more logical position to savor the final word. That word lurks in the question, where do the odds lie? That is, what is *likely* to be true? So, imagine that you are tempted to take a shortcut across someone's lawn. Out there in the middle stands a very large Doberman pinscher. Seeing you, he takes a step in your direction, bares his fangs, and makes a noise like an Army tank in low gear. Now, you don't know that he will bite you, but you don't know that he will *not*. What decision will you make? Why?

And there we'll let the matter rest.

NEWS AND INFORMATION

Television has become the dominant source of news for a majority of all Americans. Dr. Cole reminds us: "In the spring of 1980, 56.3 million people watched one or more of the three network evening newscasts every weekday, and the Public Broadcasting System's *MacNeil/Lehrer Report* had an audience of four million people." Even after some print and broadcast hoaxes in 1981, a Gallup poll found that 71 percent of the respondents believe network TV is best for accurate, unbiased news; 69 percent favor local TV.

This fact clearly endows our broadcast journalists and their decision-making superiors with several important responsibilities. As we might expect, though, there are a good many critics who believe that these responsibilities are not being accepted and fulfilled—either nationally or locally—with proper concern for the viewer's needs.

Most of the complaints fall into the two large categories of content and techniques/practices. Content refers to the gatekeeping or editorial selection of what is included and what is excluded from the newscast. Technique/practice refers to how they handle that which is included. Of course, there are numerous subcategories under each of these. We will consider a few of the most important.

Many of the complaints in both categories can be summarized as resulting from the fact that TV stations and networks compete as hard for news audiences as for other kinds of audiences. Therefore, comes the charge, TV news is more representative of show business than it is of solid journalism. Thus, a good many of the stories will be what the news bosses think we want to watch rather than what we really need to know.

An important word there is "watch." The bosses believe that people tune in to *see* something interesting, and so a story has a better chance of making the newscast if there are some good visuals to accompany the anchorperson's audio. This prompts the news assignment editor to look for predictable events—those that will permit a camera team to get to the location in time. Or, perhaps, there's some usable footage in the video morgue that can somehow be tied to the day's events. In either instance, critics complain, something other than high standards of journalism makes the selection. That something is appeal.

A communications researcher says: "States of mind are not photogenic. In translating them into visual terms, the image takes over from the cerebral and what was construed as illustration becomes the essence of coverage."[39] For example, if what we have is footage on the presidential motorcade, that becomes the story rather than the important issues of the election campaign.

Conversely, there is some evidence that the visuals can be important to some. One study finds that "people remember more facts delivered in TV news audio when those facts are accompanied by interesting video rather than by a shot of a talking head, even when the interesting video does not convey those facts." The researchers conclude: "Television news staffs can take comfort from the fact that...the exciting video for which TV news departments strive makes TV news more useful to the groups [less educated and lower-income viewers] that depend on it most."[40]

In some instances, of course, carefully written audio and interesting video which complement each other will lead to better understanding and remembering of the facts. But what makes for interesting video is not always what is most important. It may be interesting to see the mayor snip the ribbon in front of the new city building. But what does that pseudoevent or others like it really contribute?

Other consequences arise from the news-as-show-biz approach. One takes place mostly at the local level when falling ratings prompt the general manager to call in a news consultant to explain what's wrong and what to do about it. Although these consultants can point to quite a few satisfied clients, experienced journalists are likely to frown at what they believe to be essentially cosmetic changes. The new look is likely to feature young and photogenic on-camera people who may or may not be trained journalists. But they are pleasant, and they intersperse varying amounts of "happy talk" between the news items. The opinion is that this will be more appealing than another news item.

Another concern is a rather standardized appearance of most TV newscasts, whether local or network. News is prepared to be molded into a fairly rigid format, and the formats resemble each other. The people are different and the news sets are different, but the packaged products offer a glib and slick sameness.

Implicit in the show business packaging complaint is that many news items are trivial. A corollary complaint is that this same kind of packaging, along with the time constraints, makes the treatment of even important news superficial. A political science professor explains: "Life is ragged, fiction is neat. Television news tends to wrap up each story, to try to march it from the beginning through middle to end—in 90 seconds." This, he says, "requires radical editing" that eliminates "rough edges of information" so that the story can convey "an impression of patness, a finished quality."[41]

The result is that TV news becomes a headline service that makes us aware of something, but does not always help us to understand it. A former NBC newsman, Robert Goralski, is quoted as saying that TV news "has profound impact on the average American, but it tends to impress more than it informs."[42]

A good share of the problem may be that we don't differentiate correctly between what is topical and what is relevant. Daniel Boorstin made this point a decade ago. "*Topical* (from the Greek word 'topos' for place) means that which is special to some particular place or time."[43] And so, an airplane high-jacking, a hotel fire, or an earthquake is appropriate for a "Topics of the Day" program. They are special to this day and they become part of the news. But their importance (if any) to the larger picture is seldom explained. In any case, the event soon disappears as other topical events replace it.

"'Relevant' comes from the Latin 'relevans,' which means lifting or raising. To show the relevance of something is to lift it above the current of daily topics, to connect it with distant events and larger issues." And, Boorstin says, these relevant connections "will be just as valid—and even more interesting—tomorrow and the day after."[44]

What all of this adds up to is the notion that TV news should educate us. If many of us get most of our news from TV, and if many of us get *all* of our news from TV, that news should help us to understand the background and meaning of issues that affect our lives. It is not sufficient to learn that nuclear power can be hazardous. We must be able to weigh the pro's and con's of each energy-producing method. Then, when one of our elected officials makes a statement, plans a course of action, or votes on a bill, we can respond with reason rather than a knee-jerk reaction.

Nobody argues with that thinking, reply the defenders, but it ignores the uses and gratifications people get from television viewing. The typical viewer, home from a day that was physically or mentally tiring or both, doesn't tune in to be educated. Otherwise, our thoughtful documentaries would enjoy larger audiences. For example, Don Hewitt, producer of *60 Minutes,* tells us that CBS offered six documentaries in prime time in 1978. Five finished last in the weekly ratings; the other finished next to last. The audience should "put its dials where its mouth is."

We must let that argument continue elsewhere and move on to another allegation—that much of our news and information is biased or downright inaccurate. It's not surprising that some news and a good many news documentaries produce such charges from time to time. A news documentary usually occurs because the person in charge feels a need to investigate something or someone. What he/she discovers, then presents in the documentary, is often unfavorable, because there is little news value in a piece that simply describes and then meekly concludes that everything is all right. But whenever a program places a person, place, institution, or pet philosophy in an unfavorable light, an army of defenders is likely to shout "Foul!" A key question is whether the piece in fact is distorted in any way. If the answer is yes, then the follow-up question is whether the distortion is deliberate or accidental.

Bias, or unfairness, typically results when the producer includes video and audio which support the point the piece is trying to make, but excludes equally important material which weakens or refutes that point. Bias can also occur more subtly through the newsperson's delivery style: a frown, raised eyebrow, or vocal inflection can color the meaning of what the words alone seem to convey.

Inaccuracy, of course, occurs when the piece presents "facts" or creates impressions which are not true. And some have charged TV with being more interested in news values than in truth. Again, this can be a matter of content, in that the material presented simply is not true. It can also be a matter of production techniques, in that the formal nature of television permits it to abstract reality in such a way that the production emerges with an unreal result. One of the classic examples of this occurred when Chicago staged a celebration to welcome General MacArthur after his dismissal by President Truman.[45]

On occasion, some suspect, a newsperson has asked someone involved in an event—say, a demonstrator—to perform some act that the demonstrator may not have considered. If this happens, it is not usually that the newsperson wants to deceive—only to provide a little livelier video or perhaps heighten the element of conflict. Print journalist Henry J. Taylor is one who deplores this conflict notion. "Crisis is the name of the TV game," he laments. "But why is every problem a crisis?" Because "many [TV news people] feel that if they haven't a crisis to lean on, they're dead. If TV can't find a crisis, it invents one."[46]

That statement, of course, is a bit harsh and may suggest that print journalists, too, are given to hyperbole and a degree of bias. The point he makes, however, worries a number of people.

In any case, staging, whether by newspeople or by others, constitutes one of several methods of news manipulation. Another common method is to plant a news item which in reality is favorable propaganda for a vested interest. Sources of this kind of manipulation include foreign governments, our own government, various industries, and representatives of various causes.

What makes this bad, say the critics, is that the newspeople don't inform us of the fact that these items are hand-outs. There is no disclaimer which warns us that this so-called news may be designed simply to engineer our consent to some action or some way of thinking. Thus, because "seeing is believing," we tend to accept the information as truthful.

Truth, relevance, and depth are important to us viewers, partly because of the extent to which we lean on TV news for what we know of the world, and partly because TV serves what Maxwell McCombs calls the agenda-setting function of the press. This means that by covering some events and issues, while excluding others, the newscasters tacitly tell us what is important for us to think about. And the way they cover any given story may also tell us how we should feel about it.

The agenda-setting function can exert great influence on events as well as on viewers. Barry Cole reminds us that "coverage of the civil rights movement hastened passage of the Civil Rights Act of 1964 and the Voting Rights Act of 1968. The United States' withdrawal from Vietnam was influenced by television coverage which eroded public support for the conflict. Television publicity of the Watergate scandal helped precipitate President Nixon's resignation and the subsequent passage of new legislation." Then he adds that "suffering caused by the famine in Cambodia in 1979 was televised and relief efforts were promptly mobilized."[47]

With that kind of influence, everybody in TV news shares an awesome responsibility to be certain that the news and information Americans receive are as clear and accurate as is humanly possible and to avoid any possible deception. Walter Lippmann's words come to mind when, in *The Public Philosophy,* he says, "There is no more right to deceive than there is a right to swindle, to cheat, or to pick pockets."

As ominous as these criticisms and warnings sound, however, we can take great pride in the fact that the greatest majority of our TV newspeople are intelligent and dedicated journalists. And yes, TV news is part of a profit-making industry; but despite that fact, television executives invest hundreds of millions of dollars to bring us the best product they are capable of providing. And overall, along with the brickbats, they deserve a number of bouquets.

ADVERTISING

As we said regarding radio advertising, the commercial uses of the electronic media fall outside the scope of *program* criticism. And so, the following summary must suffice.

In 1980, according to FCC financial data published in the August 10, 1981, issue of *Broadcasting,* more than 2,000 advertisers invested $10.3 billion to buy TV advertising time. In addition, they spent untold millions more to produce the commercials you see during those times. When we consider that each commercial is repeated—some many times—we arrive at an incalculable number of total showings.

It is inevitable that commercials will be subject to a great deal of criticism. First of all, they are obtrusive: the typical viewer can't avoid them unless he/she leaves the room or finds another channel which hasn't yet reached its commercial break. Next, there are some tasteless juxtapositions: a commercial for a luxury product within or adjacent to a program dealing with the very, very poor, for example. Finally, there are so many commercials; not only do they total an incredible number, but they interrupt the program too often. When added to other nonprogram announcements, these commercials contribute to "clutter."

These and similar complaints we can combine under the labels "scheduling" and "salience." Tradtionally, the NAB Television Code prescribed the maximum number of commercials in a row, the maximum amount of time permissible in each daypart, and the maximum number of interruptions each half-hour. At this writing, however, the legality of Code advertising guidelines is being challenged by Department of Justice antitrust actions, and the NAB has suspended enforcement of those guidelines. If Justice wins, we conceivably could end up with an even *more* permissive advertising environment. Even so, to the extent that a program director exerts control over commercial placement, he/she should be aware of these charges and be sensitive to them.

TV AND CHILDREN

Nearly every fear expressed so far in a general way causes even greater concern when applied to television in the lives of our children. Only a few more thoughts need to be offered here in amplification, and they can be loosely summarized in this question: how large a role does TV play in the "teaching" and socialization of children when compared with the role played by parents, school, church, and peers?

Clearly, the extent of children's viewing must involve TV in some kind of role. According to A.C. Nielsen figures from spring, 1981, teenagers watched nearly 24 hours each week, while preschoolers watched nearly 30 hours per week. Even though these figures reflect a decline in viewing from the previous year, the typical young person, by age 18, will have spent more time in front of the tube than with parents, in play with other children, in school, or in church.

This probability prompts several to comment that ours is the first generation to be reared by three parents, and there is considerable fear about the impact of that third parent. The founder of the New York Council on Children's Television believes "that habitual viewing can affect a young person's basic outlook and sensibilities, predisposition to violence and hyperactivity, IQ, reading ability, imagination, play, language patterns, critical thinking, self-image, perception of others, and values in general."[48] She adds, with specifics, that habitual viewing also affects the *physical* self.

Therefore, even "Sesame Street" and other applauded children's programs may contribute to the problem of habitual viewing. Whether or not that's true, youngsters rapidly outgrow those programs and, by age four, many of them have moved on to other programs, taking their TV addiction with them. And if, by age four, "Sesame Street" has effectively taught these children the alphabet and how to count, will the more adult programs teach them other, less desirable things?

A major impediment to answering that question with certainty lies in the nature of existing research. Despite the tremendous amount of research, much of it may have questionable validity. Most experiments must be conducted in the laboratory or under other artificial conditions, because there are few opportunities to apply rigorous research methods to real-world situations. Moreover, for the same and other reasons, most of the research must be conducted over a relatively short period of time, whereas it may be more important to understand long-range consequences.

Another major impediment lies in the fact that children may perceive things differently from adults. The typical adult will perceive, selectively or functionally, only a part of all the stimuli available. Then his/her mind will organize those perceptions into a meaningful whole. The next probable step is for the viewer to make inferences, which, as in the montage theory, lead to understanding or conclusions which are greater than the sum of the perceived parts. Is a youngster able to do that? Even if able, is the typical youngster so motivated?

Obviously, this discussion oversimplifies the problems of perception, cognition, and equally complicated mental operations. But it does offer a glimpse of the problems connected with understanding the relationships between TV and viewers of any age, especially children. [By way of digression, we can mention that the same puzzles exist when we try to relate children to advertising messages aimed at them.]

Because we *don't* know, observers rightfully continue to worry about the teaching and socialization impact of television. Most agree that TV entertainment programs, advertising, and especially cartoons tend to cloud or destroy the boundaries between fact and fiction and between reality and fantasy. An important question arises as to whether children will be damaged by such constant exposure to this confusion before they are able to handle it.

How, for example, can children handle programs that some adults think are too sexy for themselves? Again, we need to know what kind of sex and how it is handled in the presentation. Much of what we place in the category of classic literature contains sexual material, some of it pretty hair-raising! So, we can ask, does anyone *really* become turned on by a sex scene in

"Soap" or when Woody Allen attempts a conquest? Perhaps not, but some say that the very portrayal of adultery contains its own negative lessons for the very young.

Irrespective of that argument, something accounts for the increase in sexual activity among the young, not to mention the problems resulting from that activity. One study reports that sexual activity "among never-married American teen-age women...increased by 30% between 1971 and 1976." Note that people who were teenagers by 1971 were among the first to be reared by television. The researchers also found that by "age 19, more than 55% of these young people have had sexual intercourse," and the 19 age level represents a drop from earlier reports. Moreover, finds the study, there was "an increase in the number of sexual partners and an alarming absence of appropriate birth control measures."[49]

An AP story of June 25, 1981, adds this: "A third of the 3.8 million American women who sought help from family-planning clinics in 1978 were teenagers." Moreover, 44,000 of those were under age 15, with 1.2 million between the ages of 15 and 19. Other stories point to the increase in reported cases of venereal disease, including one new, difficult-to-treat strain.

When a young person reaches the first-hand experience stage, is he/she really prepared to cope? How much of that sexual socialization came from TV, and how much from peers (who are probably TV-educated)? And how much of it came from parents, school, and church? Many are worried about the probable answer.

Now, how about violence? Much of the same logic applies to violence as applies to sexual material. It is difficult to reconcile the violence, say, in *Hamlet* and *Othello* and some other classics with the idea that literary violence is, in itself, damaging.

Stephen King, author of *Carrie, The Shining,* and other stories of suspense, terror, and violence, writes in the June 13, 1981, issue of *TV Guide* that the psychological violence in "Bambi," "Snow White," or the actual violence in "Hansel and Gretel" and even a Dr. Seuss story, can be much scarier than some of the worrisome TV fare.

Carol Mort replied to the King article by writing in the July 4, 1981, issue: "King's article lays it on the line. My son wouldn't eat apples for weeks after watching 'Snow White!' And he's still not convinced camping near a lean-to is safe. But when he watched a man 'explode' in a movie on TV, he said it was just a robot and never said anything else."

The point is that some children can handle sex or violence and some cannot. It depends on the child and the context in which the incident occurs. And, agree TV's defenders, the same probably can be said of anyone of any age who watches almost any program at all.

SUMMARY

Many reasoned "think pieces" and much research data conclude that danger to individuals and society lurks in the listening to and viewing of our electronic media. Although there is a great volume of contradictory data, the fears can be oversimply summarized in three general areas: lifestyle, altered values, and perception of reality.

Not only has our lifestyle changed in the sense that we time our daily habits according to our media desires, but TV, especially, has turned many of us into withdrawn spectators instead of lively doers. At the same time, some allege, we have developed higher tolerances for activities which used to cause outrage—drug use, adultery, mindless violence and killing, for examples. Not the least of the fears is that of our overall view and understanding of the "real world" beyond the tube. Spending so much time with atypical people in unusual situations, some say, can't help but subliminally "teach" us things that interfere with our abilities to cope with everyday life.

Whether or not these charges are true is unknown, because neither the opponents nor the proponents can prove a point. Otherwise, the programmer would face fewer troublesome decisions, and a chapter titled "Program Criticism" could follow a different course. Nonetheless, the astute programmer realizes that, for those who think it's true, it *is* true. And if or as their numbers increase, so do the challenges to the program decision maker.

And so, the wheel has come full circle. In the early pages of this chapter, we stated that our chief purpose was not to tell you *what* to believe, but only to convince you of the need to believe something. If it has succeeded in this purpose, then you have the foundation upon which to build a value system. And it will be this value system, when consistently followed, that will help you as a programmer to create program schedules that are appealing, pragmatic, professional, and much less vulnerable to attack in the future.

There are some other important considerations about broadcast programming in the future, too. You'll discover these as you move into the next chapter.

ENDNOTES

1. Miller v. California, 413 U.S. 15 (1973).
2. "Buttoned-Up Sequel to Topless Radio," *Broadcasting,* March 18, 1974, p. 76.
3. For a clear account, see F. Leslie Smith, "The Charlie Walker Case," *Journal of Broadcasting* (Spring 1979), *23,* 137.
4. FCC v. Pacifica Foundation, 438 U.S. 726 (1978). See also Susan Wing, "Morality and Broadcasting: FCC Control of 'Indecent' Material Following *Pacifica," Federal Communications Law Journal* (Winter 1978), *31,* 145.
5. Theodore L. Glasser and Harvey Jassem, "Indecent Broadcasts and the Listener's Right of Privacy," *Journal of Broadcasting,* (Summer 1980), *24,* 286.
6. Cited in Leona R. Busselmaier, "Television Violence: What Is the Networks' Liability?" *Glendale Law Review* (1978–1979), *3,* 100.
7. Anne Rawley Saldich, *Electronic Democracy: Television's Impact on the American Political System* (New York: Praeger, 1979), p. ix.
8. Joan Bartel, "Paddy Chayefsky: 'TV Will Do Anything for a Rating,'" *New York Times* (November 14, 1976). Cited in Winston L. Kirby, "The Influence of Television on Social Relations: Some Personal Reflections," in Frank Coppa, ed., *Screen and Society: The Impact of Television Upon Aspects of Contemporary Civilization* (Chicago: Nelson-Hunt, 1980), p. 141.
9. Cited in Timothy Green, *The Universal Eye: The World of Television* (New York: Stein and Day, 1972), p. 10.
10. Zamora v. State, 361 So. Rptr. 2d 776 (Fla 3d DCA 1978). See also Cleveland Coon, "A Mitigating Factor—Television's Influence on the Criminally Maladjusted: Diminished Capacity at Its Best," *Southern University Law Review* (Spring 1979), *5,* 249.
11. Quoted in "Brain-Numbing Time...Again," *Television Quarterly* (Summer 1980), *17,* 46.
12. Marilyn Jackson-Beeck and Jeff Sobal, "The Social World of Heavy Television Viewers," *Journal of Broadcasting* (Winter 1980), *24,* 10.

13. Iver Peterson, "Publishers Simplify College Textbooks," *The Knoxville News-Sentinel* (November 18, 1974), p. 20.
14. UPI, "Many High School Graduates Can Barely Read, Write, Army Finds," *The Knoxville News-Sentinel* (March 14, 1981), p. 5.
15. Frank Stanton, "Television and the Book," in John Y. Cole, ed., *Television: Textbook and the Classroom* (Washington, D.C.: Library of Congress, 1978), p. 30.
16. Kirby, *op. cit.*, pp. 137-138.
17. Barry Cole, ed., *Television Today: A Close-Up View* (New York: Oxford University Press, 1981), p. 238.
18. William A. Belson, *The Impact of Television: Methods and Findings in Program Research* (London: Crosby Lockwood and Sons, Ltd., 1967), pp. 225-226. Cited in Coppa, *op. cit.*, p. xviii.
19. Quoted in John W. English, *Criticizing the Critics* (New York: Hastings House, Publishers, 1979), p. 172.
20. "Rebel with a Cause," *Broadcasting* (May 19, 1980), p. 40.
21. B. Cole, *op. cit.*, pp. 3-4.
22. Christopher H. Sterling and John M. Kitross, *Stay Tuned: A Concise History of American Broadcasting* (Belmont, Calif.: Wadsworth Publishing Company, 1978), p. 460.
23. Fred E.H. Schroeder, "Video Aesthetics and Serial Art," in Horace Newcomb, ed., *Television: The Critical View* (New York: Oxford University Press, 1976), p. 261.
24. *Ibid.*, p. 262.
25. John M. Phelan, *Disenchantment: Meaning and Morality in the Media* (New York: Hastings House, Publishers, 1980), p. 25.
26. Robert Geller, "Above All, Involve the Audience," *Television Quarterly* (Spring 1980), *17,* 13.
27. Frank Mankiewicz and Joel Swerdlow, *Remote Control: Television and the Manipulation of American Life* (New York: The New York Times Book Company, 1978), p. 11.
28. Jackson-Beeck and Sobal, *op. cit.*, p. 5.
29. Quoted in *Window Dressing on the Set: Women and Minorities in Television,* A Report of the United States Commission on Civil Rights (Washington, D.C.: Government Printing Office, August 1977), p. 4.
30. Bradley S. Greenberg, Katrina W. Simmons, Linda Hogan, and Charles Atkin, "Three Seasons of Television: A Demographic Analysis," *Journal of Broadcasting* (Winter 1980), *24,* 59.
31. E.B. Eiselein, *Minority Broadcasting* (Tucson: Society of Professional Anthropologists, 1978), p. 20.
32. *Window Dressing on the Set: An Update,* A Report of the United States Commission on Civil Rights (Washington, D.C.: Government Printing Office, January 1979), p. 5.
33. John R. Silber, "Television: A Personal View," in Newcomb, *op. cit.*, p. 225.
34. "Crooks, Conmen and Clowns: Businessmen in TV Entertainment," *Business and the Media* (Spring, 1981), p. 4.
35. AP, "TV Writer Says Scripts Hide American Reality," *The Knoxville Journal* (February 9, 1972), pp. A1-2.
36. Stephen F. Rohde, "It's Unfair to Blame TV for Crimes by the Disturbed," *Los Angeles Times,* Part II (June 29, 1978), p. 7. Cited in Busselmaier, *op. cit.*, pp. 101-102.
37. Eda LeShan, "Television—The Perfect Scapegoat," *Television Quarterly* (Summer 1979), *16,* 55-56.
38. Robert Coles, "What Harm to the Children?" *Channels* (June/July 1981), p. 31.
39. George Comstock, *Television in America* (Beverly Hills, Calif.: Sage Publications, 1980), p. 43.
40. Mickie Edwardson, Donald Grooms, and Susanne Proudlove, "Television News Information Gain from Interesting Video vs. Talking Heads," *Journal of Broadcasting* (Winter 1981), *25,* 22-23.
41. James David Barber, "What Network News Should Be," *Television Quarterly* (Fall 1979), *16,* 52.
42. "Networks Need Ombudsman," *The Television Business-Economic News Index* (April 16-30, 1981), *3,* 3.
43 Daniel Boorstin, "Too Much Too Soon?" *TV Guide* (December 16, 1972), p. 14.
44. *Ibid.*
45. See Kurt Lang and Gladys Engel Lang, "The Unique Perspective of Television and Its Effect: A Pilot Study," in Wilbur Schramm, ed., *Mass Communications* (Urbana: The University of Illinois Press, 1960), pp. 544-560.

46. Henry J. Taylor, "Crisis Is Name of TV News Game," *The Knoxville News-Sentinel* (June 3, 1975), p. B2.
47. B. Cole, *op. cit.*, pp. 121-122.
48. Kate Moody, "Growing Up on Television," *Television Quarterly* (Fall 1980), 17, 41.
49. Melvin Zelnick and John F. Kantner, "Sexual and Contraceptive Experience of Young Unmarried Women in the United States, 1976 and 1971," *Family Planning Perspectives*, 1977, *9*, 63. Cited in John A. Courtright and Stanley J. Baran, "The Acquisition of Sexual Information by Young People," *Journalism Quarterly* (Spring 1980), *57*, 107.

STUDY QUESTIONS

1. Listen to the most recent big hit from each of your favorite rock groups. Summarize what the words of each "tells" you. Does each seem to uphold the "older values" or establish new ones? Why or in what way?
2. View one episode each of your two favorite action-adventure shows. Summarize the plot of each. What "lesson," if any, is implied in each? Compare your perception with others in your class.
3. View one episode each of your two favorite situation comedies. Analyze the character of the key protagonist. Would you like to be like him or her? Why or why not?
4. Watch your favorite anchorperson on the evening TV news. Restate the content of the first big issue-oriented story (not simply an event). What "understanding" of the issue does the story provide? Is that enough? Why or why not?
5. Think deeply about the role that radio and television play in your own life. List the valuable contributions each makes to you, then the disadvantages. Why do you think these positives and negatives exist for you?
6. Talk in depth with a close friend about his/her values. In what ways are they the same as yours? Different? Analyze the reasons why.
7. Consider your answer to any one of the above questions. Analyze the way(s) in which that answer can guide a program director.

SUGGESTED READINGS

Adler, Richard P., et al. *The Effects of Television Advertising on Children: Review and Recommendations*. Lexington, Mass.: D.C. Heath, 1980.

Adler, Richard P., ed. *Understanding Television: Essays on Television as a Social and Cultural Force*. New York: Praeger Publishers, 1981.

Baran, Stanley J. *The Viewer's Television Book: A Personal Guide to Understanding Television and Its Influence*. Cleveland Heights, Ohio: Penrith Publishing, 1980.

Cantor, Muriel G. *Prime-Time Television: Content and Control*. Beverly Hills, Calif.: Sage Publications, 1980.

Davis, Richard H. *Television and the Aging Audience*. Los Angeles: University of Southern California, Androus Gerentology Center, 1980.

Frank, Ronald E., and Marshall G. Greenburg. *The Public's Use of Television: Who Watches and Why*. Beverly Hills, Calif.: Sage Publications, 1980.

Himmelstein, Hal, ed. *On the Small Screen: New Approaches to Television and Video Criticism*. New York: Praeger Publishers, 1981.

Jacoby, Jacob, et al. *Miscomprehension of Televised Communications*. New York: The Educational Foundation of the American Association of Advertising Agencies, 1980.

Lull, James. "Family Communication Patterns and the Social Uses of Television," *Communication Research* (July 1980), *7,* 319-334.

Newcomb, Horace, ed. *Television: The Critical View.* 2d ed. New York: Oxford University Press, 1979.

Palmer, Edward L., and Aimee Dorr, eds. *Children and the Faces of Television: Teaching, Violence, Selling.* New York: Academic Press, 1980.

Rubin, Bernard, ed. *Questioning Media Ethics.* New York: Praeger Publishers, 1978.

________________. *Small Voices & Great Trumpets: Minorities & the Media.* New York: Praeger Publishers, 1980.

Smith, Ralph Lewis. *A Study of Professional Criticism of Broadcasting in the United States 1920–1955.* New York: Arno Press, 1979.

Spero, Robert. *The Duping of the American Voter: Dishonesty and Deception in Presidential Television Advertising.* New York: Lippincott & Crowell, 1980.

Thayer, Lee, ed. *Ethics, Morality, and the Media: Reflections on American Culture.* New York: Hastings House, Publishers, 1980.

Turow, Joseph. *Entertainment, Education, and the Hard Sell: Three Decades of Network Children's Television.* New York: Praeger Publishers, 1981.

Also check recent issues of *Index to Legal Periodicals; Journal of Advertising Research; Journal of American Culture; Journal of Communication; Journal of Popular Culture; Journalism Quarterly; Mass Communication Review; Mass Media Booknotes; Psychological Abstracts; Sociological Abstracts; Topicator.*

11

THE FUTURE OF BROADCAST PROGRAMMING

Mark Banks

Any projection about the future of broadcast programming is speculation. If we were able to work wizardry in conjuring up a completely or even closely accurate picture of the future of programming, we would not be writing textbooks—we would be heading up major network programming departments. As it is, a very large percentage of new network prime-time programs do not last a full season, and in recent years the shifting and replacing of programs in prime time has increased. Professional programmers, therefore, cannot predict the successes of their own new products with much accuracy, even on a year to year basis. For us to presume to predict large bodies of programming trends over a number of years is indeed presumptuous. Moreover, the predictions we make today are based on a media structure and potential that were quite different merely a decade ago; if we had been writing this chapter in 1972 rather than 1982, it would probably not resemble this one at all.

Nevertheless, there are a number of trends underway, many of which may well progress predictably. In this chapter, we look at some important factors and influences on programming that deserve exploration and explanation. They are potentially significant indicators of things to come.

Among the influences on programming, some are more predictable than others. For example, some technological advances are virtually inevitable, while others are less certain. It is reasonable to say that electronic equipment will continue, as it has in the recent past, to become more compact and more versatile. But when we delve into predicting public tastes or the willingness of the public to support a vast diversity of specialized broadcast programming, we are much more vulnerable to error.

We take a somewhat broad approach, therefore, in examining the many possible directions in which broadcast programming may go. Because in the real world television receives much more attention than radio, most of our discussion in this chapter is about television, although we emphasize, where appropriate, not only the changing role of radio but the changing nature of all mass media.

In the sections that follow, some major trends and influences are described, with accompanying speculation about their possibilities. These influences are:

1. Changing technology and the increased availability of channels,
2. Home communcation facilities,
3. Talent considerations,
4. Production costs as a factor of program quality,
5. Public tastes,
6. Public action and the influences of audiences,
7. The role of media critics,
8. Regulation,
9. Changes in the structure and balance of media power.

As we have seen in all the preceding chapters, influences on programming vary far and wide. The list above is not meant to be exhaustive, nor is it possible to cover each of the categories in the list completely. We can, however, develop a large picture that illustrates many of the potentials and many of the alternatives that the future of programming holds.

CHANGING TECHNOLOGY AND THE INCREASED AVAILABILITY OF CHANNELS

Since the electronic media depend on technology at every stage of communication—production, delivery, and reception—changes in technology pervade virtually all aspects of this process. For the most part, these changes operate within the established structure. Given the necessity to collect, process, and deliver media messages, there will be predictable improvements that make this procedure easier and more efficient. For example, the pioneer developments in electronic news gathering in the 1970s spurred a competition among manufacturers to make cameras and recorders lighter in weight and more reliable. Today's 40-pound equipment packages will become 15-pound or even lighter systems tomorrow. Manufacturers have already developed self-contained camera-recorder units. Computers and microprocessors have had an impact on every stage of production, including cameras, recorders, editors, character and graphic generators, and voice synthesization and electronic animation.

In the processing and recording of information, there are also a number of notable innovations. The conversion of both audio and video signals from analog to digital formats is well underway. Digital processing involves taking hundreds of thousands of samples of a signal each second. With so many

Figure 11.1 An artist demonstrates the use of the Ampex Video Art System, which enables the creation of drawings electronically

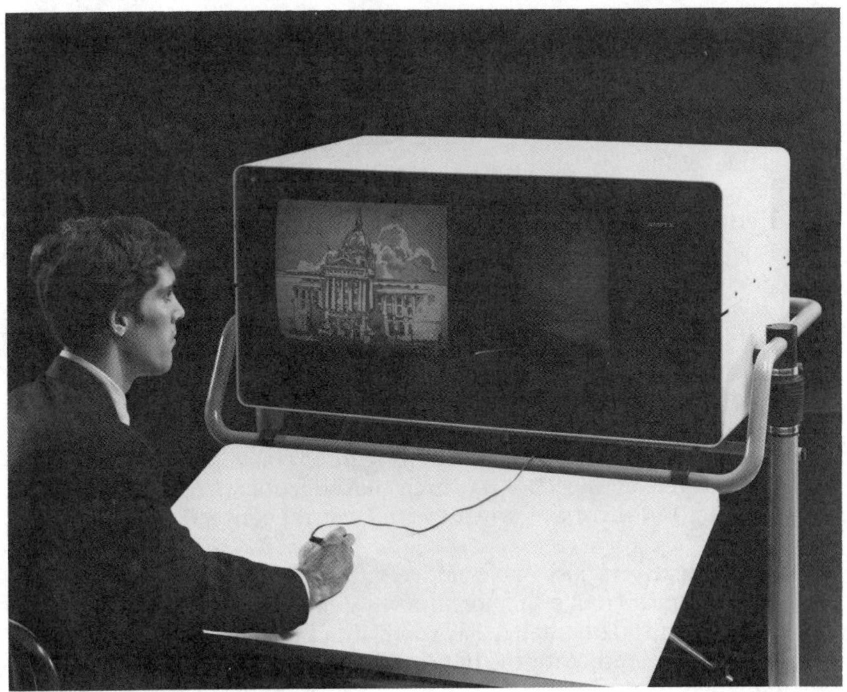

Courtesy of Ampex Corporation.

samples, each sample point can be recorded as a simple "on" or "off" electronic unit. This process enables virtually a whole new world of recording technology, wherein signals can be easily stored, copied, transmitted, and recombined into usable audio and/or video formats with essentially no loss of signal quality. Even multiple successive generations can be made of program material with little or no loss or distortion. It is difficult at this time to foresee all the many potentials of this technology, though many proponents suggest that it will revolutionize the electronic media.

One technology that may have a strong impact on the quality of programming is the recently demonstrated high definition television. In the American system, a television picture has 525 lines of definition. For conventional television, whose screens have been relatively small, this has been adequate. But as large-screen projection television becomes more common, and as large flat-screen technologies become practical, the need for better definition increases. Moreover, as the potential of video as an art form receives more attention, there is the desire for more "quality" in the technical make-up of the picture. By increasing the number of lines to over 1,000, these needs for greater definition can be met. Some movie makers are already looking at the possibility of replacing film entirely with high definition video. One of the problems for television broadcasting, however, is that the more lines in the picture, the more frequency bandwidth required to accommodate the greater amount of video information. Today's frequency allocations do not allow that luxury. The CBS network proposed that high definition television be wedded to the use of direct broadcast of programming to the home via satellites. Since both innovations are current, CBS reasoned that it would be most practical to develop them together.

At the receiving end, there is also substantial improvement and expansion of available technology. Radio receivers develop improved quality yearly. FM stereo is quite commonplace, and the popularity of FM has, in many markets, overtaken the popularity of AM. One of the most visible areas of radio receiver and system improvement is in automobile systems, which have gone "component" and which boast not only improvements in the basic receivers but also in power, speakers, and additional features such as tape recorders and graphic equalizers.

AM radio has sought to compete with the quality FM, evidenced most recently by the proposals and experimentation with AM stereo. With the FCC's approval, there will likely be a full-fledged competitive move by manufacturers to capture the market. Stations will, of course, have to reequip to accommodate this new technology, so the introduction of AM stereo will not be immediate. But there will probably be a general conversion over the next few years.

Television receivers also have undergone substantial changes in recent years, and it appears that even more dramatic changes are yet to come. Probably the most important change has come about through miniaturization of components, combined with the increased variety of functions added to the basic functions of receiving and displaying television pictures. One dramatic change has been the appearance and marketing of large screen televisions, which incorporate projection of the picture on a screen. Another important change has been the marketing of home video cassette recorders and players, and, more recently, video disc players.

Solid state technology is emerging in the last hold-out in television—the picture tube. Flat screen displays have been developed which enable pictures to be displayed without the cathode ray gun. Early models are small, but increase in size and quality is imminent, depending on successful marketing of the first.

Other refinements in television receivers include automatic control of color, electronic combing devices which give better picture resolution, and the long-awaited improvement in the sound of television.

Closely allied to changing technology is the increased availability of channels, which has already begun to make an impact. The most obvious and most developed change is that brought by cable systems, which for many years have imported signals from faraway stations. The addition of cable's own program sources, especially via satellite, has virtually caught fire and is proving to be one of the biggest drawing cards of cable. Most notable are the movie channels, but sports, special interest programming, all-news, "superstations," children's channels, and religious channels are increasing in popularity also. That the proliferation of channels will be accepted and even desired has been well demonstrated. Cable companies bidding to establish systems in markets not yet "cablefied" regularly use the appeal of a large

Figure 11.2 The Sony Betacam is one of the newer camera recorder units which eliminates the need for physical separation of recorders from the camera. The units are lighter in weight and much easier to use than predecessor models.

Courtesy of Sony Corporation.

number of imported and special channels to win franchises. Although cable penetration is still lagging in the rural areas, it had reached nearly 30 percent of American homes by 1982. Some advertisers claim that with cable penetration above 30 percent of the population, it will itself become a mass medium.

One of the key results of the proliferation of channels is increased programming variety, illustrated by the examples above. Whether that variety will continue to expand is not yet known. There will probably be a leveling off when certain boundaries of variety will be imposed. It remains to be seen if the introduction of many new channels will go in the direction that magazines have in recent years, specializing in widely diverse ways; or if it will go in the direction that radio has gone, producing a relatively narrow variety and a great deal of program overlap. We suspect that the former will occur, if the media economy fosters the viability of great programming diversity.

There are also indications of an increased availability of channels for over-the-air broadcasting. In 1981 the number of broadcast licenses—both radio and television—surpassed 10,000. Broadcasters and the FCC began in the 1970s to explore options for increasing the number of channels available. Subscription television has grown slowly, but its success suggests that there may be more opportunity for its use in many more markets. Low power television stations were also proposed by the FCC, designed to provide local markets with area-limited television service with a local community orientation.

Communication satellites have been used since the early 1960s, but experienced a spurt of growth by cable systems in the mid-1970s. Until now, these satellites have been relatively low powered, requiring large receiving antennas—"dishes"—equipped with powerful signal amplifiers for adequate reception. For the most part, they have been used by cable systems, enabling a great increase in the programming available. The Public Broadcasting System has also used satellites for signal dispersion to public television stations, and the commercial networks have begun to offer additional programming via satellite.

In 1979 the Communications Satellite Corporation (COMSAT) proposed still another possibility. By placing more powerful satellites into orbit, much smaller receiving antennas would be required at earth stations. This makes possible relatively inexpensive home satellite receivers. Though the many ways of doing this are being explored, the FCC has indicated a favorable attitude and has been receiving applications for such systems. The remote or rural home which may not have cable available for a number of years could thus have access to some of the same variety of programming that cable subscribers already have. Even today there are marketers of satellite earth stations which can receive the relatively weak signals now being transmitted for cable systems; though the investment is high for the individual homeowner, some systems are being advertised for under $3,000—far below the $25,000 price of barely a few years ago. These prices may fall even more as mass marketing and efficient fabricating techniques multiply.

Scientists and engineers have also been exploring ways to make better use of the available channel spectrums. One of the most imminent is the development of teletext. A portion of the bandwidth of the television picture is unused for the picture itself, and it is possible to put pages of text into unused portions of the 525 lines. Broadcasters are already using this for "closed captioning," allowing a specially equipped television receiver to display captions at the bottom of the picture for people who cannot adequately hear the audio portion of a program. Broadcasters and cablecasters in this country are gearing up for using the unused picture bandwidth for teletext, which allows the transmission of pages of information to receivers equipped to decode the information. Already in operation in some countries, teletext provides a whole new area of programming potential, with little alteration of existing media transmission technology.

These are but a few of the new technological developments that have or will have a direct impact on broadcast programming. Basically, they have aided in increasing programmers' accessibility to the media, as well as making programming easier to produce and of a higher quality.

In the sections that follow, many of these innovations are discussed in light of their implications for the future of programming. But first we look at how some of the technological innovations in the home itself are affecting programming.

HOME COMMUNICATION FACILITIES

A look at practically any magazine sales rack reveals that there is increasing attention to the use of video in the home. The appearance in recent years of home video publications, as well as the increased sales of home video recorders, demonstrates that the audience is willing to purchase and use them. The chief use of these machines, according to studies by researchers, is for time shift—the recording of programs off the air in order to view them later. Other increasing uses include individual recording with cameras and the purchase or rental of prerecorded programs. Researchers are exploring many other potential uses, especially in combining the use of the video disc with home computers. Since the disc is capable of storing a massive amount of information, any part of which is retrievable almost instantly, the possibility of using discs with computers provides enormous flexibility and capability for manipulation of information.

Home entertainment facilities are likely to expand even further. Large screen televisions, coupled with high definition picture recording, will probably increase both the flexibility and desirability of electronic media in the home. Add the impending improvements in the audio portion of video recordings, whether by magnetic tape or by video discs, as well as the seemingly unending improvement of audio recording technology itself, and the projections are open-ended. Even such esoteric recording and playback techniques as holographic recording will become more viable as electronic technology and decreasing prices target them toward the general market.

There is also likely to be a combination of entertainment functions with information functions, making the home entertainment center a home information center as well. Libraries and newspapers may become integrated with television and radio. Moreover, communication by telephone and electronic mail will also become part of that realm, and the integration of even more complex systems such as computers, banking, and other community services may make the traditional distinctions between broadcasting, other mass media, and personal media of communications nonexistent.

How far this development will go depends on many things. The public has evidenced a strong willingness to invest a lot of money in the equipment of home entertainment. For example, it has been estimated that consumers spend as much money yearly on the home receivers, antennas, supplies, and maintenance as national advertisers spend in the broadcast media. People also spend a great deal on stereo systems and records, magazines and newspapers, and even attendance at movies, concerts, and so on. The precedent has been established. The likelihood of this increasing is great.

Again, home media technology is having an increasing impact on programming. The home user is becoming more active, to the extent of creating his/her own programming. Interactive home terminals are proliferating, enabling the home user to "feed back" to the source, or to interact on a more personal one-to-one basis, resembling the use of the telephone. With greater activity on the part of the home user comes greater power; the user can acquire programs from more diverse sources, not depending on the scheduled feed of a limited number of channels.

These trends and others will change programming to some extent. Since the user can pick and choose more freely, program providers must accommodate increased user discrimination. For example, video clubs and tape rental centers have been successful throughout the country. Users who rent or borrow their programming (mostly movies) probably watch less broadcast programming, and the television ratings go down. One interesting additional competitive element is that video stores do a healthy business renting soft-core pornography and uncut R-rated movies that do not appear over the air.

Figure 11.3 An artist's drawing of what a direct broadcast satellite (DBS) might look like. Using powerful transponders, small-sized receiving dishes on individual rooftops make direct satellite-to-home broadcast both feasible and marketable.

Courtesy of Satellite Television Corporation, a COMSAT subsidiary.

TALENT CONSIDERATIONS

Perhaps more than any other factor, the quality of programming is directly related to the talent of writers, producers, and performers. Too much programming is mediocre, at best. One might conclude, therefore, that there are just not enough *really* talented or creative people to produce high quality programs. In short, there is a great need for an enlargement of the available pool of highly talented people in the broadcasting arts.

THE AVAILABLE POOL OF TALENT

Besides marketplace considerations that ultimately pervade all considerations of program development, the available pool of talent is one of the most critical factors in the kinds and types of programs that emerge from the broadcast media. With the increasing number of channels, there has become a critical need for good writers, creators, actors, artists, and talented technicians to meet the programming needs of those burgeoning media channels.

In some ways, the talent pool is increasing. The attraction of the broadcast media in recent years has stimulated a wealth of interest. Much of that interest is fostered, moverover, by the increased use of media for training and information in industrial and educational settings. There also has been a corresponding development of hardware that is moderately priced and relatively easily used. Indeed, the largest user of the video medium is not broadcasting—it is industry. Such a preponderance of nonbroadcast use provides the milieu for would-be programmers to learn the skills for development of their talents. In a way, this situation could be compared to the realm of popular music. Most musical stars of today began with inexpensive and readily available instruments in basements and garages, playing locally while cultivating their talents. Home video, so-called "underground" television, and consumer audio recorders have provided access for potential star programmers for both the medium and its equipment. This availability was practically nonexistent barely a decade ago.

In another area, there has been a substantial proliferation of training programs in broadcast communications not only at the college, university, and technical school levels, but also at the high school and even elementary school levels. The talented programmer of the next few years has ample opportunity to develop his/her talents along many established routes.

One of the issues that also influences the development of this pool of talent, however, is the complaint by many educators that the electronic media foster verbal and visual skills to the detriment of writing skills. A recent poll of broadcasters, for example, showed that stations would prefer to hire graduates who have strong writing skills from English or journalism curricula rather than from broadcasting departments. Indeed the value of writing ability in broadcast programming cannot be discounted. Many broadcast schools are taking note of the need to write well and are applying the appropriate emphases. Whether this will result in a more highly skilled group of programmers is still uncertain.

In addition to writing skills, however, there is still the need for media literacy in all its dimensions, and this will grow. In fact, trends are already evident in the direction of developing media skills not only in writing and traditional broadcasting, but also in cable, nonbroadcast media, and in organizational communications. There is also an increasing concern for the need to teach computer skills, since that technology is becoming quite vital to broadcasting and related media.

The pool of talent in programming, then, is expanding. More people have broadcast, audio, or video skills than ever before, and the number is increasing. Combined with the proliferation of electronic media channels and the need for greater numbers of capable programmers, it seems likely that the market for jobs in programming will remain good. It also seems likely that many will emerge to fill that need. How long this will endure, and how much money will be available to sustain a swelling of broadcast programming, is uncertain. The interest of the public in programming is indeed the crucial factor. If viewers or listeners are attracted, then available money will follow. But if there is a growing diversity of public interest, such that specialized programming becomes more important than mass programming, as has happened in the magazine medium, then the amount of money available for programmers for these specialized types of programs may be limited. The economics

Figure 11.4 High school and even elementary schools now teach programming and production skills. Here students at Fulton High School in Knoxville, Tennessee, produce a daily news program that is sent on closed-circuit TV to schools throughout the city.

Courtesy of Mark Banks.

of the situation depend on the balance of many variables. Pay television has been successful, and people have demonstrated a willingness to directly support individual programs. But there are limits to how much people will pay, and these limits will in turn have some effect on how vastly specialized programming will grow. Even if much of this specialized programming is advertiser-supported, there will be limits also, especially since the present system of advertising rates depends largely on audience numbers. Programming that is very specialized will usually attract small numbers of viewers, thereby limiting the revenues for program production.

It is reasonable to predict, then, that since the available pool of talent is strongly influenced by the marketplace, any substantial increase is predicated on the overall economic structure of the emerging electronic mass media.

PROFESSIONAL IDENTITY

Corollary to the available pool of talent is the emergence of professional identity among programmers. In history, whenever a new medium or art form appeared, it was generally ridiculed and boycotted by practitioners of the more established forms. When the piano was invented, it was considered a foul instrument, and jazz was considered profane in its early emergence. When motion pictures were new, actors of the "legitimate" stage generally refused to have anything to do with them. Later, some changed their minds and began to explore the potential of this new medium, and a whole new breed of "acting" grew. The film medium today is, at least in some of its products, considered an art form. Indeed, when television was new, film actors and producers wanted little to do with this primitive medium. But today many a movie star gets a start in television, and frequently television producers try their hands, often quite successfully, in the movies. In fact, the movie industry has been significantly supported in recent years by television.

In every new medium a time is required for its craftsmen and women to sharpen their talents and to experiment with its possiblities. After a time, what was once primitive becomes cultivated, and new professionalism emerges from those basic crafts.

Today some critics look despairingly at what is being produced at local cable access channels and in teletext and among the many new media capabilities. But if history repeats, these criticisms will diminish. For example, Ted Turner has demonstrated that a credible all-news channel is possible. Industries are rapidly improving the quality of their video training products. Some public access programs are attracting attention. Video festivals are appearing around the country, demonstrating that there is a vast potential for the medium of narrow-casting as an art form.

There will be, to be sure, a large share of "B" video, just as there is a lot of low cost/quality television and movies today. But there will emerge those who can give credence to video as a polished, intense, artistic, and probing form. And this will be an important factor in bolstering the medium.

PROGRAMMING COST AS A FACTOR OF PROGRAMMING QUALITY

An important consideration relative to all the factors mentioned above is the overall cost of program production. Traditionally, program quality has generally reflected the amount of money spent. If there is not a lot of money available to pay talent, then the quality of the work of affordable talent will be equal to the money spent.

Likewise, other costs of production will (and have) had an influence on the quality of programming. There are many variable factors in costs. New technology is expensive, but tends to decrease in cost as it proliferates. The first communication satellite earth stations were very costly prototypes. As they became more heavily marketed, their cost decreased. Now available are very costly computer animation devices, which allows artists to create not only animation but also graphics and visual representations electronically, thus saving countless hours of human work time. As these devices become more common, their cost will diminish. Perhaps it can be said that to the extent that facets of programming are facilitated by new and growing technological developments, the cost will decrease.

Quality, of course, is a changing phenomenon, and its definition is dependent in part on the current contexts of media programming. When the film medium was young, editing and filming techniques which are commonplace today were considered major breakthroughs. For instance, no one today marvels at the technique of cutting close-ups with medium shots in a paced manner designed to create a dramatic effect. But when early movie pioneers accomplished such effects, moviemakers heralded a whole new era of "quality." A more recent example is the development of stereophonic recording and broadcasting. When it was new, it foretold a quality of recorded sound which was astounding. Today, stereo is taken for granted, and quality becomes more a matter of noise suppression, sound synthesis and manipulation, and other factors that were nonexistent in the early stereo era.

One thing to consider as the number of channels for broadcast programs increases is that the amount of money available for any one program or any one channel may decrease from the relative preponderance that the three major national networks enjoy today. ABC, NBC, and CBS are already finding that overall viewing of their programs is decreasing as superstations emerge and as cable viewers choose pay channels and other alternative fare. That decrease results in lowered income for the networks, since advertising rates are based largely on ratings, which reflect the number of viewers. As money becomes scarcer for the networks, there will be a decrease in the amount of money available for programming, which, in turn, will likely affect programming quality. That is not necessarily a hard and fast rule. Many an inexpensively produced program has received much critical acclaim. But overall, the economics of the situation directly influence the quality of programming.

In the last 20 years, the variety of radio programs available has declined, primarily because of the transfer of audience attention to television. Radio has become restricted largely to recorded music and talk material. To propose that television networks will become purveyors of recorded packages, yielding little innovation and variety, is risky, since networks are also known to diversify and remain current with the marketplace. The major television networks have already become involved with cable and satellite programming, and may stay well in the forefront in producing programming of mass appeal and attractive quality.

It may be that overall television programming will achieve a "tiering" structure, where there will be a few predominant channels that cater to the bulk of public interest, much like the major networks do today. At the second and less popular levels will be the specialized programs, catering to special interests. Also at a lower level may be the equivalent of cinema's "B" movie, which will include low-budget formula programs. And it is safe to predict that old network and movie reruns, which today comprise the bulk of syndicated programming, will expand to these new channels. In some cases, they already have.

Another factor that suggests a different direction regarding the costs and quality of programming is pay television. Whether on cable channels, direct satellite broadcast, or by subscription television, pay television may revolutionize the broadcast economic structure. Conventional broadcasters have long predicted that pay television will siphon off the best programs for programming availabilities and leave them with second choices.

Some pay programming is on a per-program pay basis. The economic structure of pay television may have many ramifications. The siphoning of the best or most desirable programs is but one. Pay TV provides for more direct sale of programs than the advertiser-sponsored conventional programming and yields more money for programmers more efficiently. Pay TV may also have a rejuvenating impact on the movie industry, since movies are now the most frequently sold pay programming fare. Rather than distributing movies through the theatres, moviemakers can save the enormous costs of duplicating and circulating films by selling directly to the pay-television groups, which can distribute them simultaneously via satellite. It is expected that, with the growing success of pay programming, there will be an increased demand for new movies, giving a great boost to the movie industry. On the other hand, advertisers may suffer some loss of the ability to reach large masses of people.

And yet, one of the growing areas today in cable programming is advertising. Not constricted by short messages sandwiched between and into programs as is the case in broadcasting, advertisers are experimenting and often succeeding with lengthy product advertisements which are programs themselves. There is great optimism in the industry about the growth and refinement of this avenue of advertising.

PUBLIC TASTES

In the matter of predicting future program popularity and public tastes, there are few certainties. The number of influences on the public's likes and dislikes is great; and while gross cycles may be reasonably foreseen, predictions of specific public tastes are vulnerable to inaccuracy.

It is difficult to account for public tastes. At the same time, programs as diverse as "Three's Company," "Dallas," "The Hulk," "The Dukes of Hazzard," and "Sixty Minutes" attract large audiences. Many viewers are the same for most of these programs. In radio, audiences are attracted to a blending of jazz, rock, disco, country and western, bluegrass, and more classical music. Soap operas, game shows, situation comedies, movies, action-adventure, and other program types with substantial diversity enjoy side-by-side popularity.

On the other hand, there are some identifiable popular programming trends. In the early days of television, Westerns were quite popular, as were variety shows. In more recent times, those program types have been practically nonexistent, while situation comedies and prime-time soap operas have become popular. Part of the reason is that programmers, upon seeing the success of one program type in a season, predictably copy or "spin off" other programs of a similar type, in the hopes that the success of one will lead to the success of others. Generally this works. After the relatively bold appearance and enormous success of "All in the Family" in the early 1970s, producers created a number of copies of that show—copies which reflected the theme of boldness and relevance. Among those offshoots were "Maude," "Sanford and Son," and "The Jeffersons."

A major question, then, is whether program trends lead public tastes or follow them. That question has been asked throughout the history of popular media and has never been satisfactorily resolved. On the one hand there is a school of communication theory which postulates that media have a strong influence in determining public likes and awareness. To be sure, there is a bandwagon effect, whereby many people want to follow the likes and tastes of others. It's probably very much a part of human nature, and is perhaps best reflected by the arrival, tenure, and departure of the hits in top 40 radio. Hordes of songs are released and promoted by record companies, especially to radio stations. If they are played, they become familiar to listeners, who in turn buy them as single releases. If sales rise, then popularity lists based on record sales are circulated among radio stations, who, wanting to represent popular tastes accurately, play them even more often. After a while, sales begin to drop, the songs move down on the lists, and people stop buying the singles, which causes the popularity based on sales to diminish even further.

On the other hand, public taste will often lead the media. The recordings of Elvis Presley were banned on many radio stations in his early career, but his popularity rose dramatically and those stations had to give in to the demands of the marketplace.

Public tastes are wedded to the media in a transactional manner, it seems. Television programs are presented to the public. More often than not, they do not receive rampant public viewing or support. Those that do are usually quickly copied because history shows that, if people like one program, they will also be attracted to programs of similar structure, method, and theme. Waves of program-type popularity follow much the same patterns in both radio and television. In all cases, popular program types are usually quite varied.

It is probably safe to say that public tastes will have the same kinds of effects on program popularity in the future. If the number of channels and programs available continues to expand, there will likely be more programs of the same type, and the popularity of certain programs will be dispersed among other programs of the same type. But there may also be an overall decline in predominance of any one type of program, and many followers of one type will choose more of the same rather than a large variety. For example, sports networks on cable TV already provide a glut of sports programming to which loyal followers will devote a large portion of their viewing, at a cost to other programs they might otherwise view. On the other hand, there is probably also a saturation point, and no one type of program will predominate.

Another possibility is that public tastes will be reflected in tiers, as suggested before. There may well be a variety of the most popular programs, much as in network television today. Without some type of rural "cablefication" similar to the rural electronification that occurred earlier in this century, many viewers will not have access to the mutichannel cable services for a long time. Network and conventional broadcasting, therefore, will not disappear overnight, and are likely to provide the greatest range of mass appeal programming for most of the country for many years to come.

But the emergence of more specialized programs is likely to succeed directly according to the tastes of their potential viewers. And there will be waves of popularity even among the specialized program types. For example, in the current period of energy awareness, there has been and will be a market for programs dealing with energy conservation and alternate forms of energy production and use. If, in the near future, the energy source problem is substantially solved, programs on that topic may diminish in popularity. Magazines reflect that type of trend. Energy topics have resulted not only in a number of new magazines on the subject, but even the more popular magazines such as *Mechanix Illustrated* and *Popular Science* load their pages with energy-related features, and have virtually abandoned stories about fast cars that were so popular in the 1960s.

There are, at the same time, influences at work that lead in at least two directions relative to public tastes. Many of these influences come via the mass media, especially radio and television. On the one hand, the electronic media promote a sameness in the American society, urging standardization of speech and nationwide familiarity with the same public issues and entertainment domains. On the other hand, because the media and other public institutions have aided the increased education and awareness among the populace, they have fostered a greater variety of awareness of possibilities and cultural choices. The increased availability of television channels is likely to spur that trend, proliferating cultural and information variety among the public even more. Some may argue that this would be the best of all possible worlds, producing a more cosmopolitan dimension in the society. Critics, however, point to the dangers of "information overload," where so much information and variety serves only to confuse and destabilize society. Probably both perspectives are valid, the balance being determined by the disposition of individual viewers more than by the overall media structures.

An interesting parallel has occurred in offices. The photocopy machine and the word processor have indeed made work for the secretary easier, allowing facile production and storage of typewritten material. But in some ways these "conveniences" make the work harder. The copy machine results in many multiple copies that are often distributed widely, where before a minimum of copies sufficed. Now users of typed information are swamped with much more material to handle and file. The word processor requires higher level skills than were needed before, accompanied by higher wages and greater equipment costs. In effect, these blessings have hidden deficits.

In the electronic mass media a burgeoning of programming, along with the home recording capability, may require the average viewer to plan and to handle and store mediated information that is now much easier to use. It is quite possible that there will be a point of diminishing returns, and it is important to consider the willingness of people to be active consumers of programming as a component of public tastes.

It is certain that public tastes will change. In many sectors, they will grow and become more varied. In other cases there may be a retrenchment toward more conservative preferences. Today there is considerable public activity to stop the trend of programming toward more drug, sex, violent, and antireligious fare.

PUBLIC ACTION AND THE INFLUENCE OF AUDIENCES

Public action takes at least three forms. One is individual action, and what individuals will buy, like, etc., in large numbers but largely as individual actions. Home video recorder purchase and use is a good example of that type of action.

Another type of public action is more concerted and is usually manifested by public interest organizations or groups, often self-appointed, whose thrust of activity is oriented toward influencing the media. The issues of sex, violence, drugs, and religion mentioned in the last section are current and prime examples of the activity of this type of public action.

A third and emerging type of public action revolves around actual public access to the media as programmers. This is best manifested in television by use of the public access channels in cable systems. There is now a national organization of public access programmers, and it seems that the popularity and utility of local public programming is on the increase. It also has potential in the expected proliferation of low power television and radio stations, whose intent, according to the FCC, is to provide local organizations the opportunity to operate broadcast facilities in their own areas. Another realm of more local use of the technology of radio and television is the emergence of in-house production facilities that many industries, educational institutions, and other small organizations have been quickly acquiring. These facilities often achieve broadcast quality, and many who work in them have developed expertise, if not budget capabilities, rivaling that of major program producers. Video literacy from the production standpoint is approaching that of the print media, which has a multiplicity of levels of expertise and the vehicles to employ that multiplicity. Recent years have seen the emergence of "underground" video from a handful of people experimenting with narrowcast possibilities to literally millions of people trying out their production talents.

It is likely that this trend will continue, especially as the channels of access for small groups or individual producers proliferate. This may provide an even wider variety of programs for the public to choose from, although it may remain in the background, much as amateur moviemakers seldom reach national notoriety. In fact, with ready access to the equipment allowing individual experimentation with video, there is likely to be a number of people who become actively interested and then later lose interest or realize the limitations of their talents. This has happened in photography, moviemaking, and virtually all media forms that allow easy access. A positive offshoot of this will be the possibility for a unique producer or video artist to emerge, making it easier for the obscure artist to flex his/her talents and achieve some recognition. We have mentioned "video festivals" which resemble traditional film festivals—often local, regional, or specialized. This provides an opportunity for would-be major producers to expand their capabilities along nearby routes of growing sophistication, and today's hard-to-enter television market may become more accessible for those who need to begin competition at levels near their ability.

In the matter of direct public action to influence the broadcast media, public interest groups have been around a long time, striving to "improve" programming according to their own beliefs about how media should represent and reflect the society. In recent years, some of these have received a great deal of attention, often ironically because they have received greater media coverage. The effectiveness of these groups or organizations is varied, depending on the one hand upon whom they represent and how powerful they are within the social structure and on the other hand upon the focus of their respective causes. Recently representatives of the "Moral Majority" have crusaded to eliminate what they perceive as obscenity and profanity in broadcasting. Their impact has been amplified by a nationwide swing toward conservatism. On the other hand, a representative of a large cable corporation informs us that the one type of programming most requested by subscribers is soft-core pornography. The clash of self-appointed public protectors with the trends of the marketplace poses an interesting battle, the outcome of which is as yet unpredictable.

The action of individual citizens in influencing the media and using the media more actively is also likely to grow, though the impact of this is also uncertain. Still, one person was able to force television and radio to cease cigarette advertising. A handful of housewives formed Action for Children's Television and created waves of influence. But such instances are rare. More representative are the crusaders who attract attention to some aspect of protest, but whose effect diminishes rapidly. Often their issue is taken up by larger organizations, and they have an indirect influence. On the other hand, many fizzle out. One of the hazards of taking on the national media is that they are so large and so distant from most people that many who would crusade find themselves up against enormous odds and are often unable even to be heard. Agnostics and atheists have frequently protested the broadcasting of religious programming, citing unequal representation under fairness policies. Their voice is drowned, however, both by the media and a regulatory structure too powerful and established to be changed around and by overwhelming public sentiment in favor of religious programming.

An area where individual influence will grow is in making choices in the home about which programs to view. As the number of choices increases and as cable systems provide services that enable measurable individual choices, individuals will have a greater influence on determining the directions of programming. We already have pay television on a pay-per-program basis, and the home button-pusher in a growing number of markets can select and pay for programs on an individual basis. Even in many systems where individual program selection is not monitored or individually priced, there are tiered services made available by the cable system. Some subscribers can choose a basic movie service, for example, or a higher level movie service that provides a greater variety, or even a number of different services. Monthly rates charged by the cable company to the subscriber vary according to the tiers or kinds of services the subscriber chooses. In addition, there is a good indication that other services will grow both in cable and regular broadcasting, such as teletext, over-the-air subscription television, and extended advertising. The individual home viewer will have the greatest impact on their success by exercising the prerogative of choice. Although that influence has existed via ratings in traditional television, the number of options has been very limited. Now with many possibilities, individual viewer choice becomes potentially more influential.

In addition, many cable systems offer interactive services. In some of these cases, the viewer is able to respond, to "vote." By pushing buttons at a home console, the viewer can respond directly to questions broadcast over the programs themselves. This provides a direct opportunity for all viewers with this service to have their reactions immediately registered, and the accumulated votes enable programmers to receive tabulated feedback instantaneously. Audience research shows a trend in favor of increasing the immediacy of audience feedback, among other things. The possibilities are great. Not only are basic measures of viewing possible, but more qualitative public attitudes and reactions can be measured. The extent of growth of this type of individual influence is yet to be seen.

There are a number of cautions or dangers. One is the obvious need for the protection of individual privacy. If wired systems allow intended feedback from homes, they also allow for unintended feedback in the form of surreptitious monitoring of viewing habits. Another danger is the possibility of public opinion being determined by an elitist segment of society, since cable subscribers comprise more economically secure homes and are predominantly urban or suburban, rather than rural.

Still another danger lies in the determination of who does the polling. The choices of types of questions and/or information offered for immediate public response are vulnerable to less than objective purposes. This is a concern that public polling services have to deal with as they make up their questionnaires. There is a potential for malpractice in the use of polls, if the desires or self-interests of those conducting the polls override the necessity for objectivi-

Figure 11.5 In-home interactive systems such as QUBE allow viewers to give direct and immediate feedback by means of an array of response buttons

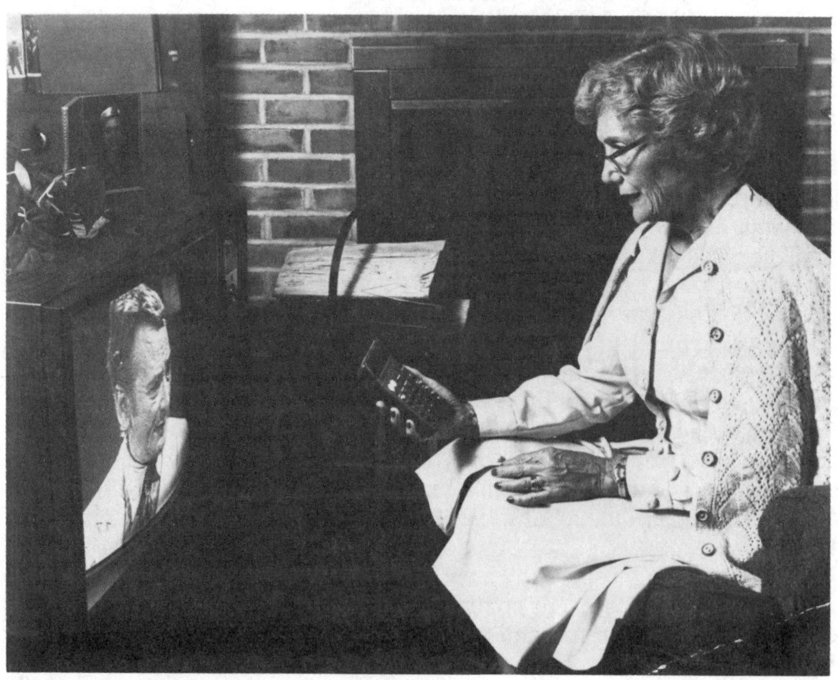

Courtesy of Warner-Amex/QUBE.

ty and impartiallity. It is easy to see how polling abuses could invade this new arena of public surveying through cable interactive systems.

Whatever the dangers, it seems that interactive systems are here to stay, and will proliferate slowly but deliberately. It is important for programmers to be aware that interactive capability requires the development of programming that is in many ways different from conventional one-way programming. For example, if viewers are asked to respond at a certain point in the program, it is possible to deliver subsequent material immediately determined in part by the response. The possibilities are fascinating but the techniques are quite different from conventional programming, both in production and in delivery.

Overall, there seems to be a growing influence by the public on broadcast programming, whether by individual action, cause crusading, or direct participation in program production. How much this influence will increase cannot be determined at this time, but it presages a new era in which substantial numbers of the viewing and listening public will participate more actively in the formation and direction of programming.

THE ROLE OF MEDIA CRITICS

As mentioned in chapter 10 on criticism, there are many distinctions between the roles of critics and reviewers. Though many of the concerns mentioned in this section apply to both, they are generally more appropriate to the reviewers.

One of the problems that professional television and radio reviewers have had with reviews of programs has been the inability to see programs until broadcast. This has led them into the necessity of critiquing programs after airing, thus producing a product of questionable value to the viewer, who has little chance to see the program again. In some cases, the problem is not great, such as when reviewers discuss series that are aired week after week and vary little in expected content, theme, or formula.

There is a growing opportunity for critics to have access to programs, especially specials, before they air. As competition increases among programmers, the role and influence of critics may also increase. Programmers will want to explore every possibility for bringing public attention to their offerings before airing. Major networks now engage in extensive over-the-air promotion of programs. As the channels proliferate, this will indeed continue. But to gain a competitive edge, they may provide critics greater opportunity to preview and influence audience choice, much as movie critics do today.

There is another corollary development relative to media writers that is not criticism per se, but is represented by various writings about the broadcast media in an ever-growing number of publications. It seems that broadcasting and its auxiliary offshoots are receiving increased attention by writers, many of whom are legitimate critics coming out of a scholarly or aesthetic criticism background; but many others of whom are writers in the popular tradition, who view media fare from the perspective of general social impact or lay person's judgment.

One can find articles about television in practically every type of publication. Religious magazines and journals grapple with the moral issues of programming. Futuristic magazines such as *Next* and *The Futurist* provoke some insights into the future trends of programming. Few popular publications have not at one time or another addressed the issue of media violence and its impact on children and the society.

Another rapidly growing group of publications giving attention to the broadcast media focus on the media themselves. Numerous home video magazines have appeared in recent years. *TV Guide,* not long ago the only lay publication on broadcasting, finds itself in the company of newer, publicly targeted magazines such as *Channels.* And, of course, critical works reviewing the programming of radio—recorded music—have enjoyed quite respectable popularity in recent years. We should mention also that critics will likely find greater opportunities to be represented in the broadcast media themselves, becoming less limited to written publications as a vehicle for their works. There are indeed increasing opportunities for critics and reviewers to be heard.

At another level, critics of video art are emerging, though they admit as an art form it is relatively new. One critic writes that the art of video has three major areas—documentary, portrait, and experimentation. As this form grows, the critic's role will be an important one both for alerting readers to what is going on and for providing some critical explanation of the meaning and value of the works.

Constraints that affect the pool of talent for programming also apply to critics. There is not a sufficient tradition thus far for a wealth of talented critics to develop. As programs proliferate, the critics have the task not only to be more sensitive in the programs they review, but also to make themselves heard, since they will be competing for public attention alongside the many new information channels themselves. It is possible that critics will serve a genuine public need in pointing toward the worthwhile things to view. But, as has happened in the recording industry, it is difficult just to keep up with the critics.

REGULATION

There can be little doubt that regulatory development will accompany the changes in media structure and content. The chapter on regulation demonstrates the rationale and procedures that regulatory agencies, notably the FCC, have followed regarding the regulation of broadcast programming.

In the future, regulation is likely to follow much the same pattern, though we cannot discount varying political climates. In recent years there has been a notable trend toward "deregulation" of broadcast and cable media. That trend is likely to continue; and where, for example, cable television had substantial restrictions regarding siphoning and the importation of distant signals, by the late 1970s those restrictions all but disappeared. Some were deliberately abandoned by the FCC; others were overturned by the courts.

On the other hand, there are also likely to be some new regulations that will have significant impact on programming. In the past, broadcasting had relatively firm control over how and when its programs were distributed. Now, with satellite distribution and home receivers and recorders, the potential for unintended distribution and use becomes more possible. Much as the recording industry has been plagued with piracy and counterfeiting of records, broadcast and cable programmers, as well as moviemakers, have already begun to have their control over their product violated by pirates and home recorders. The courts have begun to deal with this problem, and an appellate court recently held that the use of home recorders for personal recording of programming off the air or by other means is illegal. A ruling by the US Supreme Court on this matter is expected during 1982. In a related matter, despite protests from some of them, some independent television stations' signals have been picked up and transmitted via satellite to cable systems nationwide.

Protest has also come from writers and actors, who, coordinated by their respective unions, have often struck. One of the major issues of a recent Screen Actors Guild strike, for example, was that participants desired a share in the profits from sale and distribution of their programs by prerecorded video cassettes and over pay television.

The copyright disputes are swelling. Although the copyright law was rewritten in the mid-1970s, it has been undergoing reexamination and will probably need to be repeatedly amended or rewritten to reflect and protect these many new uses of programming material. This legal evolution will have an impact on programming in many ways, some of which have not been explored as yet. Foremost among the effects is that programming will be more expensive to produce, for programmers will not be as able to overextend production costs in anticipation of large future profits from these other uses. Second, the consumer may be affected as up-dated copyright regulations and agreements regain some of the control over distribution and use. Third, if copyright procedures become much more complex and protective, it may become even more difficult for would-be programmers to secure the funding necessary to take advantage of these protections. A similar problem has occurred for inventors wishing to patent new products. Patent restrictions and the need to thoroughly research existing patents make it quite difficult and often expensive for inventors to secure patents on their inventions. One of the hazy areas of copyright is that of style, theme, or general plot. As we have seen, many programs that appear are similar to existing successful programs. With new, more restrictive copyright laws, it is possible that creators of program ideas may find it necessary to be much more cautious in how closely they copy existing programs.

Perhaps another emerging area for greater regulatory control is that of obscenity or pornography. In conventional broadcasting, this type of program material has a tradition of proscription by the FCC, and has been reasonably successfully barred from broadcast, though many conservative critics today disparage the amount of sex that appears on television. Cable, however, does not have that type of restriction, except where prohibited by local or state regulations. In many areas, R-rated programming is regularly offered, and there seems to be substantial viewer interest in supporting that type of programming. Most often it is on channels that must be specially subscribed to or purchased, allowing the subscriber to control its access to the home set. Whether public sentiment will impose widespread restrictions is yet to be seen, though there is reason to believe that the recent wave of conservative protest will have some impact in this area. It seems less likely that hard-core pornography will achieve wide acceptance on cable channels, though there are already a large number of such prerecorded programs available for home viewing on video cassette players.

Figure 11.6 A send-receive satellite dish used by KTTV-TV in Los Angeles. Because satellite signals are scattered across wide geographic areas, it is possible for virtually anyone to set up receiving dishes, which complicates the copyright privileges of those who transmit the signals to authorized users.

Courtesy of Metromedia, Inc.

Wherever there is potential for abuse, or what "public standards" consider abuse, there is an accompanying potential for regulation. Perhaps one of the areas most vulnerable to abuse and attendant correction through regulation is in advertising. As mentioned before, experiments are underway with more flexible advertising on cable television, manifested in ads that run long periods and expand the practice of direct solicitation for mail-in or phone-in orders. As this advertising flexibility proliferates, unless cable and advertising interests engage in strong self-regulation, the Federal Trade Commission may produce rules designed to protect the unwary consumer. This, in turn, would have an effect on this type of programming, much like the recent history of such regulation affects the conventional broadcast media.

CHANGES IN THE STRUCTURE AND BALANCE OF MEDIA POWER

We have already explored the potential impact of cable and its proliferation of channels for viewers and programmers. In a larger sense, there may be significant changes in the overall balance of power in broadcast media, especially as it relates to programming. Networks, for example, control most of the programming today. With the increasing potential for program sponsorship and satellite distribution from virtually anywhere, programming control may substantially depart from New York, giving greater access and power not only to Hollywood, but to other programming centers as well. Nashville, for example, is a growing programming center for "country" programming. The opportunity is increasing for any local outlet, with sufficient backing, to become a significant programming source. Many of the growth areas of the country, such as Florida and Texas, may be able to support such ventures, and the distribution networks can change, and indeed are changing, such that these potentials may be realized. Already the Turner Broadcasting System activities in Atlanta have given new-found attention to that city as a major program supplier.

In addition, control over programming may become more diversified, falling into the hands not only of network giants as it is today, but also into other corporations who may wish to diversify. In the recent past, networks have found it beneficial to diversify, owning a variety of interests, both broadcast and nonbroadcast. A similar pattern occurs in the other direction, where nonbroadcast corporations buy into broadcasting. It is probably a matter of marketplace potential before many other large corporations take an active role in providing programming for these new media. Moreover, just as the movie industry's relative monopoly by the major studios was destroyed by smaller production units and so-called "runaway productions," the major networks will likely find as yet unknown programmers competing in a frontal attack.

On the other hand, powerful organizations always demand an influence. The major networks have intently made moves into the many emerging media possibilities, and have acquired satellite avenues and nonbroadcast program options. Recent deregulation suggests that they will continue to expand their ownership of cable systems. Moreover, the telephone companies persistently request the opportunity to own cable systems as well.

At the local level there is growing competition for broadcasters from community access programmers using channels provided by the local cable systems. This has grown to such an extent that there is now a national association of local programmers, which allows for affiliation and sharing of ideas and products.

The movie industry may undertake its own competitive activity. One of the big drawing cards of cable and pay TV systems is already the increased availability of current-run movies. This may have an adverse impact on the conventional distribution of movies, however, and it is possible that the practice of distributing movies through local movie theaters will diminsh, going into recession and decline. On the other hand, people dine out more today than ever before, and the number of restaurants has increased dramatically. To expect that people will want to withdraw into their homes and not attend such public events as movies may be an unrealistic expectation. Many taverns have installed large-screen televisions, and many experimental theatres have explored the potential of public receptivity to video products. There may be a resurgence of the use of video and television in public-gathering places. As the technologies of both video production and playback improve, today's movie theater and disco dance hall may become tomorrow's place to experience grand scale video events. Aldous Huxley foretold of a possibility in that direction when he wrote about the "feelies" in *Brave New World.* Indeed, current trends strongly suggest that new technologies will be coordinated with public or social events. Practically all popular music stars began by trying out and developing their style and talents before live audiences. Las Vegas, among many other places, provides performers the same opportunities. It is important to consider that the balance of media power cannot neglect the need for parallel opportunities in live events or public gatherings.

Add to these considerations many that have been described elsewhere in this chapter, such as the influence of low power television, changes in radio broadcasting structure, and the increased participation of individuals in choosing, buying, and recording programs for personal use. The balance of power is not yet finalized, and for many years will probably continue to change, especially in the context of changing patterns of government regulation and deregulation.

SUMMARY

In many ways, we have been evasive, declining to offer very many specific predictions about the future of broadcast programming. We see too many factors whose relative influence over programming is yet to be worked out.

This is a time of vast change in broadcast media, and it is occurring rather rapidly. Probably the safest prediction we could make about broadcast programming is that it will increase in diversity. But even that prediction must be a cautious one, because we do not yet know the limits of both the marketplace and human resources.

The media professional of today and of the future must take into account these many influences and trends we have described, plus many more. Old boundaries and definitions are being replaced with new ones, and the transitions themselves will likely undergo much trial, error, and success. Whatever the outcome, it is indeed exciting and challenging to be part of an era of change.

STUDY QUESTIONS

1. Chapter 11 has identified several emerging technologies which may have an impact on the future of broadcast programming. These technologies include miniaturization of equipment, digital processing, home video recording, high definition television, proliferation of channels, and direct satellite programming. In your judgment, what effect has each had to date on broadcast programming?
2. Have any other technological innovations emerged which have affected, or which may affect, programming on radio or television?
3. What changes in media usage (television, radio, newspapers, or other) due to new home telecommunications facilities have you observed during recent years? Explain the cause and the resulting change.
4. What seem to be the most promising opportunities at this time for careers in radio and television programming, in industrial television, and in cable programming?
5. What important economic shifts, if any, have occurred in the broadcasting industry during recent years? How have these changes affected programming?

6. Can you cite a type of specialized programming service that has emerged during recent years? To what extent has it been economically and artistically successful?
7. Based upon your study of telecommunications and your personal intuition, describe the broadcast and cable programming industry as you foresee it 10 years from now.

SUGGESTED READINGS

Adler, Richard P., ed. *Understanding Television*. Part Four: The Future. New York: Praeger Publishers, 1981.

DeLuca, Stuart M.. *Television's Transformation—The Next 25 Years*. San Diego, Calif.: A.S. Barnes, 1980.

Dizard, Wilson P., Jr. *The Coming Information Age*. New York: Longman, 1982.

Haigh, Robert W., Gerbner, G., & Byrne, R., eds. *Communications in the Twenty-First Century*. New York: John Wiley & Sons, 1981.

Toffler, Alvin. *The Third Wave*. New York: Morrow Publishers, 1980.

Williams, Frederick. *The Communications Revolution*. Beverly Hills, Calif.: Sage, 1982.

World Future Society. *The Futurist*. Published bimonthly.

INDEX